Shadowlands

D1596874

Shadowlands

Memory and History in Post-Soviet Estonia

Meike Wulf

berghahn
NEW YORK · OXFORD
www.berghahnbooks.com

First published in 2016 by
Berghahn Books
www.berghahnbooks.com

Library of Congress Cataloging-in-Publication Data

Wulf, Meike.
 Shadowlands: memory and history in post-Soviet Estonia / Meike Wulf.
  pages cm
 Includes bibliographical references and index.
 ISBN 978-1-78533-073-5 (hardback: alkaline paper) – ISBN 978-1-78533-074-2
 (ebook)
 1. Estonia--Historiography. 2. Historians--Estonia--Interviews. 3.
 Intellectuals--Estonia--Interviews. 4. Historiography--Political aspects--
 Estonia. 5. Post-communism--Estonia. 6. Collective memory--Estonia. 7.
 Nationalism--Estonia. 8. Estonia--History--1940-1991. 9. World War, 1939-1945-
 -Estonia. 10. Estonia--History--1991- I. Title.
  DK503.46.W85 2016
  947.980072--dc23

                                                                    2015034277

British Library Cataloguing in Publication Data
A catalogue record for this book is available from the British Library

ISBN 978-1-78533-073-5 hardback
ISBN 978-1-78920-791-0 paperback
ISBN 978-1-78533-074-2 ebook

To my beloved grandmother Herta Schaefer, née Barmer
(1920–2010)

CONTENTS

List of Figures — viii

Acknowledgements — ix

Introduction: Shadowlands — 1

Chapter 1 — 9
Understanding Collective Memory and National Identity

Chapter 2 — 35
Between Teuton and Slav

Chapter 3 — 63
Historians as 'Carriers of Meaning'

Chapter 4 — 105
Voicing Post-Soviet Histories

Chapter 5 — 143
A Winner's Tale: The Clash of Private and Public Memories
in Post-Soviet Estonia

Conclusion: Framing Past and Future — 169

Appendices — 180

Bibliography — 187

Index — 239

FIGURES

1.1   Collective Memory: Three Levels of Memory Work   12

1.2   The Connective Structure of National Identity   20

1.3   Functions of Cultural Memory for Collective
      Cultural Groups   24

4.1   Formative Historical Events Constitutive of the
      Estonian National Identity   115

4.2   Recurring Narrative Tropes of the 1990s   131

5.1   The Public Uses of National History:
      Dimensions and Functions   145

Maps

Map of the Baltic States   xi

ACKNOWLEDGEMENTS

My greatest debt is to the people who agreed to share their experiences with me, opening up to an outsider about events that shaped and often scarred their lives. All the interviewees are listed in Appendix 1, but names have been changed because of the sensitivity of the issues.

I would like to express my deep gratitude to a number of scholarship bodies for facilitating this research: Robert Bosch Foundation; German Academic Exchange Service; European Institute Research Studentship (LSE); British Federation of Women Graduates; British Association for Slavonic and East European Studies; Institute for Advanced Study in the Humanities; Baltic and East European Graduate School; Swedish Institute; LSE Conference Travel Fund; Research Stimulation Fund of the Faculty of Arts and Social Sciences (Universiteit Maastricht); and Sidney Sussex College, Cambridge.

Some of the central ideas of Chapter 1 appeared as a working paper and book chapter: 'Theory Building: Dynamics of Collective Memory in Estonia', in Department of East European Studies, Uppsala, Working Paper, No. 51, April 2000, and as 'Theoretische Überlegungen zum Begriff des kollektiven Gedächtnisses in Estland', in P. Nitschke (ed.), Sammelband: Kulturvermittlung und Interregionalitäten (Frankfurt: Collegium Polonicum, 2003). Parts of Chapter 3 were published in a joint article with P. Grönholm, 'Generating Meaning across Generations – The Role of Historians in the Codification of History in Soviet and post-Soviet Estonia', in Special Issue on 'Collective Memory and Pluralism in the Baltic States', *Journal of Baltic Studies* 41(3), 2010, pp. 351–82; and as book chapter 'Locating Estonia: Homeland and Exile Perspective', in P. Gatrell and N. Baron (eds), *Warlands: Population Resettlement and State Reconstruction in Soviet Eastern Europe, 1945–50* (London: Palgrave, 2009), pp. 231–54. Part of Chapter 4 was published as a journal article and book chapter 'Politics of History in Estonia: Changing Memory Regimes 1987–2009', in M. Neamtu (ed.), *History of Communism in Europe, Vol. I: Politics of Memory in post-Communist Europe* (Bucharest: Zeta Books, 2010), pp. 243–65 and 'The Struggle for Official Recognition of "Displaced" Group Memories in post-Soviet Estonia', in M. Kopecek (ed.), *Past in the Making: Recent History Revisions and Historical Revisionism in Central Europe after 1989* (Budapest and New York: CEU Press, 2008), pp. 217–41.

This book is based on my doctoral dissertation and I remain indebted to my supervisor Professor Anthony D. Smith for his advice and unbroken encouragement. The manuscript was revised for publication during a visiting fellowship at Sidney Sussex College, Cambridge, and I am forever grateful to Cambridge friends, particularly James Mayall and David Reynolds, for making that possible. I appreciate those at Berghahn who have worked in various ways to turn my text into a published book, especially Chris Chappell, Charlotte Mosedale, and Nigel Smith.

Close colleagues working in this field have stimulated and supported me along the way: I am especially thankful to Anton Weiss-Wendt, Augusta Dimou, George Schöpflin, Liis Ruussaar, Kristel and Tiit Kaljund, Jörn Rüsen, Allan Megill, Alon Confino, Alexander von Plato, Mladen Dolar, Bernhard Giesen, Daniel Sŭber, Richard Mole, James Mark, Michal Kopecek, Harald Wydra, Ger Duijzings, and Peter Nitschke. Finally I am grateful to my close friends, parents and family for their patience and support.

Map of the Baltic States

Introduction

SHADOWLANDS

> Yea, though I walk through the valley of the Shadow …
> – Psalm 23

> Ye who read are still among the living; but I who write shall have long
> since gone my way into the region of shadows … This year had been a
> year of terror, and of feelings more intense than terror for which there is
> no name upon the earth.
> – Edgar Allan Poe, 'Shadow – A Parable'

In his play 'Black on White', the German director Heiner Goebbels uses Edgar Allan Poe's deadly vision. When read by a ghostly voice across a dark theatre stage it evokes an ominous feeling that something extraordinary – an unpronounceable catastrophe – had taken place.[1] We who live in the present exist in the shadow of this catastrophe, which can scarcely be put into words. It is precisely this atmosphere of shadows and of terror that I encountered in many of my interviews in Estonia.

Eastern Europe – the forgotten half of the continent, whose complex history is often treated in broad-brush terms by English-language writers for whom Europe means the West – deserves more attention. That is my general claim throughout this book. But why Estonia the reader might ask? Why take us on such a 'ramble through the periphery' of Europe, to employ the title of Alexander Theroux's 2011 travelogue on Estonia? In fact why did Theroux pick Estonia for his first-ever travelogue? My perhaps far from obvious choice of country is indeed a way of slipping into the vast and troubling realities of the former Eastern bloc by a small side door. This is essentially what the historian Norman Davies did in his recent book *Vanished Kingdoms*, where he devoted a chapter on the Soviet Union (entitled 'CCCP') entirely to Estonia's dramatic history. Davies writes that when the Soviet empire imploded in the aftermath of the August coup, Estonia soared into free flight. But this was a country trapped in the borderlands between Germany and Russia, an ominous geopolitical position from which it has struggled to escape. Theroux appositely remarks that 'Mother Russia, the gigantic, authoritarian overlord ... was always Estonia's psychic or mythic opposite, its Jungian shadow', but his statement conveys only half the truth because the German 'Other' played a similarly significant role in Estonia's past.[2]

Historically Estonia has teetered between the German and Russian cultural and political spheres of influence. A relatively small nation, only 1.3 million people even today, Estonia has for most of its history been under the suzerainty of various 'landlords'. With a very short experience of independent democratic statehood (1920–40 and again since 1991) but a long-term experience of alternating foreign rulers, the country's collective identity has been fiercely contested and often in doubt. As with many nations, identity has often been shaped in opposition to a significant internal or external 'Other', but, with its complex history and contemporary ethnic composition, Estonia provides an interesting case of various 'othering' processes. Numerous traces of the Baltic-German heritage can still be found today in the language, songs, architecture, administration and legal structures, and even the food. Equally, post-Soviet Estonia retains a remarkable Soviet legacy, most visible in the form of the large Russian-speaking community, which presently amounts to nearly one-third of the total population and makes inter-ethnic relations – questions of integration and reconciliation – central issues in politics. What brought me initially to the case of Estonia was an interest in the causes of protracted ethnic conflict and the persistent stereotypes thereby generated. Later I got increasingly interested in how long-term foreign rule and military occupations shaped modern Estonian identities and in the difficult question of how this small nation managed to maintain a distinct sense of itself.

The question of what brings about social change and how this affects modern society was of key concern to sociologists of the twentieth century. Similarly, dynamics of continuity and change are also at the heart of memory studies: how does change affect memory and identity? What remains, and what gets lost over time? In the case of Estonia the dynamic process of continuity and change is amplified by a number of specific historical and political conditions, such as foreign domination, belated state formation and far-reaching demographic shifts, making the country an extremely interesting case to scrutinize.[3]

The political ruptures of the last century in particular challenged and contested group identities in Estonia. Traditions have been destroyed and the repository of collective memories threatened by forced amnesia and physical destruction. In the tumultuous twentieth century, Estonians were caught up in the cogwheels of history: virtually each Estonian family has some members who fought in the German army and on the Soviet side during the Second Word War, occasionally also in the Finnish army or with the anti-Soviet guerrilla fighters. The experience of forced exile to the West or to Siberia also affected every Estonian family. This meant that consequential choices had to be made about taking one side or the other, and often there was no grey zone. Such tragic stories find poignant illustration in the Meri family. Lennart Meri (1929–2006), who in 1992 would become the first president of re-independent Estonia, was deported to Siberia in 1941 because his father, Georg-Peeter, was a member of the political and intellectual elite. But his cousin, Arnold Meri (1919–2009), had joined the Red Army and he was eventually put on trial in May 2008 for genocide in connection with the forced deportation of Estonians in March 1949.

The cost of the occupations for Estonia is truly shocking: according to the official Estonian 'White Book' on Repression, published in 2005, in the first Soviet year alone (1940–41) the human losses (killings and deportations) are estimated at 48,000. During the German occupation (1941–44) the estimate is 32,000, before the Soviet Union regained control over Estonia a second time in September 1944. Total human losses during the whole of the second Soviet period are estimated at 111,000. In the words of the White Book, it was only on 31 August 1994, when the last Russian troops left Estonia, that the era of 'three successive occupation regimes that had lasted 54 years and 75 days' was over and 'World War II has come to an end'.[4] But the horrors inflicted by the Soviet and the German military occupations still leave the nation traumatized to this day, with many memories unresolved. In the words of Theroux: 'During an occupation, far more than a country is captured – a national soul is possessed. Brutalized. Mortified. Hurt. Made inflexible. Freedom itself, the very idea of it, becomes victim, as well. More than self is lost, a soul harmed ... A collective unconscious is left with fears and a terrible rigidity it can never relinquish'.[5]

This book is about war and cultural memory in Estonia during and after the Cold War; more specifically, about the complexity of commemorating the Second World War and its protracted aftermath – the so-called 'Long Second World War'. The events of 1940–44 were an intensely sensitive subject during the Soviet era. How are Estonians coming to terms with the memory of the war and post-war years after fifty years of a prescribed and one-sided memory regime? Memories of the war subsisted in private but, metaphorically speaking, they were frozen until the mid-1980s when they gradually assumed more fluid forms during Gorbachev's thaw. But these memories were politically charged and, since re-independence, they came pouring into the public arena, like molten lava with devastating power. Different, often conflicting accounts of the past were articulated, vying for public recognition. The revision of Estonia's history – to administer post-communist justice in the 1990s – was an important feature of the transition process. This was intimately connected to national restoration, to the redefinition of post-Soviet collective identities, and ultimately to the stuff of daily politics. Post-1991 Estonia witnessed fierce battles over the interpretation of historical reality; in such cases, history acquired an 'existential' quality, as changes in the interpretation of historical facts seem fundamentally to have challenged people's group identities. My analysis of the 1991 transition period is highly instructive for the study of collective memory and national identity because, during this time, competing interpretations of the nation surfaced in the society's debate and were 'up for grabs'. This highly public process allows a unique insight into the inner workings of Estonian society (such as the storehouse of building blocks of Estonian identity and the criteria of national membership) which under less dramatic circumstances would have remained largely invisible.

At the core of the newly constructed national narrative of post-Soviet Estonia stands the traditional trope of '700 years of slavery and 700 years of survival'. Here stories of collective suffering and resistance figure prominently, with lines of conflict starkly drawn between Estonian 'victims' and Soviet-Russian 'perpetrators' or 'invaders'. Clearly the fact that the past could not undergo critical public debate for half a century left identities contorted; as a result, issues of national identity and history are heightened and amplified in contemporary Estonia. While tracing these developments, the book also shows how, two decades after the end of the Cold War, a new national narrative and memory regime have not been solidified. It is this process of negotiating and codifying a post-Soviet national history and national identity that aroused my interest and prompted this book. But my Estonian 'miniature' illustrates a bigger picture. The Estonian case helps to provide answers to wider realities of the Eastern bloc and to questions about who is writing the new post-Soviet history there: which facts are being included and why, and whose accounts are being excluded or marginalized in this process.

To answer the question of how Estonians were able to maintain a sense of national self throughout foreign rule, I have concentrated on the role of intellectuals and historians as potential 'custodians of memory' and 'carriers of meaning'. My choice was informed by the fact that many professional historians played an important role as statesmen in post-1991 Estonia, but this was part of a larger historical pattern, exemplified by the pivotal role of intellectuals, or literati, during the national movements of the late nineteenth century in Eastern Europe. Moreover, professional historians participate centrally in the discourse on Estonian history – in writing the new national narrative and in negotiating, selecting and codifying the various historical accounts and social memories of the recent past. They make a fascinating object for research because, through their work, they transform social memories into political memories.

Therefore professional historians constitute the entry point to this study. It soon turned out that their societal role was both complex and sensitive. We have numerous examples of intellectuals in Central Europe who became implicated and compromised in relation to the ranks of power in times of non-democratic rule: Leni Riefentstahl, Wilhelm Furtwängler, Gustav Gründgens, Oskar Pastior and István Szabó spring to mind. Possible compromises of intellectuals in Estonia spurred my interest and I was eager to understand why they chose to become professional historians in the period after 1945, knowing that their research would be heavily constrained by the Soviet interpretation of history. I had in mind an image of a piano player who would only be permitted to play a hymn to Stalin, and I mentioned this in the interviews. One respondent replied directly: 'If you learn how to play the piano in a society where only certain tunes are allowed to be performed, you can still learn how to play it. And you may play on your own [and] secretly for your friends, and wait for the time when you can do so publicly' ('Oskar').

Shadowlands is a contribution to scholarship in two main areas. First, to historical theory by examining how professional historians make sense of historical change, and how the subjective experience of personal life influences disciplinary choices and narration of the past. Its second contribution is to the growing body of work on identity formation in post-communist societies. The book is organized around three main themes: first theory, through an intense engagement with the literature on collective memory (Chapter 1); second borderland identities, that is, the Estonian national identity formed in the interplay of Teuton and Slav (Chapter 2); and third the extended analysis of the historians' life stories (chapters 3, 4 and 5). The concluding chapter (6) returns to the main themes of identity, history and memory – connecting them to the wider discourse and highlighting some of the methodological and conceptual implications of this study for future research projects. Themes that I highlight in this conclusion include generational identity after empire, transcending national historiographies in post-conflict societies, and the prospects of a shared European memory bridging East and West.

To develop this outline in a little more detail: in order to establish the theoretical and methodological foundations of the book, Chapter

1 provides the reader with concise definitions of the most prominent concepts of both collective memory and also national identity. The interrelation of these two areas of scholarship is a further original contribution of this work. Shared memories are the keys to national identity; and national identity is characterized by a connective structure linking a group's common past with its present and future. Collective memory is not homogeneous; instead various collective memories are subdivided into overlapping and competing group memories, such as generational groups. There are also different formats of collective memory, such as social memories on the one hand and cultural or political memories on the other. I introduce 'generational memory' as a form of social memory and highlight this as a central category for conceptualizing intergroup relations in post-conflict societies of the former Soviet space. Such is its centrality that, as I shall show, generational solidarities can at times supersede ethno-cultural identities. *Shadowlands*, then, addresses a lacuna caused by the predominantly West European discourse on the concepts of collective memory and collective cultural identity. It thus aims to remedy some of the shortcomings produced by the Western theoretical bias through some fine tuning of the conventional concepts, to take account of the neglected East European historical experience.

The second chapter adds history to the theory. It serves as a kind of national identity overview, outlining the formation of modern Estonian identity in relation to both the German and the Russian 'Other' – from the nineteenth century up to the regained independence in 1991. Thus, I add to the recent publications on the East European borderlands such as Timothy Snyder's *Bloodlands* and Alexander Prusin's *The Lands Between*, and also Maria Mälksoo's study of the liminal space of the Baltic Three and Poland and the politics of their becoming European.[6] Here the book is also contributing to the growing body of work on identity formation in the post-communist space. In effect I am exploring the 'shadowlands' of memory that still haunt the 'bloodlands' of Eastern Europe.

Chapters 3 to 6 spell out my distinctive argument about how to do oral history – using the case study of professional historians in Eastern Europe and employing the method of life-story interview. Aside from the light this sheds on the Estonian story, the book also offers a practical guide for all historians who are interested in employing memory studies in their research. Some scholars have questioned the utility of oral history. The unique value of oral testimony in this case is the fact that history writing was highly censored during the Soviet period and that in the 1990s the climate of the 'nationalizing state' also constrained history writing. Thus, crucial personal accounts of Estonia's recent past remain largely unwritten and difficult to access, particularly for a non-Estonian readership.

The originality of this book stems from the analysis of the local material, namely over forty life-story interviews that I conducted with professional historians from Estonia (nearly half of all the country's professional historians). All these interviews are listed in the bibliography. I concentrated on the historian's personal life story to explore how the biographic experience influences their interpretation of historical reality and their self-understanding as professional historians. Developing the generational framework, I show how four different generations of historians (which I call the War Generation, the Post-War Children, the Transitional Generation and Freedom Children) remember the past, and how they generate historical meaning in the face of seismic political change.[7]

Chapters 4 and 5 illustrate the process of negotiating a new national narrative and point to its various building blocks. Here I am moving on from the analysis of the life-story interviews to consider both historiography (history textbooks) and the material culture (monuments, museums). The last chapter zooms in on momentous landmarks of post-Soviet Estonian historical culture, around which private and official interpretations of the war came to clash. In analysing these contested spaces, I highlight the wider context of private, local, national and international interests, all of which affect the formulation of the new post-Soviet memory regime. In these chapters I deploy empirical evidence to show the complexity, diversity and fragmentation of existing group identities in contemporary Estonia, and demonstrate how collective memory both restricts and informs day-to-day politics.

What makes the analysis of the political developments in Estonian society over the past twenty years valuable to a wider readership is that it demonstrates some of the specific challenges faced by a great number of Soviet successor societies when trying to overcome their historical legacies and move forward to a new Europe. Because, as we shall see again and again, in 'framing the past' nations are also defining their future.

Notes

1. Performed by the Ensemble Modern at the Barbican, London, in 1999.
2. Norman Davies. 2011. *Vanished Kingdoms: The History of Half-Forgotten Europe*. London: Penguin; Alexander Theroux. 2011. *Estonia: A Ramble through the Periphery of Europe*. Seattle: Fantagraphics, 10.
3. George Schöpflin. 1993. *Politics in Eastern Europe, 1945–92*. Oxford: Blackwell; Wydra in Alexander Wöll and Harald Wydra (eds). 2008. *Democracy and Myth in Russia and Eastern Europe*. London: Routledge, 15–18.
4. Estonian State Commission on the Examination of the Policies of Repression. 2005. The White Book. Losses Inflicted on the Estonian Nation by Occupation Regimes 1940–91. Tallinn: Estonian Encyclopedia Publishers, 16, 19, 22, 23.

5. Theroux, *Estonia: A Ramble*, 14.
6. Timothy Snyder. 2010. *Bloodlands: Europe between Hitler and Stalin*. London: Bodley Head; Alexander Prusin. 2010. *The Lands Between: Conflict in the East European Borderlands, 1870–1992*. Oxford: Oxford University Press; Maria Mälksoo. 2010. *The Politics of Becoming European: A Study of Polish and Baltic Post-Cold War Security Imaginaries*. London: Routledge.
7. See Meike Wulf and Pertti Grönholm. 2010. 'Generating Meaning across Generations: The Role of Historians in the Codification of History in Soviet and Post-Soviet Estonia', *Journal of Baltic Studies* 41(3): 351–82.

Chapter 1

Understanding Collective Memory and National Identity

> Remembering in order to belong.
> – Jan Assmann, 'Erinnern, um dazu zugehören'[1]

> When a big power wants to deprive a small country of its national
> consciousness it uses the method of organized forgetting ...
> A nation which loses awareness of its past gradually loses its self.
> – Milan Kundera (in interview about *The Book of Laughter and
> Forgetting*)[2]

> A nation is a soul, a spiritual principle.
> Two things, actually, constitute this soul, this spiritual principle.
> One is in the past, the other is in the present.
> One is the possession in common of a rich legacy of remembrances;
> the other is the actual consent, the desire to live together, the will to
> constitute to value the heritage which all hold in common.
> – Ernest Renan, 'Qu'est-ce qu'une nation?'[3]

Estonian history in the twentieth century inevitably poses questions
about the effects of war, military occupation, authoritarian rule and
socio-political rupture on collective memories and identities. In
this chapter I will discuss these issues on a conceptual level. Which
memories can be preserved, which will be transformed and which
are permanently lost? How far is collective memory important for
the continuity of a group, such as a nation? Understanding the social
dynamic of continuity and change in modern societies has been the
main focus of sociologists, but it is also a key concern in the field
of memory studies. This opening chapter intends to provide a good
theoretical understanding of the interrelated concepts of collective

memory and national identity, as well as history and generation, and to lead – as a sort of 'toolkit' – into the case study of identity formation in post-Soviet Estonia. The relation of collective memory to processes of national identity formation forms the logical axis of this chapter as well as the next. To be sure, memory and identity are highly elastic concepts that need to be clarified. Whereas this chapter sets up the concept of collective memory as a synthesis of the works of founding figures Maurice Halbwachs, Pierre Nora, Jan and Aleida Assmann, Jacques Le Goff and Jeff Olick, Chapter 2 will discuss Estonian collective identity formation between Teuton and Slav. I will add my own theoretical refinement to the discourses on memory studies and nations and nationalism in three ways: understanding national identity through collective memory and establishing the link between the two concepts; launching the concept of generational identity as an alternative to ethnically defined collective cultural identities; and rethinking collective memory for the East European context. In addition I shall tackle questions of the social and political functions of collective memory in modern society, and the mechanisms of its transmission.

Mechanisms of Collective Memory

The anthropologist Elizabeth Tonkin's aphorism 'memory makes us and we make memory' captures well the intertwined mechanisms underlying the concept of memory and points to its socially constructed nature. To start with, memory is embodied individual memory because there is no living entity such as a 'collective memory', there are only collective memories.[4] The first part of Tonkin's quote – 'memory makes us' – hints at the social framework of memory, which both informs and restricts its group members' thoughts and actions. Thus, group members perceive and interpret the past, present and future through these social frameworks, a process that Francis A. Yates referred to as seeing through the 'eyes of memory'.[5]

However it was the French sociologist Maurice Halbwachs who in the 1920s first placed individual memory within the larger framework of society, claiming that individual memory requires the support of a collective for its existence, maintenance and reconstruction. He further argued that it is only through group membership that individuals acquire, localize and recall their memories. These socially prescribed cognitive frames are systems of conventions that, due to their partial and biased nature, impact on how and what the group remembers. Because of this the social framework of society is essential to processes of individual remembering, which is the main reason Halbwachs coined the term 'social memory'. It is because social memory is inextricably connected to a specific social framework that it is limited in time and space. In other words, human life is finite and groups vanish. Another reason for labelling individual memory as social memory is that it is structured through language and based on communication. It is indeed language that forms the link between the collective and the individual enabling conversation and sharing, including even those group members who lacked the first-hand experience of certain events in the imagined reconstruction of the group's collective memory. Here the mechanisms of transmission of memory can either be familial and unmediated or mediated through public institutions, such as schools and libraries. Recognizing that we participate in a range of different groups throughout our lifespan and that individual memory is an agglomerate of various group memories, Halbwachs introduced the term 'collective memory' in addition to social memory. He later also employed collective memory in the plural to emphasize the many different social memories coexisting in a society at any one time.[6]

'We make memory', the second part of Tonkin's quotation, stresses the constructed and constantly reprocessed nature of social memory. This means the past is not merely preserved but is continuously and selectively reconstructed in the light of present interests, needs and aspirations.[7] To make more explicit the point that collective memory is a social process, Jay Winter prefers the term 'remembrance' instead of collective memory. This social process or activity of reconstructive 'memory work', to employ Freud's term, takes place in the aforementioned social frameworks and comprises three levels: first, collective conversation; second, categorizing and conceptualizing past events; and third, more abstract processes of re-construction and selection.[8] As we move from the first level of collective memory work to the third, we are also moving from more unmediated forms of personal sharing of the past to mediated forms of institutiona-lized interpreting of the past. These multilevelled processes of collective memory are made visual in Figure 1.1.

Levels of Collective Memory
Third Level of Memory Work **Collective reconstruction**, reinterpretation and selection of past events (mediated in institutions).
Second Level of Memory Work **Categorizing**, conceptualizing and describing of past events (unmediated and mediated).
First Level of Memory Work **Collective conversation** and sharing of personal embodied memories (unmediated).

Figure 1.1 Collective Memory: Three Levels of Memory Work

Continuity and Change in Collective Memory

To give a preliminary definition: collective memory constitutes a repository of shared cultural resources (such as language), which guarantees continuity of a group. Change lies in the continuous process of reconstruction, reinterpretation and selection of these cultural resources; in the how and what is remembered at any point in time. Halbwachs explained changes in the collective memory through an altered social framework, but it was Friedrich Nietzsche who pointed out that forgetting the past is as vital as remembering it for the endurance of a group. Forgetting, he argued, is the capacity of a people to accommodate change and to recreate and transform themselves in the light of present and future challenges.[9] To understand continuity and change in collective memory, we need now to consider more carefully the different aggregate states of collective memory: it can manifest itself in more fluid and fluxionary forms or turn into forms which are more durable and lasting. Oral traditions, for example, can be classed as fluid, whereas archives and monuments constitute more crystallized forms of collective memory.[10]

Halbwachs' way of accounting for continuity and change in collective memory was to distinguish between 'historical' and 'autobiographical' memory. Whereas the former is periodically re-enacted through commemorations, festivals and rituals, the latter refers to the personal memory of events. But this autobiographical memory will fade over time unless regularly reinforced through contact with other group members who have shared past experiences.[11] It is important to note also that Halbwachs did not employ the term 'cultural memory': launching the dual concept of communicative and cultural memory to account for the dialectic interplay of continuity and change in collective memory can be credited to the Egyptologist Jan Assmann. Because communicative memory depends on language, it is ephemeral; but this also gives the group flexibility to adapt to the changing requirements of modernity. Communicative memory encompasses all experiences that are personally communicated over a time span of up to four generations. On the other hand it is through its long-lasting, institutionally manifested and thus externalized forms of memory that cultural memory ensures continuity. Cultural memory is recorded, codified and transmitted through literary tradition, cultural artefacts and forms of institutionalized communication, and is therefore trans-generational and long lasting, externalized from the individual embodied memory. We can therefore conclude that language plays a pivotal role for communicative memory, while tradition forms the backbone of cultural memory.[12]

The shift from oral traditions to script cultures profoundly transformed collective memory. It was particularly the innovations of print technology, a central bureaucracy and the ideology of nationalism as features of European modernity that had deep effects on the development of cultural memory. For instance, the French Revolution, with its new calendars and festivals, all in the service of its own remembrance, can be seen as a benchmark in the secularization and multiplication of public commemorations.[13] Similarly in the late nineteenth century it was the creation of national archives, public record offices and historical research institutes after the national unifications of Italy and Germany that formed notable manifestations of cultural memory. After the First World War, monuments to the dead – such as the tomb of the Unknown Soldier – but also photography and film, further revolutionized cultural memory.[14] With these developments in mind, the literary scholar Aleida Assmann has argued for a further differentiation of cultural memory into an active 'functional memory' and a more latent 'stored memory', two terms that can be understood as foreground and background of cultural memory. In other words, while the functional memory contains only a selection of the resources and traditions of a society's cultural memory depending on its present needs and interests, the stored memory contains the larger pool of knowledge independent of political currents and short-term developments.[15]

Time in Space: Sites of Memory

We have seen that collective memory is anchored and unfolds in a social framework, but groups locate and solidify their collective memory also in a spatial framework, helping them to retrieve memories through landmarks.[16] Anthony Smith holds that the homeland, as an ancestral land of saints and sages and historic battles, constitutes a repository of historic memories aiding national reassertion in times of foreign domination.[17] Certainly in Estonia, a country that has been under foreign rule for most of its modern existence, the landscape was linked to the history of the community and to collective identity. In Chapter 5 I shall examine various landmarks of cultural memory in contemporary Estonia, such as monuments and memorial sites connected to the wars.

Although Halbwachs began to develop ideas on topographical memories in *The Legendary Topography of the Gospels in the Holy Land* (1941), it was Pierre Nora who in the 1990s brought the related concept of 'sites of memory' to prominence by developing a new spatial history of France, built around various lieux de mémoire in which the country's cultural heritage had crystallized.[18] Nora's starting point is a critique of modern historiography and our 'disenchanted' times in which memory is uprooted and the equilibrium between past and present disturbed.[19] In analysing these sites of memory, Nora's objective was to go beyond historical reality in order to discover the symbolic world of things and to recover the memory that they sustain. Nora's endeavour is informed by a binary opposition of history and memory; he wants to salvage memory from history, because he considers memory alive, whereas history is turning memory into stone, and thereby distorting it. In this line of thought, history (and the work of the historian) begins when the past is no longer the lived reality of a group.[20] Nora's precursor, Halbwachs, shared this understanding of history as positivist and rationalized. According to him, memory emphasizes inner-group similarities and continuity, whereas history highlights only differences, breaks and discontinuities, and is abstracting historical facts from its specific group context to reorganize them in a universal history (alienated and detached from the people).[21] Nora clearly holds a romantic notion of past times, when, for instance in peasant cultures, memory formed an intimate part of a group's everyday experience with 'real environments of memory' (in French, milieux de mémoire) constituting an abundant reserve to support the group's active remembering. All that we are left with today are, according to him, those sites of memory that preserve only a residual sense of continuity with the past.[22]

From the 1960s this fact-based idea of history – in the traditional Rankean sense of '*wie es eigentlich gewesen*' – has been replaced by social and cultural approaches to history, so that Nora's critique appears to be less adequate.[23] And yet, even after the recent memory boom, memory continues to be under suspicion by professional historians and others for being subjective and fictitious.[24] This is in part to do with earlier attempts by professional historians to separate memory from history, but is also founded in the very limitations of memory: our capacity to remember is limited, as details get lost over time and are distorted, while new material is imported and integrated in a process of constant reconstruction and reframing.

In light of this discussion, I propose that while it is necessary to establish and understand what happened – the 'factual' history – we must also consider subsequent narratives and memories. I also argue that any clear-cut distinction of history and memory is not useful. This is why I adopt historian Jörn Rüsen's integrative approach, which understands both phenomena – history and memory – as expressions of 'historical culture'. In broad terms, historical culture encompasses every articulation and contestation of history, and all the ways in which memory is processed in the daily life of society.[25]

Group Conflict and Counter-Memories

Even though Halbwachs acknowledged that collective memory is differentiated into many subgroups, he did not consider the potential for conflict and fragmentation inherent in collective memory but regarded the latter primarily as a source of social cohesion. In his thinking, groups would remember their pasts under the aspects of cultural continuity, while blanking out all that is not in support of that positive group image.[26] But most communities display significant divisions, which would indicate that a group's collective memory is indeed a product of constant inner-group struggle over competing versions and images of the past. Therefore collective memory serves a double function: it not only endows the group with stability, but bears a subversive potential of resistance and conflict as well.

The cultural historian Peter Burke discusses defeated groups, who cannot afford to forget their history but have to work on alternatives to the status quo in an attempt to rectify putatively false interpretations of the historical past, while the victorious contestant writes the tale of the dominant group and can afford to forget.[27] When a group experiencing deficiency and inequality, caused for instance by foreign domination, counterposes its current predicament against memories of cultural and economic prosperity, sovereign statehood, and military power, these memories acquire a subversive potential and can thus be labelled counter-memories. In particular such memories of liberation, a golden age, victories and defeats with subsequent heroes and martyrs can become a social Utopia for the future, a counter-memory that raises hopes and expectations and mobilizes people to call for change.[28] These sets of counter-memories can be better described as myth (and will be discussed in a later section as formative or foundational narratives).[29] Myth and history are often used as opposing categories – similar to memory and history – but I propose to go beyond this binary thinking that tends to equate myth with fiction and history with reality.[30] Myths in their revolutionary function were utilized in the national liberation movements of the late nineteenth and early twentieth centuries: after 1870 Kaiser Wilhelm I was equated with Frederick Barbarossa (in German myth supposedly sleeping under the *Kyffhäuser* mountain) because he united the German Reich in 1870.[31] Another example, this time from Eastern Europe, for the creation of a national epic to mobilize national consciousness, is the Kalevipoeg (Kalev's Son). Inspired by the publication of the Finnish national epic, the Kalevala, in 1835 and 1849, the Estonian Friedrich Robert Faehlmann set out to create a work about the legendary figure of Kalevipoeg to help the Estonians in their struggle for national self-esteem in the late nineteenth century.[32] Based on folk tales and songs, Kalevipoeg was believed to be 'marrow and bones, flesh and blood of the Estonian people', constituting 'the only indigenous verbal monument to this people's past'.[33] Finally nostalgia – the longing of homecoming or towards a particular time in the past – can also be defined as a powerful counter-memory; a way of cultural resistance to maintain one's identity in the face of change.[34]

But group conflict and counter-memories point us also to the political dimension of collective memories. Aleida Assmann has introduced the political format of memory, along with the individual, social and cultural formats. According to her, political memories are (bottom–up) individual or social memories which are transformed into (top–down) institutionalized forms of remembrances. While she employs the concepts of individual and cultural memory similarly to Jan Assmann, her usage of the term 'social memory' is also specific (and different from Halbwachs) in that social memories are shared by a generation. Adding the social and political format to our discussion on collective memory is a significant contribution for two reasons: first because it makes clear that memories can indeed be highly political, and second because it points us to the importance of generations, a theme I will begin to explore in the next section.

Generational Group Memory

In societies divided by war and conflict, such as Northern Ireland, Spain, South Africa, Israel, and also Estonia, I shall argue that it can be helpful to find more inclusive categories of group identification such as 'generation' to supersede exclusive definitions based on ethnicity and descent.

So far we have seen that a group's collective memory is differentiated into many – at times overlapping – subgroups which can hold competing and conflicting accounts of the past. Building on this I introduce the concept of 'generational group memory'. The interview with an Estonian sociologist born in the late 1940s, whom I refer to here as 'Ülle-Mai', prompted my decision to scrutinize the generational dimension of memory in contemporary Estonia. To the question of whether she would term Estonia's recent past until 1991 a 'Soviet occupation', she alerted me to the fact that there are indeed 'several social times in Estonia, and [that] in one time line, it was truly occupation all throughout'. It was, she said, an occupation 'in the memories of those who were teenagers or older at the beginning of the 1940s. In their minds it was an occupation the whole time'. Ülle-Mai's response pushed me further in suspecting that group memories in Estonia are not only defined by the social framework of language, religion and indeed ethnicity – as emphasized by Halbwachs – but that generational differences figure prominently as well. Although the post-Soviet Estonian national narrative represents the Estonian collective memory as unified and opposed to that of the Russian-speaking community, this insight makes it crucial to contrast the official narrative with various conflicting 'social times' or social group memories existing *within* the Estonian collective memory (which I will be examining in the empirical chapters 3 to 5).

In the process of continuous renegotiation of a group's collective memory each generational group holds a set of beliefs. While most beliefs remain relatively constant across generations, some generations develop new opinions and attitudes that press to be integrated into the group's self-image, which poses a serious challenge at the time.[35] In her work on the memory of the Holocaust across three generations (in Israel and Germany) the sociologist Gabriele Rosenthal pointed to the importance of studying generations in context, that is to say, always considering the dynamics of inter-generational transmission and interaction. Moreover memory scholars hold that societies reflect on and reconstruct their pasts after thirty to forty years because this time span allows sufficient 'psychological distance' from the past, the accumulation of 'generational resources' to establish commemorations and a diminishing likelihood of repercussions from the authorities. Adding to this, Jan Assmann argues that after forty years the generation of eyewitnesses aims to codify their social memories in more lasting cultural forms.[36]

The sociologist Karl Mannheim saw the generational factor as crucial in the social dynamics of change. Due to the centrality of the concept of generation for this book, let us now take a closer look at how he defined it. Because Mannheim conceived of generation as a sociological phenomenon, he distinguished between the 'location of a generation', including all people born around the same time and into the same community and space (coming close to the biological concept of generation), and the concept of 'generational context', constituting a 'community of destiny' through participation in the *Zeitgeist*.[37] According to this, a generation is formed by collective historical experiences, particularly during the formative years of youth; for instance, fighting side by side in the First World War functioned as a unifying point of identification for a generational context. Any heightened socio-historical dynamic, such as a revolution or economic crisis, he claims, creates a generational context, because it gives rise to new impulses and demands fresh answers. In this scenario a generational context may give rise to different 'generational units' that are distinguished by their specific 'generational style' (or *entelechy*); that is, a new paradigmatic outlook to pressing questions of the time.[38] But Mannheim concedes that not every generational context produces a 'generational style'; we do not have a 1967, a 1968 and a 1969 generation. Instead – and this is Mannheim's main argument – only certain socio-political conditions bring about distinct generations.[39]

Connecting Mannheim's concept of generation to what has been said so far about collective memory, we may argue that a generational context and a generational unit both qualify as social group memories, or what I term 'generational group memory'. In the empirical chapters I shall be analysing four such generational group memories to highlight the complexities of post-Soviet Estonian collective memory and also shed light on contemporary Estonian national identity. Although I consider it important to have outlined Karl Mannheim's concept of generation in some detail, I will apply it somewhat more loosely in the empirical part.

Tying together Collective Memory and National Identity

In this section I show how national identity is a powerful 'cultural collective identity', sharing similar structures with collective memory. Understanding national identity through collective memory is what I am therefore proposing. Starting first with individual identity: the individual needs the social group not only as a social framework for his or her memory but also for identity. Individual identity comes into being when a child begins to experience his/her self as an entity separate from the rest of the world. Therefore identity originates in the 'self and Other' distinction, in the separateness of the self from the outside world. Inherent in the very concept of identity is the duality of 'us' and 'them' but, as political theorist Bhikhu Parekh made clear, identity is logically and ontologically *prior* to difference, and difference per se cannot be the basis of identity.[40] Because identity is both dialogic and relational in character, we need – in a second step – to turn to the social group: group identity is based on social interaction and communication, and on degrees of felt commonality and of felt sameness among group members distinguishing them from the Other. Consequently collective identity is always contested, be it by an internal Other within the group or by an outsider.[41] It is this process of collective identification which I will turn to in Chapter 2 when discussing the formation of Estonian national identity between Teuton and Slav.

Let us now look more closely at the link between collective memory and collective identity: similar to collective memory, collective identity is also a social construct, or as Jan Assmann put it, a 'social *imaginaire*' – depending on the collective imagining of its individual members.[42] Consequently a group's identity can only be reconstructed through the conscious activity of remembering, because it is through remembering that groups imagine themselves. And this remembering has to be done together as a group for a collective identity to come into being, and for it to be maintained and reinforced over time. Essentially group members sustain and preserve the common stock of knowledge inherent in collective memories out of a need for identity.[43] This prompts me to think about social groups under the conditions of foreign domination with collective celebrations and commemorative rituals heavily curtailed: what are the effects on their collective identity? It is these kinds of questions that I will tackle for Estonia in the later chapters.

Collective memory and national identity are both located in the wider field of culture and are connected to a particular community. Culture I understand as a shared system of symbols that forms the basis of all social identities. As a pool of cultural resources it provides the *forms* through which collective memory can be transmitted and preserved; and it is also the *medium* through which a sense of collective identity can be created, reproduced, communicated and maintained. Jan Assmann argues for culture's 'connective structure', tying collective memories to group identity and group continuity.[44]

The sort of function that Anthony D. Smith attributes to national identity is quite similar to the connective function Assmann gives to culture – and indeed to cultural memory – which is why national identity is more accurately described as a 'collective cultural identity'. Smith maintains that national identity serves as a powerful means of defining and locating individual selves in the world through a prism of collective personality and distinctive culture. National identity provides the group with a sense of belonging and a means of orientation over time, because it helps to provide answers to questions about who we are, where we come from, and where we are going. By offering answers to these questions of descent and membership, national identity bestows on the group an enduring element of common legacy that links it to a presumed collective past and a destiny that provides it with some vision of a common future. Nations, ethnic communities, and religious groups are examples of collective cultural identities. These are communities of a longer lasting and more binding quality for the individual members than those based solely on common needs or interests, such as for instance occupational identities. Smith further suggests that there are certain cultural elements, such as symbols, values, memories, myths and traditions, inherent in all collective cultural identities, and that they meet the community's need for a sense of continuity, distinctiveness and mission.[45]

In sum, national identity equips a people with a sense of belonging through a shared legacy, with orientation for the present, and a common purpose for the future – in short with a 'connective structure'. It is therefore on the functional level that national identity and collective memory converge: collective memory has an identity-reinforcing function in that it strengthens the bonds of solidarity among group members by forming an integral part of the 'connective structure' that underlies national identity. The crucial factor of time, and thus of collective memory, in processes of national identification becomes evident in Figure 1.2.[46]

But how can we justify defining these communities of longer lasting and more binding quality such as a national community? I suggest the definition by Parekh as a starting point: 'a territorially concentrated group of people bound together by their acceptance of a common mode of conducting their collective affairs, including a body of institutions and shared values'.[47]

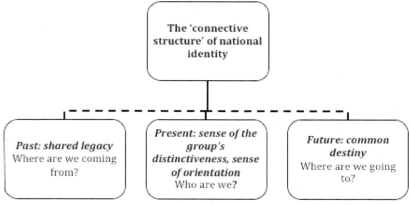

Figure 1.2 The Connective Structure of National Identity

Parekh's definition makes us acutely aware of the ambiguity the term 'national' holds, in that it refers to the nation as cultural community and its political institutions. And yet it is impossible to neatly separate the political from the cultural community, because what is the base of the political community if not the specific culture of a polity? How else can solidarity among the members of a community, societal coherence and loyalty towards state institutions be generated except through culture? In other words, a political community can virtually never be entirely stripped bare of any culture. Therefore I am adopting a rather open definition of the 'nation' as a cultural and political community. This is also an attempt to bridge the prevalent but problematic dichotomy of civic versus ethnic nationalism. In fact I am following Brubaker's argument against the strict usage of the civic–ethnic schema as an analytical tool, because we are left with only a few clear instances of each of these cases and a large middle ground that involves both the civic and the ethnic.[48]

So far I have shown that the term 'nation' holds a conceptual ambivalence in that it simultaneously refers both to the cultural and the political community. Several scholars of nationalism stress the subjective, emotional or affective dimension of national identity, linking this to culture or ethnicity. The French philosopher Ernest Renan, for example, regarded suffering and sacrifices as great national unifiers as they contain a strong emotional charge: 'A nation is a grand solidarity constituted by the sentiment of sacrifices which one has made and those that one is disposed to make again'. Likewise Smith asserts that without the 'subjective element' of shared memories the sense of being part of a collective group would be absent, and no passionate identification by individual citizens with a particular nation would be possible. And Schöpflin gives ethnicity the function of a 'binding agent', forming an important pillar of modern democratic nationhood (together with the state and the civil society), which in my reading, comes close to culture itself. All this makes clear how culture and ethnicity are often used as overlapping terms in the discourse on nations and nationalism.[49]

Let us think a little more about the notion of positive and negative group identity. Due to the need for a positive group identity, all groups produce flattering self-images and, as the converse, demeaning images of those 'other' nations.[50] Arguably the biggest attraction of belonging to a nation is that it acts as patron of the group's positive self-image, group worth and collective self-esteem. But what if a national community has difficulty in deriving such a positive group image out of its recent past, due to divisive or even shameful collective experiences?[51] I would like to highlight two common social strategies for regaining a positive national self-image. First, there is the selective omission of disagreeable facts and the development of a publicly prescribed amnesia.[52] The circumstances under which European nations came into being were mostly violent. This is why Renan pointed to the tendency of political leaders to screen out of the national genealogies recent historic events from the national past that are still in the active memory of the community and too divisive to be revived, while including, on the other hand, historically remote ancient massacres. The latter are, to employ Charles Maier's term, 'cold memories' with no explosive charge.[53] The second frequently employed strategy for cultivating or regaining a positive national self-image is blaming the Other. One familiar case in Western Europe would be the long enmity between Germany and France, culminating in the polemics of 1914–18 about the struggle between *Kultur* and *civilization*. Another example was the way eighteenth-century British national identity developed in conscious self-definition against the values of France – as a nation that was Protestant and parliamentary rather than Catholic and absolutist.[54]

Functions of Cultural Memory: Canon, Myth and Wisdom

So far I have discussed the relationship between collective memory and collective cultural identities on an abstract level. But how does it operate in more concrete terms? We have established that collective memory consists of cultural and communicative forms of memory. Due to their extensive size, nations cannot be based on communicative memory alone but rely also, in their persistence, on the effective organization, tradition and circulation of cultural memory. Because we will be discussing processes of national identification for the case of Estonia later on, it is the practical functioning of cultural memory for national communities and national identities that we will now turn to more closely.

Communicative memory is transformed into cultural memory through 'canonization' – that is, through selection of traditions containing both formative and normative knowledge.[55] Canonized cultural knowledge offers a highly condensed and idealized account of what the community takes to be its values, organizing principles and collective identity constituting the cultural level of national identity.[56] According to Jan Assmann cultural memory conveys norms and values, presenting the group with 'common sense knowledge'; this sort of knowledge needs to be circulated and articulated through communication and group interaction, and regularly reinforced, re-enacted and recalled in rituals, ceremonies and texts. Common sense knowledge, or canon, can further be differentiated into 'wisdom' and 'myth'; through this distinction Assmann identifies a normative and a formative dimension: wisdom conveys normative knowledge including rules and moral guidelines for the shared way of life (*what should be done*), whereas myth holds formative knowledge which is conveyed through legends and foundational histories, feeding into a group's self-defining processes, because it answers questions about the meaning of life (*who we are*).[57]

Olick and Levy provide us with a more differentiated view of several cultural constraints through which collective memory's normative dimension functions in a society. They point out that this dimension is both prescriptive and restrictive. On the one hand, cultural memory gives prescriptions in the form of duties and requirements (*what should be done*); on the other hand, it restricts present political claim making in the form of taboo topics, for instance (*what should not be done*). These taboo topics or proscriptions involve moral constitutive principles and also claims that are absolute and unquestionable so that their transgression means pollution: they cannot be discussed and are complete taboos. As an example of such proscription the authors analyse the ways the Holocaust figured in West German politics before reunification, arguing that neo-conservatives attempted to alter and transform the 'ontological taboo status' of the Holocaust in the *Historikerstreit* into a prohibition that could then be openly and rationally debated.[58] In chapters 4 and 5 I will be looking at taboo themes in relation to the Second World War in contemporary Estonia, and will also be discussing the limits of historical comparison between the two totalitarian experiences.

Let us turn once more to the formative function of cultural memory. Historical events with a constitutive or formative function for a group's distinct identity I call myth (we have discussed the function of myth already in the context of counter-memories). It does not matter whether these foundational narratives are based on fact or fiction, what distinguishes them is their formative function.[59] Examples of such powerful myth are that of *Romulus and Remus*, the *Kiev Rus'*, and the Polish *Piast*.[60] Assmann describes the transformation of certain historical events into these foundational narratives as *mythogenesis* and relates this process to Claude Levi-Strauss' notion of *mythomotorik*, a concept which describes how groups internalize their historical knowledge to make it the 'motor' of their development.[61] In chapters 2 and 4 I will provide examples of such *mythomateurs* for the context of the Estonian struggle for national independence. Based on this theoretical discussion of the formative knowledge inherent in cultural memory, I will single out foundational narratives of significance for Estonian collective identities in Chapter 4.

Jan Assmann points out that the *canon* of a group – its common traditions, guidelines and values – constitutes the nexus between individual and collective identity, because the individual has to know

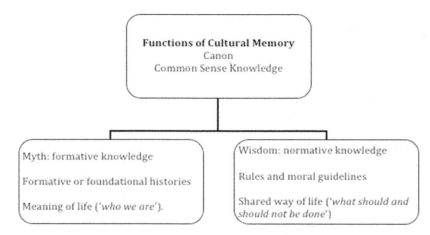

Figure 1.3 Functions of Cultural Memory for Collective Cultural Groups

and accept it in order to acquire membership of the group.[62] He also alludes to the etymological proximity between canon and conversion: only by understanding and remembering the condensed essence of a group's collective identity – its canon – is an individual able to convert and become a group member. However, the canon contains the criteria for inclusion as well as exclusion; in other words, it sets up group boundaries, determining what is remembered and what is forgotten.[63] It may not always be possible for an individual aspiring to become a group member to achieve membership; because while it may be possible to obtain group membership in a community defined on cultural grounds, this is more complicated for communities based on genealogical or racial conceptions. When we think of those modern German Jews who converted to Christianity and who, like the poet and writer Heinrich Heine, saw in baptism the 'admission ticket to European civilization', we know that there was no admission ticket to the German *Volk* after identities had been politicized, and heightened racial conceptions of the nation rendered conversion impossible. This shows how a canon can take the function of a boundary marker, fulfilling the need of groups concerned with their survival in diaspora or in relation to other minority groups in the homeland for a more distinctive cultural and political demarcation against the Other. In this process of enhanced canonization, all that is 'alien' to the group's identity is erased from the canon, and all the rules about the shared way of life sacralized.[64] This mechanism is relevant for processes of national identity formation discussed in the Estonian example in the next chapter.

Beyond the West: Collective Memories in Contemporary Eastern Europe

By and large, theoretical concepts of 'collective memory' and 'national identity' were essentially formulated within and for the West European and American context. They have not been systematically reassessed for twentieth-century societies that have alternated between periods of independence and renewed foreign rule – and equally important, rule by two rival powers, in this case the Germans and the Russians. I therefore argue that certain idiosyncratic conditions of East European societies have an important bearing on the structures of collective memory and national identity. These can be grouped into pre-communist and post-communist legacies.

Let us begin with the pre-communist legacies: first the fallout from multinational empires which left the region with highly complex inter-ethnic relations; second, latecomer nations with a limited experience of independent democratic statehood; and third, long-standing oral, vernacular traditions. My discussion here is based primarily on George Schöpflin's analysis of politics in Eastern Europe in which he pointed to the very different nature of the relationship between state and society, namely the absence of a separation of powers and the lack of civic traditions, a pronounced *étatism*, or state domination, and the essentially personalized nature of politics.[65] Unlike Western Europe, it was the state in the East that acted as agent of modernization from above while society was characterized by a certain 'backwardness' consequent on late urbanization, a small urban middle class, and no home-grown class of literati prior to the late nineteenth century. More will be said in due course about the distinctive role of intellectuals in Eastern Europe. The impact of foreign rule (that is German, Magyar and Russian domination) and the comparatively recent break-up of the multi-ethnic empires left many East European societies with weak civic identities, resulting in a more ethnically defined conception of nationhood as well as mistrust of official institutions and an abidingly negative view of the state. For countries such as Estonia, Latvia and Lithuania the emancipative founding moment of 1920 was followed swiftly by a re-imperialization, unseen in the West European context; here we can think of Italy breaking irrevocably away from the Habsburg rule in the 1860s.[66]

I argue that the first two legacies (multinational empires and latecomer nations) introduce a political dimension rather different from the West European historical experience. In the West, the national states of Portugal, Spain, France and Britain emerged in the early modern period and their empires were oceanic rather than continental. Turning to the third

legacy: East European societies are characterized by long-standing vernacular traditions and a greater trust in oral testimony than in the written
word or institutionalized forms of cultural memory. The description by
historian Jacques Le Goff of societies whose social memories are primarily
oral, because they are still in the process of establishing a literate culture, shows they have certain similarities with the transitional processes
of post-communist societies, because here too we can find a struggle for
domination over remembrance.[67]

Having discussed the historical character of East European society in
general, let me now focus on the particular legacies of Soviet communism. By this I mean first the polarization into the private and the public spheres, and secondly issues of complicity and collaboration. On the
first point: Stalinist communism was characterized by a specific desire to
control. In an attempt to deprive people of their collective identity and
to homogenize them into Soviet citizens, the Stalinist system cut people
off from their historical memory through forms of organized or enforced
forgetting. This happened for instance through the destruction of historical monuments and books (including whole libraries), even the 'urbicide'
of entire cities (Königsberg/Kaliningrad in Russia, and Narva in Estonia,
serve as examples), as well as the imposition of a new Soviet architecture, novel commemorations and reformed school curricula.[68] Therefore a
people's struggle against Soviet rule can be read as an effort to keep their
'counter-memory' alive. This was an existential need, because remembering meant nothing less than survival as a nation.

Everyday life under the conditions of Soviet communism underwent a
strong polarization into a public realm – with a censored history disseminated through the education apparatus and political propaganda – and a
private realm, with its family memories and small clandestine circles. In
these societies the public sphere was intensely expanded and ideologically
standardized, whereas the private sphere was profoundly constrained.
Individuals who wanted to participate in the public sphere – that is at
the workplace or in the Komsomol youth organization – had to accept
the prescribed 'double talk', although they were fully aware of the bogus
nature of 'real existing' socialism. The adaptive mechanisms that people
under post-totalitarian rule appropriated to cope with these 'incongruous
public and private scripts'[69] had a profound effect on people's identity.
The Polish sociologist Piotr Sztompka, in his post-1989 reflections on the
socialist mindset, remarks that in societies under Soviet communism the
dissociation of the public and the private sphere was the basic founding
principle from which all other dichotomies had derived.[70]

In this book I will scrutinize how the politicization of all aspects of life
and the stark private–public divide affected the social memories of four

different generational groups of intellectuals in post-Soviet Estonia: I call them War Generation, Post-War Children, Transitional Generation and Freedom Children. For example 'Ülle-Mai', a Post-War Child, described many members of the older generation of intellectuals in Estonia – those born before the Second World War – as people who were able to switch consciously between public and private ways of talking. She used the example of a telephone switchboard to illustrate her point; whereas she characterizes her own generation – those born shortly after the war – as 'fundamentally doubled' in that they were less consciously aware of the divide between the two worlds, 'Ervin', an Estonian dissident born in the early 1950s, tells me rather emphatically at the outset of the interview: 'We knew it, in our inner mind. Maybe it was suppressed ... but we were not ... a totally level-minded society such as depicted in Orwell's *1984*. We had our history, our culture. We did and still have [*he laughs*], which made it easy for us to survive these changes'. The question that needs addressing is whether individuals at the time of Soviet occupation experienced this split in their identity, or whether that rupture has only been conceptualized *ex post facto*, that is, after the interpretive frame has changed from communism to post-communism.

The second and related post-Soviet legacy is that of collaboration during the war and complicity with the '(post-)totalitarian' regimes after Stalin's death – something that Vaclav Havel discussed in his book *Power of the Powerless*. The resulting bad conscience and divisive memories complicate discussion on responsibility and accountability in these transitional societies to this day. The sensitivity is heightened by the significant temporal delay of half a century (1945–91 in the case of Estonia) before open and democratic ways of coming to terms with the past could even begin. In fact, many societies of Eastern Europe had to come to terms not only with the recent Soviet communist legacy but also with that of the Second World War – that is the double legacy of totalitarian rule. What are the effects of these pre- and post-Soviet legacies on the mechanism and functions of collective memory in Eastern Europe?

Rethinking Jan Assmann's dual concept of cultural and communicative memory for the East European context, I argue that cultural memories were less affected by the Soviet regime than the more fluid aggregate states of collective memory – those communicative memories that are personally passed on over several generations.[71] However due to the specific East European experience – here in particular the long-standing oral tradition and the high degree of politicization of memories – a further differentiation of Jan Assmann's dual concept is useful in my judgement. Therefore I adopt Aleida Assmann's two formats of memory, the social and the political, in addition to the concept of cultural and communicative memory. I prefer the term social to communicative memory because it stresses somewhat more the bottom–up process and the struggle for public recognition of this type of memory. I also use the term political memory more extensively than cultural memory, although both refer to codified official memories, because the political struggle over the codification of social memories played an important role in the transition politics of Estonia.

During times of foreign rule, and above all during the Soviet period, collective memories were split into private and public memories. While in the public sphere memories were highly politicized, memories held in the private of the family realm did not undergo much critical revision, but remained as what we might call 'frozen memory crystals' in a sort of hibernation until the late 1980s. In Soviet Estonia the boom of social memories in the second half of the 1980s was in part triggered by Mikhail Gorbachev's go-ahead to critically assess the blank pages of Soviet historiography; but interestingly, forty years after the end of the Second World War, this time span also constituted a transformative turning point with regard to collective memory – because forty years constitutes the benchmark after which the generation of eyewitnesses who experienced interwar Estonia and the war began to fade. Consequently it was exactly at this moment in time that they felt the need to transform their social (counter-)memories into more enduring forms of political or cultural memory.[72] But the political circumstances of the late 1980s still posed great obstacles to this process, which in turn produced various counter reactions and which fuelled the political transition process. This book will illustrate how the dynamic between private social memories and public political memories gradually began moving again after the 'memory crystals' were defrosted, and how, from the late 1980s onwards, these social counter-memories began to emerge from the private sphere, influencing public political debates on the nation's past, present and most importantly future (fulfilling the formative and normative functions of cultural memory). The continuous social processes of negotiation and reconstruction of collective memory in post-Soviet Estonia show how once the official framework of political memories – or the memory regime – shifted from an anti-fascist to an anti-communist interpretation, political memories that no longer fitted the official interpretation were erased (such as Soviet era monuments from the post-Soviet cityscape). Equally, bottom–up approaches of social groups to transform their memories into official political memories were hampered if they did not concur with the official interpretive post-communist framework (such as the social memory of groups that sympathized with communist ideology or were complicit with the former regime).

Conclusion

By way of conclusion I offer a revised definition of collective memory for the East European experience: collective memory constitutes a 'storage' of shared cultural resources which guarantees the cultural continuity of a community's identity due to its formative and normative functions. Change lies in the continuous process of functional selection and reinterpretation of these stored cultural resources; in other words, in *what* is remembered and *how* at any point in time. In the East European context this dynamic of collective memory was distorted due to foreign domination and institutionalized practices of forced forgetting. Collective memory consists of many overlapping social group memories which are competing over the codification of what is the official interpretive framework of memory. The transformative process of social memories into cultural memories was highly politicized and curtailed in various ways in the East when compared to Western Europe. Because of weak civic traditions, a complicated ethnic mix and contorted identities in Eastern Europe, the 'generational group memory' can serve as a more inclusive category of group identification, superseding exclusive definitions based on ethnicity.

Next I point to some of the theoretical ideas discussed in this chapter that are particularly relevant for *Shadowlands*: overall this book will analyse the dynamic of the transformative process of social (counter) memories into official political memory regimes. The discussion of the formation of Estonian national identity formation between Teuton and Slav (in Chapter 2) will show how the canon inherent in cultural memory can function as boundary marker in these processes of national identification and 'Othering'. Chapter 3 utilizes the generational category for the Estonian case. In Chapter 4, three sets of foundational narratives constitutive of Estonian national identity are singled out, hinting at the formative function of cultural memory. Various social strategies for maintaining and recreating a positive self image after war and occupation are elaborated in chapters 5 and 6. In these later chapters I also provide examples of taboo themes in the contemporary Estonian political discourse on the war and the Soviet period, and show the proscriptive and prescriptive functions of cultural memory. Thus the theoretical apparatus outlined in this chapter will inform the rest of this book.

Notes

1. J. Assmann. 1995. 'Erinnern, um dazu zugehören. Kuturelles Gedächtnis, Zuge-hörigkeitsstrunktur und normative Vergangenheit', in K. Platt and M. Dabag (eds), *Generation und Gedächtnis. Erinnerung und Kolleltive Identitäten*. Opladen: Leske & Budrich, p. 51.
2. P. Roth. 1980. 'The Most Original Book of the Season', *New York Times*, 30 Nov. 1980.
3. E. Renan. 1994. 'Qu'est-ce qu'une nation?', in Hutchinson and Smith (eds), *Nationalism*. Oxford: Oxford University Press, p. 17.
4. *Pace* the claims of Carl Jung for a collective unconscious and Emile Dürkheim who proposed a collective consciousness.
5. E. Tonkin. 1992. *Narrating our Pasts: The Social Construction of Oral History*. Cambridge: Cambridge University Press, 97; Frances Yates, in Jacques Le Goff. 1992. *History and Memory*. New York: Columbia University Press, 77.
6. M. Halbwachs. 1966. *Gedächtnis und seine sozialen Bedingungen*. Berlin: Luchterhand, 195, 200, 366; also J. Assmann. 1997. *Das kulturelle Gedächtnis. Schrift, Erinnerung und politische Identität in frühen Hochkulturen*. Munich: C.H. Beck, 37.
7. M. Halbwachs. 1985. *Gedächtnis und seine sozialen Bedingungen*. Revised edn. Frankfurt a. M.: Suhrkamp, 19–24; quoted in L.A. Coser (ed.). 1992. *Maurice Halbwachs: On Collective Memory*. Chicago: University of Chicago Press, 119; cf. E.J. Hobsbawm. 1972. 'The Social Function of the Past: Some Questions', in *Past & Present* 55(1): 3–17.
8. J. Winter. 2006. *Remembering War: The Great War between Memory and History in the Twentieth Century*. New Haven, CT: Yale University Press, 3; M. Fulbrook. 1999. *German National Identity after the Holocaust*. Cambridge: Polity Press, 44ff.
9. M. Halbwachs. 1980. *The Collective Memory*. New York: Harper & Row, 24–30; Halbwachs, *Gedächtnis und seine sozialen Bedingungen*, 368; Assmann, *Das kulturelle Gedächtnis*, 40; F. Nietzsche. 1995. 'On the Uses and Disadvantages of History for Life' (1874), in Nietzsche, *Untimely Meditations*. Cambridge: Cambridge University Press, 62.
10. A. Assmann and D. Harth (eds). 1991. *Kultur als Lebenswelt und Monument*. Frankfurt: S. Fischer, 11–25.
11. Halbwachs, *Collective Memory*, 50–59; Halbwachs, *Gedächtnis und seine sozialen Bedingungen*, 243–96; Assmann, *Das kulturelle Gedächtnis*, 45, 64.
12. Assmann, *Das kulturelle Gedächtnis*, 12, 50, 56; J. Assmann. 2007. *Religion und kulturelles Gedächtnis*. Munich: C.H. Beck, 29–32, 115.
13. Le Goff, *History and Memory*, 86.
14. B. Anderson. 1991. *Imagined Communities: Reflections on the Origin and Spread of Nationalism*. London: Verso.
15. A. Assmann. 1999. *Erinnerungsäume: Formen und Wandlungen des kulturellen Gedächtnisses*. Munich: C.H. Beck.
16. M. Halbwachs in Coser, *Maurice Halbwachs*, 175; Jan Assmann (*Das kulturelle Gedächtnis*, 59–60) introduces the term mnemotop to describe such sites of cultural memory.
17. A.D. Smith. 1997. 'Nation and Ethnoscapes', *Oxford International Review* 8(2): 11–18; A.D. Smith. 1991. *National Identity*. Harmondsworth: Penguin, 9.
18. The French word lieux approximates to the English word 'root'.
19. P. Nora (ed.). 1996. *Realms of Memory: Rethinking the French Past, vol. 1, Conflicts and Divisions* (translated by Arthur Goldhammer). New York: Columbia University Press, Introduction.

20. As noted in Assmann, *Das kulturelle Gedächtnis*, 44.
21. Halbwachs, *Collective Memory*, 78–87, 101, 205ff.
22. Nora, *Realms of Memory*.
23. Assmann, *Das kulturelle Gedächtnis*, 75ff.; P. Burke. 2004. *What is Cultural History?* Cambridge: Polity, 126.
24. See Winter, *Remembering War*, 17–51, on the memory boom(s) of the twentieth century.
25. J. Rüsen. 1994a. *Historische Orientierung: über die Arbeit des Geschichtsbewußtseins, sich zurechtzufinden*. Cologne: Böhlau Verlag, 213; J. Rüsen. 1994b. 'Was ist Geschichtskultur? Überlegungen zu einer neuen Art, über Geschichte nachzudenken', in J. Rüsen, Klaus Füßmann and H.T. Grütter (eds), *Historische Faszination. Geschichtskultur Heute*. Cologne: Böhlau Verlag, 3–25; J. Rüsen and F. Jäger. 2001. 'Erinnerungskultur', in Karl-Rudolf Korte and Werner Weidenfeld (eds), *Deutschland TrendBuch: Fakten und Orientierungen*. Opladen: Leske and Budrich, 404.
26. Noted by Assmann, *Das kulturelle Gedächtnis*, 40.
27. P. Burke. 1989. 'History as Social Memory', in Thomas Butler (ed.) *Memory: History, Culture and the Mind*. Oxford: Blackwell, 97–113.
28. A.D. Smith. 1998. *Nationalism and Modernism: A Critical Survey of Recent Theories of Nations and Nationalism*. London: Routledge, 191; G. Bellelli and M. Amatulli. 1997. 'Nostalgia, Immigration and Collective Memory', in J. Pennebaker, Dario Paez and Bernard Rimé (eds), *Collective Memory of Political Events: Social Psychological Perspectives*. Mahwah, NJ: Lawrence Erlbaum Associates, 209–20.
29. Jan Assmann cites Deuteronomy as an example of a powerful counter-history of an ethnic resistance movement (Assmann, *Das kulturelle Gedächtnis*, 24, 79ff., 227; J. Assmann and D. Harth, 1992. 'Frühe Formen politischer Mythomotorik. Fundierende, kontrapräsentische und revolutionäre Mythen', in Jan Assmann and Ditriech Harth (eds), *Revolution und Mythos*. Frankfurt a. M.: Suhrkamp, 52; cf. M. Walzer. 1982. *Exodus and Revolution*. New York: Basic Books).
30. Assmann, *Das kulturelle Gedächtnis*, 75ff., 89–96, 140ff. Joanna Overing (1997. 'The Role of Myth: An Anthropological Perspective, or the Reality of the Really Made-up', in Geoffrey Hosking and George Schöpflin (eds), *Myths and Nationhood*. London: Hurst, 1ff.) notes that it was during the fourth to eighth centuries BC that muthos was increasingly seen as a form of speech opposed to the reasoned discourse of logos. It was in the local debates of ancient Greece where the dualism equating history with truth and myth with fiction originated. Privileging *logos* over *muthos* was directly associated with a stronger emphasis on the written text over the tradition of oral poetry, and also connected to the democratization of speech. Jack Snyder and Karen Ballentine (1996. 'Nationalism and the Marketplace of Ideas', *International Security* 21(2): 5–40) define myth as assertions that would lose credibility if exposed to rigorous, disinterested public evaluation.
31. M. Flacke. 1998. 'Die Begründung der Nation aus der Krise', in Monika Flacke and Rainer Rother (eds), *Mythen der Nationen: Ein Europäisches Panorama*. Munich: Koehler & Amelang, 101–28.
32. E. Jansen. 2000a. 'Cultural or Political Nationalism? (On The Development of Estonian Nationalism in the 19th Century)', in Anu-Mai Köll (ed.), *Time and Change in the Baltic Countries: Essays in Honour of Aleksander Loit*. Stockholm: Stockholm University Press, 69.
33. F. Kreutzwald (ed.). 1982. *Kalevipoeg: An Ancient Estonian Tale*. Moorestown, NJ: Symposia Press, 293, 300.

34. Assmann, *Das kulturelle Gedächtnis*, 209; see also Halbwachs, *Gedächtnis und seine sozialen Bedingungen*, 149ff.
35. M. Conway. 1997b. 'Inventory of Experience: Memory and Identity', in James Pennebaker, Dario Paez and Bernard Rimé (eds), *Collective Memory of Political Events: Social Psychological Perspective*. Mahwah, NJ: Lawrence Erlbaum Associates, 21–45.
36. G. Rosenthal. 1997. 'Zur interaktionellen Konstitution von Generationen: Generationenabfolgen in Familien von 1890–1970 in Deutschland', in Jürgen Mansel, Gabriele Rosenthal and Angelika Tölke (eds), *Generationen-Beziehungen, Austausch und Tradierung*. Opladen: Westdeutscher Verlag, 57–73; J. Pennebaker and B.L. Banasik. 1997. 'On the Creation and Maintenance of Collective Memory: History and Social Psychology', in James Pennebaker, Dario Paez and Bernard Rimé (eds), *Collective Memory of Political Events: Social Psychological Perspective*. Hillsdale, NJ: Lawrence Erlbaum Associates: 14ff. 'Codification' refers to the classification and reduction of meaning to a broadly accepted code.
37. K. Mannheim. 1928. 'Das Problem der Generationen', in *Kölner Vierteljahreszeitschrift für Soziologie* 28(7): 309.
38. Mannheim points out that some generational units are at the time fully conscious of the fact that they are creating or have created an *entelechy*, while others act more intuitively, not yet aware that they constitute a generational unit (Mannheim, 'Das Problem der Generationen', 317).
39. Mannheim, 'Das Problem der Generationen', 310–19.
40. M. Scott Peck. 1990. *The Road Less Travelled*. London: Arrow, 90; B. Parekh. 1995. 'The Concept of National Identity', *New Community* 21(2): 256.
41. See H. Tajfel. 1981. *Human Groups and Social Categories*. Cambridge: Cambridge University Press; H. Tajfel. 1982. *Social Identity and Intergroup Relations*. Cambridge: Cambridge University Press; D. Abrams and M. Hoog (eds). 1991. *Social Identity Theory*. New York: Springer; J. Schotter and K.J. Gergen (eds). 1989. *Texts of Identity*. London: Sage.
42. Assmann, *Das kulturelle Gedächtnis*, 132.
43. Ibid., 160.
44. Ibid., 16. In German, *konnektive Struktur* or *Bindungsgedächtnis*.
45. Smith, *National Identity*, 17, 25; A.D. Smith. 1995a. 'The Formation of National Identity', in Henry Harris, *Identity*. Oxford: Clarendon, pp. 130, 131, 140ff.
46. Figure 1.2 is based on Jan Assmann's concept of 'connective structure', as well as on the elaborations on collective cultural identities in Smith, *National Identity*, 25; Smith, 'Formation of National Identity', 131ff.; and Fulbrook, *German National Identity*, 17, 232ff.
47. Parekh, 'Concept of National Identity', 260; B. Parekh. 1994. 'Discourses on National Identity', *Political Studies* 42(3): 501.
48. R. Brubaker. 2004. *Ethnicity without Groups*. Cambridge, MA: Harvard University Press, 138ff. For Brubaker the bone of contention is the uncertain place of culture in the civic–ethnic divide scheme. He argues that if we equate ethnic with 'common descent' most nationalisms would be defined as 'civic', whereas if we adopt the Smithsonian's usage of cultural and ethnic as interchangeable it would make virtually all nationalisms 'ethnic'. By the same token, a purely acultural model of civic nationalism does not exist. In reference to Renan, Brubaker concludes that nationhood is given (ethnic) as much as it is chosen (civic). In Chapter 2 I shall settle on the term 'ethno-cultural nationalism' to describe Estonian nationalism as being based on language and common descent, as well as a shared history and memories.

49. Renan, in Hutchinson and Smith, *Nationalism*, 17; G. Smith (ed.). 1996c. *Nationalities Questions in the post-Soviet States*. London: Longman, 384; George Schöpflin. 2000. *Nations, Identity, Power: The New Politics of Europe*. London: Hurst, 35–50.
50. Tajfel, *Human Groups*, 56.
51. Smith, *Nationalism and Modernism*, 166; Donald L. Horowitz, 2000. *Ethnic Groups in Conflict*. Berkeley: University of California Press.
52. R.F. Baumeister and S. Hastings. 1997. 'Distortions of Collective Memory: How Groups Flatter and Deceive Themselves', in J. Pennebaker, Dario Paez and Bernard Rimé (eds), *Collective Memory of Political Events: Social Psychological Perspectives*. Mahwah, NJ: Lawrence Erlbaum Associates, 277–94.
53. C. Maier. 2002. 'Hot Memory … Cold Memory: On the Political Half-Life of Fascist and Communist Memories', *Transit* 22: 153–65.
54. See L. Colley. 1992. *Britons: Forging the Nation, 1707–1837*. New Haven, CT: Yale University Press.
55. C. Wischermann (ed.). 1996. *Die Legitimität der Erinnerung und die Geschichtswissenschaft*. Stuttgart: F. Steiner Verlag, 66.
56. Parekh, 'Concept of National Identity', 257; Bhikhu Parekh. 1999a. 'Defining National Identity in a Multicultural Society', in Edward Mortimer (ed.), *People, Nation and State: The Meaning of Ethnicity and Nationalism*. London: I.B. Tauris, 67.
57. Assmann, *Das kulturelle Gedächtnis*, esp. 103–29, 140. The term 'common sense' as 'cultural system' was coined by C. Geertz. 1973. *Local Knowledge: Further Essays in Interpretive Anthropology*. New York: Basic Books, 73–93.
58. J.K. Olick and D. Levy. 1997. 'Collective Memory and Cultural Constraint: Holocaust Myth and Rationality in German Politics', *American Sociological Review* 62(6): 925–34.
59. F. Bédarida. 2000. 'The Historian's Craft, Historicity, and Ethics', in Joep Leerssen and Ann Rigney (eds), *Historians and Social Values*. Amsterdam: Amsterdam University Press, 72; Burke 1989.
60. The conventional starting date of Polish history is 966, when Prince Mieszko (963–992) – the first ruler of the *Piast* Dynasty – converted to and accepted Christianity in the name of his people; for myth making in Ukrainian history, see A. Wilson. 2000. *The Ukrainians: Unexpected Nation*. London: Yale University Press.
61. Levi-Strauss in J. Assmann, *Das kulturelle Gedächtnis*, 75, 78. The term mythomoteur is also used by John Armstrong (1982. *Nations before Nationalism*. Chapel Hill: University of North Carolina Press, 283), who attributed to such figures a crucial role in the emergence of national identity.
62. J. Assmann, 'Erinnern, um dazu zugehören', 51–76; J. Assmann, *Das kulturelle Gedächtnis*, 126ff.; Abrams and Hoog (in M. Billig. 1997. *Banal Nationalism*. London: Sage, 66) link group identification to stereotyping; by that they mean that (new) group members have to accept the stereotypic norms associated with the group identity.
63. J. Assmann. 1988. 'Kollektives Gedächtnis und kulturelle Identität', in Jan Assmann and Toni Hölscher (eds), *Kultur und Gedächtnis*. Frankfurt a. M.: Suhrkamp, 13; J. Assmann, *Das kulturelle Gedächtnis*, 153. The word 'canon' has a strong Christian connotation referring to a body of statements concerning faith or morals proclaimed by the Church. A more secular use of canon can refer to a record arranged according to some system or to an accepted principle of rules.
64. J. Assmann, *Das kulturelle Gedächtnis*, 151, 159.
65. Schöpflin, *Politics in Eastern Europe*; see also Wöll and Wydra, *Democracy and Myth*, 16–20.

66. J. Szacki. 1994. *Liberalism after Communism*. Budapest: Central European University Press, 106.
67. Le Goff, *History and Memory*, 98.
68. See D. Crowley and S.E. Reid (eds). 2002. *Socialist Spaces: Sites of Everyday Life in the Eastern Bloc*. New York: Berg.
69. V. Skultans. 1998. *The Testimony of Lives: Narrative and Memory in Post-Soviet Latvia*. London: Routledge, 142.
70. P. Sztompka. 1991. 'The Intangibles and the Imponderables of the Transition to Democracy', *Studies in Comparative Communism* 24(3): 300.
71. If we employ Aleida Assmann's differentiated concept of cultural memory (involving both a functional and a stored memory), then at the foreground the functional memory in Soviet Estonia was impaired by practices of Soviet-communist domination, but stored memory – the background – was less affected, and although communist rule limited recourse to the stored memory as well due to the widespread destruction of the cultural heritage, this larger pool of resources could be reconstructed. Forbidden libraries often 'survived' in summer houses, and the literary body produced by Estonian exiles was fed back into Estonian society after re-independence.
72. J. Assmann, *Religion und kulturelles Gedächtnis*, 29–32.

Chapter 2

BETWEEN TEUTON AND SLAV

We must not forget that the Estonians ... have no culture of their
own and will hardly ever possess one.
– Georg Dehio, 'Vom baltischen Deutschtum'[1]

One slaughters an animal by breaking its backbone. The estates were
the backbone of the Baltic Barons.
– Aleksander Veiler, left-wing Estonian politician in 1919[2]

Stalin, Khrushchev and Brezhnev are travelling in a train. The train
breaks down. 'Shoot everyone!' orders Stalin. They shoot everyone but
the train doesn't budge. 'Rehabilitate everyone!' orders Khrushchev.
They rehabilitate everyone, but still the train won't go. 'Close the
curtains', orders Brezhnev, 'and just pretend we are moving'.
– Famous anti-Soviet joke[3]

Estonia's history of century-long foreign rule prompts the question of
whether a culture is sufficient to hold a people together. This chapter
will illustrate how Estonian national identification was shaped by the
complex conditions of the East European borderland, a sort of 'shatter
zone' where the parallel existence of different national groups has been a
characteristic feature. In this region identities were more contested than
in much of Western Europe because of the East European legacies of ethnic diversity and frequently shifting borders discussed in the preceding
chapter. But it is in more modern times that this borderland crystallized as a focal point of political tension in the power struggle between
the German and Russian empires – Teuton against Slav.[4] Consequently
the fate of Estonia depended largely on the outcome of the competitive
relation between these two powers. Estonia, and this will be my argument, had to develop a modern national identity in opposition to a

'double Other'. For the British, by contrast, the role of the historic Other was assumed by the French and for America by the Old World – that is to say, in each case essentially by a 'single Other'.

I shall trace here the main lines of development of modern Estonian national identity from the declaration of independence in 1918 to re-independence in 1991. The First World War had a crucial impact on the course of Estonian history, because it was when the country proclaimed its independence for the first time. Yet it is the social experiences of the Second World War – that is, the first Soviet year (1940–41), the Nazi occupation and the Holocaust (1941–44) – and the ensuing Soviet period that are of key importance for *Shadowlands* – for historical reasons and also because events from that era are still in the living memory of the historians interviewed for this book. This is why I move from the more geographically defined notion of 'borderland' to the idea of 'shadowland': a land marked by the experience of double occupation – Soviet communist and Nazi German – and overshadowed still by unresolved memories of subordination and collaboration resulting in conflicted identities. Likewise the specific form of the Soviet domination left deep traces on Estonian society, with Stalin, Khrushchev and Brezhnev serving as shorthand forms for the Soviet-imposed experiences of terror, thaw and stagnation. I shall be asking what kind of social counter memories and cultural symbols fired the process of the Estonian 'Singing Revolution' from 1987 onwards, which was in part sparked by the 'Gorbachev moment'. How did Estonian national leaders reinterpret and use history to mobilize the people for independent statehood?

In sketching the main lines of development of modern Estonian national identity formation in relation to the double Other, this chapter also looks at the Estonian national movement. Although the first Estonian awakening of the 1860s was predominantly cultural, it progressively changed into a political empire-subverting and state-creating force.[5] Yet Estonian nationalism is non-expansive and rather protective, in this way characteristic of a small nationalism.[6] Due to the lack of a long-standing state-bound tradition and the impact of the Soviet institutional legacy – alluded to at the end of the last chapter – Estonian national identity is mainly defined by language and culture, which is why we can speak of it as a cultural nationalism.[7] Chapter 1 highlighted how a group's cultural memory can function as a boundary marker in processes of enhanced canonization, triggered through foreign domination or inter-ethnic conflict. In Estonia these ethno-linguistic markers were effectively employed as justification for independent statehood, and they also shaped the processes of negative 'Othering' during times of state building after 1918 and again after 1991. We may therefore classify Estonian nationalism as a divisive ethno-linguistic nationalism.[8] This chapter provides the reader with the historical toolkit needed to contextualize the social memories of the wars and the Soviet period which are discussed in the life-story narratives of historians in Estonia in subsequent parts of the book. In other words the four generational groups of respondents whom I analyse in detail in Chapter 3 are formed by the historical events outlined in this chapter.

The Double Other in Estonian Collective Identity Formation

'Estonia cannot be considered a borderland in the classical sense of the meaning, because the country belongs historically and integrally to the sphere of the so called Lutheran German civilization.' This tendentious statement by the political scientist Rein Ruutsoo serves as an entry into my assessment of the conflicted heritage of the Baltic German and Russian Others for processes of Estonian identity formation.[9] To achieve independent statehood the Estonians had to get rid of a ruling elite that was ethnically different: this makes it essential to turn to the dialectic between national self and Other in Estonian national identity formation. The sociologist Pille Petersoo points out that often more than one significant Other figures in a group's identity construction; in other words, various Others, negative and positive, exist simultaneously and may be functional in different periods.[10] While Petersoo suggests a total of four ideal types of Other – the external versus internal and negative versus positive Other – I shall limit my focus largely to the Russian-speaking community who settled in Estonia after 1940, treating it as negative internal Other (and the Russian neighbour as negative external Other), and secondly the Baltic Germans, considered as negative internal Other that was transformed to an external positive Other after 1945.[11]

I shall begin by illustrating the ambivalence inherent in Russian and German rule of Estonia. During the long nineteenth century under Tsarist rule, the Russian impact on Estonian society was not always negative but at times proved modernizing and liberalizing. Conversely, although some consider the Baltic German heritage – with the Reformation, Enlightenment thought and the nationalist philosophy of Johann Gottfried Herder – to be Estonia's cultural foundation, the German influence also meant autocratic feudal rule. My point here is to probe the established account in Estonian historiography after 1991 of both German and Russian rule being only times of suffering and occupation, threatening the Estonian nation. Instead I ask whether the impact of the double Other also provided Estonians in some ways and at some points with a framework conducive to the development of national identity.

My brief discussion of the Other and the borderland form the conceptual frame of this chapter. Before I turn to the German influence on Estonian identity, I shall give some background on the establishment of the 700-year rule of the German landed elite of the Baltic borderland. In 1200 Bishop Albert von Buxhöveden of Bremen led the Sword Brethren (or Teutonic Knights) east to convert Europe's last pagans, thereby establishing the north-eastern frontier of Latin Christendom and marking the territory referred to as 'Mary's Land' (in Estonian *Maarjamaa*). Estonians were subsequently forced into serfdom and Christianized after defeat in what is commonly termed by their descendants as the 'ancient fight for freedom'.[12] There ensued the Livonian Wars (1558–1629) between Russia, Denmark, Sweden and Poland for control of the Baltic provinces, out of which Sweden emerged as the dominant power. But all along it was the Baltic German landed elite who ruled the country as intermediaries for the big powers.

Similar to other colonial rulers, such as the British in India, the Baltic German Other is viewed by Estonians with an intrinsic ambivalence, having imposed serfdom while also bringing high culture. With regard to the latter we need to mention the Protestant Reformation and its encouragement of standardizing the vernacular language, the role of the Moravian Brethren in promoting education, and the introduction of Herder's idea that language forms the basis of national identity – which deeply stimulated the Estonian cultural awakening of the late nineteenth century. In 1523 the Reformation reached Estonia: church services were conducted in Estonian, raising its prestige to that of a 'language of God', on a par with Latin or German, and giving a major psychological boost to the status of the native population.[13] The Reformation was coupled with the formulation of a standard written language. One of the first Estonian-language books, a fragment of the Lutheran catechism, was published in 1535 by Simon Wanradt and Johann Koell in Wittenberg, Germany.

In the 1720s, with the spread of Pietism, the Moravian Brethrens' Enlightenment beliefs regarding the equality of man took root among the locals, in particular encouraging the Estonian people to see the worth and unique quality of their culture. The Moravians found many open ears among local peasants, who rejected Lutheranism as being an institution of the Baltic German landed nobility.[14] To encourage individual Bible study, the Moravians recruited clergy from among the local population and promoted peasant education, with the result that by the end of the eighteenth century adult literacy in (southern) Estonia had climbed to 66 per cent of the population – a higher level than in Russia.[15] This development coincided with the first full translation of the Bible in 1739 into the (north) Estonian dialect, which later formed the basis for standard written Estonian.[16]

Herder's ideas on nations expressed in his *Voyage in the Year* 1769 inspired the creation of national consciousness and a striving for cultural autonomy among the indigenous people of the Baltic region. To Herder, nations were language communities, because it is through language that the 'consciousness of the nation' is articulated. His thoughts on nationhood focused on those national cultures that did not possess a state of their own, or whose cultural autonomy was endangered in other ways. Herder valued folklore as the repository of the national spirit, and folk songs as 'the archive of the people, the treasury of their knowledge, religion and theogony, and the cosmologies of their fathers' deeds and of events in history'. Consequently, he argued, an oppressed nation could only recover its national identity through the rediscovery of its folklore.[17]

At the end of the nineteenth century the Estonian rural population saw themselves controlled by the Baltic German landed elite, who, although constituting only 1 per cent of the rural population and with no support base among the peasants, maintained their power on grounds of medieval privileges granting them land and regional domination within a status-bound social structure. In their social roles as feudal masters, pastors, teachers and physicians, Baltic Germans considered themselves to be on a Teutonic mission: as the 'vehicle of culture and civilization' and as a 'bulwark against Eastern barbarism', they upheld paternalistic notions about their 'duty to their homeland [*Estland*]'.[18] The Baltic Germans never actively pursued cultural assimilation – or Germanification – of the native population; instead German culture served as an important social boundary marker between 'master and servant'.[19] As elsewhere in Eastern Europe, social mobility required the command of German; even so, upwardly mobile Estonians who had a command of German were dismissed as 'wannabe Germans', which reflects the essential haughtiness displayed by the Baltic German nobility and clergy vis-à-vis Estonians, as well as the limits of breaking the exclusive code of German cultural prestige.[20] Yet the Baltic German Other could potentially be considered also as 'awakeners' or even 'engineers' of the Estonian 'high culture' because the Estophiles among them helped to standardize the modern Estonian language out of the regional vernaculars.[21] But whereas the majority of Estophiles viewed the Estonian process of self-assertion as a predominantly cultural awakening, driven primarily by the idea of education, they opposed any politicized version of Estonian nationalism. We can therefore conclude that they propagated the ideas of Herder but omitted Kant's ideas of the 'autonomous will'. Peasant uprisings against the reactionary 'grey Barons' occurred across the Baltic borderland from 1343–45 right up to the anti-Tsarist upheavals of 1905, but the Baltic German landed elite cannot be regarded as modernizers. Instead they resisted the socio-economic modernization process of the old agrarian system – triggered by peasant emancipation, for instance – and continued to deny the indigenous population their calls for democratization and political participation.[22]

Before we turn to the impact of the Russian Other on Estonian national identity formation, I shall make a few observations about the Estonian cultural awakening of the late nineteenth century, which is important because it forms the memory basis for future national independence movements. Baltic German and Germanized intellectuals, such as August Wilhelm Hupel and Garlieb Merkel, disseminated Herder's ideas in the late eighteenth century. But it was the first generation of home-grown Estonian intellectuals, notably the journalist Carl Robert Jakobson, one of the most radical figures of the 'Estonian awakening' (in Estonian *ärkamisaeg*), who openly denounced the German conquerors for having imposed nothing less than the yoke of slavery upon the Estonians for seven hundred years, bringing about the degeneration of their splendid old culture. Jakobson delivered three patriotic lectures between 1868 and 1870 in which he divided Estonian history into a time of light prior to the thirteenth-century conquest, then a time of darkness signifying the '700 years of serfdom', and finally a renaissance or dawn of a new era – in other words, the contemporary cultural awakening. Another nationalist leader of the same era, Pastor Jakob Hurt, explained to his Estonian audience that nationality was determined solely by descent, and that 'Estonian' did not mean 'peasant', just as 'German' did not signify a person of higher social status.[23] A fine example for the direct influence of Herder's ideas is the creation of Kalev's Son (in Estonian *Kalevipoeg*): Friedrich Robert Faehlmann (and his successor Friedrich Reinhold Kreutzwald) produced Estonia's national epic about the legendary figure of *Kalevipoeg*, based on thousands of songs, fables, sagas and fairy tales of the common people, which had been collected by public appeal in the late nineteenth century.[24] All the ideas referred to here would have lasting influence on Estonian cultural memory.

The year traditionally held to mark the beginning of the national awakening is 1857, when Johann Voldemar Jannsen, an elementary schoolteacher and parish clerk, first published the *Pärnu Courier*, an Estonian-language weekly, using the term 'Estonian' as a self-ascribed category instead of 'people of the country' – the vague identity label used in many parts of Eastern Europe before the First World War. It was only in the 1860s that a larger number of home-grown Estonian nationalists emerged who addressed their message in their Estonian mother tongue directly to the common man – notably the free peasant – via a flourishing periodical press. Education in the vernacular, both at school and university level, thereby became the cornerstone of the national movement.[25]

The Estonian language – not Slavic but Uralic, like Finnish or Hungarian – became a central symbol of Estonian nationalism in the nineteenth century, and this is why I refer to the movement as cultural nationalism. Lines of demarcation between a cultural and political nationalism are, of course, fluid: the Estonian awakening was initially a cultural awakening and only in the second stage an awakening of the national consciousness among Estonians. In the 1850s, Estonian was still a language of peasants, not yet used as the medium of higher education. By 1900, Estonian standard language-building had assumed the character of a collective national undertaking, which took place amid the crossfire of German and Russian cultural and linguistic influences.[26] Estonia is known for a strong singing tradition: in 1869 the first 'Song Festival' was held, and the Estonian Musical Society was founded that same year. The founders' intent was to use an interactive performance to forge a sense of solidarity and national consciousness (social *imaginaire*) among the participating masses. The song festival has proved another important building block of Estonian cultural memory.

But Estonian nationalism was not defined simply against the (Baltic) German heritage. After the Great Northern War of 1700–21, Estonia – together with Livland, Ingermanland and south-eastern Karelia – were transferred to Tsarist Russia. And although Estonia, along with Livland and Curonia, became an autonomous Russian province governed ultimately from Petrograd, the Treaty of Nystad (1721) continued to guarantee Baltic German control over the local administration.[27]

So let us now turn to the Russian influence on Estonian identity formation: Tsarist Russia pursued cultural Russification policies to assimilate non-Russians into the administrative, juridical and educational system – with the aim of creating a base for a Russian nation defined in a political sense (in Russian *rossiyskiy*) rather than an ethnic sense (in Russian *russkiy*).[28] It may sound paradoxical given the later impact of Soviet power, but Tsarist Russia played the role of a modernizer by providing Estonians with the opportunity to take up professional positions and thus encouraging greater upward social mobility. The abolition of Estonian serfdom by Tsar Alexander I in 1816 – well ahead of the general peasant emancipation in Russia in 1861 – helped to unshackle the Estonian people from the tight grip of their local Baltic German masters, and transformed the country from an exclusively agrarian society into one with a small emergent middle class.[29] Later Tsar Alexander II supported the spread of education and enabled farm purchases in Estonia.³⁰ Subsequently a small class of Estonian peasants was prosperous enough to send their sons to universities, a development crucial to the crystallization of the Estonian nation and the emergence of an Estonian national movement. Estonian politicians found a parliamentary platform in the Petrograd Duma for articulating ideas about autonomous Estonian self-government, the agrarian reform and universal franchise. In October 1905 the Tsar's manifesto granted new civil rights, such as freedom of speech and assembly, and permitted the creation of political parties faithful to the new constitutional monarchy of Nicholas II. In response, the Estonian Jaan Tõnisson founded the Estonian National Progressive Party, as the first legal party of Estonia.

This is not, of course, to deny the negative effects of the Russification policies of Alexander III (1881–1904), which censored the national press and imposed Russian as the language of the schools and law courts, nor to gloss over the brutal reaction of the Tsarist authorities after the peasant revolts of 1905.³¹ But my overall point remains, namely that the Tsarist regime – in its efforts to break the dominance of the German Baltic elite over Estonian national life – served at times as a modernizing and liberalizing force. I therefore depart somewhat from the blanket statement by Alexander V. Prusin that 'the Russian government consistently resisted any constitutional experiments, and the concepts of autocracy, rigid Orthodoxy, and the estate-based order remained key foundations of the imperial order'.³²

And so, by the end of the nineteenth century, there existed a clear ethno-cultural base for Estonian national identity. The etymological proximity of the Estonian words for 'people' (*rahvas*) and for 'nation' (*rahvus*) points to the fact that an ethnic conception of the Estonian nation is deeply entrenched in Estonian self-understanding.³³ *Rahvas* signifies a community of shared descent, history, language and culture, while *rahvus* holds an additional meaning of 'a political community'. Following Anthony D. Smith's definition, Estonians did not possess a national identity until the late nineteenth century because that requires 'some sense of political community based on common institutions and a single code of rights and duties for all the members of the community'.³⁴ But because the Estonians existed with a collective cultural identity separate from the ruling class, living on a more or less clearly defined territory and cherishing a rich folklore and distinctive vernacular, they qualified as an *ethnie* – to employ Smith's term. Although there were some full-blooded nationalists at the turn of the century – for instance, the 'Congress of People's Representatives' declared in November 1905 that the Tsarist regime should be overthrown and committees of self-government formed in its place – the main demand, more modestly, was for greater autonomy within a federalized Tsarist empire. This moderation possibly reflected Estonian experience of Russia as to some extent a positive external Other, but it was mostly because autonomy seemed the maximum to be hoped for from the Tsarist regime. But new opportunities opened up once the German Reich and the Russian Empire became locked in a titanic struggle that would tear both regimes apart.

Foundational Moment: The First Estonian Republic

For some nations, winning independence was a once-for-all moment, as in the war between the United States and Britain in 1776–83. For Estonia, however, independence has required repeated struggles, not only throughout the twentieth century but also against multiple enemies. This pattern was strikingly foreshadowed in the foundational moment of Estonian independence, when the First Republic had to fight for its new life against both Russians and Germans, amid conditions of internal civil war.

Let me briefly summarize this chaotic period. In March 1917, after the Tsar was overthrown, the new Russian provisional government under Aleksander Kerensky granted autonomy to Estonia. The Russian civil war swept through Estonia, but there was also an internal civil war raging between local Bolshevik sympathisers, Estonian national patriots and German volunteers. Taking advantage of the Bolshevik coup in November 1917, Estonian nationalists proclaimed an independent and democratic Estonian Republic on 24 February 1918, under a new provisional government led by Prime Minister Konstantin Päts. This audacious gesture turned out to be of mainly symbolic value, because the Bolshevik government, embattled in civil war, signed the Brest-Litovsk peace with Germany, and Estonia was overrun by German troops seeking to turn the country into a Baltic Duchy in union with Prussia.[35] During the German military occupation the activity of Estonian political parties was banned and the representatives of the Estonian provisional government imprisoned; Estonian newspapers were closed down, Estonian national military units dispersed and the Bolshevik organizational network destroyed. But then the tables turned again. The reinstalment of Baltic German control was stopped short by the collapse of the German Reich and the Armistice of 11 November 1918. Rather ironically the Entente powers encouraged the German volunteers to remain in the Baltic borderland to ward off the Bolshevik threat.[36]

In the eyes of many Estonians the German occupation during the war discredited any paternalistic Baltic German claims to protect the 'common fatherland' because they were now seen as 'traitors' and 'fifth

column' threatening Estonian ambitions of independent statehood.
This is reflected in Georg Eduard Luiga's graphic statement: 'What they
[*the Germans*] have done in the course of 700 years we can forget, but
what they now have done in the last seven months, to forget this is
impossible'.[37] The new Soviet government invaded the region to support
local communist sympathizers and to establish an Estonian Commune
in November 1918. It claimed to be liberating the Baltic people from
the 'German imperialist yoke' but its invasion served to add a Bolshevik
element to the perception of the Russian Other.[38]

For Estonia, 1918 was the beginning of the War of Independence
(1918–20), which pitted the Estonian provisional government with weak
national forces against Estonian Bolsheviks, the invading Red Army
and German volunteers. In January 1919 Estonian troops under General
Juhan Laidoner (together with the German Baltic regiment and Finnish
volunteers, armed with British weapons) managed to turn the tide and
push the Red Army back. The victory of Estonian and Latvian troops
(again joined by the German Baltic regiment) over the German volunteers
and other Baltic German forces at the battle of Cesis (in Estonian,
'Võnnu') resulted in the complete German withdrawal from Latvia on
23 June 1919.[39] The experience of German occupation during the war
elevated the radical expropriation of the Baltic German landed elite to
the top of the Estonian political agenda. In October 1919, dressed up as
agrarian reform, this revolutionary act of decolonization was executed,
reflecting the staunch determination of the young and vulnerable state
to undermine their former subjugators' claim to Estonian territory by
breaking their 'backbone'.[40] This redistribution of land provided Estonian
war veterans – the so called 'Freedom Fighters' – with plots of land in
an attempt to create loyal citizens of the new state and as a pre-emptive
strike against feared Bolshevik communist agitation.

The end of Estonia's first struggle for independence was now in sight.
Although the Red Army emerged victorious in 1920 from the Russian
civil war, the Soviet Union was still willing to sign the Tartu Peace Treaty
with Estonia on 2 February 1920, possibly to cut its losses and concentrate
forces on waging war with Poland. Some scholars argue that Estonia's
independence came into being more as a consequence of the collapsing
German and Russian empires,[41] whereas Norman Davies insists that
'Estonia's independence … was achieved almost exclusively by Estonian
efforts'.[42] I would adopt a middle position: in 1918 Estonians achieved
independence through their own efforts, but the new state took shape in
the spaces opened up by the defeat and demise of the German Reich, the
collapse of the old Tsarist regime, and the relative weakness of the new
Bolshevik leadership.

Nevertheless, democratic stability was short lived and, as elsewhere during the 1920s in Europe, Estonia saw an economic depression and growing anti-democratic movements. On the radical left, communists attempted a coup in 1924, while on the right an ex-combatants' interest group – the War of Independence Veterans' League – also agitated against the young parliamentary democracy.[43] In response, President Päts declared a state of emergency, dissolved the state assembly and ruled by decree, ushering in the so-called 'era of silence' (1934–40) during which all democratic life was frozen.[44] With the political objective of renewing national unity, Päts promoted traditional national values, summoning up romantic notions of the countryside, the farmstead and the territorially bound peasant. Song festivals were now performed by choirs in traditional peasant dress, while experts from the Estonian National Museum laid out correct rules for the costumes for each region, in a clear case of the 'invention of tradition'.[45]

We have discussed the events culminating in the founding of the first Estonian republic in some detail because the social memories of a free interwar Estonia would later serve as a potent counter-memory for many Estonians opposing Soviet rule. The political figures such as President Päts and General Laidoner acquired almost mythical quality, and the foundational narrative of the battle of Võnnu, which is commemorated as Victory Day on 23 June, became an important formative cultural memory. Likewise the idealized ethnic rural Estonian (in Estonian, *asunik*) – who together with his family toiled on his own piece of land – came to serve as a normative cultural memory upholding certain pre-war traditions and values against Soviet ideas of collectivism.

Double Totalitarian Rule of Estonia

The second half of the twentieth century left the East European borderland overshadowed with the experience of double totalitarian rule. As in 1917–20, the pattern was chaotic. In 1939 the secret protocols of the Molotov–Ribbentrop Pact carved up the region between Soviet Russia and Nazi Germany. This gave Stalin carte blanche to invade the Baltic countries in the summer of 1940. But then Hitler broke the pact and invaded the Baltics in the summer of 1941, only to be pushed out in 1944. This curt narrative cloaks terrible horrors. The local population fought on both sides, leaving people with traumatic memories of fratricidal war and collaboration for decades to come. Also during the German occupation (1941–44) the Nazi project to exterminate the European Jewry (*Endlösung*) took place in part on Estonian soil. Members of the

'War Generation' were most affected by the events of the Second World War, as I shall show in the next chapter.

Let us now turn to the course of historical events in some detail, because this helps to show the intense horror of this period for Estonians. In October 1939 Hitler had called for the repatriation of the Baltic Germans to the Wartheland ('Warthegau', the Reich territory in Poland), which created an eerie feeling amongst some Estonians as they watched more than 14,000 Germans leave by January 1941.[46] The Soviet occupation of Estonia in June 1940 and the establishment of the Estonian Soviet Socialist Republic (ESSR) were immediately followed by mass arrests among members of anti-communist organizations, the political elites, high state officials, the police, landowners and industrialists in order to destroy Estonian society.[47] The Estonian standing army was broken up, its officers executed or deported, and over 20,000 Estonian men were drawn into the Red Army – several thousand of these, however, subsequently deserted to the German side.[48] Others had already formed anti-Soviet partisan units as German troops approached in 1941, fighting a guerrilla war against the retreating Red Army and Soviet 'shock battalions' who were implementing Stalin's 'scorched earth policy'.[49] Soviet repressive operations throughout its Western borderlands resulted in the mass deportation of 11,000 Estonians to the hinterland of Russia.[50]

In the summer of 1941 the German army was greeted as 'liberators' from Soviet rule, but hopes that Estonian independence would be regained were soon dashed. Nazi Germany granted Estonia limited self-governance as part of the 'Occupied Eastern Territories' (State Commissariat Ostland).[51] On their arrival the Germans created an 'auxiliary police' (in Estonian, Omakaitse), eventually numbering nearly 40,000, formed from 'trustworthy' elements of the former Estonian self-defence militia, the Estonian anti-Soviet partisan units, and those former Estonian army and police personnel who had escaped Soviet deportation. In the National Socialist conception of race, Estonians were inferior to the Germanic race.[52] Nevertheless from 1942 Estonians were admitted into the local branch of the 'Hitler Youth', and German authorities began to progressively mobilize young Estonian men into various armed formations.[53]

A snapshot of the winter of 1943/44 reveals the full effect of the war between Teuton and Slav in dividing the local population. Approximately 50,000 Estonian men in the Estonian SS Legion, the Estonian brigade, the auxiliary police, the battalions, and other smaller national units, were fighting to hold back the Soviet advance.[54] Facing them, the Red Army at this time included the 20,000-strong Eighth Estonian Rifle Corps. To avoid the German draft, over 5,000 Estonians had earlier fled to Finland to volunteer for service in the Finnish armed forces; following the renewed Soviet advance westwards in August 1944 up to 3,500 of these 'Finnish Boys' returned to defend their homeland. Meanwhile, at the end of the war, about 80,000 Estonians fled to the West in the face of the Soviets' imminent arrival in September 1944 – a huge number given the small total population of some 1.1 million.[55] Canada and Sweden were the principal destinations of Estonian refugees. In this precarious geopolitical position, Estonians tried to exploit the rivalry between the two great powers and also developed strategies of complicity and muddling through. Yet ultimately they were caught in the middle and became the frequent losers in the struggle between Nazi Germany and Soviet Russia.

By January 1945 Estonia had lost between 10 and 25 per cent of its pre-war population through deportations, military and civilian fatalities, political executions, emigration and territorial transfer. And the country also became the arena for the *Endlösung* of around 1,000 local Jews and approximately 15,000 European Jews during the Nazi occupation.[56] Estonia gained notoriety at the Wannsee conference of 1942, where it was scheduled to be the first country 'free of Jews'.[57] The auxiliary police's objective was to clear the occupied territory of Jews, communist activists and anti-German partisans, thus carrying out the arrests and executions of the Estonian Jewry. In this the Germans depended on the collaboration of the locals to find Jews, anti-German partisans and communists. At the time, SS Oberstrumbandführer Martin Sandberger – head of the special detachment 1a of mobile killing unit A – complained about the poorly developed 'racial viewpoint' among the Estonians.[58] Evidence suggests there was a greater hatred of communists (and Russians) among the Estonians after the first Soviet year than of Jews. For example, during the opening month of the German occupation an attempt by the auxiliary police to deport the Russian population of the coastal villages of the Peipus Lake was thwarted by the German authorities. Yet no organization for the rescue of Estonian Jews existed, so that at most five Estonian Jews survived the German occupation, all others being killed between August and December 1941.[59] The second phase of the Holocaust in Estonia began in the autumn of 1942 when Jews, mainly from Germany, Occupied Lithuania and Czechoslovakia, were deported to the country; the old and sick were killed in the forests, while the young and strong were sent to prisons or forced labour camps.

Soviet-Style Domination

In 1944, Estonia was recaptured by the Red Army and incorporated into the USSR as a Soviet republic with a restructured economic, administrative and political system. In this section I shall summarize the changing phases of Soviet rule from the 1940s to the 1980s, some harsher than others but all of them based on domination.

The first post-war decade, the last years of Stalin, witnessed intensified Soviet repressions through the military apparatus and KGB, as well as guerrilla warfare by an Estonian pro-independence resistance movement comprising at its peak approximately five thousand men, mainly former Estonian soldiers in the German army or members of the auxiliary police who may have failed to escape to the West. Apart from the structuring of all societal spheres, Sovietization also meant shock industrialization, including the influx of Russian-speaking immigrants and the exploitation of natural resources, such as phosphate, oil shale and uranium.[60] Between 1948 and 1950, over 93 per cent of all Estonian farms were forcibly collectivized (*kolkhozes*), transforming Estonia from a predominantly agricultural economy to one that was much more industrial and urban. In March 1949, as part of a Baltic-wide secret operation, Soviet authorities deported to Siberia over 21,000 Estonians, and also other so-called 'enemies of the people'.[61] By the early 1950s the Estonian Communist Party (ECP) was dominated by Russians and 'Russified' Estonians – that is Estonians who had lived in Russia – while most of the nationally orientated Estonian *nomenklatura* had been dismissed as 'bourgeois nationalists'.[62]

Stalin finally died in 1953. Khrushchev's critique of Stalin's cult of personality in 1956 ushered in a period of de-Stalinization and relaxation of authoritarian rule. The post-Stalin era in Estonia was a time of accommodation to the Soviet regime, and it proved particularly formative for the generation of Post-War Children (as I shall discuss in the next chapter). Overall decentralization allowed for necessary reforms, for instance in the agricultural sector, such as the introduction of a wage system and private ownership of machinery. Estonia (together with Latvia) enjoyed the highest standard of living in the USSR, yet many Estonians complained about their 'backwardness', blaming it on the involuntary incorporation of their economy into the all-Soviet Union.[63] In the course of liberalization, most of the deportees were allowed to return from the gulag camps in the mid-1950s, and a renaissance in cultural life was noticeable in the 1960s. The opening of the new Tallinn to Helsinki ferry in 1965 and the fact that small numbers of Estonians were allowed to travel to the West increased this sense of freedom. Initial hopes raised by the wave of liberalization were reflected in a rise in the number of ethnic Estonians in the Estonian Communist Party (ECP) – up to 50 per cent in the last twenty-five years of Soviet rule.[64] But ultimately hopes were dashed by the crushing of the Prague Spring in 1968 – a moment referred to by many of my interviewees.

Leonid Brezhnev (1964–82) tried to stabilize the Soviet system after the upheavals of the Khrushchev era. His enforced 'Sovietization' policies, such as linguistic Russification, and the dramatically changed demographic situation due to the mass influx of Russian-speaking immigrants – who mostly worked in the military-industrial complex – aroused widespread concern among Estonians. Many Estonians in the late 1970s asked plaintively: 'Will the people disappear?'[65] Within the ESSR the titular nationality dropped from 94 per cent after the war to 68 per cent in 1970 (and 62 per cent in 1989). From the 1980s onwards the Russian-speakers came to represent the repressive Soviet regime. Kolstø states that the majority of Russians had been indoctrinated to believe that they had the moral and historical right to control and 'Russify' the whole of the Soviet Union.[66] Russophones effectively controlled key party and state institutions in the ESSR. The native Estonian elite were under-represented in the ruling organs of the CP on all-Union and republic levels. Consequently Soviet Estonians felt politically deprived in their own country, yet at the same time many Estonians despised the Soviet political institutions.[67] When an Estonian addressed a local Russian in Estonian, he often received the answer 'Speak a human language' – in other words speak Russian. The reply this provoked (on the Estonian side) was, 'Why don't you go back to your Russia?'[68]

As elsewhere in the Eastern bloc, the Final Act of the Helsinki Conference on Security and Cooperation in Europe (1975) prompted a new form of dissent based on demands for Human Rights. Four Estonian signatories supported the Baltic Appeal to the UN in 1979 demanding the publication and repudiation of the secret protocols of the Molotov–Ribbentrop Pact. A year later, well-known Estonian writers and intellectuals – many of them party members – in the 'Letter of the Forty' showed public disapproval of Russification policies and of the ECP leadership for suppressing a spontaneous youth demonstration in Tallinn.[69] The obligatory two-year military service for all male Soviet citizens in general and the Afghanistan War in 1979–80 more specifically were also important issues for the generation growing up in the 1970s, which I will discuss in the next chapter as the 'Transitional Generation'.

How did the experience of the wars and Soviet rule impact on the Estonian view of the double Other? Baltic Germans had long figured as a negative internal Other for Estonians, although I pointed out that in fact their role was ambiguous. In the twentieth century Estonians came to view the Baltic German Other as a threat to the newly established republic. In particular the German occupation during the First World War irreversibly discredited the Baltic German claim of serving as a 'midwife' to the first Estonian Republic (based on the fact that Baltic Germans were instrumental in forging a high culture and introducing the legal, educational and administrative structures to the country). After their radical expropriation in 1919, Baltic Germans left the Baltic borderland in great numbers, so that their influence as negative internal Other began to dwindle (a tendency that continued until 1939 with the repatriation of Baltic Germans). Certainly the Nazi occupation revived hostile Estonian perceptions of things German, but after 1941 the former negative internal Baltic German Other was irrevocably replaced by the Soviet occupying power as an internal negative Russian Other. After the traumatic experience of the first Soviet year and of renewed Soviet occupation of Estonia from the summer of 1944, the perception of Russia itself shifted from that of a potential liberator and modernizer to that of an exploiter and oppressor, and Estonians came to view Soviet aggression as synonymous with 'Russian aggression'.[70] At the same time the historical view of the Baltic German villain at the core of the Estonian narrative of '700 years of suffering and survival' changed to a more positive external Other; in fact the negative internal Baltic German Other was now replaced by Soviet Russians, while the German role during the Second World War was viewed as the lesser of the two evils. So I can only partly follow Petersoo's contention that the Baltic German Other transformed from a negative internal Other to a positive internal Other.[71] I argue instead that the Baltic Germans could be transformed into a positive Other only because they were no longer physically present on Estonian territory (other than as a ghostly presence after 1945) and did not constitute a threat of any kind; which is also why the term 'external positive Other' appears to be more accurate.

In their fear of becoming a minority in their own country due to cultural colonization, Estonians needed to draw on potent boundary markers inherent in their cultural memory. These included their conversion to Christianity in the thirteenth century and the key experiences of Lutheran Reformation in opposing Russian Orthodoxy, even though this meant forgetting that the Lutheran Church was considered by many as an alien Baltic German institution and that numerous (ethnic) Estonians had converted to Orthodoxy in the past.[72] Other markers included the Estonian use of the Roman not the Cyrillic alphabet, and the fact that serfdom was abolished forty-five years earlier in Estonia than in Russia; though again this meant blanking out the fact that the peasant emancipation was initiated by the Russian Tsar to weaken the Baltic German landed elite in their Western provinces. All these cultural referents served to place Estonia in the 'historic Western borderland' while the Soviet Russian Other was stigmatized as 'uncivilized' and 'Asiatic'.[73] To this day objects and buildings from the Soviet period are frequently considered by Estonians as a 'Russian thing' (in Estonian: *vene värk*), implying its inferior quality and tendency to malfunction. As for exclusive boundary markers, Estonian ethno-cultural identity became a potent oppositional symbol of cultural resistance to the Soviet regime, being an apolitical category uncorrupted by Soviet power. By employing the term 'ethno-cultural identity' for the case of Estonia, I point to the fact that group membership is not just defined by culture and history but also by a more exclusive conception of ethnicity – in other words, that group membership is restricted by ethnicity. In a way the perceived threat of Soviet Russification unified Estonians in ethno-cultural resistance, and provided an effective way to mobilize a national mass movement around such an *ex negativo* identity. In this vein, Vetik describes the Estonian identity as 'reactive', aiming to reinforce the collective group worth in a hostile environment.[74]

Estonia's Path to Independence

Which cultural symbols and cultural memories from the past functioned as *mythomateurs* in Estonia's national independence movement (1987–91)? What kind of historical arguments and interpretations of history have been employed since the late 1980s? What can we say about the 'double Other' during this transition period? These are the main issues in this section.

Gorbachev's twin policies of *glasnost* and *perestroika* legitimized increasingly open dissent and unleashed a groundswell for independence. Over the course of this 'new awakening', grass-roots organizations such as the green movement voicing environmental concerns and the 'Estonian Heritage Society', concerned primarily with non-Soviet interpretations of the past, quickly gained prominence. Both represented the nucleus of an emerging civil society. The love of the countryside and the desire for its preservation were expressed in the very first Estonian mass protests in 1987 against a planned increase of phosphate mining and oil shale extraction in the north-east of Estonia. This green activism contained ethnic overtones because an increase in phosphate mining would lead to a further influx of the Russian-speaking workforce, and also because mining policies typified the Soviet pattern of colonial-style exploitation of natural resources.[75]

As the 1980s progressed, nationalist resurgence gathered pace. Gorbachev's 1987 go-ahead to unveil and assess the blank spots of Soviet history triggered dissident groups such as the 'Estonian Group for the Making Public of the Molotov–Ribbentrop Pact' to organize annual demonstrations to publicly commemorate the illegal incorporation of 1939 and the victims of Stalin's mass deportations. By 1988 this had achieved a turnout of thousands. The secret protocols of this pact (hereafter 'MRP') were perhaps the greatest taboo of Soviet history because they pointed to the illegality of the Soviet occupation of the Baltic States, and it was this argument from history that became the focus of the Baltic independence movement. Already in August 1987 Estonian dissidents were publicly demanding their country's self-determination in a demonstration in Tallinn, employing the legalistic argument that they wanted to exercise their republic's constitutionally enshrined right to leave the Union; but Estonian national activists soon realized that the Soviet authorities would not agree to this line of argumentation. In May 1989 the Supreme Soviet of the Estonian SSR formally asked the Soviet Union Congress of People's Deputies to investigate the problems related to the MRP. References to the past were increasingly used to secure mass support for the Estonian independence movement. Memories and symbols of the First Estonian Republic turned into potent *mythomateurs* to destabilize the communist regime by, for instance, displaying the national colours or singing the unofficial national anthem. The Estonian independence movement was termed the 'Singing Revolution' in analogy to the first song festivals of the 1870s and, more generally, to the long-standing Estonian struggle for cultural self-assertion.[76] During the summer of 1988 growing numbers of Estonians, reaching up to thirty thousand, flocked to the Singers' Ground outside Tallinn to chant together for freedom.[77]

During this time a number of alternative political structures were emerging as potential pathways to attaining independence: the Estonian Popular Front, the aforementioned Estonian Heritage Society, and the Citizen's Committee. Each of them used symbols from the past in their struggle for the future. Let us first turn to the Estonian Popular Front, which was established by Edgar Savisaar in 1988 and which did not challenge Soviet authority in principle but supported demands for greater autonomy *within* the Union. In a short time this organization gained a broad base support, and in large-scale demonstrations requested the replacement of the old-guard ECP leadership. Addressing these claims Gorbachev appointed the reformist Vaino Väljas as new first secretary of the ECP, who then declared the political demands of the Popular Front to be those of the party. Candidates of the Popular Front were very successful in the first semi-democratic elections to the USSR Congress of the People's Deputies held in Moscow in March 1989. During sessions of the congress, deputies from all three Baltic states cooperated closely, establishing the Baltic Assembly and the Baltic Council. These bodies also coordinated joint activities such as the 600-kilometre continuous human chain from Tallinn to Vilnius, comprising over two million people, on the fiftieth anniversary commemoration of the MRP in the summer of 1989.

The second political organization, the Estonian Heritage Society, can be labelled a form of cultural resistance. It organized public celebrations of Estonia's history in April 1988 that were attended by thirty thousand (its work will be discussed in more detail in the next chapter). The independence movement began to split between the Popular Front, advocating autonomy within the Soviet Union, and more radical groups who employed the historical argument of the illegitimacy of Soviet institutions. Latching on to the idea of *de jure* continuity with the political institutions of the interwar republic, the Citizen's Committee under Trivimi Velliste – who also was the leader of the Heritage Society at the time – pursued the path of institutional restoration. This committee organized elections to the 'Congress of Estonia' in which only citizens of the interwar period and their descendants enjoyed the right to decide Estonia's future – over eight hundred thousand Estonians had registered by February 1990.

What can we say about the Russian Other during this critical time? In June 1988 the Russian-speaking minority, fearing discrimination in an Estonia less controlled by Soviet Russia, established the 'interfront' movement. Together with the United Council of Workers' Collectives, these were powerful organizations with hundreds of all-union enterprises standing behind them, and also good contacts with Moscow.[78] Their provocations ranged from commemorative gatherings to mark the annexation of Estonia in 1940, general strikes, and the rallying for a separation of north-east Estonia (a region where the Russian-speaking population amounted up to 97 per cent), but it was the attack on the Estonian parliament on 15 May 1990 by 'interfront' demonstrators that made real the worst fears of those Estonians who regarded the Russian-speakers as a 'fifth column' – fundamentally disloyal to the Estonian cause of independence.[79] Their fears were not, however, shared by the whole population, with probably only a minority avidly in favour of independence.

Somewhat similar to the events leading to Estonia's first declaration of independence in 1918, the internal power struggle among the leaders of Soviet Russia created a power vacuum that was soon filled by Lithuania declaring its sovereignty on 11 March 1990. Estonia and Latvia were inspired to follow suit on 30 March and 4 May respectively.[80] After demonstrations in Vilnius and Riga had been violently smashed by 'special units of the Soviet Interior Ministry' while planning a coup, Estonians feared that they would be next. But in January 1991 Boris Yeltsin, then chairman of the Russian parliament, flew to Tallinn calling on Russian troops not to act against civilians. What followed was a stalemate situation that ended only with the abortive August coup in Moscow, which in turn functioned as a catalyst for Estonia's full independence. In the uncertain crisis situation, the Estonian Supreme Council and leaders of the congress unanimously voted for immediate national independence on 20 August. Over the next few months the last vestiges of Gorbachev's power ebbed away, while Yeltsin, who had decisively confounded the plotters, set about establishing an independent Russia. Gorbachev agreed to dissolve the USSR and handed over his prerogatives as commander-in-chief to Yeltsin, president of Russia. By the end of December 1991, the Soviet Union – a key feature of European politics for three-quarters of a century – had disappeared into history.

The uses of the past by Estonian nationalists in the 1980s would play a significant part in domestic political battles after 1991. Let us take a closer look at what I have earlier referred to as the legal continuity argument pursued by organizations such as the Citizens' Committee and the Estonian National Independence Party (founded by dissidents in 1988). The Estonian writer Jaan Kaplinski saw in the pragmatic juridical argumentation for the re-establishment of Estonian statehood and the legalistic course taken against the Russophone community (which I will discuss in the following chapter) a kind of 'rationalism' quite different from other forms of romantic or hot irrational nationalism. This does not mean however that Estonia of the 1990s cannot be termed a 'nationalizing state'.[81] Important legislation passed on this 'restorationist path' (1989–93) comprised a new law determining that annual immigration was not to exceed a quota of 1 per cent of Estonia's total population, and the citizenship law of 1992 according to which only citizens of pre-war Estonia and their direct descendants were granted 'automatic citizenship' (all others had to apply for naturalization of their status).[82] It was this law particularly that effectively disenfranchised the majority of the Russophone community and made the referendum on the new constitution and the first post-independence parliamentary elections in June 1992 an (ethnic) Estonian endeavour.[83] In 1992, Trivimi Velliste, the minister of foreign affairs, proclaimed that it was wrong to call Russians a minority, as 'legally, the word "minority" applied only to those Russians who settled in Estonia before 1940: the rest are colonists'.[84] Estonian nationalists refused to conceive of their country as a bi-national or bi-cultural one, and instead labelled the Russophone population as a minority, immigrants, settlers, 'aliens' or non-citizens, disregarding the demographic changes since 1940 – namely the hard fact that the Russian-speaking community constituted up to 32 per cent of the total population.[85] The 'Alien Law' of 1993 obliged non-citizens to seek residence permits. Finally a new 'Language Law' was also passed during this transition period, which made Estonian the official language, to secure the firm foundation for 'the preservation and development of the Estonian people and its culture'.[86] Some of the effects of these laws on the Russophone community in post-Soviet Estonia will be discussed further in later chapters.

Conclusion

Gorbachev's liberalization of formerly oppressive laws and Estonians' sense of economic and cultural deprivation were important in making Estonian national re-independence possible. But I have also showed that there are three other structural conditions, namely a national mobilization largely based on the existence of formative cultural memories, the legacies of a specific style of Soviet domination, and finally the role of the German and Russian Other. In concluding this chapter, I would like to return to these three themes.

The Estonian national movement of the twentieth century saw an increasing mass politicization of the cultural community (and its cultural memories). It also changed from a more cultural movement to a political empire-subverting and state-creating force.[87] In this process, ethno-linguistic markers were progressively employed to bolster political claims for independent statehood via divisive ethno-linguistic nationalism.[88] In other words, the Estonian nation was being defined more in ethno-cultural terms than as a political community of citizens based on voluntary membership. With regard to the language, immigration and citizenship legislation of the early 1990s we can say that this ethno-linguistic nationalism opposed liberal democratic principles with regard to the treatment of non-dominant ethnic groups in the new state, such as the Russophone community.[89] This is why Brubaker's term of a 'nationalizing state' aptly captures the social practices of Estonia's independence movement and of the transition politics.

Reasons why Estonian independence activists found the 'national card' the most effective one to play are manifold. We can find answers in part by looking at the legacy of Soviet-style domination. Estonia had only limited civic traditions due to its belated statehood, and its state institutions were discredited as symbols of oppression during the Soviet period, making many Estonians revert to more ethno-cultural categories of collective cultural identification. The paradoxes of Soviet nationality policies were another contributing factor in this equation, because these policies institutionalized personal nationality based on ethnic descent to function as a legal category in the internal Soviet passport system. Although created as an official instrument of heightened control, it was Soviet nationality policy that engraved the national category in each (Soviet) individual's consciousness.

How then were the German and Russian Other seen during and after the 'Singing Revolution'? First, the Baltic German heritage figured increasingly as a positive reference point – along with the Nordic countries of Sweden and Finland, and Western Europe more generally, in the course of Estonia's westward orientation.[90] I would argue that the cultural memories of the Baltic German as 'colonizer' and 'oppressor' have been neutralized as they have grown cold and lost their negative charge. Particularly in the course of EU accession (achieved in 2004), positive allusions were made to the Baltic German heritage, albeit mainly for instrumental reasons – an important point to which I shall return in Chapter 5. Finally the revaluation of the external German Other was bolstered by the idea of the 'lesser of two evils' and by an anti-communist narrative emerging from the private social memories into public debate. With regard to the Russophone community of post-Soviet Estonia, it is possible that in time this can be transformed into a positive internal Other.[91] Here I would suggest, however, that due to the numerical strength of the Russian-speaking community, Estonia's geographic proximity to Russia, and Russia's strong 'homeland nationalism', it is rather unlikely that Estonian Russians will cease to be a perceived threat to Estonian collective identity.

This rapid survey of Estonian history shows how the Other can serve in overcoming the crisis of national identity because it unites the people against a common enemy, highlighting a communal sense of distinctiveness. In that vital sense German and Russian rule helped to create a framework conducive to the development of the modern Estonian nation.

Notes

1. Quoted from a Baltic German intellectual, and translated by author from the German: 'Zunächst ist nicht zu vergessen, dass die Esten und Letten keine eigene Kultur besitzen undschwerlich jemals besitzen werden' (G. Dehio. 1927. 'Vom baltischen Deutschtum', *Mitteilungen der Akademie zur wissenschaftlichen Erforschung und zur Pflege des Deutschtums* 10: 345).
2. V. Vasara. 1995. 'Das estnische Parlament und die Deutschbalten. Zu den Debatten bis zur Verabschiedung der Kulturautonomie 1925', *Nordost-Archiv* 4(2): 481.
3. A. Chubarov. 2001. *Russia's Bitter Path to Modernity: A History of the Soviet and Post-Soviet Eras.* London: Bloomsbury, 149.

4. On shatter zones and borderlands, see Armstrong, *Nations before Nationalism*; Prusin, *The Lands Between*; and Snyder, *Bloodlands*.

5. M. Mann. 1995. 'A Political Theory of Nationalism and its Excesses', in Sukumar Periwal (ed.), *Notions of Nationalism*. Budapest: Central European University, 44–64.

6. On small or mini-nations, see R. Alapuro (ed.). 1985. *Small States in Comparative Perspective: Essays for Erik Allardt*. Oslo: Norwegian University Press; W. Leitsch. 1991. 'Die Esten und die Probleme der Kleinen', in Manfred Alexander et al. (eds), *Kleine Völker in der Geschichte Osteuropas: Festschrift für Günther Stökl zum 75. Geburtstag*. Stuttgart: Franz Steiner Verlag, 149–58; A. Park. 1995. 'Fighting For the Mini-State: Four Scenarios', *Nationalities Papers* 23(1): 67–78; R. Ruutsoo. 1997. 'The Estonians: Identity and Small Nation in Past and Present', *Anthropological Journal on European Cultures* 6(1): 73–100. Nations that lack their own ruling class and are dominated by an elite of a different nationality are categorized by Miroslav Hroch (1985. *Social Preconditions of National Revival in Europe: A Comparative Analysis of the Social Composition of Patriotic Groups among the Smaller European Nations*. Cambridge: Cambridge University Press, 9) as 'small nations'. Small nations lack continuous tradition of cultural production in a literary language of their own, and have been subjected to a ruling class over long periods, leaving them without an independent political unit or social structure at the dawn of the era of modern nationalism.

7. J. Hutchinson. 1987. *Dynamics of Cultural Nationalism: The Gaelic Revival and the Creation of the Irish Nation State*. London: Allen & Unwin.

8. See Eric J. Hobsbawm. 1990. *Nations and Nationalism after 1780*. Cambridge: Cambridge University Press, 101–11.

9. R. Ruutsoo. 1995. 'Introduction: Estonia on the Border of Two Civilizations', *Nationalities Papers* 23(1): 13.

10. P. Petersoo. 2007. 'Reconsidering Otherness: Constructing Estonian Identity', *Nations and Nationalism* 13(1): 117–33. More generally, in these Othering processes, an argument against one Other is simultaneously an argument in favour of another Other. For example, similarities between Estonians, Finns, Latvians, Danes and Germans are emphasized on grounds of a shared Protestant religion and set against Russian Orthodoxy (ibid.: 122, 129).

11. Finland, Sweden, Latvia, the Jews and Romani also figured as Others at various times in Estonian history, but I limit my analysis to the Russophones and Baltic Germans because they were most significant for processes of Estonian identification.

12. M. Laur et al. 2002. *History of Estonia*. Tallinn: Avita, 38–52; T. Raun. 1987. *Estonia and the Estonians*. Stanford, CA: Hoover Institution Press, 19.

13. Raun, *Estonia and the Estonians*, 24.

14. Ibid., 80.

15. By 1850 adult literacy was close to 90 per cent of the Estonian population over ten years of age, but only 77 per cent could write, consequently there was little Estonian-language-based literature apart from translations of the Bible.

16. Raun, *Estonia and the Estonians*, 32ff.

17. H.B. Nisbet. 1999. 'Herder's Conception of Nationhood and its Influence on Eastern Europe', in Roger Bartlett and Karen Schönwälder (eds), *The German Lands and Eastern Europe: Essays on the History of their Social, Cultural and Political Relations*. London: Macmillan, 116–25. In this sense, folklore takes on the role of a potent counter-myth, as discussed in Chapter 1.

18. K. Brüggemann. 1995. 'Von der führenden Schicht zur nationalen Minderheit. Zur Klärung der Rolle der estländischen deutschen Minderheit bei der Begründung der

Republik Estlands 1918–1919', in 'Estland und seine Minderheiten: Esten, Deutsche, Russen im 19. und 20. Jahrhundert', *Nord Ost Archiv* 4(2): 475ff.

19. Gert von Pistohlkohrs. 1993. 'Inversion of Ethnic Group Status in the Baltic Region: Governments and Rural Ethnic Conflict in Russia's Baltic Provinces and the Independent States of Estonia and Latvia, 1850–1940', in David Howell (ed.), *Roots of Rural Ethnic Mobilisation*. Dartmouth: European Science Foundation, New York University Press, 180.

20. D. Kirby. 1995. *The Baltic World, 1772–1993: Europe's Northern Periphery in an Age of Change*. London: Longman, 54. 'Wannabe Germans' in Estonian is *kadakas saksa* (or 'juniper German' in direct translation).

21. With the terms '(social) engineering' and 'high culture' I am employing Ernest Gellner's (1983) vocabulary about nations and nationalism. See also Kirby, *The Baltic World*, 69, 126ff; and Jansen, 'Cultural or Political Nationalism?', 62.

22. von Pistohlkors, 'Inversion of Ethnic Group Status', 196; see also E.M. Simmonds-Duke. 1987. 'Was the Peasant Uprising a Revolution? The Meanings of a Struggle over the Past', *EEPS* 1(2): 187–223.

23. Jansen, 'Cultural or Political Nationalism?', 61ff., 75.

24. Ibid., 69.

25. E. Laul. 1985. 'Die Schule und die Geburt der Nation', in Aleksander Loit (ed.), *National Movements in the Baltic Countries during the 19th Century*. Stockholm: Centre for Baltic Studies, 293–309.

26. R. Raag. 1990. 'The Linguistic Development of Estonian between 1900 and 1914', in Aleksander Loit (ed.), *The Baltic Countries 1900–1914*. Uppsala: Centre for Baltic Studies, 425–42; R. Raag. 1999. 'One Plus One Equals One: The Forging of Standard Estonian', *International Journal of the Sociology of Language* 139: 17–38.

27. Livonia encompassed the present-day Latvia and Estonia.

28. G. von Rauch. 1986. *Geschichte der baltischen Staaten*. Hannover-Döhren: Harro v. Hirschheydt, 28; M. Geistlinger and A. Kirch. 1995. *Estonia – A New Framework for the Estonian Majority and the Russian Minority*. Vienna: Braunmüller, 94. Another aspect of Russification was the attempts to persuade Estonians to convert from Protestantism to Russian Orthodoxy in an endeavour to unite all subjects of the Russian empire and to undermine the power of the Lutheran Church (Raun, *Estonia and the Estonians*, 80).

29. T. Miljan. 2004. *Historical Dictionary of Estonia*. Lanham, MD: Scarecrow, 97f.

30. In 1866 local self-government for peasant communities was introduced and *corveé* labour abolished. In 1877 a small Estonian middle class was able to participate in an urban self-government as well (Jansen, 'Cultural or Political Nationalism?', 68ff).

31. Jansen, 'Cultural or Political Nationalism?', 76; von Pistohlkors 'Inversion of Ethnic Group Status', 192.

32. Prusin, *The Lands Between*, 39.

33. A. Loit. 1998a. 'Nationale Bewegungen und regionale Identität im Baltikum', in *Nordost-Archiv: Zeitschrift für Regionalgeschichte*, Neue Folge, 7(1): 221.

34. Smith, *National Identity*, 9. A position supported by the Estonian historian of the awakening, Ea Jansen ('Cultural or Political Nationalism?', 77). Whether or not Estonians have a 'navel' – a primordial cultural lifeline – has been contested by A.D. Smith and Ernest Gellner in the so-called Warwick debate (A.D. Smith. 1996b. 'Memory and Modernity: Reflections on Ernest Gellner's Theory of Nationalism', *Nations and Nationalism* 2(3): 371–88).

35. Raun, *Estonia and the Estonians*, 106.

36. von Pistohlkors, 'Inversion of Ethnic Group Status', 194; Rauch, *Geschichte der baltischen Staaten*, 62ff., 70.

37. Quoted in K. Brüggemann. 1997. 'Die deutsche Minderheit in Estland und Konstituierung des Estnischen Staates', in Boris Meissner et al. (eds), *Die Deutsche Volksgruppe in Estland. Während der Zwischenkriegszeit und Aktuelle Fragen des deutsch-estnischen Verhältnisses.* Hamburg: Bibliotheca Baltica, 17.

38. Rauch, *Geschichte der baltischen Staaten*, 57.

39. Brüggemann, 'Von der führenden Schicht', 467, 470.

40. More than 50 per cent of the Baltic German nobility left Estonia; see von Pistohlkohrs, 'Inversion of Ethnic Group Status', 200.

41. von Pistohlkors, 'Inversion of Ethnic Group Status', 195; R. Kionka and R. Vetik. 1996. 'Estonians', in Graham Smith (ed.), *Nationalities Questions in the Post-Soviet States*. London: Longman, 131.

42. Davies, *Vanished Kingdoms*, 706.

43. At its peak, the War of Independence Veterans' League had about sixty thousand members with a broad-base support that cross-cut all class lines (A. Kasekamp. 1999. 'Radical Right-Wing Movements in the North-East Baltic', *Journal of Contemporary History* 34(4): 596). Their ideology comprised a mixture of militant nationalism, anti-Marxism and anti-Semitism (R. Marandi. 1991. 'Must-valge lipu all, Vabadussõjalaste liikumine Eestis 1929–1937, I. Legaalne periood (1929–1934)', *Studia Baltica Stockholmiensia* 6: 521, 546ff.; R. Marandi. 1997. 'Must-valge lipu all, Vabadussõjalaste liikumine Eestis 1929–1937, II. Illegaalne vabadussõjalus (1934–1937)', in *Studia Baltica Stockholmiensia* 18: 225–37).

44. Many contemporary and Western observers regarded Päts' coup and subsequent 'guided democracy' as pre-emptive and legitimate, pointing to the mildness of his authoritarian rule (Raun, *Estonia and the Estonians*, 117, 122).

45. A. Lieven. 1994. *The Baltic Revolution: Estonia, Latvia, Lithuania and the Path to Independence*. New Haven, CT: Yale University Press, 112ff.; E.J. Hobsbawm and T. Ranger (eds). 1983. *The Invention of Tradition*. Cambridge: Cambridge University Press.

46. The Warthegau was the largest administrative district of the Reich.

47. S. Myllyniemi. 1979. *Die baltische Krise 1938–1941*. Stuttgart: Deutsche Verlagsanstalt, 143. On 24 September 1940, Moscow pressured Estonia into agreeing to a mutual-assistance pact, which permitted the stationing of twenty-five thousand Soviet troops across Estonia (along with naval and air bases). Faced with increasing Soviet pressure, President Päts gave in to elections for a new pro-Soviet government and the stationing of more troops (Raun, *Estonia and the Estonians*, 140).

48. Raun, *Estonia and the Estonians*, 158.

49. S. Myllyniemi. 1973. *Die Neuordnung der baltischen Länder 1941–1944: Zum national-sozialistischen Inhalt der deutschen Besatzungspolitik*. Helsinki: Suomen Historiallinen Seura, 73.

50. M. Maripuu. 2002. When compared to the other Baltic Republics, the mass deportations in Estonia amounted to the highest proportion in relation to the total population. I would argue that there is a nexus between the Soviet memory of the futile Finno-Russian Winter War (1939–40), Finland's siding with the axis powers in June 1941 and a pronounced hatred of Estonians (based on Finnish and Estonian Finno-Ugric kinship). A further reason for greater purges and deportations of Estonians may have been their support for General Yudenich and the Whites during the Russian Civil War (S.V. Vardys and R.J. Misiunas [eds]. 1978. *The Baltic States in Peace and War 1917–1945*. University Park: Pennsylvania State University Press, 13).

51. The country was placed under a local self-government headed by the Estonian and former leader of the Veterans' League, Hjalmar Mäe, who was under the command of the high commissioner of Estonia, Karl Litzmann.

52. Nazi plans for Estonia saw the 'Germanization' of the racially worthy elements, the 'colonization' by Germanic peoples and the 'exile' of undesirable elements (Myllyniemi, *Die Neuordnung der baltischen Länder*, 145–57; Raun, *Estonia and the Estonians*, 161).
53. J. Keegan. 1981. *Die Waffen SS*. Munich: Moewig, 223.
54. Myllyniemi, *Die Neuordnung der baltischen Länder*, 255.
55. Raun, *Estonia and the Estonians*, 158, 166.
56. T. Parming. 1977. 'Roots of Nationality Differences', in Edward Allworth (ed.), *Nationality Group Survival in Multi-ethnic States: Shifting Support Patterns in the Soviet Baltic Region*. New York: Praeger, 24–57; Raun, *Estonia and the Estonians*, 165; Israel Gutman (ed.). 1990. *The Encyclopaedia of the Holocaust*. New York: Macmillan, 448ff. For a concise treatment of the Holocaust in Estonian history, on which this paragraph draws, see A. Weiss-Wendt. 2009. *Murder without Hatred: Estonians and the Holocaust*. Syracuse, NY: Syracuse University Press.
57. M. Gilbert. 1995. *Endlösung: Die Vertreibung und Vernichtung der Juden*. Ein Atlas. Hamburg: Rowohlt, 85; *Ereignismeldung* der UdSSR (des Chefs der Sicherheitspolizei und des Sicherheitsdiensts, UdSSR), Nr. 155, 14.01.1942, Bundesarchiv Berlin, R 58/220.
58. In E. Gurin-Loov. 1994. *Holocaust of Estonian Jews 1941*. Tallinn: Eesti Juudi Kogukond, 225.
59. Gurin-Loov, Holocaust of Estonian Jews, 225–300; E. Gurin-Loov. 1996. 'Verfolgung der Juden in Estland (1941–44) Rettungsversuche und Hilfe', in Wolgang Benz and Juliane Wetzel (eds), *Solidarität und Hilfe für Juden während der NS-Zeit, Regionalstudien 2, Ukraine, Frankreich, Böhmen und Mähren, Lettland, Litauen, Estland*. Berlin: Metropol, 305ff. Prior to the German arrival, however, large numbers of Estonian Jews were evacuated eastwards along with communists, apparatchiks and unionists, where they survived in the interior of the Soviet Union.
60. Until 1953 the influx of the Russian-speaking work force amounted to approximately forty thousand per annum; for the rest of the 1950s numbers decreased to about twenty thousand per annum (A.M. Kõll. 2000. 'The Narva Region in Soviet Industrialisation, 1945–1952'. Conference paper presented at 'Narva in the Mirror of History' conference, Narva, 17–20 November 2000).
61. A. Rahl-Tamm. 2007. 'Deportations in Estonia, 1941–1951', in K. Kukk and T. Raun (eds), *Soviet Deportations in Estonia: Impact and Legacy*. Articles and Life History. Tartu: Tartu University Press, 9–54.
62. Whereas prior to 1945 the ECP consisted overwhelmingly of Estonians, the share of the titular nationality had been reduced to 48.1 per cent by 1946. In 1981 Estonians constituted 51 per cent of the total members of the CPE (Raun, *Estonia and the Estonians*, 170ff.).
63. S.R. Bollerup and C.D. Christensen. 1997. *Nationalism in Eastern Europe: Causes and Consequences of the National Revivals and Conflicts in Late 20th Century Eastern Europe*. London: Macmillan, 68.
64. During the 1960s and 1970s the profile of the party membership body changed from one dominated by representatives of the working class to one dominated by university graduates.
65. Kionka and Vetik, 'Estonians'. Many Estonians experienced Sovietization as Russification, and equated Russians with Soviets (K. Kallas. 2002. 'The Formation of Interethnic Relations in Soviet Estonia: Host–Immigrant Relationship'. MA thesis. Budapest: Central European University). In the ESSR a cultural division of labour existed, inasmuch as the Russian-speaking community mainly worked in the

industrial sector (and in the military) whereas the Estonians were employed in light industry, agriculture, or white collar jobs (Bollerup and Christensen, *Nationalism in Eastern Europe*, 71; C.W. Mettan and S.W. Williams. 1998. 'Internal Colonialism and Cultural Divisions of Labour in the Soviet Republic of Estonia', *Nations and Nationalism* 4(3): 363–88).

66. P. Kolstø. 1995. *Russians in the Former Soviet Republics*. London: Hurst & Company, 16.

67. Bollerup and Christensen, *Nationalism in Eastern Europe*, 69.

68. Kallas, 'Formation of Interethnic Relations', 59, 64.

69. Raun, *Estonia and the Estonians*, 196.

70. My empirical research did not substantiate Petersoo's claim ('Reconsidering Otherness', 128) that Soviet and Russian are not used synonymously by Estonians.

71. Ibid., 120–22.

72. Parming, 'Roots of Nationality Differences', 30. Also in Soviet Estonia the Lutheran Church was implicated by complicity with the regime (A. Kasekamp. 2010. *A History of the Baltic States*. New York: Palgrave Macmillan, 153) and rather different from the role of the Catholic Church – as a bastion of nationalism and of anti-Soviet dissent, providing a subculture and a space for non-conformists – in Socialist Poland and Soviet Lithuania (H. Johnston. 1992a. 'Religion and Nationalist Subcultures in the Baltics', *Journal of Baltic Studies* 23(2): 133; Raun, *Estonia and the Estonians*, 52, 366; B. Törnquist-Plewa. 1992. *The Wheel of Polish Fortune: Myth in Polish Collective Consciousness during the First Years of Solidarity*. Lund: Lund University).

73. I.B. Neumann. 1996. *Russia and the Idea of Europe: A Study in Identity and International Relations*. London: Routledge; Ruutsoo, 'The Estonians: Identity and Small Nation', 13ff.

74. R. Vetik, G. Nimmerfelft and M. Taru. 2006. 'Reactive Identity versus the EU Integration', *Journal of Common Market Studies* 44(5): 1085.

75. K. Gerner and S. Hedlund. 1993. *The Baltic States and the End of the Soviet Empire*. London: Routledge, 47ff., 70ff. These sentiments were aggravated further by the fact that thousands of young men from the Baltic republics were drafted for the clean-up of the nuclear site of Chernobyl (Kasekamp, *History of the Baltic States*, 158, 161).

76. M. Lagerspetz. 1996. *Constructing Post-Communism: A Study in the Estonian Social Problems Discourse*. Turku: Turun Yliopisto, 67–72; Hank Johnston. 1992b. 'The Comparative Study of Nationalism: Six Themes from the Baltic States', *Journal of Baltic Studies* 23(2): 95–103.

77. Lieven, *The Baltic Revolution*.

78. Gerner and Hedlund, *The Baltic States*, 107–14.

79. A trigger for the attack on the Estonian parliament building was the declaration by the Estonian Supreme Soviet in 1989 that Estonian was to be the single state language. See ibid., 148.

80. Ibid., 43.

81. R. Brubaker. 1996. *Nationalism Reframed: Nationhood and the National Question in the New Europe*. Cambridge: Cambridge University Press, 55–78; K. Hallik. 2002. 'Nationalising Policies and Integration Challenges', in Marju Lauresin and Mati Heidmets (eds), *The Challenge of the Russian Minority: Emerging Multicultural Democracy in Estonia*. Tartu: Tartu University Press, 65–88.

82. Bollerup and Christensen, *Nationalism in Eastern Europe*, 61, 72, 209.

83. A. Park. 1994. 'Ethnicity and Independence: The Case of Estonia in Comparative Perspective', *Europe–Asia Studies* 46(1): 73.

84. Lieven, *The Baltic Revolution*, 307.

85. According to the 1989 census the Russian-speaking community amounted to 471,000 of Estonia's total population. It is more accurate to speak of a qualitative minority instead. In this book I tend to use the term 'Russian-speaking community' to denote a group that is unified by language and also by and large by social experience, but is of diverse ethnic backgrounds.
86. P. Järve. 2002. 'Two Waves of Language Laws in the Baltic States: Changes of Rationale', *Journal of Baltic Studies* 33(1): 99.
87. Mann, 'Political Theory of Nationalism'.
88. A.D. Smith. 1986. The Ethnic Origins of Nations. Oxford: Blackwell, 50–58; Kasekamp, *History of the Baltic States*, 171.
89. S.L. Burg. 1994. 'Nationalism Redux: Through the Glass of the Post Communist States Darkly', in Minton F. Goldman (ed.), *Russia, the Eurasian Republics, and Central Eastern Europe*. Guilford, CT: Dushkin, 162–66.
90. See essays in N. Götz and J. Hackmann (eds). 2003. *Civil Society in the Baltic Sea Region*. Aldershot: Ashgate. In the successful marketing campaign 'Welcome Estonia' in the course of the country's EU accession it was branded as 'Nordic plus'.
91. Petersoo, 'Reconsidering Otherness', 125.

Chapter 3

Historians as 'Carriers of Meaning'

> For indeed strange things shall happen, and secret things be known,
> and many centuries shall pass away, ere these memorials be seen of
> men. And, when seen, there will be some to disbelieve and some
> to doubt, and yet a few who will find much to ponder upon in the
> character here graven with a stylus of iron.
> – Edgar Allan Poe, 'Shadow – A Parable'

> If you learn how to play the piano in a society where only certain tunes
> are allowed to be performed, you can still learn how to play it.
> – 'Oskar'

The life-story interview is a unique and very useful research method
to capture the ephemeral social memories of societies that endured
long-term foreign rule and momentous socio-political transition.
This is particularly true in an era when these social memories have
not yet been transformed into more lasting forms of cultural memory.
Professional historians are carriers of meaning, but during the Cold
War period Estonian historians were 'frozen', with the exception of
their colleagues in exile.[1] This chapter creates a detailed profile of four
different (generational) groups of professional historians active at the
time of the restoration of Estonia's independence in 1991. Applying
Karl Mannheim's concept of 'generational context' in a rather generous
fashion, I characterize these four groups as the 'War Generation', the
'Post-War Children', the 'Transitional Generation' and the 'Freedom
Children', drawing out some of the key social experiences formative
for the identity of each one.[2] This analysis sets the stage for Chapter 4,
which will discuss how historians from the 1980s onwards came to take
a more political stance. But, before going on to examine the various
official narratives in the next chapters, I shed light on the personal

outlook of some of the professional historians involved in rewriting the post-Soviet Estonian historiography.

Why Historians, Why Life-Story Interviews?

Through the writing of national histories, professional historians play a crucial role in the construction of national identities and are often actively involved in nationalist movements and politics. It is well known that under communism the deterministic science of historical materialism dissolved the distinction between history as a discipline and history as sheer propaganda; history was promoted as the 'Truth' with historians as its 'official bearers'.[3] Many Estonian historians became active in politics in the early 1990s, such as Mart Laar, Lauri Vahtre and Tunne Kelam, which exemplifies my argument that the struggle over historical truth played a decisive role in Estonia's re-emergence as a sovereign state, and also validates my choice of historians as a case study. Estonian historians stand in the tradition of the sixteenth-century chronicler Balthasar Rüssow, a Protestant minister of Tallinn's Church of the Holy Spirit who was famous for criticizing the nobility and the Catholic Church.[4] Intellectuals played a pivotal role in the vernacular mobilization of national movements in nineteenth-century Eastern Europe. The previous chapter elaborated the role of Estonian village schoolteachers, parish priests and philologists in Estonia's national awakening during the 1860s. In this era nationalism was a historicist movement par excellence, and historians passionately engaged in writing 'ethno-history' could have a bearing on contemporary affairs.[5] Contrary to more 'domesticated' variants of professional history, ethno-history does not come in the guise of scientific language.[6] Many of my interview responses can be subsumed under the heading of 'ethno-historians'.

But we also see in these interviews a more complex picture. In twentieth-century communist Europe some intellectuals helped to legitimize the system, and others subsequently de-legitimized its ideological superstructure.[7] Intellectuals such as Hanns Eisler, the composer of the East German national hymn, who remarked to an associate that he was proud to live in a country where books were taken so seriously that they were feared and at times banned, may have felt empowered and flattered by the system. In 1991 the former Hungarian dissident György Konrád stated: 'Today ... only the dissidents conserve the sentiment of continuity. The others [the rest of society] must eliminate remembrances; they cannot permit themselves to keep the memory'.[8] Konrád's provocative statement alludes to the important question of who are the 'rightful bearers' of a society's collective memory. Notions of 'custodianship of memory' are quintessentially based on moral claims to integrity and authenticity, and these claims are clearly heightened in periods of military occupation, totalitarian regime and socio-political transition. Can historians in Estonia after 1945 be described as custodians of a 'counter-memory', transmitting and preserving alternative accounts of Estonian history? This question flows from the overall understanding that historians hold an intellectual, social and moral responsibility. Wolfgang Mommsen has argued that 'it is the historian's foremost task to act as a bearer of the group's memory, to preserve the traditions and collective memories of the former, but simultaneously to critically analyse them and assess their pertinence and accuracy in the light of empirical facts'; while François Bédarida states that the historian should become a spokesman for justice, but not pass judgements. Jacques Le Goff even goes so far as to say that historians only really fulfil their role when they become moralists.[9]

Professional historians are also interesting conceptually because they constitute an interface between the remote past as absolute history and the recent past as contemporary history, over which the battle over interpretation and definition is still raging. In the interviews with historians, both the communicative and cultural dimensions of memory are revealed. It is in the telling of personal life stories that the intertwined levels of communicative memory and cultural memory (as codified in historical narrative) become apparent. A lot of what is related in the interviews is social or communicative memory – in other words, that which has not yet been transformed into cultural memory; but at the same time historians are chroniclers of the past, writers of annals and keepers of archives, who actively debate, frame and codify cultural memory. We have seen how, in the twentieth century, world historical events dramatically affected personal lives in Estonia, with almost every family caught in the cogwheels of history. One respondent's starting line, for instance, was that Estonians had been peasants and slaves for seven hundred years. I was interested in the historian's personal life story and its effect on his or her professional work. In biographical interviews, official history can provide the interpretive frame for understanding one's life. This is why some of the biographical narratives (the ego-history) follow a personal periodization, in which world historical events are merely adumbrated. At other times it is world history providing the structure, while the personal details merely flesh out the 'big picture'.[10] Mostly what I found in the interviews was a mix of the two patterns. Frank Ankersmit writes that 'personal recollections and the facts of history are inextricably linked together', emphasizing the inseparability of the observer and that which is observed.[11] In interviewing historians, the life story method –

which will be discussed in a subsequent paragraph – ensures a way of going beyond the subject–object dichotomy, because it permits the historian (as historical subject) to speak about the personal life story and the individual interpretation of historical reality. This allows respondents a form of unpremeditated expression, the freedom to air speculations, attitudes and allusions, because nothing needed to be immediately documented.

Historians also personify the tension between story and history, because they speak both as professional historians and as contemporary eyewitnesses. A tension inevitably arises between personal stories, in other words anecdotal evidence, and expert talk, which is the academic domain of history.[12] When professional historians assert their impartiality and objectivity this may be to cover up a hidden scholarly insecurity. Ankersmit points out that deep in their hearts historians know that, despite their emphasis on the need for accurate investigation of sources and on prudent and responsible interpretation, history ranks lowest in scientific status of all the disciplines taught at university [and thus they] feel more insecure about the scientific status of their discipline than do the practitioners of any other field of scholarly research.[13]

Part of this insecurity is caused by the fact that the domain of history writing uses natural language, which prevents it from being confined to specialists alone. Reflecting on the historian's task in 1821, Alexander von Humboldt proposed that all history writing is subjective. The historian is supposed to describe and explain the facts, but also to understand and interpret them, which inevitably introduces an element of subjectivity or 'guesswork'. Similarly, Nicola Gallerano describes historiography as 'a scientific activity *sui generis*, whose cognitive dimension touches and mingles with the affective dimension, which is steeped in values, predilections, and non-scientific or pre-scientific choices'.[14] This subjectivity of historians gives rise to certain sensitivities, which I encountered when conducting the interviews. For example some respondents contended that history is a scientific discipline while oral history is not. At other times my respondents felt uneasy about being turned into objects of research, and some suspected that my methodological approach automatically questioned their codes for representing the historical past.

How, then, to justify oral history? In the countries of Eastern Europe with a legacy of long-term foreign rule, a strong oral tradition, such as folklore, songs, and family memory persisted as a 'source of truth'.[15] This reflected long-standing dichotomies between the peasants and the landlords, with their sets of institutions such as the church and the German language. The pattern was repeated in the dichotomy between the public and the private spheres of the Soviet period, pitting the totalitarian state against the family home as a place of refuge and resistance.[16] In the case of Soviet Latvia,

Vieda Skultans points out that great importance was attached to personal testimony for the preservation of national identity, and that trust was given more to the spoken than to the written word.[17] Similarly in Soviet Estonia it was individual lives that bore witness against the state. Jokes, allusions, and anecdotal evidence were part of the repertoire of counter-accounts in the private sphere, which were transmitted mostly orally.[18]

The Life-Story Method

The methodology employed is based on the biographical interview or 'life-story interview'.[19] The origin of oral history as a discipline stems from the attempt to write the history of the marginalized 'underdog' but it can as well be applied to interviewing political elites. The oral testimony of professional historians in Estonia provides fresh insight into their personal lives and into the conditions of history production during the Soviet period, when historical research, access to archives and teaching were hugely restricted by censorship.[20] But such testimony is equally revealing in throwing light on the post-Soviet transition when professional historians in Estonia faced new constraints in a 'nationalizing state' intent on national restoration and consolidation.[21] Likewise, the interviews captured some of the rich accounts of the older professional historians as well as the recollections from narrators of mixed background – the postwar children and young generation – who were under-represented in the official debates of the 1990s and early 2000s on Estonia's recent past.

Over the course of telling one's life story the construction of identity becomes apparent, as well as the importance for that identity of certain formative past events. In summary, 'human individuals conceive of their identity in terms of the historical narratives that they tell themselves about their past'.[22] It is precisely the biographical method which lends itself to the recording of fundamental reorientations of post-Soviet societies.[23] It enables the researcher to obtain information about an individual's experiential patterns, interpretive frameworks and handling of the past. In these in-depth interviews, I was guided by a set of questions, which were formulated in a rather open fashion and mostly designed to generate conversational narrative. In practice I wanted to elicit *how* the respondent interprets the world – that is the interpretive and explanatory systems he or she deploys over time. Once the traits have been established for the individual it is then possible to look for collective patterns within a wider group.

But interviewing is not a one-sided process. In the course of a biographical interview both the interviewer and the interviewee partake in the interactive construction of a narrative identity that depends largely on their verbal and non-verbal rapport, and is thus highly situational. We can therefore speak of the listener as co-author. When analysing an interview we have to remember that it is *not* a text but the spoken, evanescent word, highly contingent on the particular context. Due the situational character of the 'construct' the interviewer must maintain a high level of self-reflectivity with regards to cultural, generational and experiential differences. It is the ethical responsibility of the researcher not to pre-empt, or jump to conclusions: indeed, good conduct means continually reflecting and challenging one's own conclusions. Also in terms of positioning in the field, my vantage point was that of a 'professional stranger', to borrow Michael Agar's term – an insider outsider – which is that of neither an ethnic Estonian nor a Russian speaker living in Estonia. Ideally, the interview situation is characterized by an asymmetric communication; in other words, the researcher is there to listen and at times guide the interview, whereas the respondent does most of the talking.

In some interviews, when the respondent touched on emotionally sensitive issues or traumatic memories that had been bottled up for a long time, I came to feel like an unprepared therapist – and we could easily speak of 'interview therapy'. I had learnt to sit through the initial defence mechanism, such as prolonged periods of silence, even if it was uneasy. Often the most interesting facts were voiced after pauses. Likewise with traumatic experiences: I did not gloss over them, but was empathetic and attentive. I encountered various limitations caused, for instance, by cultural and generational differences and linguistic misunderstandings. Experiences that respondents found almost impossible to convey were those of terror during the war years and the conditions of living under occupation.

Critics may point to the difference between lives lived and lives remembered. In other words, when the respondents recall their lives in retrospect and with hindsight, the interpretive frame changes. Others may complain that the method is based on memories, which are never simply stored in a neutral medium but instead change over time and through increasing life experience. Indeed memory can be fallible, distorted or false, and people often simply forget. However, I am focusing more on *how* rather than *what* the respondent remembers in the interview; for instance, ways of talking about the past. Also it is not the aim of life-story interviews to prove the interviewee wrong or to judge the information entrusted to the interviewer; it is rather to learn about his or her strategies for coping with change. Therefore, questions of authenticity, credibility or plausibility are not raised in the interview context. Instead, I chose to interpret the biographical interviews by contextualizing and contrasting the accounts with regard to the different ways in which the past is narrated by the various groups *within* the Estonian collective memory.

Returning to the activity of 'memory work' discussed in Chapter 1, it is through relating the past in the interview situation that personal experiences are put into words and made comprehensible, memories are reflected upon and processed.[24] Also in the interview the respondent does not merely recount his or her life by stringing together an accumulation of events, but he or she is also concerned to craft coherence, a logical narrative structure that makes sense, something Hayden White calls 'emplotment'. Although a chronological order normally exists in the narratives, one often finds that streams of memory, temporal disparities, leaps in time, back-tracking, and anticipations frequently occur.[25]

The Empirical Case Study

The primary source of my research consists of biographical interviews with over forty members of Estonia's intellectual elite, mostly professionally trained historians, and a smaller number of philologists, social scientists and 'local historians'. I conducted these interviews (1.5 to 4 hours in length) in English, German, Estonian and Russian (in the latter case with the help of simultaneous translation by colleagues) between 1996 and 2004. Most of the interviewees lived in Estonia, but about a quarter resided abroad. However, all partake in the discourse on Estonian history – be it as researchers, university lecturers, memory agents in museums, local historians, politicians or journalists.[26] Most of my respondents are still active in their working lives and many are public figures, so the information disclosed in the interviews was at times sensitive, for instance regarding issues of collaboration or complicity with the Soviet-era regime. I therefore chose to give all respondents fictitious names, distinguished by only first names.[27] My knowledge of Estonian history and of some biographical facts about my respondents was essential. This knowledge functioned as a matrix, allowing me to quickly detect inconsistencies, breaks and omissions in their life narratives, and to request clarification at a suitable point during the course of the interview.

To standardize my conduct of all the interviews I developed what I call the interview questionnaire. This is an attempt to turn the theoretical concepts of 'social and cultural memory', 'collective cultural identity' and 'generational group' into analytical categories for the purposes of oral history. In the interviews I aimed to establish which past events were formative for an individual's identity, and how the years of occupation, the Soviet period, and the political transition had affected their personal lives, their self-understanding as professional historians and their interpretation of historical reality. I developed a questionnaire that allowed for personal identifications, subjective explanations, emotional reactions, and intellectual conceptualization of the past, and that made apparent the different dimensions that historical experience can have for an individual.[28] This helped to probe how historians made sense of change and of the loss of meaning it can entail. The questionnaire became my hidden (mental) agenda. I refined it as I went along, particularly after the initial interviews; however to ensure degrees of comparability I stuck to a sequence and number of questions for all interviewees. Generally the questions were primarily meant to trigger and encourage the uninterrupted flow of life-story narrative.

At the start of the interview the informant was asked to talk about turning points and changes in life experiences during childhood, youth and adolescence. I asked what parents had conveyed about the interwar period, the Second World War and the post-war years. Did such knowledge cause conflict in school (or university); did respondents encounter any teachers conveying critical accounts of history? Another question concerned the motives for choosing history as a university subject. While the first part of the interview was very loosely guided, more specific follow-up questions could be asked in the second phase, but only after the interviewee came to a logical end of the natural flow of his or her life-story narrative. I questioned how and if Estonians were able to maintain a sense of cultural identity during foreign rule, and whether my informants could identify the carriers of counter-memory. I wanted to know when they felt the Soviet occupation effectively ended and who had been rewriting history since 1991. I invited my respondents to identify controversial topics during the Soviet period and after re-independence. I asked for interpretive shifts in the discussion of Estonia's recent past after 1991. Finally I enquired which events of Estonian history should be made mandatory in history textbooks. The set of questions was altered slightly to match the life experiences of Estonian exiles and the Russophone respondents, including, for exiles, questions of memories of flight, the new host country and return to the homeland; or, for the Russian speakers, the theme of inter-ethnic relations.

Four Generational Group Identities among Estonian Historians

Based on the earlier theoretical discussion of generational group identities (Chapter 2), I identified four generational identities among Estonian historians and intellectuals in post-1991 Estonia.[29] As mentioned earlier,

I describe these as the 'War Generation', the 'Post-War Children', the 'Transitional Generation', and the 'Freedom Children'. I shall summarize their profiles in turn.

The 'War Generation' was born in the Estonian Republic in the 1920s and early 1930s, and educated in either the late Estonian Republic or Soviet Estonia. Their most poignant experiences were the loss of independent statehood, the Second World War and its concomitant occupations. Their university studies were delayed due to the war, so most of them graduated in the late 1940s and early 1950s. They worked throughout the Soviet period or emigrated in mid-1940 and continued their careers abroad. Born between the late 1930s and the early 1950s, the 'Post-War Children' were the first generation to be raised, educated and fully socialized in the new Soviet system; in that sense they constitute the first Soviet generation and, as we shall see, they internalized a 'double consciousness'. I argue that due to the socio-political changes of the 1980s, Estonia saw an 'Intermediate' or 'Transitional Generation'. Born between the late 1950s and early 1960s, these historians underwent their schooling and university education, as well as their first years of professional work as historians, in the Soviet system. They were shaped by experiences such as Brezhnev's enforced Sovietization policies of the late 1970s and the protracted war in Afghanistan. My last group is the 'Freedom Children', a generational identity of younger historians born in the late 1960s and early 1970s, who had commenced their university studies in newly independent Estonia.

In what follows I list the main collective experiences shaping these four generational contexts. To reveal some of the facets of these generational group identities I contrast them with accounts of different subgroups such as Estonian exiles, Estonian Russians, Russians and Estonians of mixed background – leading to a complex fabric of various personal narratives that exposes contested and divided identities. Essentially this is to establish whether we can discern specific generational styles (in the Mannheimian sense) and secondly to show that these generational group identities may well transcend ethno-cultural boundaries. In subsequent pages considerable space is allocated to 'personal voice' through lengthy quotation: this is because the original interview transcripts always seem to be much more revealing, vivid and authentic than all the researcher's attempts at 'over-interpretation'.[30]

Context: History Production in Soviet Estonia (1945–91)

Before turning to the four generational profiles in more detail, something should be said about the conditions under which history was produced

– that is the work setting of the historians of the first three generational groups, including their researching and teaching of history. As discussed in Chapter 1, to enhance their position rulers form intellectual alliances with both memory and forgetting: they do so through genealogies, commemorations and memorials, which work both retrospectively and prospectively.[31] It is well known that in the ESSR as elsewhere in the USSR, history was the most politicized subject of all, because it served as a powerful device for legitimizing Soviet institutions.[32] Estonian history was taught as a part of the history of the USSR, and certain motifs were elevated to key positions in the new Soviet historiography. These included the 'liberation' of Estonia by the Red Army;[33] the 'historical friendship' between the 'great Russian nation' and the Estonian people; the 1940 revolution in Estonia against the 'reactionary bourgeois government' (intended to indicate the existence of home-grown Estonian leftist organizations who sympathized with Soviet ideology); the alleged pro-German orientation of all three Baltic peoples as collaborators with Fascist Germany; and lastly the supposed treachery of Baltic émigré circles and their anti-Soviet activities in the West after 1944.[34] These themes were often interlinked. In Soviet propaganda it was *kulakism* that provided a base for the German occupation regime, an allegation that legitimized the subsequent fierce policy of collectivization in the late 1940s.[35] After the war every expression of nationalism by Estonians was easily linked to their supposed Nazi leanings. In verbal confrontations, Russians called Estonians 'Nazi collaborators'.[36]

In the early 1950s, schools and institutions of higher education were purged and 'Estonian-minded' teachers replaced by Estonian-speaking teachers who were mainly from Russia. March 1950 constitutes a watershed, because this was when a great purge was carried out affecting, amongst others, some historians from the interwar period.[37] A direct effect of this, according to Ea Jansen, was that the quality of education at the University of Tartu was low. In fact Litvin, a historian and contemporary witness, writes: 'Party historians formed a special group whom one can scarcely place within the historical profession'.[38] 'Hanneleen' of the War Generation recollects:

the minister of education was Ferdinand Eisen. He was a communist, already an old man. He received his education before the [Second World] War. During these twenty years he tirelessly aimed at upholding the Estonian language and Estonian textbooks ... very many teachers were sent to Siberia ... or they lost their work. And [replaced with] the communists ... especially from Russia, Russian Estonians, who had lived in Russia. Estonians, [except that] their Estonian language was already bad, but the Russian occupier's policy brought them here.

The quote illustrates how she struggles to define those Estonians who returned from Russia. To describe them, other respondents used the term 'jestlase', often while laughing quietly, perhaps embarrassed due to the derogative connotation of the term. While the correct spelling of the term for Estonians would be *eestlased*, the wrong spelling (*jestlased*) denotes the Russian accent of these newcomers.

During the time of the ESSR, history teachers had a very limited scope for teaching a more critical history. Schoolteachers had to use available textbooks and teach the prescribed curriculum. Some teachers 'kept the books closed' and conveyed more critical tones verbally. Here jokes, exaggerations, allegories and 'talking between the lines' were the most common expressions of dissent.[39] Jokes can be a form of resistance, depending on the setting in which they are voiced: uttered in private, these demonstrations of detachment from the despised system assume a quality of whitewashing whereas, expressed in public, they can be considered acts of open dissent. An Estonian Russian respondent of the War Generation, 'Hariton', recalls that behind the scenes the head of the Department of Scientific Communism 'used to say communism is all a big lie. It is all rubbish and that he doesn't believe in the discipline. These paradoxes were quite common'. Teachers may have feared awkward questions from pupils who had heard different accounts of Estonian history at home. Asked whether history teachers were able to voice dissent, Haneleen, who belongs to the generational context that experienced Stalinist terror, stated that 'most of the people decided that they didn't want to be in prison'.

The following interview illustrates how it was essentially down to the courage and initiative of individual teachers to keep alive the scholarly tradition and heritage of interwar Estonia. It also shows the importance of private space in that transmission. 'Nora', a Post-War Child whose father worked in a publishing house, recalled a very personal conversation with her Estonian language teacher when she was about eleven or twelve years old: 'I said what a great catastrophe it has been for the Estonians when the Germans came to us in the thirteenth century. And ... she [the teacher] replied, 'well, but much worse occupying powers followed'. The teacher, who had been educated during the so called 'Estonian time', considered Nora to be her favourite pupil and invited her home. There, Nora continued:

> She openly spoke to me about the past, also about 1939 and 1940. She was puzzled and asked me if my parents didn't put things straight to me? And I said no ... It was a talk in confidence, times weren't as tough anymore. Stalin had died. [It was] 1956 or 1957, already after Hungary. We spoke about history and literature ... what it means to be a state without

an occupying power, independent … so that I would understand what independence really means … Perhaps she simply wanted to explain to me what it takes to have a state … self-confidence and all that.

Subsequently, Nora's parents brought her to their summerhouse in the countryside where their private library had been relocated. According to Nora, 'this is where I spend almost my entire holiday … I have discovered all that [the forbidden books and journals] in one summer, and afterwards a whole different life for me began'. After her discovery she returned to the normal patterns of her childhood life; however, following that summer she attended church on Sundays, which may have functioned as a counter-world for her.

'Oskar', an Estonian historian born in 1960, with a patriotic-minded family background, describes how he learned more from other children than through explicit stories from his parents:

I was very young, maybe four or five, when … I was beginning to be pro-grammed like a Soviet kid. Perhaps I had watched some movie about the Second World War on good Russians and bad Germans and then I said to a neighbour boy who was four years older than me, 'How lucky we are that the Russians won this war', and he looked at me and said, 'Why … lucky? It was a very great misfortune'. I clearly remember this moment. I thought, well maybe things are totally different, maybe reality is different from what we are told. This goes back on how kids influence kids. How the slightly older ones influence the younger.

At the time of the interview, Oskar had young children of his own. 'Zahkar', born 1963 of mixed background, recalls his high school days in the 1970s:

I belong to this generation that was raised with Soviet War movies. I was socialized through these war movies … The German occupation was depicted as the worst thing imaginable … When I was six or eight years old I realized that my mother may hold some wartime memories, so I asked her: 'Mother have you seen a real German soldier? Were there Germans in your village?' 'Yes!' 'And what happened?' 'Nothing', mother said, 'nothing happened'. No pillage, no executions, nothing. This was a shock for me. Thereafter I asked other family members … but they implied that the Soviet occupation was different from the German one. It was cruel, because of the deportations and the expropriations … In the history class at school, I was taught that during the German occupation in Estonia … 100,000 people were killed and as a little boy I said, but my mother and my grandmother told me something else … My parents were asked to come to school and they [the KGB] had a serious talk … about their ideological stance … In my elementary school years I could sense this fear with my older teachers – a fear that we [might] ask inappropriate questions.

One of the questions I posed to respondents of the Post-War and the Transitional Generation was why they chose to be trained as professional historians, when they knew full well that their research would be restricted and they would have to teach only the Soviet interpretation of history. I suggested that they would be much like a piano player who would only be able to play a hymn to Stalin. Oskar, of the Transitional Generation, picked up on this metaphor in his reply: 'If you learn how to play the piano in a society where only certain tunes are allowed to be performed, you can still learn how to play it. And you may play on your own [and] secretly for your friends, and wait for the time when you can do so publicly'. Similar to his colleagues, Oskar's motivation to study history, despite all the difficulties, was to gain a better understanding of his autobiographical experience, in a sense, to generate meaning. In his words: 'History isn't just a big bag of facts and numbers, it is a system to know that there was the Thirty Years War and the Northern War … The whole civilization has some structure and some logical build-up and that was the thing I went to university for … Because there are large areas in history, which you can't deny, which even Soviet communist rule allowed to be taught and studied'.

Optimists among the War Generation hoped for the Soviet system to vanish before the completion of their studies.[40] A respondent of the Post-War Generation, 'Ervin', states:

We did not have four years of occupation like the French, Danish or Dutch, but we had fifty years of occupation. And to survive [this] in order not to be destroyed [or] expunged, somebody had to collaborate … This is understandable, because if all the people [had] refused to teach at the universities, what would have happened to us?

Clearly, historians were all faced with the ethically precarious choice between political pragmatism and 'historical truth'. Although their lives were no longer under immediate threat after the early 1950s, voicing dissent still endangered their position and impeded their career or the possibility of publishing their work. There were several institutions for the study of history in Soviet Estonia: the Department of History at the University of Tartu was responsible for teaching history, while the Institute of History and the Institute of the History of the Communist Party, both part of the Academy of Science in Tallinn, were designated solely for research. 'Vilma', born in 1921, had joined the CPE in the 1950s because she believed that by joining the party she could contribute to the liberalization of the Soviet system. Vilma had worked at the Institute of History all her life, and described the process of writing the 'History of the ESSR' as

> the main work that the Institute of History was engaged in … it took a lot of trouble. I was a young historian and I was made to write it. It was so difficult. It was edited and changed several times, and criticized from ideological positions. It was a terrible work … The Institute of History wasted its time with the compilation of this generalizing work based on the Soviet model. [pause] It was most difficult and nobody read it. Of course the students had to read it, but … I think, the common people never read these books.

Vilma went on to describe the difficulties imposed by censorship, particularly over publication of the third volume, which dealt with the interwar period or 'bourgeois Estonia'. Due to its never-ending revision process, Vilma and her colleagues simply named it an 'egg' in endless gestation.[41] She concludes: 'The rigid principles of class and absolute class struggle … weren't the worst. The absolutely worst [thing] about Soviet manipulation was that the whole history was looked upon as a prologue to [the creation of] the Soviet State'. In the same context, 'Vilhelm', an Estonian history professor born in 1932, admonishes: 'These half-truths were far more detrimental than downright lies … total falsifications of textbooks are completely innocent, they have a different impact, but to write a text where some long-established facts are inserted into an overall fabric of lies is very bad … It is the liability and duty of every honest human being and historian to stay away from these things'.

The web of compromise was all-embracing. With any academic publication, historians in the ESSR had to insert the obligatory quote from Lenin, Engels or the like in the preface, adhere to Marxist–Leninist rhetoric and apply the overall concept of class struggle.[42] The alternative would have been to write only for the private drawer. Nevertheless, there was a degree of choice about joining the Communist Party. Evidence suggests that even without party membership one could become a lecturer and even a professor. During the time of the ESSR, a small number of history professors served as figureheads of resistance for the students, among them Sulev Vahrtre and Helmut Piirimäe. The decision to acquiesce to the system thus depended on one's ambitions, because those who dissented in the 1970s and 1980s still put at risk future career advancement or opportunities to travel abroad.[43]

Also historians had the option to revert to 'apolitical' research topics, such as ancient or medieval history. For many of the older Estonian historians, the end of the First World War constituted the great divide after which they avoided teaching any topics. Vilhelm stated: 'It was impossible to write modern history. All those [historians] who can be taken seriously … researched older periods. My research in agrarian history was absolutely innocent. It could have been carried out in any country at any time'. Similarly 'Urmas', a history professor at the University of Tartu, born in 1926, said: 'Dangerous were all topics of modern history. Already at university I researched the older times. Also later when I was teaching, [I taught] the older history of Estonia up until the middle of the nineteenth century'. Consistent with this, 'Pauls', a historian born in 1948 in Germany to a Latvian exile family who subsequently settled in Sweden, recalled: '[Soviet] Historians themselves say, when you are researching the medieval ages you could write 90 per cent truth, but the closer one got to the modern times, this was decreasingly so. It was hardly possible to research the history after 1918'.[44] Estonian respondents explain that generally Estonians from Russia or Russians (that is, the *jeestlased* discussed earlier) were designated to teach 'Red subjects' such as party history and historical materialism. An Estonian Russian philologist and former MP born in 1933 concluded that, because these Estonians grew up in Russia, to them the party history came close to the true history.[45]

In contrast to the majority of historians in Soviet Estonia, who tended to conform, Estonian historians in exile, such as Evald Uustalu (born in 1952) and Toivo Raun (born in 1987), were active in academic institutions worldwide to inform the West of their country's fate, campaigning openly against the 1940 annexation. In particular, the Estonian exile community in Sweden kept alive the idea of the Estonian Republic's legal and political continuity through the Estonian exile government in Stockholm, which existed until 1992, and the Estonian National Committee (established in 1944). Sweden became the centre of the literary life of Estonian refugees, with lasting consequences. As the linguist Raimo Raag has noted, while the majority of Soviet Estonians were rarely able to read exile literature, this body of work met the need of post-Soviet Estonian society to learn more about their own culture.[46] The cultural and political activity of Estonian exiles fulfilled two objectives: firstly to maintain their cultural traditions and preclude the danger of their community's full assimilation into the host society, and secondly to act as custodians of an 'untainted' Estonian identity for their compatriots in Soviet Estonia.[47] 'Simon', who had spent five years in a labour camp in Perm for 'anti-Soviet propaganda', looked up to these Estonian exile historians. He felt they were 'surviving without collaborating … they were alternative Estonia, I truly believed that when we are all finished they would still be there and one day they will come back ... it was really some kind of moral support ... We thought, this is the real Estonia'. However, Simon subsequently conceded that their publications were one-sided because they were written in clear opposition to the Soviet regime that had forced them to leave their homeland.

The 'War Generation' – Carriers of the Pre-Soviet Tradition

I turn now to the first of the four generational groups that I have identified in order to begin a more comprehensive discussion. The War Generation is frightened by the war years and Stalinist terror – the repressions, mass deportations and forced collectivization. For this group the past is filled with the painful experience of loss and even trauma, which is why I agree to refer to them also as 'Lost Generation'.[48] Vilhelm recalled the bloody events of the summer of 1941 from a boy's perspective:

> Yes, the story goes that a couple of our people drove to Wesenberg, Rakvere, the county capital, to complain to the [German] commandant that order needed to be restored. My father's position was that this is unlawful, that one needs some kind of proper investigation and jury. But at the time, I remember, I was eight years old; I believed that this was normal. An old woman eighty or ninety years of age from the neighbouring village asked me if it was right that this and this person shot the blacksmith. I replied that it was correct and then she asked me whether they will be arrested. I only smiled inside, being only eight years old, which means that although I was no more than a child, I approved of such deeds. That shows that after having survived the first Soviet year, I believed that all the bad things one could inflict on them [the Soviets] were justified. And I still hold this belief today.

Most men of this generation faced limited and stark choices during the war years such as conscription into the Red Army, fighting as anti-Soviet partisans or in the German army, or flight abroad to Finland or elsewhere – often with enormous consequences for their own lives and the futures of their families. Memories of the war may have also been physically embodied through injuries.[49] While none of my respondents of the War Generation related their experiences of fighting in the Red Army to me, Urmas did describe how he got conscripted into the German army in 1944 and worked in close proximity to the Klooga concentration camp:

Yes, I saw Jews there. They were not from Estonia. They came from Poland … well dressed, very pretty women … Yes, but, we heard this: how they got shot in September 1944. No, we did not hear it. I know it, because we saw it. This was a Sonderkommando that came. And this was the reason why I did not want to go to Germany. I was in Klooga then. The camp was evacuated to Paldiksi. I ran and drove back to Tallinn. And on the 22nd of September [1944], when the Russians came, I was in Tallinn, still in German uniform.

Urmas mentioned this rather profound war memory only after I had probed him about temporal gaps in his life story. But it was this particular experience that informed his choice to stay in Tallinn (even though dressed in the wrong uniform) and not to flee to Germany in September 1944. The Estonian exile, 'Illar' recalled how he chose a third way: 'I fled to Finland [in 1942], as did many others of my age. We wanted to fight against our Russian enemy, but not in the German army. There we formed our own regiment on foot, the so-called I R 200. I then came back to Estonia in 1944, only to leave again via Finland to Sweden, where I arrived in September 1945'.[50]

This generational group was faced with a genuine threat to their lives up to the early 1950s; consequently its members present the sharpest private–public divide in their social memories because they preserved their personal accounts in opposition to the official Soviet version of historical reality. On the whole, the War Generation can be described as normative in outlook, putting substantial emphasis on education, which they often equate with moral integrity. Their view of interwar Estonia tends to be nostalgic, with great admiration for high moral standards, communal values and the national spirit prevailing in Estonian society at the time. Because members of the War Generation retained personal childhood memories of the interwar period they became an important living link to pre-Soviet Estonia, which is why the sociologist Aili Aarelaid-Tart and political scientist Li Bennich Björkmann refer to them as the 'Republican Generation'.[51] 'Pille', a social scientist born in 1971, remembers the highly moralistic stories she found in children's books from this period. Vilhelm explains that to him, and to those born in the 1920s, these values were still palpable and real. He recalls how his father

was a man from the first awakening, by that I mean totally altruistic, working in a number of non-profit associations and enterprises. In the 1920s he returned from the War of Independence. Still a young man, he established a co-operative dairy farm … I asked him once why he did not do something for himself instead; he replied that this would have been the easiest of things, but that he had not even given it a thought ... Candour, conscientiousness, [these are values] today's people are lacking.

Vilhelm adds how in the 1960s and 1970s these societal values had been completely devalued. But as quotations from members of the Post-War Generation will reveal, an unexpected proximity between the War Generation and the Post-War Children does exist, in that when the latter rather enthusiastically described the Pioneer and Komsomol life of their youth and the project of building a new society, they made reference to exactly the same set of communal values, albeit under a different prefix; which would speak for a re-evaluation rather than devaluation. 'Ülle-Mai', a sociologist born into the next generational context, sees those born in the late 1930s as the most innovative in amalgamating pre-Soviet values with the new socialist ideas such as schooling for poor working-class families. From her own school days in Tallinn she recalls that many of her teachers 'from the first Republic were ... carriers of that mentality', which she describes as 'being active, honest, with respect for others; very humanistic. To be correct, to do your schoolwork correctly ... It is our cultural heritage because we belong to the German cultural realm ... This was the mentality'. This relates back to the 'Baltic German backbone' of Estonian culture discussed in Chapter 2.

In fact there is a noteworthy convergence here of remnants of collectivism based on corporatist nationalist values promoted during interwar Estonia together with socialist or communist ideas endorsed during the Soviet period.[52] A study by the social psychologist Anu Realo, conducted after re-independence, gives us some insight: while Estonian culture includes both individualist and collectivist tendencies, 70 per cent of her Estonian sample chose the self-description 'individualist'. Nevertheless, and similar to my findings, collectivism also carries positive meanings, such as thinking of the common good and teamwork – values that were associated by her respondents with patriotic efforts such as peasant uprising or the War of Independence. This leads me to conclude that old communal values from the interwar period were still a part of the cultural memories in post-Soviet Estonia. Ultimately the fact that the Estonian national self-image appears to be premised on a belief in extreme individualism may be an attempt also to draw a line between Estonians and Russians in an act of Othering – setting images such as the Estonian farmstead against the Soviet kolkhoz.[53]

Respondents from the War Generation would often describe themselves as 'peasant sons' or 'peasant boys', illustrating how the connection to the countryside or the farmstead still holds significance for this group's identity – their parents were the first generation of city dwellers.[54] Land ownership was an important factor in determining the political outlook of Estonians: those who were poor in interwar Estonia tended to gain from the political changes brought about by the war and post-war years, while landowners were likely to suffer forced collectivization or even deportation.[55] Ülle-Mai's father was a self-made man from a poor background, and therefore 'a bit leftist'; in contrast, her mother was from a well-off background. Based on this distinction their views of the Estonian Republic differed. This essential connection to the land also sets natives apart from the post-1945 settlers. Vilhelm even employs the analogy of Native American Indians to describe the Estonians' battle against Soviet military occupation: 'The red activists were entrenched in various buildings. They acted just like white squatters on Indian land. They came out to do some raids and killings. Hard to believe, you can read this in Karl May or [James Fennimore] Cooper'.

I shall now widen this characterization of the War Generation by adding accounts offered by different subgroups of Estonian exiles, Estonian Russians and Estonians of mixed background.

In as much as the members of the War Generation had to adapt to the new conditions of Soviet Estonia, Estonian exiles of this generational context had to get accustomed to the new setting of their host countries, for instance Australia, Canada, Germany, Sweden and the USA. In the face of this challenge, exiles preserved an often-idealized memory of interwar Estonia.[56] The notion of loss also figures strongly amongst Estonian exiles from this generational context. While members of the Estonian War Generation forfeited their political freedoms and, not infrequently, property and personal liberty, the exiles lost their homeland, extended family, material possessions and their language community. They also had to cope with the ethical dilemma of deserting their home country. Moral questions about who suffered the most, or who can claim to be the custodian of 'Estonianness', are at stake here. One respondent, a journalist born in 1960 to Estonian parents in the USA, said they needed to legitimize *why* they had left Estonia and became political refugees through something akin to a 'daily plebiscite'.[57] Issues of envy and mutual accusations between those Estonians who had fled and those who remained in the ESSR existed. After 1991, many Estonians saw their compatriots from abroad as arrogant know-it-all *Wessis*, out of touch with Estonian realities and trapped in a 'time warp'. One respondent, a historian born in 1963 of mixed Estonian–Russian background, 'Zahkar', criticized the obsolescent perception of Estonian exiles, who could not contribute positively to the political process since they would not face the fact that the Russian-speaking minority in Estonia had become a full part of contemporary Estonia.

A careful positioning between Estonians, on the one hand, and the new Russians, on the other, also became apparent in the interview with the Estonian Russian respondent 'Hariton'. Estonia's historic Russian community (which I refer to as Estonian Russians or local Russians) amounted to up to 10 per cent of the total population before the Second World War, and consisted mainly of Russian peasants living in the Transnarva and Pechory regions, plus 'Old Believers' and the Whites. Hariton argued passionately for the historical place of Russians in Estonia. He explained that it was mostly Russians of his generation who value the protection of traditional Russian culture, language and education, whereas the new Russians in Estonia have adopted a Soviet identity with little interest in their roots. These fervent identity claims can be explained by the fact that the local Russian community had been in a precarious situation for centuries, experiencing prejudice and open discrimination by the Estonians. As has been discussed in Chapter 2, after 1941 they became a negative internal Other for ethnic Estonians, who began perceiving them as representatives of Soviet power. And after 1944 these local Russians ran the risk of falling between the cracks, because the new Russian settlers were also antagonistic, considering them as 'Whites'. Nevertheless, Estonian Russians and new Russians concur on certain interpretations of historical reality. Hariton states:

> For the majority of Estonians it's still a very clear-cut picture that those Estonians who fought on the German side are true patriots and those who fought on the Russian side weren't. From the Russian point of view the opposite is true ... [they] consider those Estonians who fought on the Soviet side [to be] true patriots and the SS [Legions] of course have a very negative image ... This is one of the issues where the local Russians, those Russians who lived here from the interwar period onwards, agree with those Russians who came to Estonia after 1945.

Hariton voiced a moderate criticism with regard to the treatment of the Russian-speaking minority in post-Soviet Estonia:

> They [the Estonians] just want the Russians to learn the Estonian language and to internalize the Estonian culture, and [they believe] this would re-solve all problems. In my opinion – and I am certain that ... most Russians in Estonia would support this – integration is a two-way street and that a one-sided process cannot really bear any fruits ... This makes Russians think that integration is just a hollow concept and they perceive integra-tion as 'Estonization'.

To shed light on another facet of the experience of the War Generation I turn to 'Paula', an emeritus professor of sociology from a mixed ethnic background. Born in an Estonian settlement in the St Petersburg *oblast* in 1933 and resettled in Estonia during the German occupation, she describes the loss of her family's farm through collectivization and subsequent near starvation as decisive early childhood memories.[58] Unlike the idealized picture of interwar Estonia held by many Estonians of that generation, she associates the period with the experience of social inequality and exclusion. She recalls how in 1943 her family initially stayed with a wealthy Estonian farmer, who made them live in the cellar with the foodstuff for the animals. He was a veteran of the War of Independence, who had been rewarded with a piece of land, and was probably seen as national hero by many Estonians, but was then possibly expropriated and deported as kulak after 1944. Paula's family subsequently stayed with a traditional Estonian peasant family who, though on the breadline, shared what little they had. For her the Soviet period meant a gain in social standing, which is why she believed in the project of communism and socialist ideals (in the interview she used the collective 'we' for the group of intellectuals who joined the ECP). Yet, like other respondents of the War Generation, Paula felt high esteem for education and its concomitant moral integrity. She recalls that, back in the Estonian settlement, 'the teachers in the village were the only educated and [well-]respected people … I admired them, they were *real* teachers'.

However Paula's mixed background and the lack of specific shared experience set her apart from the majority of Estonians of the War Generation. She says this was due not only to her Russian maiden name but also because she did not share with the majority of Estonians the experience of interwar Estonia and the traumatic loss of independence during the first Soviet year of terror; she had, however, witnessed the bombing of Tartu in 1944. This feeling of exclusion reached its peak in 1991, when Paula was asked to apply for Estonian citizenship, despite the fact that she had lived and worked in Estonia all her adult life. She uses the collective 'we' at several points during the interview. For one when explaining that 'forty thousand ethnic Estonians have been born in Russia, the second generation or our children', but 'a lot of them had to be naturalized' because they had become stateless after 1991. She continued: 'I am sure that these people … feel that they have been humiliated, that they have to pass an examination to become [a] citizen'. Like the Estonian Russian Hariton, she criticizes the treatment of the Russian-speaking community after 1991, stating that the citizenship legislation is about power interests legitimated by ethnicity: 'Our politicians are not thinking about democracy in terms of participation of all people; perhaps [the legislation] is an easy way to hide egoistic interest in the name of the nation, our culture, our language'.

Paula described how, during her doctorate in Moscow in the mid-1960s, lectures critical of Soviet Russian politics of the 1920s and 1930s (that is, the agrarian policies of forced collectivization) and on Soviet military history, turned everything she thought to have understood until this point into a 'historical hole', a void that dissolved all attempts at historical interpretation. In the interview, her recollections of the crushing of the Prague Spring were particularly agonizing and shameful for her because she held high positions in the ECP. She relates: 'Knowing about the events in Budapest and unfortunately later in Czechoslovakia it was awful, it was a real trauma ... I always wanted to visit Czechoslovakia, but after that ... I am afraid to go there, because I am from that place [pause, *she is sobbing*] or at least in Soviet times [pause, *she is sobbing*] it was personally impossible to go there'.

After she displayed such strong emotions in relation to the painful destruction of her political ideals, it struck me that she mentioned the death of her daughter in a calm and composed fashion. Her involvement in politics stands in a striking contrast also to a childhood memory of the deportation of her classmate:

> And then in 1949, I experienced personally what deportations ... [meant].
> I was living with other students in a dormitory, ten girls in one room, and very late at night the soldiers came in and one of our friends, M. R. was her name, was arrested and taken away. Her story was that her family ... had been deported in 1941, and after the War children were allowed to come back to Estonia and she was an excellent student at the teachers' training school ... and in March she was deported once more to Siberia. I remember that morning; it was awful. My initial reaction was to drive home. My family was there, but a lot of people around me were taken away. But people have to live!

Again it is astonishing how immediately after recalling this traumatic event, Paula goes on to describe how she was co-opted into joining the Young Communist League and later the Komsomol. Paula continued her attempts to democratically reform the system from inside with an unremitting idealism up to her involvement as a Baltic deputy in 1989 (even though the Afghan War meant another degree of disillusionment for her).[59] She frames her political activity in the 1970s and 1980s as 'semi-dissident work', the gathering of information on demilitarization, peace and justice. Paula's experience of shattered ideological beliefs, as well as the apparent dissonances in her life story, moves her closer to the next generational context of Post-War Children, for whom this mindset is characteristic. In her own words, it is common for the successive generational context: 'A bit younger than I am ... that the families and relatives tried to create a safe environment for their children, [and] not to push them into the past'. With this comment she hints at two important topics that come to a fore in the next generational context: complicity with the regime and inter-generational tension.

The 'Post-War Children' – A Doubly Betrayed Generation

Estonia's Post-War Children grew up in an atmosphere that was quite extraordinary: a catastrophe had clearly taken place not long before, yet it seemed unfathomable and even unpronounceable. As children they experienced the horrors of the War or the Stalinist terror, and they were young adults under Khrushchev. To protect their children from harm the War Generation often conveyed only scant information about the 1940s, and instead encouraged their children's socialization into Soviet society. A degree of alienation between to two groups was therefore to be expected: in this sense the Post-War Children might be considered a 'betrayed' generation. This generational context can also be labelled 'fatherless', because in most of my respondents' childhoods their fathers had been absent – they had died in war, had been imprisoned, had fled abroad or had been sick and unapproachable. However, most Estonian families also had relatives returning from Siberia in the mid-1950s, which constituted a potential subversive source of non-verbal information on the recent past. Ülle-Mai recalls the family photographs and suitcases of deported relatives in her home; and 'Nelli' remembers how she just 'knew' (without anybody being explicit) that her aunt and other relatives had perished in Siberia. When asked about her childhood, Ülle-Mai replies:

Aha, I [was] born in Tallinn during the after-war period and it is quite meaningful. It is the generation of after-war children ... It is a special child-hood. The first part of this was the Stalin period with those deportations ... The other part is when I was in my teenage years, the Khrushchev thaw. Everything was a bit easier and a bit better; all the society came out from the war mentality ... When I came to university it was like a conclusion to these two earlier periods, because then we first understood that we lived under some kind of extraordinary condition; that something had happened before us and we must now understand what really happened; because at home what really had happened wasn't told to us.[60]

Whereas issues of collaboration with the occupying powers were most pertinent within the first generational context, and they created a predisposition towards forgetfulness, not least in the interview situation, the second generational context was more affected by issues of accommodation to and complicity with the Soviet regime. With Khrushchev's 'Soviet consumerism' came rising living standards, making this generation inclined to forms of acquiescence in the system, such as career advancement through party membership. But what also united many of its members was a shared belief in the grand narrative of building a new society based on equality (which is why I refer to them as a doubly betrayed generation). To my cautious question about membership in the communist youth organization, Ülle-Mai responded:

> I was a pioneer, a young communist and later a party member. I have done it all [*she laughs*]. But it was not about ideology, each and every step of it. It was not about the great Lenin being our idol. No, it was all very practical. It was interesting to do something together with other children … Those who were not members of the pioneer organization – there were two in my class – they were not in our group, they were a little strange … But our Komsomol life at school was very active, all these summer camps and every kind of competition and … discussions on youth problems, on love problems.

'Nora', an Estonian writer and literary critic, rather ironically refers to herself as belonging to the 'Stagna-generation', shorthand for the 'stagnation' label ascribed to her generation by the wider Estonian society.[61] The term holds a derogatory meaning, implying that these people are not to be trusted. To express her experience as a Post-War Child, Nora drew on the melancholic image of a bird that, though it appears to be flying, is in fact standing still. This alludes to what the East German playwright Heiner Müller, in *Leaden Time* (1978), characterized as 'the throes of late socialism'. It also reminded me of Bob Dylan's lyrics: 'The only thing I know how to do, was to keep on keepin' on, like a bird that flew, tangled up in blue' – not unreasonably, because this was also the generation listening to 1960s rock music. Nora remarked: 'What makes things difficult is that we [*pause*], that when somebody of our generation makes a statement that elicits controversy, people can just say "you are a Stagna. This is why you think this way". And this is why many Stagna, or older people, simply restrain themselves [from participating in the public debate], to avoid being stigmatized [as] Stagna, even when they are right'.

Some members of the Generation of Post-War Children feel they have to reclaim their lives after 1991, when the entire period was being labelled as Soviet occupation. Merle Karusoo, an Estonian theatre director of this generational context, describes how presently existing 'memory blocks' do not even allow her to remember her own life lived in the Soviet period.[62] It is such memories of their youth that the Stagna are keen to salvage from the rubble of the Soviet bloc. Nora, for instance, says:

> This was 1968, [in] spring [it] was at its peak and in the autumn of the same year it was all over. I was studying at the time and all came together: something happened in my life. I fell in love. I studied. I married. I believed that, quite naturally, I am the centre of the world. I was twenty-two … And the world around me does what I do, it's opening. [That was] 'Socialism with a human face' … The shock and depression when all was shattered was immense.

'Zbigniew' drew a negative image of the stagnation period, as a time with 'no opportunities available … one just had to kill time … If it had been "Estonian time" throughout, then, of course, I would have done something else as well'. Instead, he chose not to engage with the system during the 1960s, and became a tailor – leading, it occurred to me, a 'Huckleberry Finn' sort of existence at his grandmother's summerhouse. 'Pille', a Freedom Child, claimed that many of those born in the 1940s had been effectively brainwashed in the 1950s because they continued to believe that they lived in the 'happiest country in the world'. She added her unease about the fact that this generation forms a large part of the political elite in Estonia today.

Many Estonian respondents of the Post-War Generation used expressions such as 'I did not actualize or realize it, but I knew it all the time', suggesting they did not find the courage to draw such conclusions at the time. This is also the reason why respondents of the Post-War Children less frequently considered the Soviet period an occupation: 'I did not consider it an occupation until the 1990s. I don't know how it would have been if we had known right from the start that it was an occupation? … You cannot live then. It's too much pressure to think that you are living under occupation all the time'.[63]

Ülle-Mai explained that while the War Generation were adept at shifting consciously between public and private ways of talking (she uses the example of a telephone 'switchboard' to illustrate this), members of her generational context of Post-War Children had already internalized a sort of 'double consciousness', or set of 'double mental standards'. She describes her group as 'fundamentally doubled by birth' because they were less aware of the divide between the two worlds. She then employed the analogy of a radio station broadcasting all stations in chorus (possibly with reference to the widespread Soviet practice of systematically jamming foreign radio stations) to convey this state of mind. One respondent related how the Soviet authorities attempted to jam the transmission of foreign radio stations after 1979, but said that he and his friends had managed to listen to them despite the jamming: 'It was painful, but it was possible'.[64]

These 'double mental standards' made the reorientation after 1991 particularly painful. Ülle-Mai recalled the early 1990s: 'I began to ask myself what was right and what was wrong. How can I explain, or can I even explain, why certain things were wrong and others were right? Is it possible that both were wrong and right at the same time?' If the ending of the Hungarian uprising meant the shattering of the last hopes for a free Estonia for the War Generation, the crackdown of the Prague Spring had a similarly strong impact on the Post-War Children, leading some of them to reassess their moral standards and belief systems and forced a re-signification of cultural norms to regain meaning. Yet others went through an agonizing process of disillusionment with the system in the late 1970s or late 1980s. It can thus be argued that the Post-War Children experienced the shattering of their ideals and the deconstruction of their previous worldview most profoundly, and can therefore be considered 'doubly betrayed' – both by their parents for keeping the truth about the horrors of Stalinism from them and again by the end of the Soviet system that had framed their conscious lives. As a result they turned into a highly self-conflicted generational group, which is reflected in astounding inconsistencies, dissonances and pervasive strategies of self-justification in their life stories.

Before moving on to the Transitional Generation, let us turn briefly to another group of Post-War Children, those born in exile, a group I would rather characterize as Cold War children of Estonian exiles. It is their stories of visits before 1991 that are the most striking. The opening of a regular Tallinn–Helsinki ferry connection in 1965 allowed limited numbers of Estonians to travel directly to the West. The opening of Soviet Estonia to foreign visitors now meant that the children of Estonian exiles, who had learnt about interwar Estonia only through parental stories, could reassess their views through first-hand experience. Conservative circles among the Estonian exile community, predominantly from the older generation, regarded visits to Soviet Estonia with great hostility, believing them to represent tacit recognition of the political status quo.

'Siim', a historian and politician, born in Estonia in 1943 but grew up in Sweden, described how on his visit to Soviet Estonia in 1979, he was faced with the dilemma of how to act towards Soviet officialdom:

> I remember my brother's birthday on July 17. We were in Tallinn then. He plays the piano and is an old singer. I sing sometimes too. Our cousin Tõnu

... is also a singer. A musically gifted family. We decided to celebrate his birthday in style and invited Tõnu and his wife to the Hotel Viru ... Since I still had a bottle of whisky in my room, we all decided to go upstairs. But a uniformed bouncer wanted to prevent our guests from joining us ... I persisted and asked him in Estonian what he wanted ... but he kept grunting ... The Tallinn Estonians stood shyly by my side. Then I tried it in English, in German, and finally in French ... My relatives on the other side [of the glass door] got worried and told me to stop it ... Later when we all sat outside again, the bouncer cruised around us breathing heavily. At that point Tõnu and my relatives turned to me: 'Now you see how it really is in this country!' I replied: 'So is this the space you've been boxed into?' Still followed by the bouncer... bellowing behind my back, I asked the hotel receptionist in Estonian to tell me exactly what the man wanted. She replied: 'I can't tell you' ... This incident was typical for the time and it stands for the dilemma of whether to give in when you travelled back to Soviet Estonia, the old home, and behave like Soviets or the way the native people had to behave – that is, to give in to those 'gorillas' ... [or] continue to behave like you were in the West.

Siim's narrative illustrates some of the stereotypes held by Estonian exiles about life in Soviet Estonia. 'Pauls' recalled his first trip to Soviet Latvia in 1975:

We arrived and [the tour guides] let us out at the Freedom Monument [the Milda]. I went to the kiosk close by to get the local paper ... I observed that the man before me bought Ziņa, the party paper. I needed to go to the public toilets [which are located below the public square]. The man went there also and I saw him tearing up his paper, in very long, single strips of paper, all evenly measured of exactly the same length. I had never seen something like that before. He used the paper, sheet by sheet, as toilet paper [laughs]. That I never forgot: my first experience in Riga. Really, his skill, snap, snap, snap, perfectly even strips of paper [laughs again] ... An expert in his field! They had a shortage of paper at the time. There was no toilet paper, not until the 1990s ... I thought: life teaches you, life shapes you, life makes experts. That he tore the paper in pieces, so fast, so perfectly, I truly admired the man![65]

This narrative of transgression is multi-levelled. Pauls' first impression of the Latvian stranger buying the Communist Party newspaper probably was that of a stereotypical 'Soviet man'. But once he went underground to the public toilet, he witnessed a different reality. To buy this particular newspaper and use it as toilet paper may well have been a conscious act of defiance. This vivid initiation to his parents' home country gave him an insight into the 'double standards' of life in Soviet Latvia – that is, the coexistence of public conformity (represented by behaviour in the main city square) with the possibility of ambivalent or perhaps deliberately subversive private acts (as represented by behaviour in the underground lavatories). Both accounts of travelling between the two political systems are particularly informative because they also shed light on misperceptions held by the children of Estonian exiles during the 1970s and 1980s (some of whom would return to Estonia after 1991 to engage actively in the reconstruction of society).

Building on the earlier discussion on Estonian identity formation in relation to the (Baltic) German and (Soviet) Russian Other, I would like to turn briefly to hybrid identities among the War Generation and the Post-War Children. With the War Generation we saw signs of 'cultural hybridity' emerging among the Estonian Russian respondents and those of mixed ethno-cultural background. The concept of cultural hybridity, as introduced by Homi K. Bhabha in his discussion of post-colonial identities, signifies the 'construction of cultural authority within conditions of political antagonism and inequity'.[66] It describes the (post-) colonial subject, who has partly taken on the habits, cultural traits and even language of the former oppressor and has interwoven them into his or her own identity structure (resulting in uneasiness or shame).

A concept closely connected to cultural hybridity is that of 'liminality'. The liminal state is characterized by ambiguity, indeterminacy and often a distorted self-understanding.[67] This liminary state, or diaspora identity, is also evident for the Post-War Children among the Russian settlers. For them the year 1991 meant a loss of their collective (Soviet) identity and the frightening, even traumatic, process of becoming a minority of stateless foreigners as happens during a process of decolonization. A respondent from this group, 'Elena', a municipal politician born in 1941, described herself as 'a child of Narva', opting for a local identity. She called herself 'a stranger among my own people [Russians in Russia], and on my own among strangers [Estonians in Estonia]'.

Another identity strategy deriving from this liminality is to become even more Estonian than the Estonians, similar to the Estonian 'juniper Germans' or wannabe Germans a century earlier. 'Eduard', a linguist, who was a Post-War Child of Russian-Armenian background born in 1950, demonstrated a critical attitude towards Russia and its tradition of destroying other cultures and creating chaos, violence and suffering: he labelled this the principle of the 'continuous return of Ivan the Terrible' or the 'Genghis Kahn tradition'. Essentially Russian society to him is non-functional because Russians have an authoritarian type of personality. Distancing himself from this, he portrayed his group of friends as:

Really democratically minded Russian people [who] disliked the stamp 'Russian' ... freely thinking Russians ... tend to mix with the locals. They tend to seek for their roots ... When I was younger I had a period when I said: 'No, I am not Russian'. Now, I am a little older ... and I accept my identity as Estonian, Armenian and Russian. [*Towards the end of the interview, Eduard speculated:*] Estonians have been efficiently assimilating oppressors without applying violence. Perhaps this experience of living under Danish, Swedish, Russian and German rule ... produced some ... defence mechanism among the Estonians effective in ... situations of subjugation.

From Rein Taagepera we learn that persistence, endurance, spite and stubbornness, captured in the Estonian word *jonn*, is considered a characteristic trait of many Estonians.[68]

We will return to the theme of liminary identities once again at the end of the chapter when discussing newly emerging post-Soviet identities in Estonia, but let us now turn to the Transitional Generation.

The 'Transitional Generation'

I argue that due to the socio-political changes of the 1980s in Estonia one can discern a third generational context, the 'Transitional Generation'. Those born in 1960s were affected by the events of the Afghan War and the Solidarity movement.[69] I would argue that no generational context among Russians in Estonia exists that would parallel the Transitional Generation among Estonians, which was – as we shall see – activated by the very specific social dynamic in the Soviet Estonia of the 1980s. One respondent, 'Oskar', who became a professional historian and politician, commenced his history studies at Tartu University in 1978, but was expelled in the early 1980s. He recalls: 'I became famous. I happened to be a martyr ... People repressed by the KGB got a sort of quality certificate: "These are honest and fair people [who have] been accused by KGB"'. The reason for Oskar's arrest was his activity as a founding member of a small movement called 'Young Tartu', which opposed the intensified use of Russian in institutions of education in the late 1970s and early 1980s; this was experienced by many Estonian intellectuals as a threat to their identity. Rather than teachers and professors, it was high school and university students who took to the streets in protest at Brezhnev's enforced Sovietization policies – possibly because these groups felt that they had less to lose, not yet having career or family. Siim, the Estonian exile born in 1943, was in the country at the time. He remarked that in these student street demonstrations the youth shouted 'Heil Hitler'; the Soviet authorities classified them as 'rioters' and 'hooligans'.

The 1970s were arguably the most formative period for this generational context, although Oskar's childhood recollections of earlier political events also marked him:

> I knew there were ... people who had fought against the Soviets with arms in their hands. I was eight years old when the Prague Spring was 'killed'. I remember people were quite open, especially when compared to the later period ... [It] was a very memorable lesson for me that there are people who want to change things. That there is even an entire nation which tried to do something and there was no question anymore, to whose side I belonged, at least mentally.

While the Post-War Children joined the Communist Party hoping to reform the system from within, the Transitional Generation had only 'disgust' (a frequently used word) for the corrupt client–patron system, and viewed the Stagna as morally corrupt, despising their conformity. They took a far more pragmatic view than the previous generational context, rejecting the idealism of their predecessors and any belief in ideology. Even though there might not have been a full break in the generational chain, the degree of accommodation with the Soviet regime certainly created a rift between the Post-War and Transitional generations (resulting in the marginalization of the former, generationally). Instead the Transitional Generation found themselves closing ranks with members of the War Generation in an intergenerational alliance of historians functioning as engineers of the independence movement.

Let us examine this concrete intergenerational dynamic further. Although private student organizations were forbidden in Soviet Estonia, small groups of teachers and students met throughout in clandestine circles, exchanging and reading forbidden literature.[70] Dissidents attended these meetings as well. One of them, 'Ervin', recalls:

> As I understand it, they [the university teachers] had knowledge about everything, but they ... only began to make use of it when the occupation ended. The historians, true historians, were very good and they were informed, because we 'resistance fighters' were not isolated from society. We knew the intellectuals, we passed our information, our material, on to them and they gave us their books and material. It was an exchange of information.[71]

In the 1960s and 1970s the 'History Circle', ran by Helmut Piirimäe and Sulev Vahtre, played an important role in promoting a less ideological interest in history. They organized excursions to places of ancient and medieval Estonian history. It was in this context that respondents of the Transitional Generation were taught by the War Generation about the Estonian past, and found support in their efforts to expose the falseness of the Soviet–Marxist narrative of Estonian history. At the time of perestroika, members of both generational contexts were among the founding members of the 'Estonian Heritage Society', including the later statesmen Lennart Meri and Mart Laar who set as their goal 'to become masters of their own past', and drawing up an agenda for a new national history writing.[72] Modelled closely on its precursor, the 'History Circle', the Estonian Heritage Society organized excursions to the countryside to restore graveyards and ancient battle sites – settings that yet again facilitated free and informal communication about the recent past. According to the recollections of one participant, history came alive as a direct consequence of participating in these workshops – the past became palpable, people came together and became more active. It was particularly the younger members of the heritage society who, between 1987 and 1991, gave ad hoc teachings on Estonian history in classrooms and who authored the first new history textbooks.

'Pille', who graduated from High School in 1989, remembered this:

> During the last year new history books were published. [It was] sometime around the second half of 1988. I still have a copy of the very first edition; it was written by Mart Laar and Lauri Vahtre [both members of the heritage society], it is a small book … and it gives you a brief history of Estonia, how it actually happened. So we were taught both versions.

The 'Freedom Children'

This brings me on to my last generational context. While elements of the political liberalization of perestroika were already noticeable during the last high school years of the Freedom Children (born between the late 1960s and mid-1970s), most of them commenced their university studies and entered their working lives in a free Estonia. Still, they share an understanding of both worlds. Early in interviewing I referred to this group as the 'Gorbachev Generation', but one of my respondents, 'Zinovij', born in 1973 in Russia of mixed background, disliked the term as 'one of these over-simplistic academic concepts imposed in retrospect'. It is, of course, true that these ascriptions are often made with hindsight. In fact members of the respective generational context may not have even been consciously aware of belonging to or constituting a generation; they assumed this label *ex post facto*. I came to choose the label 'Freedom Children' for this generational group, because, as we shall see, the regaining of independence is undoubtedly the most significant experience for them.

In 1987 party history was no longer an obligatory subject, and a new curriculum for history textbooks was being launched. Zinovij described how that year liberalization also became noticeable in the classroom, although still tentatively: 'It was no longer a "sin" to listen to Western radio stations. I would not be arrested for it. I could do it freely. I could even speak about it at school. The teacher said, "Zinovij is spreading anti-Soviet propaganda", but nothing happened, nobody expelled me from school'.

With regard to the worldview of the Freedom Children, an Estonian sociologist (generationally of the Post-War Children) says that they quote cultural symbols such as 'Fatherland', 'Soviet Union', 'Civil War' and 'War of Independence' in a playful mix-and-match fashion, because for them all of these representations have lost their original meaning.[74] Ülle-Mai described almost jokingly the phenomena of 'double reality' and of the Freedom Children's 'anything goes' mentality: 'The first Republic was reality, the shoe size of the first prime minister was reality, 1945 and 1946 was reality, the deportations were reality, as were Stalin's statues and their demolition. All of this was reality'. We can note an interesting proximity here, because it is not immediately clear from the interview as to whether Ülle-Mai is describing the mindset of her own generational group or that of the Freedom Children.

In fact, by and large my interviews with members of this generational group do not support Aarelaid-Tart's assessment that the coexistence of two controversial worldviews was perceived as normal by the Freedom Children or that they lacked a belief in any of these versions of the past.[75] Because if the majority of this generation held a distinctly laid-back view of current Estonian affairs, how did they become involved in the Singing Revolution? Tulviste and Wertsch found out that this generational group is in fact less deeply affected by official accounts of the past than the preceding one.[76] Pille, a Freedom Child, recalls:

> I never questioned the official history of the time, although my parents and grandparents had told me about the Republic of Estonia, the time prior to the occupation; and my family always celebrated Christmas. I had no moral conflict … I knew … about the occupation, although it took me some years before I realized that [during] my happy childhood – and I can say I had a very happy childhood – we were actually living under occupation. Personally I felt I was in a cage all these years; not able to travel, something I had wanted to do from very early on.

Pille's recollections indicate that the picture is more complex, and we cannot simply talk of 'double reality' for her generational group.

As stated earlier, the Singing Revolution was probably *the* formative event for the Freedom Children. 'Niils', a professional historian and politician born in 1969, recalled how the wave of the independence movement meant a big change for his personal life, transforming him from someone who 'grew up blind' to a young man who, in 1988, read out the historic Estonian declaration of independence of 1919 under a waving Estonian flag in his hometown of Valga. That year he had also joined the local heritage society. He experienced the return to independence as natural, yet as something that had been unthinkable to them just a few years earlier. Likewise, 'Pille' also remembered flags, songs, ethnic upsurge and nationalism all around her, and said that it felt natural to go along with it. 'Tiina', a social scientist born in 1970, provides a window into the *Zeitgeist*:

> I told you about this emotional time of learning about history at the end of the 1980s … at sixteen … I was participating in what we call the 'Singing Revolution' … afterwards, I could really see what a sensitive time it was for many people, especially for young people … You were given a very special pride … [*pause*] I was proud, and I think that most of the people were very proud of being Estonian in the Soviet Union. Because it was [*pause*], I mean everybody knew that it was better to be Estonian than to be Russian. At the time we didn't compare ourselves with the rest of the world, but we just had a comparison within the Soviet Union … We were very proud of who we were … I think you could feel this special pride of being Estonian at the end of the 1980s. I think the people were endowed [with it] [*pause*]. You were still the same person, but you were given an additional value.

With regard to the intergenerational transmission of stereotypes, it is interesting to note the outlook of Niils, who in the early 2000s headed an independent think tank on Russian Studies. He expressed strong anti-Russian sentiments, warning me that, although Russians look like Europeans, they will always remain Russians. Similar statements were voiced in interviews by historians of the War Generation.

With regard to the youngest Russian-speaking generation in Estonia, my interviews left a rather pessimistic impression. Ülle-Mai explains that even though Russian parents, born in the 1960s, are more tolerant towards Estonians, their children are greatly influenced by their grandparents' generation: 'These elderly people in their sixties and seventies, they are "sovietized", [they are] absolutely against this Republic. Of course the grandmother is cooking the soup at home, telling of the good old Soviet times. And now the youngest generation of sixteen or seventeen-year-olds are chauvinists'. This rather gloomy outlook was substantiated by the social riots surrounding the removal of the Bronze Soldier Statue from the centre of Tallinn in April 2007 – discussed further in Chapter 5.

Emerging Post-Soviet Identities

Following on from the earlier discussion of hybrid identities among the War Generation and the Post-War Children, I turn now to various emerging post-Soviet identities (or liminary identities).[77] Inter-ethnic marriages were considered a progressive development by the Soviet regime, leading to the merging of nationalities (in Estonia in 1979 the figures for inter-marriage were 18.6 per cent of the urban population and 9 per cent of the rural), but there was only a small number of inter-ethnic marriages in Estonia compared to Latvia. Members of the War Generation viewed inter-marriage as 'collaboration' or 'treason'.[78] The strong nationalist current of the early 1990s more or less demanded that intellectuals of mixed ethno-cultural background had to choose whether they were Russian or Estonian.

Like many intellectuals of mixed ethnic background, 'Zahkar' had long grappled with his identity. Until the age of ten he had tried to be a good Estonian, an 'orthodox nationalist', but the neighbourhood boys of his age picked on him because of his Russian name. In adolescence he reacted against this by embracing being Russian and hating all that is Estonian. It took him until his mid-thirties to reach a middle ground. Today he has to define his position carefully when it comes to commenting on current socio-political affairs in his professional work because he is easily called a traitor, 'a strange creature that does not belong to us, but still it dares to criticize us'. Afterwards he drew up a list of dualisms between Russians and Estonians, and concluded: 'See how many dichotomies I have in me. I am in constant agony as to where I belong. I find certain Russian traits disgusting, but the same goes for some Estonian traits. I see that communism holds a healthy core, something I do like about the doctrine; but Estonians act as if they are standing above all of it, [as if] pure'.

Zinovij only began to study Estonian when he moved to Narva with his Russian-Estonian parents in 1988. He soon developed an interest in the local history and joined the local branch of the heritage society: '[it was] more like nostalgia, … you try to find refuge in this old golden age … It was a beautiful town and of course the grandparents, mostly grandmothers, told all these romantic stories … very sweet stories about Narva'. At the time he rejected his own Russian side. He recalled that, 'particularly in Narva, [because] it is a "pro-Soviet town", you felt very bitter. Old Narva had been destroyed ... I felt really bad in the early 1990s, and this [joining the heritage society] was my attempt to join the other side'. Looking back, he understood the late 1980s and 1990s to be a personal identity crisis. When he came to study in Tartu in the mid-1990s, he was confronted with a feeling of inferiority once more: 'I was the only one there who was not a purely bred Estonian'. Finally, he overcame this state of abeyance: 'My first language is Russian. If I had to choose, it would be Russian. Once I realized that for myself, things got so much easier'. Like Zahkar in his journalistic work, Zinovij encountered emotionally charged reactions from public audiences when he delivered a conference paper on Estonian collaboration with the Germans during the war: he was reviled as a 'Russian spy' and a 'genocide denier'.

'Polina', who was born in 1976 to an Estonian father and a Russian mother, and grew up in a bilingual environment in Estonia's north-east, displays great sensitivity towards the challenge posed by the Russian-speaking community in Estonia:

> I remember how, in 1993, when the 'Alien Law' was adopted and there was a crisis in society because of it – Russians really took it very badly – I was clearly on the Estonian side, feeling that we had a right to do it to them for what they did to us ... But now ... I am thinking, it has been ten years, and it's time for a revision ... We need to have a new law that reflects the new situation. Now, I acknowledge that what we did in 1993 was not fair [*laughs*]. Most of the Estonians I talk to about this don't like to hear about it, and they start the old argument that we were the victims. And they ask me why I call the Russians a victim of our policy. It takes a long time for them to realize that the positions have in fact changed, that they are now in a position of power. And then they begin to understand and that things need to change, but it's still hard for them to admit that what we did in 1993 was wrong.

Polina picks up the same issue raised by members of the first generational context from Russian or mixed background:

> If you talk to Russians here [in Estonia], they tell you why they are different from Russians in Russia. They say, it's the tidiness, the correctness, the punctuality of Estonians, and they already consider themselves as Estonian, because they want to be tidy, correct and punctual, and that this is not a part of the Russian identity at all ... They have taken on a lot of the Estonian [forms of] social conduct without speaking Estonian or having Estonian friends. The society around them has been teaching them how to behave in this context ... How then can you tell them that 'you are not Estonian'? That would mean they are lost, because this is the only place in the world where they feel at home. This is the only place where they know

what they are required to do, how to behave, perceptions, expectations. When you go somewhere else, you don't feel at home ... you are neither at home here nor there. Is this a question of language?

Based on such statements I suggest that intellectuals of mixed background born in the 1960s and 1970s embody a great potential as newly emerging post-Soviet identities in Estonia, because these are individuals who were forced to reflect on and define their identity more carefully.

Conclusion

I have argued for the oral history method as being particularly useful when researching post-dictatorial transition societies. But I have also emphasized the need for a precise methodology, sensitive to what is said by the respondent but also conscious of the reciprocity between interviewer and interviewee. My choice of professional historians as respondents was substantiated in part conceptually, because they constitute the critical interface between social and cultural memory, between memory and history. I outlined four generational contexts among historians in post-Soviet Estonia, arguing that the third generational group is particularly germane to the transition process, which had possibly already begun in the late 1970s (in reference to the Afghan War and Solidarity in Poland). I shed light on the inter-generational dynamics with regards to the 'doubly betrayed' Post-War Children (and potential rifts in the generational chain), and on the teaming up of members of the War Generation and the Transitional Generation who formed an alliance as engineers of the independence movement: they can be identified as founding fathers of the newly independent Estonian state. I listed some of the formative experiences at the base of these four generational identities and alluded to the fact that these group identities can cut across ethno-cultural identities. I constructed a multifaceted picture of each generational group identity, contrasting it with various subgroups such as historical Russians, Estonian exiles, descendants of Russian settlers, and respondents of mixed Russian Estonian background. Finally I pointed to forms of cultural hybridity as a result of Soviet communism, and of liminarity among newly emerging post-Soviet identities, which are still in the process of becoming.

Having analysed these four generational groups and the varying social memories of the Soviet era, I now move on to the period after 1991. How did these historians and intellectuals address the challenges of constructing a national narrative for post-Soviet Estonia?

Notes

1. Anything that did not fall within the ideological framework of Soviet historiography could not be published but only produced for the drawer.
2. I am building on the scholarly work of A. Aarelaid-Tart (2006. *Cultural Trauma and Life Stories*. Helsinki: Kikimora Publications, University of Helsinki), L. Bennich-Björkmann (2007. 'Civic Commitment, Political Culture and the Estonian Inter-War Generation', in *Nationalities Papers* 35(1): 1–21), and E. Kõresaar (ed., 2011. *Soldiers of Memory: World War II and its Aftermath in Estonian Post-Soviet Life Stories*. Amsterdam: Radolphi) on generations in twentieth-century Estonia and Latvia. While I am taking on some of their generational labels, I favour the term 'War Generation' over 'Republican Generation', and I have also introduced the term 'Transitional Generation' (Wulf and Grönholm, 'Generating Meaning across Generations', 351–82). I also diverge from Aarelaid-Tart (2003. 'Estonian-inclined Communists as Marginals', in R. Humphrey, R. Miller and E. Zdravomyslova (eds), *Biographical Research in Eastern Europe: Altered Lives and Broken Biographies*. Aldershot: Ashgate, 71–100; 2006) and her early collaborator, Johnston, in their ways of organizing these generations. Both of them single out only three generations, specified by birth cohort (Aarelaid-Tart) or formative years (Johnston), and periodized as follows: 1940–55; 1956–69 and 1970–85. See also H. Johnston and A. Aarelaid-Tart. 2000. 'Generations, Microcohorts, and Long-term Mobilization in the Estonian National Opposition 1939–1991', *Sociological Perspectives* 43(4): 671–95.
3. N. Gallerano. 1994. 'History and the Public Use of History', in François Bédarida (ed.), 'The Social Responsibility of the Historian', *Diogenes* 42(4): 94; see also the essays in G. Alexopoulos, J. Hessler and K. Tomoff (eds). 2011. *Writing the Stalin Era: Sheila Fitzpatrick and Soviet Historiography*. Basingstoke: Palgrave Macmillan.
4. Jaan Kross's *Between the Three Plagues*, written between 1970 and 1980, tells Rüssow's life. The 'plagues' refer to Swedish, Polish and Russian rule of Livonia. As chronicler of his times, Kross saw himself as the 'collective memory' of Estonians (T. Salumets. 2000. 'Introduction', *Journal of Baltic Studies* 31(3): 225–36).
5. A.D. Smith. 1999. *Myths and Memories of the Nation*. New York: Oxford University Press, 16, 29.
6. F.R. Ankersmit. 1998. 'Hayden White's Appeal to the Historians', *History and Theory* 37(2): 190. See also J. Fentress and C. Wickham (1992. *Social Memory*. Oxford: Blackwell) who equate oral history and ethno-history.
7. See Z. Baumann. 1987. 'Intellectuals in Eastern Europe: Continuity and Change', in *East European Politics and Society* 1(2): 162–86; Schöpflin, *Politics in Eastern Europe*.
8. Quoted in Coser, *Maurice Halbwachs*, 22.
9. W. Mommsen. 1995. 'Die moralische Verantwortlichkeit des Historikers', in Kristin Platt and Mihran Dabag (eds), *Generation und Gedächtnis: Erinnerung und Kollektive Identitäten*. Opladen: Leske and Budrich, 131; Bédarida, 'The Historian's Craft', 69, 71–76; also Le Goff, *History and Memory*.
10. G. Lucius-Hoene and A. Deppermann. 2002. *Rekonstruktion narrativer Identität. Ein Arbeitsbuch zur Analyse narrativer Interviews*. Opladen: Leske and Budrich, 63. A further factor impacting on the individual's narrative is the 'master narrative' of his or her respective generational context.
11. Ankersmit, 'Hayden White's Appeal', 191.
12. See K.H. Jarausch. 2002. 'Zeitgeschichte und Erinnerung. Deutungskonkurrenz oder Interdependenz?', in Konrad Jarausch (ed.), *Verletztes Gedächtnis: Erinnerungskultur*

und Zeitgeschichte im Konflikt. Frankfurt a. M: Campus Verlag, 9–38; A. von Plato. 2000. 'Zeitzeugen und die historische Zunft: Erinnerung, kommunikative Tradierung und kollektives Gedächtnis – ein Problemaufriß', BIOS 13(1): 5–29; H. Welzer. 2000. 'Das Interview als Artefakt. Zur Kritik der Zeitzeugenforschung', BIOS 13(1): 51–63.

13. Ankersmit, 'Hayden White's Appeal', 183.
14. Bédarida, 'The Historian's Craft', 73ff.; Gallerano, 'Public Use of History', 91.
15. Fentress and Wickham, Social Memory.
16. J. Sharp. 2000. 'Women, Nationalism and Citizenship in Post-communist Europe', in Angela Dimitrakaki, Pam Skelton and Mare Tralla (eds), Private Views: Spaces and Gender in Contemporary Art from Britain and Estonia. London: WAL, 100–9.
17. Skultans, The Testimony of Lives, 28.
18. Anecdotes are well-tested, standardized key narratives that point beyond the actual event they are narrating (Lucius-Hoene and Deppermann, Rekonstruktion narrativer Identität, 152); see also S. Greenblatt and C. Gallagher. 2000. Practicing New Historicism. Chicago: University of Chicago Press, 49–74.
19. For background, see P. Alheit and E. Hoerning (eds). 1989. Biographisches Wissen. Beiträge zu einer Theorie lebensgeschichtlicher Erfahrung. Frankfurt: Campus Verlag; P. Alheit. 1996. 'Changing Basic Rules of Biographical Construction: Modern Biographies at the End the 20th Century', in Ansgar Weymann and Walter R. Heinz (eds), Society and Biography: Interrelationships between Social Structure, Institutions and the Life Course. Weinheim: Deutscher Studien Verlag, 111–28; D.K. Dunaway and W.K. Baum. 1996. Oral History: An Interdisciplinary Anthology, 2nd edn. Walnut Creek, CA: Altamira Press; G. Michel. 1985. Biographisches Erzählen – zwischen individuellem Erlebnis und kollektiver Geschichtentradition. Tübingen: Max Niemeyer Verlag; A. von Plato. 1991. 'Oral History als Erfahrungswissenschaft: Zum Stand der "mündlichen Geschichte" in Deutschland', BIOS 4(1): 97–119; T. Wengraf. 2001. Qualitative Research Interviewing: Biographic Narrative and Semi-Structured Methods. London: Sage; for interviewing, see N.K. Denzin and Y.S. Lincoln. 2000. Handbook of Qualitative Research, 2nd edn. London: Sage; G. McCracken (ed.). 1988. The Long Interview (Qualitative Research Methods). London: Sage Publications.
20. A.L. Litvin. 2001. Writing History in 20th Century Russia: A View from Within. Basingstoke: Palgrave, 10ff., 17.
21. Brubaker, Nationalism Reframed.
22. Rüsen, in Ankersmit, 'Hayden White's Appeal', 192.
23. For examples of oral history research in the former Soviet Union, see T. Kirss, E. Kõresaar and M. Lauristin (eds). 2004. She Who Remembers, Survives: Interpreting Estonian Women's Post-Soviet Life Stories. Tartu: Tartu University Press; T. Jaago (ed.). 2002. Lives, Histories and Identities: Studies on Oral Histories, Life and Family Stories. Tartu: University of Tartu Estonian Literary Museum; A. von Plato. 1990. 'Einleitung zum Schwerpunkt: Oral History in der SU', BIOS 3(1): 1–7.
24. Lucius-Hoene and Deppermann, Rekonstruktion narrativer Identität, 31ff.; G. Rosenthal. 1995. Erlebte und erzählte Lebensgeschichte: Gestalt und Struktur biographischer Selbstbeschreibungen. Frankfurt a. Main: Campus, 167ff.; P. Ricoeur. 1999a. 'Memory and Forgetting', in Richard Kearny and Mark Dooley (eds), Questioning Ethics. London: Routledge, 5–11.
25. White, 'Historische Modellierung'; Lucius-Hoene and Deppermann, Rekonstruktion narrativer Identität, 21ff.
26. I give the exact breakdown of the forty interviewees (based on age, gender, profession, residence) in Appendix A.

27. At the outset of the interview I asked each person for permission to record them. I guaranteed their anonymity, and protection of their personal data. I also explained that the information entrusted to me would be used solely for my academic research.
28. The questionnaire can be found in Appendix B.
29. This is an ideal typical construction of the four coexisting generational identities that I found amongst historians in the late 1990s and early 2000s, while in actual fact their boundaries are overlapping and porous. I did not analyse the transmission of memories within a specific family, but concentrated more on intergenerational transmission and interaction within the group of historians. In another study we also included the generation of Estonian historians that had emerged in the interwar period, and referred to them as 'Founding Fathers' (Wulf and Grönholm, 'Generating Meaning'); see also R. Helme. 1995. 'Die estnische Historiographie', in Michael Garleff (ed.), *Zwischen Konfrontation und Kompromiß, Oldenburger Symposium: Interethnische Beziehungen in Ostmitteleuropa als historiographisches Problem der 1930er/40er Jahre*. Munich: Oldenbourg, 139–54; J. Kivimäe. 1999. 'Re-writing Estonian History', in Michael Branch (ed.), *National History and Identity: Approaches to the Writing of National History in the North-East Baltic Region, Nineteenth and Twentieth Centuries*. Helsinki: Finnish Literature Society, 205–11.
30. U. Eco. 2000b. 'Overinterpreting Texts', in Norman K. Denzin and Yvonna S. Lincoln (eds), *Handbook of Qualitative Research*. 2nd edn. London: Sage Publications, 45–66.
31. The conviction that the past makes us what we are in the present 'is the root of the importance that political power has always given to the control of the past as a privileged instrument for the control of the present'. Hence 'the political function of historiography is to regulate memory and oblivion' (Gallerano, 'Public Use of History', 90).
32. J. Connelly. 2000. *Captive University: The Sovietization of East German, Czech, and Polish Higher Education, 1945–56*. Chapel Hill: University of North Carolina Press; M. Kerner and S. Stopinski. 1991. 'Vom Umgang mit der eigenen Geschichte', *Osteuropa* 6(41): 602–10; J. Lipinsky. 2000. 'Sechs Jahrzehnte Geheimes Zusatzprotokoll zum Hitler-Stalin-Pakt: Sowjetrussische Historiographie zwischen Leugnung und Wahrheit', *Osteuropa* 50(10): 1123–48.
33. This goes back to the Russian assistance against the Germans by Alexander Nevsky in the battle on the Ice of Lake Peipus (1242), which was repeatedly referred to in Soviet propaganda, such as Sergei Eisenstein's famous movie about the battle that was first screened in 1938.
34. The Baltic governments' alleged plans to turn their countries into German colonies prior to the signing of the mutual assistance pacts with Soviet Russia (September and October 1939) formed the basis for this claim (K.F. Shteppa. 1962. *Russian Historians and the Soviet State*. New Brunswick, NJ: Rutgers University Press, 276).
35. R.J. Misiunas. 1978. 'Soviet Historiography on World War II and the Baltic States, 1944–1974', in V. Stanley Vardys and Romuald J. Misiunas (eds), *The Baltic States in Peace and War 1917–1945*. Univerersity Park: Pennsylvania State University Press, 179ff.
36. Kallas, 'Formation of Interethnic Relations', 56.
37. Helme, 'Die estnische Historiographie', 153; S. Kivimäe. 1995. 'Estland unter der Sowjetherrschat 1941/44–1954', *Nordostarchiv* 4(2): 597; J. Kivimäe, 'Re-writing Estonian history', 209.
38. Jansen, 'Autobiographical data', 224–39; Litvin, *Writing History*, 22.
39. Soviet Estonian historians attempted such writing between the lines by contrasting Russian imperial dominance with the so-called 'good old Swedish time' (1600–1710), or by historical references to the French Revolution or the struggle of the Irish.

40. 'Urmas'.
41. The History of the ESSR (*Eesti Nõukogude Sotsialistliku Vabariig Ajalugu*, shortform: *Eesti NSV*) was published 1955–71 and replaced Hans Kruus' Estonian History (published 1936–40). The periodization of the *Eesti NSV* is interesting because the first volume covers the ancient times to the 1850s, the second volume stretches from the 1850s to the Bolshevik revolution, and the third volume goes from 1917 to the 1950s.
42. Even though S. Kivimäe (1999. 'Were These the Same Women? Life in the Socialist Structures in Estonia', in S. Bridger (ed.), *Women and Political Change: Perspectives from East-Central Europe*. London: Routledge, 21) suggests that while the concept of 'class struggle' had been accepted in principle, it was never implemented in historical research in any orthodox fashion between the 1960s and 1991; this would suggest a pseudo-Marxism among Soviet Estonian historians.
43. Vilhelm.
44. Pauls is the only respondent of Latvian background. Because of the poignancy of some of his recollections, I felt it apt to include his life-story account; however, as a professional historian, he also worked on Estonia.
45. Hariton.
46. R. Raag. 2010. 'Eestlased ja eesti keel rootsis', in Kristina Praakli and Jüri Viikberg (eds), *Eestlased ja eesti keel välismaal*. Tallinn: Eesti Keele Sihtasutus, 385–432.
47. M. Wulf. 2009. 'Locating Estonia: Homeland and Exile Perspectives', in Peter Gatrell and Nick Baron (eds), *Warlands: Population Resettlement and State Reconstruction in Soviet Eastern Europe, 1945–50*. Basingstoke: Palgrave Macmillan, 231–54.
48. According to the ethnologist Ena Kõresaar (2003. 'Lapsepõlv kuiajaloopilt. Rahvuse ja riigi metafooriline kujutamnie vanemate eestlaste lapsepõlve mälestustes', in E. Kõresaar and T. Anepaio (eds), *Mälu kui kultuuritegur. Etnoloogilisi perspektiive*. Tartu: Tartu Ülikooli Kirjastus, 60–91) the term 'lost generation' is also used as a self-marker by this generation.
49. I thank Dr Kai Junge for this comment. Clearly memory can play tricks and can be false, but these war scars are unambiguous.
50. The 3,500 Estonians conscripted into the Finnish army formed the 200th Infantry Regiment – the so-called Finnish Boys.
51. Aarelaid-Tart, *Cultural Trauma*; Bennich-Björkmann, 'Civic Commitment'.
52. M. Lauristin et al. (eds). 1997. *Return to the Western World: Cultural and Political Perspectives on the Estonian Post-Communist Transition*. Tartu: Tartu University Press, 40.
53. See A. Realo. 1998. 'Collectivism in an Individualist Culture: The Case of Estonia', *Trames* No. 1, Vol. 2(52/47): 21 ff., 61–69.
54. Elsewhere I refer to the parents' generation as Founding Fathers (Wulf and Grönholm, 'Generating Meaning').
55. As discussed briefly in the previous chapter, those Estonians who fought in the War of Independence were given a piece of land (formerly owned by the Baltic German elite) in recognition of their contribution to independent Estonian statehood.
56. With notable exceptions of rather critical accounts of interwar Estonia voiced by one exile, 'Iivo', in Sweden.
57. Henrik.
58. Tsarist laws encouraged people from European Russia to colonize Siberia, with economic privileges granted to the new settlers. By the 1920s around forty thousand Estonians lived in settlements in Siberia. The watershed event in the life of the Estonian settlements was their destruction by forcible collectivization from 1928

onwards, followed by cultural Russification. Between 1940 and 1949, about twenty-five thousand Estonians were repatriated to Estonia from all across Soviet Russia.

59. The Congress of People's Deputies of the USSR was first convened in May 1989; its ultimate purpose was to facilitate the amendment of the Soviet Union Treaty (see also Chapter 2).

60. Ülle-Mai uses the term 'after-war' instead of 'post-war' in the interview, which was conducted in English. This leads me to think that there might be a difference between the two terms, which would need further exploration.

61. From Russian *Stagnatsia*, denoting the period of Brezhnevite stagnation.

62. M. Karusoo. 2002. 'Kein Mainstream', Forum Festwochen, Vienna, 48–50.

63. Ülle-Mai.

64. Ervin.

65. The kiosk was located near the famous and highly symbolic Freedom Monument, the Milda, a Latvian site of memory for the soldiers killed during the struggle for national independence (1918–20).

66. H.K. Bhabha. 1996. 'Culture's In-Between', in Stuart Hall and Paul du Gay (eds), *Questions of Identity*. London: Sage, 58.

67. The concept of liminality goes back to Arnold van Gennep's ideas on the rite of passage, which generally involves a change in the participant's social role and consists of three distinct stages: first, the preliminary stage, involving the separation from the rest of the social group; second, the active transition, or the liminal state; and third, the post-liminal state in which the new social status is confirmed and re-incorporation has taken place; see Mälksoo, *Politics of Becoming European*.

68. R. Taagepera. 1993. *Estonia: Return to Independence*. Boulder, CO: Westview Press, 6.

69. Janusz Lewandowski, born in 1951 and a political activist in the *Solidarnosc* movement, referred to his generation as the 'generation of solidarity', distinguishing it from the earlier alienated and fearful generations and suggesting some line of comparison between the transitional generation in Soviet Estonia and the Polish generation of solidarity (interview, BBC World Service, 28 August 2005).

70. The Estonian University Organization (EÜS) – which carries the blue-black-white tricolour that became the colours of the national flag in 1918 – was banned from 1940 onwards, but its members continued to meet underground until its rehabilitation in 1988.

71. Ervin describes their network as consisting of émigrés, foreign radio stations, Finnish tourists, foreign journalists stationed in Moscow and Leningrad, and contacts with Soviet dissidents made when serving in the political prison camps.

72. Lagerspetz, *Constructing Post-Communism*, 69. The Estonian name for Estonian Heritage Society – *Eesti Muinsuskaitse Selts* – means in direct translation 'society for the protection of antiquities, or of relics of old times'. Interestingly the organization displays similarities to eighteenth-century historical societies in Germany (*Geschichtsvereine* or *Heimatschutzvereine*) and may well have been modelled on the German examples.

73. Hanneleen.

74. Ülle-Mai.

75. Aarelaid-Tart ('Estonian-inclined Communists') uses Levi-Strauss's notion of 'bricolage' to come to grips with the phenomenon of double reality. Bricolage signifies improvised structures that come about by appropriating pre-existing materials that are ready-to-hand. The term is also used in semiotics where it is seen as operating through several key transformations, such as addition, deletion, substitution and transposition.

76. P. Tulviste and J.V. Wertsch. 1994. 'Official and Unofficial Histories: The Case of Estonia', *Journal of Narrative and Life History* 4(4): 317, 320.
77. Mannheim ('Das Problem der Generationen', 310) uses the concept of emerging or becoming identities – what he calls the '*aufgelockerten, werdenden Neuen*'.
78. Kallas, 'Formation of Interethnic Relations', 62.

Chapter 4

VOICING POST-SOVIET HISTORIES

> The past is not dead; it has not even passed away. We separate it
> from ourselves and play at being estranged.
> – Christa Wolf, *Kindheitsmuster*[1]

> When my father died. They put him in the ground.
> When my father died. It was like a whole library burnt down
> World without end. Remember me.
> – Laurie Anderson (Old African Song)

Times of socio-political upheaval, such as the end of an undemocratic regime and the subsequent transition during which independent statehood is restored, are highly instructive for the study of collective memory and collective cultural identities, because this is when competing interpretations of the nation are 'up for grabs'. During this time, national identity becomes a highly politicized category, because different groups battle for the privilege and power of transforming and codifying various competing social memories into national history, and of thereby formulating national identity. This is why I am examining in particular the first fifteen years after independence was regained in Estonia: probing the process of national history-writing through my interviews with historians. This allows me to go behind the books, highlighting the conflicting voices in this process to obtain insight about the otherwise hidden 'building blocks' of collective cultural identities.

In 1989–91, the tables finally turned in Estonia and the established Soviet interpretation of the past was overthrown; old verities were rejected, taboo topics lifted and historical figures rehabilitated. As has been shown in the previous chapter, historians of the 'War' and 'Transitional' generations in tandem played an important role in the restoration of national statehood through history teaching and writing. Through these they aimed to set right historical wrongs in a negative response to the previously dominant Soviet historiography. It would be fair to say that in 1991 Estonia did not have a long-standing tradition of independent historical research to offset the long shadow cast by Baltic German scholars and by fifty years of Soviet historiography.[2]

Previously I indicated that many historians took a more political stance from the mid-1980s onwards; in this chapter I will explore why. I will also take a closer look at the kind of social memories that are gradually being codified into the cultural and political levels of the new national narrative in post-Soviet Estonia (utilizing the concepts, analytical tools and insights developed in the preceding chapters). Based on the long-standing but ever potent narrative of '700 years of slavery and 700 years of survival' introduced by the nineteenth-century journalist and politician C.R. Jakobson in the context of the first Estonian awakening, I single out two fundamental categories of events that were consistently highlighted in my interviews with the historians, and in their writing, as being formative of Estonian identity. These are events of 'collective suffering' and of 'collective resistance'. But because national history writing is based on dynamics of inclusion and exclusion, I shall also point to events that elicit controversy – that is, certain taboo topics that constitute my third category of events (relating back to the normative function of cultural memory, pp. 22–24).

Towards a New National Narrative

This new national narrative was authored by, for example, three young history students, Mart Laar, Maria Tilk and Eha Hergauk (all members of the Transitional Generation) in books such as *Homeland History* (written in the early 1980s, published in 1989). How did it take form? Kivimäe and Kivimäe describe the content of these books as anti-Baltic German, anti-Russian, populist and nationalistic. They also remark that *Homeland History* first presented Estonians as fighting on the German side against the Red Army.[3]

Whereas the official Soviet historiography had treated the period of Estonian independence as an aberrant interlude and insisted on the continuity from the 'Baltic Soviet regimes' (1918–19) to the communist governments re-established in 1940 and on to the ESSR, the post-1991 reinterpretation of history in Estonia saw the 'Soviet time' as a rupture from the 'normal' course of events – a period characterized by calamity, grief and fear – which had to be overcome to make way for the cultural regeneration of independent Estonia. The aim was to set the 'Estonian time' against the 'Soviet time'. Mikko Lagerspetz notes that the new interpretation of history shares a common basic structure with Messianism: there was a 'golden age' of the independence period, then the collective road of suffering (characterized by exile, humiliations, mass arrests and deportations) and finally a return to the 'Promised Land' – that is, to an independent Estonian State.[4] 'Estonia goes back' was the slogan indicating that the Estonian Republic was built on the notion of temporal continuity. This newly constructed narrative sets an Estonian, non-Soviet, non-Russian normality (in the shape of an idealized interwar period) against the Soviet period, claiming that the latter had made little impact on Estonian identity. Through this narrative the events of the War of Independence were reframed and previously unmentionable historical facts adumbrated, such as the annexation in 1940, the mass deportations, and the armed resistance of anti-Soviet guerrilla fighters ('Forest Brethren'). Examples of the attempt to construct an unbroken temporal continuity with the interwar period can be found in the shape of a plaque on the wall of the president's palace in Kadriorg Park in Tallinn, which lists all the non-Soviet communist Estonian presidents from 1920 onwards, including the heads of the Estonian exile government – thus effectively eliminating traces of the Soviet period. But some argue that the Soviet interpretation lives on, inasmuch as the newly constructed national narrative is a direct response to previous Soviet interpretations of Estonian history.[5]

Any periodization of historical events already conveys meaning, since it provides a 'cognitive framing' through which past events are understood or recovered. For reasons already alluded to, the periodization of modern Estonian history is a highly political matter: in my interviews the more moderate Estonian historians argued that the Soviet occupation and the totalitarian nature of the regime ended with Khrushchev's 'thaw', whereas others claimed that the Soviet occupation did not end before 1991; still others contend that its final conclusion occurred only when the last Russian troops pulled out of the country in 1994. Even more radical voices hold that the Russian-speaking community in Estonia still represents a 'civil occupation' ('Kalev'). Apart from political colouring, these different perceptions of when the Soviet occupation ended can also be explained by the generational factor.

The reconstruction of national identity involves destruction. The Soviet account of Estonian history was deconstructed, and with it much of the history of the Russian-speaking community in Estonia. 'Zahkar', born in 1963 of mixed background, notes on this process of deconstruction: 'This is another taboo! They speak about integration, but they think really of assimilation. This means that the Russian identity must be deconstructed'. It is arguably fears of further eroding the Estonian national self – particularly in the face of the perceived threat posed by the close proximity of Russia – that deterred historians from fully accounting for the Russian-speaking community living in Estonia. Yet the withdrawal of the last Russian troops from Estonia in August 1994, which signified the beginning of societal consolidation, did not immediately lead to a more pluralistic discourse on the past and a more inclusive national narrative. Instead, the writing of the nation remained hegemonized by the Estonian core nation, resulting in new forms of historical orthodoxies. The debate on whether the new Estonian history is exclusively that of ethnic Estonians (in German, *Volksgeschichte*) or a more inclusive history of the state and territory (in German, *Landesgeschichte*) was decided in favour of the former,[6] although the civic concept of *Estländer*, encompassing all people living on Estonian territory, existed as historical precedent for the latter. However, from the late 1990s onwards a turn towards a territorial concept of national identity is noticeable.

One thing that struck me about post-Soviet Estonia's historical culture is that the former prime minister, Mart Laar, while being an active politician, authored a standard Estonian history textbook, History for the 5th grade (1997) (together with Maria Tilk and Eha Hergauk). 'Evgeny', a Russian historian born in 1957, who discussed the book, notes: 'It is a book about destruction ... of creativity; the destruction of history as such'. When I ask whether he is referring to the destruction of the ways people used to live together in Estonia up until 1991, he replies: 'It's in the nature of people who come to power; they create their own history and destroy the history that had been previously created. They just tear down forty years ... and of course three hundred years of existence of the Russian Empire as well, eliminating the facts. Some Estonians say "it is not our history". They have their history starting from 1918 to 1940. You know, the other history is not their history'.

History textbooks are almost certainly the most prominent means through which national identity is constructed, especially in formative years.[7] For our purposes, that means the first fifteen years after Estonian independence had been regained. The sociologist Meril Ümarik analysed whether textbooks portray an exclusive ethno-cultural identity, or whether Estonia is represented as a multicultural society allowing for a civic notion of identity to take root.[8] According to this research, the majority of the fifteen textbooks examined promoted an ethno-cultural concept of identity, whereas the rest allow for the coexistence of different nationalities in Estonia. Seven of these textbooks were published between 1974 and 1987 by, for instance, such historians as Juhan Kahk, Karl Siilivask, Hillar Palamets and Sulev Vahtre, while eight books were published during transition or shortly after re-independence (1989–95), authored by, among others, Mart Laar, Mati Laur, Tõnis Lukas and Silvia Õispuu.[9] Ümarik concludes that a hostile attitude towards Russian speakers can be found throughout the textbooks. Indeed post-Soviet Estonian history textbooks tended to portray a negative stereotype of Russia and Russian speakers by equating 'Russian' with 'Soviet', using the two words interchangeably, with the result that the youngest generation of Russian speakers grow up with a negative self-image.[10] 'Hariton', a Russian professor emeritus, remarks that the picture of Russians as 'intruders', 'oppressors' or 'occupying power' does not motivate them to learn about history. But 'Hannelen', an Estonian of the War Generation, contends that the negative image of Russians in Estonia is an irrevocable consequence of their past behaviour and that the truth needs to be documented in the history textbooks. Only with time, she adds, can the negative image of the Russians be altered. 'Evgeny', a Russian from Narva born in 1957, talks about the corollaries of this negative textbook image: 'It finds its expression in fights between Russian and Estonian youth in Tallinn and also ... in Paldiski. These facts are known, but they [the government officials] are trying to silence them. That is one of the extremes where it shows up. Another is the destruction of monuments and cemeteries, Russian orthodox cemeteries'.

Our earlier discussion in Chapter 1 about the differences between social and political memories in relation to the stark division of private and public spheres under Soviet rule is now relevant to understanding the emergence of the newly constructed official national narrative in post-1991 Estonia. During the Soviet period, social memories that were preserved in the private family realm or through other atomized small groups – as 'frozen memory crystals' – constitute unofficial accounts that frequently run counter to the official take on the past. Tulviste and Wertsch explain that these unofficial and official historical accounts differ in content, sources, structure and ways of transmission: whereas the official or dominant history of the nation is presented as a coherently structured narrative, unofficial accounts are characterized by fragmentation, and often lack an overarching narrative. Rather they consist of strings of anecdotes and observations, a number of statements, comments and attitudes based more on personal experience – in other words, much of what has been expressed in my interviews. Consequently what Tulviste and Wertsch label as 'unofficial accounts' comes close to what I have termed so far as 'social memories', and what they refer to as 'official history' is closely linked to the concept of 'cultural or political memory'.[11]

Reverting, then, to the construction of the new national narrative in post-1991 Estonia: was the previously dominant Soviet interpretation of history simply replaced by the counter-accounts of the formerly repressed?

We can answer this with a firm 'no'. Instead of merely replacing the Soviet interpretation of history by these various counter-accounts, only *some* unofficial accounts were transformed into cultural memories as part of the new official national narrative, while other unofficial accounts remained excluded. The metaphor of 'frozen' family memories brings out how these counter-accounts did not undergo a lot of critical reflection among the wider public during the Soviet period, but were merely reproduced over time. Hence, some facets of the Estonian national identity appeared almost anachronistic and bygone after their 'defrosting' in the late 1980s. And finally, because the fragmented unofficial histories were in fact structured by the former official Soviet discourse, reflecting what Mikhail Bakhtin has called 'hidden dialogicality' between the official and unofficial sphere, in consequence traces of the former dominant narrative also remained in the new one.[12]

Freedom Child Veera's family further illustrates how private memories were 'frozen' in time, because up until 1991 her parents did not confide to her their experiences of deportation to Siberia.[13] However memories of terror were transmitted non-verbally as well. Consequently an overall atmosphere of fear was conveyed to next generations. Pille, of the same generational context, relates how she came to understand her grandmother's behaviour as a result of the war years:

> My grandparents' house was just by the road ... what I remember from my childhood is that my grandmother always had to close all curtains as tightly as possible once darkness set in, and this really annoyed me as a child. I mean it was so nice to look out of the window and watch the twilight ... But of course the idea was that no one from the outside could peek in ... and this had something to do with the 1940s and 1950s ... I mean you could get shot. She [the grandmother] did not feel safe in the 1970s and she kept this tradition ... even in the early 1980s.

Mart Laar, then chairman of the History Task Force of the Estonian Heritage Society, encouraged Estonians so 'that in writing down one's own [social] memories or those of one's parents and grandparents, everyone would have the opportunity to help give back our history to the people'.[14] In response to this, the Estonian Literary Museum undertook attempts to rehabilitate memory by calling upon those Estonians ready to bear witness to what had long been hidden to participate in a series of nationwide life-story competitions launched in 1989 and published simultaneously in newspapers. This led to a large-scale Estonian 'life history' project, which promoted autobiographical sources as highly constructive for the study of the recent repressions in Estonia. Initially only ethnic Estonians (and Estonian citizens) were encouraged to participate in these life-story competitions. Eventually, in 2003, a life history collection was launched for the Russophone community of Estonia, aiming to preserve 'the historical experience of the Russian-speaking minority in Estonia'. This runs counter to what has been noted for the 1990s, when the accounts of the Russian-speaking community were rather marginalized (for instance in history textbooks). A further competition on memories of life under the German occupation was initiated in that same year.[15] The memory work coordinated by institutions such as the Estonian Life History Organization, the Estonian Cultural History Archive, and the Estonian Heritage Society collected 6,000–10,000 autobiographical texts (memoirs, letters, diaries, etc.) in a project that went on until the mid-2000s.[16]

While *written* autobiographical texts form an important complementary source in the study of the recent political transformations in Estonia, the nature of them confronts us with what Tiina Kirss rightly refers to as the 'paradox of intentionality', namely the fact that the autobiographical text represents an intentional historical source that can indeed be edited by the author *ex post facto*.[17] The context of the construction of the source, that is the national competition, inevitably shapes the outcome as well. The narrator's intention to give testimony was coupled from the start with the wish to be chosen from the numerous contributions in order to achieve recognition for the personal story. The narrator may have attempted to fulfil public expectations and therefore chose to employ certain narrative templates that were likely to be successful. The Estonian Heritage Society left the impression among survivors of Siberia that it valued only those accounts reflecting the experience of mass repression and martyrdom.[18]

There is however another important point with regard to *written* autobiographical sources pointing up the post-Soviet context that the researcher would have to consider: when employing written autobiographical material in the former Soviet bloc one needs to be acutely aware that writing an effective autobiographical account was a common social practice during the communist period. In the words of Miriam Dobson, 'crafting a compelling life story was an essential skill for all Soviet citizens'; such successful templates were, for instance, the 'conversion model' from non-believer to believer or 'tales of heroic martyrdom', about faith sustained by endlessly devoted self-sacrificing communists.[19] James Mark also points to the common activity of remaking one's written autobiography in reaction to de-Stalinization or to the post-communist context.[20] Consequently we must assume that post-Soviet life stories are indeed crafted in relation to earlier (Soviet) templates. While I hold that this may be less relevant for verbally transmitted life stories, it is much more so for those that are written and rewritten.

Due to their long-term links with communist power and a lack of professional training, the great majority of historians in the former USSR did not contribute to a critical analysis of the Soviet regime in the late 1980s.[21] Also, it became more expedient for them to advance non-Soviet, pre-communist history rather than to set off a critical debate about the Soviet legacy which may have involved controversial questions about their own compromises. As elsewhere in the former Eastern bloc, all institutions of party history were disbanded and several research institutions reorganized as part of the phasing out and the process of post-socialist justice with the old regime.[22] One respondent, 'Pauls', related to me that when compared to post-Soviet Latvia, Estonia saw no investigations of historians or re-evaluations of their (Soviet) degrees and competences in the early 1990s.[23] Other respondents told me how, after 1991, many former party historians became political scientists; likewise teachers of historical materialism and scientific communism became sociologists.[24] Others did not reinvent themselves so deftly. For instance, 'Hanneleen' told me that 'the most important scientist, a doctor of history, who compiled books about the so-called revolutions of 1940 … now works as a cloakroom attendant'.

Another legacy of the Soviet period is the reticence about all officially prescribed theoretical and methodological frameworks in post-1991 Estonian history writing.[25] In fact Soviet historiography lacked a methodological and theoretical stronghold, because communist ideology did not allow for critical reflexivity.[26] As a consequence, historians and social scientists were not trained in methodological diversity (although the Tartu School of Semiotics had some influence). It became apparent from the interviews that my respondents often reverted to a positivist understanding of history instead, with evidence from the past treated as 'facts'.

More than a decade after independence, no extensive history of Estonia, comparable to the old 'History of the ESSR', had been written. This is partly due to lack of resources, but the deeper reason, I think, is the unresolved question of how to write Estonian history after 1991.[27] In the new millennium there still exists the rift between more traditional historians who hold fast to national stereotypes, and the younger generation of Freedom Children critical of national mythologies and stereotypical Others.[28] One of those younger historians is Magnus Ilmjärv. A specialist in Estonia's foreign policy during the 1930s, he triggered the Estonian historians' debate in 1999 by publishing his findings on President Päts from the Moscow archives in the major Estonian daily *Postimees* (*The Postman*). Ilmjärv claimed that Päts was one of the most prominent informants to the Soviet embassy in Tallinn on internal political affairs during the late 1920s and 1930s, and was paid by the Russians thousands of U.S. dollars over several years to do so. Ilmjärv raised the sensitive question of whether or not the structural changes brought about by Päts' authoritarian rule in the mid-1930s facilitated the Soviet takeover in 1940. Ilmjärv concluded that, even if Päts compromised his conscience and 'rode the tiger' for Estonia's best interests, he also did so for personal gain. Päts, a national symbol of Estonia's independence, was effectively being charged with nothing less than high treason. Ilmjärv's article sparked an emotionally charged public debate, with the honourable memory of Päts at stake, in which the young historian was branded a traitor. To some his attempt to dishonour the former president seemed an attack on Estonia itself. Ilmjärv could not defend his thesis in Estonia, but had to do so in Helsinki. While at the end of the 1990s the historical figure of Päts had undergone critical revision among professional historians, this was not the case among the general Estonian public.[29] The controversy revealed a generational rift in Estonian society, with especially the War Generation, but also members of the Transitional Generation, unwilling to disfigure their national icon.

Another proponent of this younger generation is the journalist and writer Andrus Kivirähk, born in 1970, whose writings were treated like the Bible by history students in Tartu in the mid-1990s. His first major book, *The Memoirs of Ivan Orav* (in Estonian *Ivan Orava mälestused*), is a parody of the rewriting of Estonian history in which the author assumes a Russian identity. The opening of the book reads as follows:

> Before the time when a professional brood of vipers, from the trade of robbers and murderers, divided Estonia among themselves and hit the spit in her body, our Land of Mary experienced a time of prosperous flourishing. This was the time of the Estonian Republic. Only a few are still alive who experienced this Golden Age and preserve the memory of a time when nightly violin tunes descended from the moon and even the birch trees bore apple fruit. Let me tell you a few words about these long-gone times. It was the time when animals and birds could still speak, before boots of Soviet soldiers drowned out their every sound. It was in the Estonian Republic where everybody could speak their mind openly and freely. Often one could see the wolf and the sheep walking together in the streets in sweet conversation. People were friends, they knew each other, and in the streets one would greet with a handshake – always.[30]

'Zahkar' enthusiastically remarks: 'This is not humour; it is satire, sarcasm against Estonian sacrileges. This writer [Andrus Kivirähk] did ten times more to break through taboo issues than did all of Estonia's historians together. For him sacrileges don't exist, he knows no fear of taboo issues, he is just laughing at all that is sacred to Estonians'.[31] Kivirähk also commented on the psychological dimension of the Estonian historians' debate of 1999 around the allegations against Päts. According to him, the debate painfully reminded the wider Estonian public about the compromises everyone had had to make with the Soviet system.[32]

Having discussed the process by which official and unofficial post-Soviet Estonian histories were voiced – by using the unique interview material as my source and comparing it to existing secondary material on the rewriting of the national narrative – I now move on to outline a typology of historical events that were formative for framing the new national narrative and new post-Soviet identities in Estonia.

A Typology of Formative Historical Events

A distinctive feature of Estonian history is the cyclical feel of historical events, for instance the circumstances surrounding the emergence of the Estonian Republic in 1920 and the re-establishment of independent statehood in 1991. As described in Chapter 2, in each case Estonians had to rid themselves of a foreign ruler, and towards the end of the War of Independence and during the Second World War they were subjected to an alternation of German and Russian military occupations. Georges Gurvitch coined the term 'cyclical time' to denote the sociological phenomenon 'where the past, present and future are mutually projected into one another with an accentuation of continuity and a weakening of contingency'.[33] Therefore the experience of the occupations during the twentieth century echoes in Estonian collective memories as far back as the German conquest; similarly Brezhnev's Russification policy of the late 1970s taps into the collective memories of the Russification during the late 1890s. Deportations to Siberia also have a long tradition; for instance, the great uprising of 1858 was ended with corporal punishment and sentences to Siberia.[34] In people's minds the collective memory of these different formative events can blend into one 'grand narrative'. On the level of practical life this 'cyclical nature' of historical circumstances meant that Estonians lost their homes or farmsteads more than once within fifty years. Virtually all Estonian families got caught in the cogwheels of history: they lost relatives during the war years, in combat, through deportation or flight abroad. 'Simon', an Estonian historian and dissident born in 1956, describes the fate of his own family as representative of most Estonian families:

My father was in prison, my mother had been deported ... She was in the Novosibirsk oblast. My parents met [there], because my father was released in 1955 but he was unable to come to Estonia, because his parents were deported and therefore he travelled to his parents, who were also in Novosibirsk ... My grandmother was ... in prison and deported. My grandfather was shot ... So, the day-to-day talk about how it was in the places people got deported to and in the prisons ... was nothing uncommon ... you heard it here and there all along.

Let us turn more closely to the national narrative in an attempt to identify those 'formative historical events' that figure in ways both constructive and restrictive in the processes of Estonian national identification. Chapter 1 outlined that formative or foundational histories have a mythical quality and function as *mythomoteurs* encapsulating cultural knowledge of who constitutes the group and what its purpose is in life. These histories can be identity-reinforcing, or function as a subversive counter-myth. The categorization in Figure 4.1 represents (next to the questionnaire discussed in the previous chapter) a further step in the utilization of the theoretical concepts of 'national identity' and 'collective memory'.

At the core of the Estonian national narrative stands Jakobson's slogan of '700 years of slavery and 700 years of survival', developed to indict the German conquerors for having imposed the yoke of slavery upon Estonians.[35] In the modern version of this narrative the negative internal Baltic German Other was replaced by the negative Soviet Russian Other

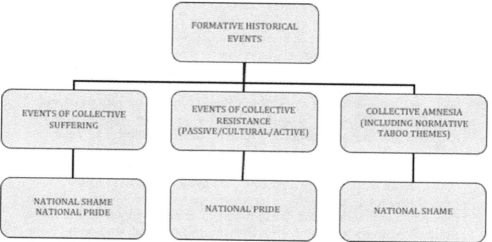

Figure 4.1 Formative Historical Events Constitutive of the Estonian National Identity

after 1940–41, which was a seismic shift because during all the previous centuries Estonians had been anti-German (as discussed in Chapter 2). This re-evaluation allowed the Estonians to view the Germans 'as the lesser of two evils', which had a particular pertinence with reference to Estonians legitimizing their fighting alongside the Germans against the Red Army. Throughout, this 700-year narrative has simultaneously been one of suffering and of resistance and resilience, because Estonians both endure and survive. From this I concluded that the formative building blocks of Estonian identity appear to be memories of collective suffering and resistance – my first two categories of formative historical events.[36] Because cultural memories are based on the logic of remembering and forgetting (or inclusion and exclusion), the collective amnesia of non-events or taboo issues is introduced here as a third category of historical event.[37] These connect to the normative knowledge about what should and should not be done inherent in cultural memory – which was labelled 'wisdom' in Chapter 1. There we also established that taboos in particular can function as prescriptive or proscriptive moral guidelines to society.

Formative Events of Collective Suffering: Trauma, Loss and Humiliation

Next I turn to events of collective suffering, the first category in Figure 4.1. These are closely linked to trauma, and certainly the events from 1940 onwards left Estonia traumatized. Freud defined 'trauma' as the impact of events that exceed the assimilative capacities of the human psyche. In the case of trauma, he explained, the intensity of traumatic events does not allow for a transformation of lived experience into conceptual experience, instead these pre-conceptual experiences remain recurring, haunting memories of traumatic events.[38] The term 'trauma' was for a long time entrenched in the European Holocaust discourse, but after 1989 it has also been used increasingly for describing the effects of the other genocides east of the Iron Curtain.[39] The mass deportation of 1941 stands out as the quintessential event of collective suffering for Estonians. The period of the second Soviet occupation until Stalin's death also figures as a time of great fear. Among its dramatic elements are the scorched-earth operations of the 'shock battalions' (who fought side-by-side with the regular Soviet troops); the total destruction of the north-eastern border town of Narva; the bombing of Tallinn and Tartu; the flight of eighty thousand Estonians to the West in the face of the Soviets' imminent arrival; the second wave of deportations in 1949; and the forced collectivization of agriculture. The harassment of Estonians in the Soviet army in peacetime has been mentioned as another example of suffering.[40] Because memories of events of collective suffering tap into the historic slavery-survival narrative and the collective fear of cultural extinction, as has befallen the Old Prussians and the Livonians, they hold such resonance. It is these events of collective suffering that shape and unite a group as a 'community of common destiny' (in German, *Schicksalsgemeinschaft*).

According to 'Vilhelm', born in 1932, one 'fault line' within the Estonian society runs between those who experienced the interwar republic and fought for a free Estonia during the Second World War – that is alongside the Germans, or in Finnish uniforms or in the forest – and those who either lack that experience of independent statehood or who were on the 'other side'.[41] Vilhelm employs the term 'community of common destiny' in conjunction with the term 'brotherhood in arms' (in German *Waffengemeinschaft*) to describe those Estonians who fought alongside the Germans against the mutual enemy. He then provides a very vivid example for this 'fault line': 'Some were those who threw [people] in the back of the trucks, others were thrown onto the trucks'. Later he remarked that he would always choose to be on the side of the deported – that is, of those who were thrown onto the trucks.

The lack of logic of Stalinist terror was astounding to several of my respondents of the War Generation. 'Kalev', born in 1930, relates an anecdote on the arbitrariness of Stalinist terror:

> There was a committee in 1949 that had to send a number of kulaks to Siberia. But how could one determine who is a kulak and who is not? ... I have seen the members of the committee walking around our house. My father had begun to build a new house in 1938 ... In 1939 the War had begun ... and so it was not completed. The head of the committee noted: 'great house, two Morgen,[42] a kulak'. But another member of the committee intervened, 'Don't you see the house has no window grate'. And now I wonder, what if he [my father] had started to build the house just a year earlier and it would have been ready!

By contrast, the Post-War Children and the Transitional Generation tried to reinsert a certain logic into the course of historical events. To them a lack of material wealth was cited as the main reason why their families would not have suffered from the mass deportations – 'we were not rich'.

The notion of loss forms an integral part of this first category of events. It figured strongly in the interviews with the War Generation, whose members had to struggle to adjust to profound loss in post-war Estonia and in exile. While Estonians in exile lost their homeland, extended family, material possessions and language community, those Estonians who stayed behind forfeited their political freedoms as well as, not infrequently, their property and personal liberty. Vilhelm recalled how he was only permitted to travel to Sweden in 1984, when his hair had already turned grey. He reminisces about life in Soviet Estonia:

> Well, to me the whole situation right until the end [of the Soviet occupation] was totally abnormal. It was no life all these decades. It was something disgusting. It was far more horrible than Hitchcock's movies and scripts. 'The Birds', do you know it? What one could watch there was like a children's game, not horrible at all. But what one could experience here [post-war Estonia], that was really horrible. For instance, the first weeks of September 1944 when they [the Soviets] came back. Those days full of uncertainty. 'Will we all be slain or deported?' … I believe my parents could not sleep and I was sleepless too … My family was not deported, but I witnessed it all: the train wagons and trucks and the despair all around.

As Vilhelm's vivid words indicate, these were traumatic moments, of almost unreal quality, which he could never forget. But he goes on:

> I can well understand that the younger generation, those born later, they couldn't realize this. It would be impossible to live like that, right? They were born into the situation … [to them] this really is … the *real* life. I lived with such a sentiment, a kind of certainty that this 'empire of evil' must crumble. Absolutely! But I was just as convinced that my eyes would not see this happening.

The Post-War Children also expressed notions of loss and resignation, although more in relation to a loss of ideological meaning and the shattering of ideals – hence my description of them in the previous chapter as the betrayed generation. Grief, or its more active form, mourning, is caused by such loss of meaning. Mourning about a loss experienced in the past is what Rüsen defines as 'work of suffering', or more simply the work of memory as discussed in Chapter 1.[43] Through mourning, the individual aims to transform the experienced loss in order to regain meaning. Some claim that it is only by way of *public* mourning that a national trauma can be transformed.[44] As Agnes Heller observes, 'one can only authentically forget what is first authentically remembered'.[45] This sort of forgetting, I think, is connected to the notion of forgiving, whereas authentically remembering entails public recognition of what has been done, both by one's community and by one's perpetrators.[46] In the ESSR the process of mourning was suppressed, and public memory work involuntarily delayed, until the late 1980s, after which an official recognition of the suffering caused by the Stalinist regime was gradually permitted.

Events of collective suffering affect feelings of group worth, because suffering can be interpreted as 'national shame'. Collective memories of suffering imply negative notions of defeat and also humiliation. Therefore nations deliberately attempt to suppress and purge the historical memory of these events and turn them into a collective taboo (my third category of formative events). But memories of collective suffering can also represent sources of collective pride. 'Pille', of the Freedom Children, said that Estonian boys and girls are often reminded that, despite all the suffering, Estonians managed to go ahead and do well; that they are survivors and can be proud of it. She recalled that whenever she did not want to eat her breakfast, her mother told her stories about her great aunt who was a child in Siberia with nothing to eat.

It nevertheless appears to be important to acknowledge the other group's suffering as well, that is not to view Russians solely as representatives of a repressive and alien system.[47] I found insightful here Zahkar's recollections of his father's life as a victim of Stalinism:

> When I asked my father, 'What do you remember from the War', he replied, 'Hunger'. Only four years ago I learned that he had also [similar to Zahkar's mother] been deported by Soviet authorities. It is an Estonian saying that 'from Siberia to Siberia you cannot be deported' ... He was deported from east Siberia to the west of Siberia, which was no improvement, and he was born to a, you could say, slave family. My grandfather worked in a copper mine in Krasnojarsk ... The deportations done with the Russian population were much harder than the deportations later on. You take an entire village and send them to a different region, with no infrastructure and the people dug holes in the ground in which they lived for years. My father was born into such a hole in 1936. He never told me about that during the Soviet time ... He was very loyal to the Soviet Union and Stalin. He was a Stalinist, personally he never blamed Stalin. This is another difference between Estonians and Russians. My father suffered much more by the Soviets than my mother, but my mother as an Estonian spoke about the crimes committed by the Soviets, whereas my father didn't. He simply accepted that, as a Russian.

Most telling were also the biblical references employed by 'Nicolaij', a Russian born in 1961, linking Russian peasants, who were uprooted and 'enslaved' for forty years, to Moses' endeavour to lead the Israelites out of Egypt. Almost at the opposite end stands 'Oskar', an Estonian of the Transitional Generation, who closes his eyes to the fact that Russians had been victims of Stalinist terror: 'This is when I get very angry when someone tells this idiotic story that Russians too are victims of communism. I admit, if you talk about individuals it's very true, but as a whole the [Russian] nation cannot be [called] a victim of its own deeds. No one brought communism to Russia except for the Russians'.

Formative Events of Collective Resistance: Sources of National Pride

This leads me into my second category: events of collective resistance against foreign rule or a dictatorial regime – be they active military confrontation, political dissent or passive cultural resistance – that are linked to an individual's moral integrity, a positive national self-image, and national pride.[48] The War of Independence still features as the key event of victorious resistance, because it led to the first independent Estonian state. The Battle of Võnnu on 23 June 1919 is particularly significant: it is celebrated as a national holiday, known as Victory Day. During the military occupations and Soviet rule, the interwar Republic as a whole figured as a powerful symbol of national resistance and pride. Dates marking events such as the founding of the Estonian Republic and the Tartu Peace Treaty of 1920 were unofficially commemorated during these 'Years of Dependence'.[49] The social memories of resistance resonate in the cultural memory of Estonians due to the long tradition of peasant revolts against foreign landowners. 'Siim' recalls how as a boy he was impressed by *The Avenger*, a novel about the peasant uprising on St George's Night of 1343 against Baltic German rule, written by the eighteen-year-old Eduard Bornhöhe at the time of the first cultural awakening in the nineteenth century.

Let us turn first to active military or armed resistance. Here the 'Forest Brethren', who carried on underground until the mid-1950s, became the stuff of legend.[50] 'Iivo', an Estonian exile born in 1925, remarks that the 'Forest Brethren … fought the battle against the Soviets that we [the exiles] couldn't fight. Even if they killed people, mostly it was those working for the Soviet authorities. Sometimes they pillaged villages, but they needed food to survive … I believe that they are and will act as a positive symbol'. 'Vilhelm', too, has only words of support for the actions of the 'Forest Brethren' because they had to 'keep the surroundings clean' of vagabonding Red Army soldiers, dangerous gangs, partisans and parachutes in self-protection and self-defence. 'Ervin', a dissident and historian who was born in 1952, explains: 'Compared to us [the dissidents, born in the 1940s and 1950s] they had no choice, they fought in the German army and then had to hide [in the woods] to save their lives'; so the heroic resistance against the Soviets turned into a matter of sheer survival after 1944. The full context of this quotation reveals how Ervin realizes that his generation had more freedom of choice to either subdue to 'organized Soviet lives' or to chose anti-Soviet dissident activities.

'Illar', another Estonian exile of the War Generation, points to the fact that, compared to the Estonian anti-Soviet partisans who resorted to armed resistance in 1941, the 'Continuation War' of the 'Forest Brethren' was a 'hopeless case'. It should be noted that usage of the term 'partisan' needs careful decoding and contextualization: when ethnic Estonian respondents speak of 'partisans' they denote anti-Soviet resistance. In contrast, when respondents of Russian or Jewish background used the term 'partisans', they were presupposing, I understood, that there was only one possible form of paramilitary resistance, namely against the Nazi Germans.[51] The memory of the Forest Brethren lived on in their songs but changed over time: whereas for 'Kalev' their songs were 'forbidden songs of resistance', they had already lost their original meaning for many of the Post-War Children. 'Ülle-Mai', born 1948, stated that 'the songs were not holy for us; ... for our parents they meant something positive, but for us it was something to take ironically'.

When I asked 'Polina', an Estonian Russian born in 1976, about collective events of resistance, she remembered:

> When we were kids, I found my father's journals from when he was young. They were kept [on] the second floor of our house. We would always like to look at them and there were many songs of the 'Forest Brethren' which I think my father and his schoolmates sang when they were gathering together drinking [and] playing guitar. 'I went to fight for my freedom, for my ideals' ... So my father is from the Sixties generation. He was a huge Beatles fan, so to some extent this put him against the State as the State was anti-Western, anti-American.

Polina ended up laughing about the fact that her father would simultaneously be a Beatle fan and cherish the songs of the Forest Brethren.

Next, open political dissent: the dissident circles in Soviet Estonia and some of the organizations of Estonian exiles stood for open political resistance. Estonia had a relatively small number of twenty to thirty outspoken dissidents, among them Mart-Olav Niklus, a prominent human rights activist, who signed the Baltic Charter in 1979 and who was arrested in 1981 for signing a statement on the Molotov–Ribbentrop pact. Another was Jüri Kukk, who had protested against the Soviet intervention of Afghanistan.[52] In 1983 massive raids were carried out in Estonia against dissidents, and among those arrested were Lagle Parek and Enn Tarto.[53] 'Simon', a former dissident who promoted the publication of the secret protocols of the Molotov–Ribbentrop Pact and who helped to organize the first political demonstration in Hirvepark in central Tallinn to mark the 48th anniversary of the signing of the pact in 1987, stresses his duty to voice dissent:

> Some people simply have more courage, more curiosity to touch the borders of what is allowed and what not, because in fact in the 1970s and the 1980s nobody was killed anymore. I mean there were accidents and people died, but no mass repression. So, actually it was a duty from my point of view that the teacher or educator tried to widen these limits, but most people are cowards. Most people only think about themselves. So, you cannot demand courage from everybody. It's a virtue that most people don't have.

An equally pragmatic view was expressed by 'Ervin', who had spent six months in the Tatari prison in Tallinn, two years in a prison camp in the Urals, two years in external exile in Siberia, and four years under strict surveillance in Estonia. When questioned whether he was resentful, he responded: 'No, absolutely not! It was my free choice and I know what I did and I know I had to pay for it ... I don't think people should all think like me ... How can I decide what other people really want? ... I wanted my freedom. What other people want ... is not my business. I'm not the Messiah'.

Over time, the dissident movement in Estonia shifted from a preoccupation with civil and human rights to a focus on achieving national self-determination. Consequently the reality of dissident activity in the ESSR was complex. The Russian Estonian 'Hariton' remarked on the relation of Russian and Estonian dissident activities:

> Initially Russian and Estonian intellectuals were united in the desire to become a democratic society and to overcome the Bolshevik system. What divided them right from the start however was that the Estonians wanted the establishment of Estonian independence, and considered this to be even more important than to achieve general democratization ... They said 'let us first regain our independence and then democracy will follow naturally'. While for the Russian dissidents the issue of Estonian independence was secondary ... [To them] the achievement of a general democratization in the Soviet Union was of primary importance. They held the belief that if you stressed the claim for independence in any particular Soviet Republic, then you may set different ethnic groups against each other, which may lead to the opposite of the intended effect.

'Simon' described the group of Estonian dissidents as:

consisting of engineers, technical intellectuals, but on a sort of lower level … and there were various generations. There were people who were already in prison during the Stalin and Khrushchev era, but got away relatively easy. They did not spend twenty-five years [in camps], but usually five years or something, and then there were younger people like me … who were disgusted by the Soviets … This dissent in its known form, [such as] writing letters … came from Russia … Of course our dissidents have their national aspects but generally it was the same … Before us there were groups which were very secret, very conspiratorial, and they mainly worked on various programmes and after they finished these programmes they got arrested, and basically they didn't do more than spending all their time on [writing] papers … From my point of view the main idea of dissent was simply to demonstrate that somebody is outspokenly in opposition. This gives others the possibility to be not quite as openly opposing, but … to do something in [the field of] literature or art, and so on. We stepped into the line of fire, although it was not a war situation.

Simon sets his own Transitional Generation against various preceding older groups of Estonian dissidents, emphasizing that they had practised different, perhaps less pragmatic, forms of resistance. 'Ervin', of the Post-War Children, makes a number of additional interesting distinctions: 'We were mainly "Freedom Fighters" not "dissidents", because dissidents were those who didn't want to change the basis of the state, especially "human rights fighters" in Moscow and Leningrad. They didn't want to decolonize [Estonia] … they didn't even want to introduce a multi-party system'.[54] It is interesting to note that Ervin employs the positive term of 'Freedom Fighters' for his group, thereby linking their cause to the potent narrative of Estonian soldiers fighting for the liberation of Estonia in the War of Independence; at times he also labels his group as Resistance Fighters. Ervin points to a further contrast between these groups of dissenters: 'The final aim of the Soviet [Russian] dissidents was to leave the country. We did not want that'. He also distinguishes his group from the publicly known, official writers in Estonia, who engaged in 'mild public action', such as the 'Letter of the Forty', whereas his group did not consist of intellectuals, but of unknown, ordinary people, such as heaters, chimneysweepers, and students. We can therefore draw a line between this group of 'Freedom Fighters' and the 'Russian dissidents'. The latter did not aim at the de-Sovietization of society, but focused on economic and human rights issues instead. Contrary to that, the group of Estonian dissidents, according to Simon, envisioned 'an ending of the occupation, the withdrawal of Soviet troops, the restoration of independent Estonia on the grounds [borders] of the pre-war Estonian Republic of course of the democratic Estonian Republic!'

Let us finally turn to passive cultural resistance, which was the most widespread form of collective resistance, and which is related to some of the sites and forms of counter-memory discussed previously. The long tradition of folklore and the more recent 'song festival' tradition, together with the important role of a distinct language, can be considered as forms of cultural resistance under foreign rule. This is the reason why the independence movement was commonly referred to as the 'Singing Revolution'. Under Soviet rule the song festivals represented a rare opportunity for larger numbers of people to show their national allegiances. On the 11th of September 1988, at a peak moment of the Singing Revolution, over two hundred thousand people gathered at a special event called the song of Estonia (*Eestimaa laul*). The preservation of sites of counter-memory is also an act of passive cultural resistance. For instance, after the Soviets destroyed monuments for the War of Independence, Estonian villagers frequently collected bits of rubble and kept them in cellars and gardens. 'Pille' recalls an incident from the 1980s:

> I remember we were in our farmhouse when my grandmother was still alive. And in [the journal] *Looming* a poem was published in which the first letters of each row gave the words blue, black, white, which are the colours of the Estonian flag. And of course that was a major taboo. Not in my lifetime, but I remember how the old people told stories that one could not even put on a black suit and white shirt and blue tie, because of the combination. And I remember that … the old people, my parents, were whispering about it [the poem]: hush-hush-hush. This is something I really remember.[55]

That education was considered the most important asset for many Estonian historians across the generations was illustrated in the previous chapter. Educational institutions were linked closely to the consolidation of Estonian national identity, and high levels of literacy in the 1920s constituted a source of national pride. The 'free spirit' of the university town of Tartu constituted a further symbol of cultural and political resistance, and was pitted against the 'corrupted' capital city of Tallinn, seat of the government, the ECP and KGB. One interviewee cited a well-known Estonian saying that Tallinn is the capital (*pealinn*) but Tartu is the city with brains (*peaga linn*).[56] From my interviews with older Estonian historians particularly, I understood how using the Estonian language was itself a form of cultural resistance. The language served as a kind of 'protective shell' in which criticism could be voiced. It functioned almost like a code that signalled people's like-mindedness and even trustworthiness; in contrast, those who spoke 'broken' Estonian, such as the so-called '*jestlased*' (discussed in Chapter 3) could not be trusted.[57] Pille, a Freedom Child, makes the point that rather than being an act of conscious resistance, the decision by Estonians not to speak Russian was more due to the great differences between the two cultures and languages: it was simply too hard. The majority of Estonian respondents are of the opinion that the retention of Estonian as the language of instruction in schools and higher education during the Soviet period ensured that their cultural identity could be preserved. 'Vilma' explains: 'We had Estonian schools and whatever the ideological direction of the subjects taught, ... it was done in Estonian nonetheless, and it was the main thing that this medium survived. And the interest for the Estonian language was most vivid. The Mother Tongue Society ... was an organization that worked very intensively'. All respondents, when asked about the constitutive building blocks of a modern Estonian identity, referred to the language as fundamental. Ervin also comments: 'We are not like the Irish, who lost their language ... the Irish, the Scottish [sic], or the Welsh ... if one took our language, we are no longer'.

Books were feared by the Soviet regime, well aware of the potential danger that a strong cultural memory posed for the system. Vilma remembers:

> The cellar of a house that held the books of the private collections of teachers and professors ... who had emigrated, and all these books were assembled in the cellar and then one worker of our university library informed us that they are there ... It was in high Stalin time, forty something ... [We] could go there to take some books on the sly ... and we all [went], because they would destroy these books. Soviet authorities will destroy these books. And then we went there several times ... she [the librarian] opened the door for us and then we took these books. Many books.

Oskar, whose mother worked in a publishing house and whose father is a retired history professor, learned about the destruction of books by the Soviets when he was a schoolboy. He recalled: 'There was a room full of books, encyclopaedias for example ... My mother simply stole as many as she could and brought them home ... They had been brought there from the libraries. They were on the list and they were taken and sentenced to burning'. The way Oskar described it, the books acquire an almost human quality and needed to be saved; for instance, those kept in summerhouses such as the hidden collection of books that enabled Nora to discover all the censored knowledge about her country's recent past. It is evident, then, that these were not just books: they had an enormous cultural and existential value after the war. If only with regard to the importance attributed to these books, it seems to run analogous to the account of the miraculous rescue of the Institute for Jewish Research (YIVO) Archive from the Vilnius' Ghetto to New York City (which is couched as part of the Holocaust narrative).[58] In a similar way the Latvian scholar Vieda Skultans equates the destruction of books to that of the textual community itself, remarking that in Latvia under Stalin thirty million books were destroyed.[59] To her the Soviet occupying power managed to obliterate the shared significance of Latvian literature; and because literary traditions can be seen as a way to remember the past, a breakdown of these traditions implied that Latvians were decreasingly able to draw on the shared cultural repertoire of the community and to recall their lives in a meaningful way.

One of these dangerous books was the *Estonian Encyclopaedia*. Eight volumes of the 'EE' – as it is widely known in Estonia – were published during the interwar period and fell under the category of censored books in Soviet Estonia. Simon showed me a volume of the EE (now part of the permanent exhibit at the Museum of Occupations (*Eestimaa lau*)) in which many pages had been blackened or removed due to censorship. From 1985, during the Gorbachev era, the *Soviet Estonian Encyclopaedia* ('ENE') was published. In 1990, in the midst of political change, the fifth volume of the ENE was once again published under its former name, in other words as EE. Vilma, one of the authors of the ENE, deems the *Soviet Estonian Encyclopaedia* an 'act of national will' that it was written in Estonian, and recalled that it 'became a national initiative. People subscribed in masses … It turned into a manifestation of national ability … although … historical articles were quite often written according to Soviet standards … the enterprise as a whole gained national meaning'.

Another form of silent or passive resistance during the Soviet period was the cultural tradition of celebrating Christmas, about which the Stalinist authorities were deeply sensitive. Vilhelm, a respondent from the War Generation, recalls: 'I know of people who after they had returned from Siberia never celebrated Christmas again … Officially Christmas and fir trees were forbidden. When I was a student in Tartu in 1950, I went to the market to buy a small sapling and I went home with this little tree, but I could not buy candles prior to Christmas. You could only buy them after December 26'. Kalev, of the same generational context, also talks about Christmas: 'We were not allowed to go to Church … for the Christmas celebrations. I knew that there were special groups in Church to make sure that nobody from the students or professors was there. They were not in the Catholic Church. So me and my wife, [although] we are Lutheran, were allowed to go to the Catholic Church'.

In contrast to the first two accounts, a member of the Transitional Generation, Oskar, expounds how during the Soviet period the Christmas celebration

> was more or less tolerated, but it was laughed at and mocked. Of course there were no holidays ..., but you could not deny people the right to visit the graves of their parents and to put candles there. All the graves were lit that evening [Christmas Eve]. A dark winter's night and then the sea of flames and this ... was silent resistance. People looked at each other's faces and felt they belonged together ..., total strangers. The graveyard was full of people ... At the same graveyard there was a monument dedicated to the soldiers of the War of Independence. It was the same graveyard where my grandfather and grandmother ... were buried. The monument itself had been taken away and there was no inscription, but there were big granite stones and there were always candles there as well. I was very young when on each visit we put candles there, and my mother said it is for the men who fought for Estonia.

Pille related that her family celebrated Christmas, though only at her grandparents' village church, but as a Young Pioneer she did not understand the meaning of Christmas. As a child she was surprised that she got her presents when other kids got them a week later. Another Freedom Child, 'Zinovij', of mixed background, recalls:

> It was a taboo that our school was not far from the only functioning Russian Church [in Narva]. There was a cemetery too and every Easter they had a small procession around that Church ... The teacher always said that 'I know that you are going, but be careful, you better not'. These religious things were taboo ... Many guys went just out of curiosity, not because they were very religious or wanted to express their dissent. It was fun, they were just curious. I am sure they were ridiculing these elderly people participating in the procession.

Collective Amnesia of Hidden Events: Taboo and National Shame

Let us now turn to my third category of historical events: these constitute sources of controversy because they are connected to national shame. They are consciously or unconsciously put aside or forgotten, and as taboos they often carry normative knowledge (in this way we may also refer to this third category as 'normative' historical events).[60] On shame, 'Nikitor', an Estonian Russian born in 1952, contends that you only understand another culture when you are able and willing to feel and relate to their collective shame. He continues: 'I think in very many cultures and nations, national shame is more important than national pride … It is very crucial for our understanding of identity, that identity is not what we think or speak about, [but instead] it is to do with what we hide'.

I previously argued that it is in periods of cataclysmic social change that these taboos or 'hidden events' can become public. I distinguish between forced institutionalized amnesia, deliberate amnesia and mere forgetfulness. Each period has its own specific taboo topics: what had to be forgotten in the ESSR differs from the events that were screened out after 1991. For instance, the greatest taboo topics throughout the Soviet era were the Molotov–Ribbentrop Pact and the Great Terror of the 1930s in Soviet Russia (as cases of forced institutionalized amnesia), whereas the Nazi atrocities committed in the Baltic region constituted 'the easiest and safest topic' of Soviet historiography.[61] As discussed earlier in this chapter, President Päts was only selectively remembered after his rehabilitation in post-Soviet Estonia, because one of the contentious issues of his legacy was his abstention from armed resistance on the eve of the Soviet invasion (1940). This needed to be forgotten (a case of deliberate amnesia) because the interwar republic is of high symbolic importance for Estonian national identity. A similar example, from Lithuania, of partial deliberate amnesia in the reconstruction of post-Soviet national history can be found in the Lithuanian independence movement's insistence on the illegality of the Soviet occupation, while not discussing the return of Vilnius to Poland, even though the city had been awarded to Lithuania by Stalin in 1939.[62]

The first complex of events that constitutes a taboo in today's Estonia concerns questions of complicity and collaboration with the foreign regimes.[63] Here it is interesting to note that in contemporary Estonia the term 'collaboration' is connected mostly to the Soviet period (and not to the German occupation). The first key taboo topic, however, is 'indigenous collaboration' with Nazi Germany in the killing of Jews, Gypsies and alleged communists as well as a great number of prisoners of war, who died in Estonia. Not many of the Estonian respondents were willing to speak openly about the current taboos, because they did not want to foul their own nest. The decisions made in the war years still have a profound impact upon social relations in present-day Estonia. Thus it was rather with the Estonian Russians, Russians and exiles, as well as with the younger Estonians, that these taboo topics within the collective memory of historians in post-Soviet Estonia were raised.

Nevertheless, among the War Generation, 'Urmas' did mention that he knew about the destruction of the Estonian Gypsy community of

Laiuse, because they had their bases close to his home village. He related that he had witnessed their deportation, and displayed regret that they had all been liquidated during the German occupation. Another respondent of this generational context, 'Vilma', recalled the days in September 1944 when the Klooga camp was liquidated: 'I just came from Tallinn to our summerhouse, and I smelled this terrible smell. I did not see it, but I smelled this terrible smell and I can't forget this terrible stench'. She conceded that there were Estonians who worked for the German liquidation units but that they were few in number; and then concluded that there had not been any anti-Semitism or pogroms in Estonia prior to these events. Somewhat contrary to this, Urmas explained: 'In the year 1940–41, many Jews, more than Estonians and Russians, participated in the KGB and the destruction battalions ... Somebody told me: "We shall fear the Jews more than the Russians". That means that the Jews are our enemy, even more so than the Russians'. When I asked him who disseminated such ideas, he replied: 'This was some spoken information. All knew it. Many Jews were deported by the Soviets [in 1941], but very many others were in support of the Soviets at the time, which means that they were against Estonians'.

Taboos about collaboration involve Soviet Russia as well as Germany. The fact that not only were 'Russified' Estonians – the so-called *jestlased* – members of the ECP but that an 'indigenization' of the party took place in the 1970s has been another sensitive issue. In an attempt at explaining Estonian membership in the ECP, Estonian respondents sometimes referred to Estonian communists as 'our communists' or as 'national communists'.

That Estonians were killing other Estonians in a fratricidal war constitutes the second complex of controversial events: Estonians fought in the Red Army or were members of the notorious 'shock battalions'. On the other side, the self-defence units and the 'Forest Brethren' fought against these shock battalions, anti-German partisans and alleged communists; they also committed atrocities directed against Estonian villagers who agreed to the collectivization. Estonians also assisted in the deportations of their fellow countrymen. 'Naturally they were Estonians,' Zahkar tells me, 'because who else was able to denounce? Estonians denounced Estonians. You are talking in today's Estonian about denunciators? This is a taboo!'

The playwright and director Merle Karusoo, a Post-War Child and practitioner of memory theatre, found a public way of dealing with this taboo by putting on a play about those Estonians who assisted the deportations of their fellow Estonians, for instance in 1949. The play, entitled *Waggoners* (in Estonian *Küüdipoisid*), was first performed at the Estonian Drama Theatre in 1999.[64] Through it, Karusoo aimed to deconstruct the commonly held myth that it was only Russians who deported Estonians, showing that Estonians and Estonian Russians (or *jestlased*) also participated. During the play she encourages the audience to decide whether these Waggoners can be seen as victims as well, since they were blackmailed and forced by the Soviet regime into following orders. The power of the 1999 play was enhanced because many of these collaborators played themselves, which added authenticity to this biographic play and gave these people actors the opportunity of public confession.

It is one of my findings that the memory of Estonians who were mobilized into the Waffen-SS has not been a cause of taboo or shame in the realm of private memories. Instead, fighting in the Wehrmacht against the Red Army was largely seen as fighting for the cause of Estonia's national independence. Indeed fighting with the Germans was understood as a form of 'national resistance' and 'national collaboration'. For instance, in post-communist Latvia, 'resistance' when used in the public discourse virtually always refers to 'national resistance'.[65] And in the Lithuanian national narrative, collaboration has been romanticized to the extent that some are dubbed 'patriotic traitors'. The complexity of the issue becomes apparent when collaboration is interpreted simultaneously as 'national treason' and 'national resistance'.

Although I came across a range of defensive reactions from the respondents, their willingness to make their pasts comprehensible to me prevailed over such protective attempts. At times, however, respondents seemed to be struggling at their own limits in making me grasp how people lived in the Soviet system. Estonians of different age groups told me that they themselves do not understand how they survived the terror and coped with the double standards of the split private and public spheres during the Soviet period.

Narrative Tropes and Social Strategies in the Reframing of Estonian History

Having considered in detail the three categories of formative historical events outlined in Figure 4.1 – those of collective suffering, collective resistance and collective amnesia – I now look more systematically at the content of the interviews. In the next sections I highlight various recurring narrative tropes, such as 'the Return to Europe', 'the Long Second World War' and 'David fighting Goliath', which have come to represent events of collective suffering and collective resistance. I conclude that, in articulating the new national narrative, my respondents employed these narrative tropes to advance three different social strategies: 'distancing from the Other', 'blaming the Other' or 'whitewashing', and, thirdly, 'strengthening of group worth'. Whereas the strategy of distancing follows the objective of restoring Estonia's normalcy, the strategy of blaming the Other (and whitewashing) is there to corroborate Estonia's moral high ground. Finally, the strategy of strengthening group worth is intended to shore up national pride. These themes are displayed diagrammatically in Figure 4.2.

Let us turn to the first social strategy, that of distancing from the Other, which finds its expression in the narrative tropes of the 'Return to Europe' common amongst most states of the former Eastern bloc. This narrative posits an 'Estonian time' against a 'Soviet time', a dichotomy set along ethnic lines; it understands the Soviet time as frozen and constituting a detour in history (this relates back to the notion of lost time). Connected to the narrative trope of return is the sub-trope of catching up or overcoming backwardness. The idea of a return to Europe was connected to the understanding that Estonia lies at the 'border of civilizations' acting as a 'bulwark of Christianity' – in other words employing the polarity of Teuton versus Slav discussed in Chapter 2. This is an interpretative frame found also in other East and South East European societies since the fourteenth century. The political debates of the 1990s reframed and placed Estonia in the Protestant Scandinavian or German cultural spheres. That is to say, the return to Europe went hand in hand with the official re-evaluation of the centuries-long Baltic German rule, involving a shift from viewing the Baltic Germans as an internal negative Other to a positive external Other that helped to bring Estonians within the ambit of European culture.[66] Here the introduction of the Cross of the Virgin

Narrative Trope	Social Strategy	Objective
'Return to Europe' 'Estonian time' vs. 'Soviet time'	Distancing from the Other	Normalcy
'No collaboration under occupation' 'Estonian Holocaust' 'The Long Second World War' 'The white ship' 'The white goose' 'The radish'	Blaming the Other or whitewashing	Moral high ground
'Resistance fighter' 'David fighting Goliath' 'Wiggling or muddling through'	Strengthening of group worth	National pride

Figure 4.2 Recurring Narrative Tropes of the 1990s

Mary's Land by President Lennart Meri in 1995 as the highest national decoration of the State, serves as a poignant example of this attempt to re-elevate Estonia into the European cultural domain. Because this Cross harks back to the Catholic mission of the twelfth century, the Estonian public also voiced protests, since it was also a reminder of Estonia's defeat by the Teutonic Knights.[67]

Turning now to my second set of narrative tropes, it is a common conviction among people in post-Soviet countries that they have been solely victims – a mythology of innocence. In post-Soviet Estonia the memory of collective suffering and Estonian victimhood was employed as a social strategy of blaming the Other and of whitewashing in order to regain a moral high ground. Estonians, it is argued, cannot be made accountable for any of the events that took place during the Soviet period, because they had no freedom of choice; in other words, there is 'no collaboration under occupation'.[68] 'We have suffered, we feel no shame or guilt, we have done nothing wrong', says 'Pille', exemplifying the strategy of whitewashing. Raun refers to the Great Northern War of 1700–1721 as a holocaust because 170,000 of the total population died.[69] In similar vein, 'Vilhelm' called the mass deportations of 1941 the 'great Baltic holocaust'. Maintaining the myth that the Estonians kept their moral integrity in their collective suffering also sustained the 'collective ego', which aided the process of restoring national identity after independence. Kaari Siemer demonstrates how Soviet Estonians emphasized their suffering to prove their anti-Soviet credentials and pro-Estonian mindset, and thereby to refute charges of complicity with the Soviet system.[70] In other words, after 1991, Estonians could employ their victimhood as a cathartic process, cleansing them of all (alleged) sins. There are more prominent examples of the glorification of defeat as a road to transcendence – as in the Serbian use of the battle of Kosovo Polje in 1389 – or claiming the high moral ground by reason of having suffered in the ways Jesus Christ had to suffer, as found in Polish political myth making.[71]

The narrative trope of the 'Long Second World War' implies that the war did not end for Estonia in 1945 but lasted until 1991, or even 1994 when the last Russian troops withdrew from the country.[72] This is connected to the moral argument of betrayal and of blaming the Other, in this case the West. This narrative trope has been widespread among Central East European intellectuals, and is encapsulated, for example, in Milan Kundera's notion of the 'kidnapped Europe' and in the Croatian writer Slavenka Drakulić's recollections of her mother: 'She experienced World War II and ever since, like most of the people in Eastern Europe, she behaves as if it never ended'.[73] It is thus important to note that these narrative tropes are premised upon certain political agendas. For instance, the figure of the 'white ship', which at the end of the war expressed the hope of Estonians that the Western Allies would intervene to restore their independence, soon came also to signify that the Allies had 'sold' Estonia to the Soviets, and thus evoked the idea of betrayal.[74] 'Vilma' described their hopes for liberation in the following terms:

> In Estonia after the ... Second World War ... nearly all Estonians hoped that the Americans would come and free us, or that the English would come. But they didn't. We had a neighbour in the countryside where my father lived who always listened to German radio ... and then everyday this neighbour came by [and we asked], 'Say, are the Americans coming?' And he replied that he had no information, but that they would come very soon.

Aigi Rahi-Tamm's research on the Baltic deportees shows that many were hoping another war would soon break out between the Soviet Union and the West, which would allow them to return home.[75] Even the Estonian deportees deep in the Soviet interior entertained hopes for rescue by outside forces. 'Nelli' recalled speaking to her aunt, a returnee from Siberia, sometime in the early 1950s: 'I remember that I began to ask about life in Siberia, and I remember her answer that they were working in the forest; and every morning when they were going to work they took all their most precious belongings with them because every morning they hoped that a helicopter would come to take them back home. Somebody will come and rescue them, every morning the same [procedure]'.

Historical references to Estonia's sell-out by the Allies were frequently made in political speeches prior to the country's NATO and the EU accession.[76] This highly moralized argument of betrayal and retribution for historical wrongs is exemplified in Enn Sarv's reproachful speech of 14 June 2000 directed at a Western audience in remembrance of the victims of the June 1940 deportation: 'The culprits behind our war were Churchill and Roosevelt, who signed the Atlantic Charter in 1941. A charter which promised to restore the independence of all European States that had lost their freedom in the Second World War ... Estonians believed in it, hoped for it, and waited and fought'.[77]

The social strategy of whitewashing is closely connected to that of blaming the Other, and serves the same objective – that is, to regain the moral high ground. This usually involves two narrative tropes: 'the white goose' and 'the radish'; these are employed to establish that there were only a small number of native Estonians in the ECP nomenclature and that complicity with the Soviet regime was rare. On my question of whether there were Estonian communists, 'Simon' replies: 'No, don't be ridiculous … A party with one hundred and thirty members, most of them in prison, one could claim that this was a mass movement, but it wasn't'. Evidently my respondent related the question to the time of the Estonian Republic (before the events of 1940). Similarly, 'Kalev' stated: 'A revolution [in 1940], it was a theatre! You know how many members were in the CP? There were a hundred and nineteen. Somebody wrote [that] there were [a] hundred and thirty-three … They could not have carried out a revolution!'[78] In the same vein, David Smith writes that 'Soviet-imposed communism never acquired any genuine legitimacy amongst an Estonian population'.[79] Many respondents of the War and Post-War Generation deployed narrative tropes of the 'white goose' and the 'radish' to maintain their claim to 'true' Estonianness. In her interview, 'Vilma' invoked the image of the 'white goose' representing Soviet Estonians as unscathed, despite all attempts by the new rulers to corrupt them. She explained her use of this metaphor as follows: 'We have an Estonian saying … "if you empty buckets of dirt over a goose, that goose comes out unsullied". Likewise, the [Soviets] exerted their influence over Estonians … but they remained largely intact'.[80] According to this metaphor, Estonians have been overpowered and helpless when confronted with the two great foreign powers, Nazi Germany and Soviet Russia, but they have kept their moral integrity, or even reinforced it, through their collective suffering. By maintaining this myth, Estonians have striven to ensure that their group esteem remains intact, which has greatly facilitated the reconstruction of an Estonian national identity since 1991. The image of the goose makes one think of a passive, sacrificial lamb devoid of any choice; it also conveys the notion of innocence. But looking back to Roman history one can find the goose as a symbol of watchfulness and vigilance. Geese were kept as holy animals in Rome, and it was famously said that in 387 BC their cackling saved Rome from an approaching horde of Gauls.

'Vilhelm' deployed a different narrative strategy of whitewashing when stating that as a boy he was already 'immune' from any form of ideology, as if medically shielded from any possibility of 'ideological contamination'. 'Zahkar' describes such attempts at self-victimization as another strategy of whitewashing:

The entire nation needs this lie. This is like the last line of defence. Estonians make it very easy for themselves … of course it is not very comfortable to live between Russia and Germany, the two great powers. On the other hand it's very easy to say that in everything bad that happened we were only victims. The Russians and Germans did all that. We are a snow-white nation. We have always been abused; nobody ever asked us what we wanted … please leave us alone and don't ask about the Holocaust, fascism, or about collaboration.

The trope of the 'radish' is also used in the strategy of whitewashing. 'Ülle-Mai' makes the distinction between those who were red on the outside *and* the inside – that is, 'real Communists' and 'guys from the war' – and those who were red *only* on the outside but, similar to a 'radish', remained white inside; the latter, my respondent asserted, was the case for the majority of Estonians who joined the ECP. I could discern an ethnic dimension in this strategy of whitewashing: the red were the Russian Estonians – that is, the so-called '*jestlased*' discussed in Chapter 3 – together with the new Russian settlers and other Russophones, who supported the ECP and Soviet regime. When asked about the Russian Estonians, 'Ervin' explains:

At the end of 1944 they invaded Estonia and stayed here. And many of them … were recruited as Soviet party officials. There were two kinds of officials: native Estonian communists who had fled from the Germans, and the Russian Estonians. And they didn't like each other. But the party leaders were Russian Estonians. And there was a power struggle between them. The main struggle was in 1950 at the plenum of the CP when native Estonian communists were blamed as 'nationalists' and expelled from their places … [After that], the *jestlased*, the Russian Estonians … took over and filled all the leading posts in the CP, in the government, in the Soviets … Estonian national communists were rehabilitated after Stalin's death, but they never reached the top level. They were rehabilitated on the medium level of office … but never [on the] high level [of the nomenklaturura]. These positions remained in the hands of the *jestlased* … until 1988 when the last leader of the CP, Väino, was sacked and replaced by the native Estonian Väljas.

Other respondents used the term 'Estonian-minded communists' to explain how those Estonians who joined the ECP did this only to reform the party from within, or did so in order that Estonians rather than Russians held these positions. The strategy of whitewashing was also achieved through narratives of 'semi-dissent' – that is, genuine efforts to improve and reform the Soviet system from within, by respondents of the War Generation and Post-War Children. 'Ülle-Mai', a Post-War Child, elaborates:

From my point of view there were thousands of other options to demonstrate that you were against Soviet power rather than to do it so very openly. To say that Soviet power is bad was no more than self-destructive. You knew what would await you at the end! The end is Siberia! And why choose this way, when you have all the other ways at hand? You may write poetry or make theatre performances and express just the same. This was our idea.

Her attempt to justify her relative inaction by stressing the threat of Siberia imposed by the Soviet system is partly disingenuous because by the 1970s voicing dissent was no longer a life or death issue. The argument of 'pragmatic accommodation', in other words 'people have to live', was also used frequently by Estonians of both generational contexts in the interviews.[81]

The third set of narrative tropes is connected to notions of resistance and resilience, and is employed in the social strategy of strengthening group worth to regain national pride. Respondents of the older generation stated that being Estonian almost automatically means to be a 'resistance fighter'. 'Kalev' contends 'most Estonians resisted [the Soviet regime]'. Contrary to this, 'Zakhar', a younger historian of mixed background gave a polemical reply: 'if you speak with people in Estonia today, everybody was a dissident; already by definition an Estonian is a dissident'. This respondent went on to remark that Estonians commonly hold that Estonia triggered the break-up of the Soviet Union, because Estonia was the first Soviet Republic to declare independence, just like 'David fighting Goliath'. There are more critical voices also among the Estonian historians of the War Generation; 'Vilhelm' comments: 'This is a little ridiculous. I like to compare it with the Dakota Indians, with the brother of Sitting Bull, the one who knew how to conduct spiritual dances. He could dance as much as he liked, [but] he could not destroy the troops of the enemy. Likewise the Singing Revolution and the Baltic Chain did not draw out the Russians'.

What is blanked out in the construction of this national myth of resistance and resilience is its converse side, that accommodation and complicity with the system were commonly the price of survival (as discussed in the earlier section on collective hidden or taboo events). The Post-War Child 'Nora' explains with a telling smile that Estonians always had to 'wiggle their way through'; and 'Niils', born in Sweden to Estonian parents, understands 'surviving to be making compromises'; this 'wiggling or muddling through' finds its expression in the Estonian concept of *rehepaplus* ('old-barnyism'), which in the 2000s acquired the meaning of always thinking of the easiest way to appropriate something to one's own use; a kind of conduct that, as some would claim, may have helped Estonians to survive the century-long foreign rule. The concept of *rehepaplus* gained prominence with Kivirähk's book *Old Barny aka November* (in Estonian, *Rehepapp ehk November*) published in 2000; a story on the common theme of Baltic German gentry dominating Estonian peasants, but in a humorous setting, almost like a fairy tale.[82]

Conclusion

Based on the interviews with professional historians who related their personal and professional interpretation of Estonian history to me, I singled out three categories of formative historical events constitutive of the post-Soviet Estonian identity: events of collective suffering, events of collective resistance, and hidden – often taboo – events that are related to critical counter-accounts in Estonian historical culture and often possess a moral (normative) function. Here interpretative differences can be related to generational identities and also to differences in ethno-cultural background. Connected to these three formative historical events are various recurring narrative tropes, such as: 'the Return to Europe', 'the Long Second World War' and 'David fighting Goliath'. In articulating the new national narrative my respondents employed these narrative tropes in conjunction with three social strategies: 'distancing from the Other', 'blaming the Other' and 'whitewashing', and, thirdly, 'strengthening of group worth'.

This chapter has made apparent the Babel of voices and counter-voices all eager to interpret and define Estonia's recent past. These competing accounts are at the heart of the newly emerging national narrative. The next chapter moves from the private to the public sphere of history making since 1991. It concentrates on the struggle of various societal groups for the inclusion of their social memoires in the official narrative (and thus for public recognition of their story), and on various contested landmarks in the new memorial landscape of post-Soviet Estonia.

Notes

1. 'Das Vergangene ist nicht tot; es ist nicht einmal vergangen. Wir trennen es von uns ab und stellen uns fremd' (C. Wolf. 1999. *Kindheitsmuster*. Munich: dtv, 1). Wolf's book *Kindheitsmuster* (Patterns of Childhood), first published in the GDR at the end of the 1970s, is an autobiographical account of the recent history of her family, which was expelled from Poland at the end of the war and repatriated in the GDR, where their memories of the life left behind soon became a political taboo.
2. See J. Kivimäe and S. Kivimäe. 1987. 'Estnische Geschichtsforschung an der Universität Tartu 1920–1940: Ziele und Ergebnisse', in Gert v. Pistolkors et al. (eds), *Die Universitäten Dorpat/Tartu, Riga und Wilna/Vilnius 1529–1979. Beiträge zu ihrer Geschichte und ihrer Wirkung im Grenzbereich zwischen Ost und West*, 277–92; J.

Kivimäe and S. Kivimäe. 2002. 'Geschichtsschreibung und Geschichtsforschung in Estland 1988–2001', *Österreichische Osthefte* 44(1/2): 159–70.

3. Kivimäe and Kivimäe ('Geschichtsschreibung und Geschichtsforschung'). In 1997 Laar then co-authored a history text book for the 5th grade (*Ajalugu 5. klassile*). This is considered to be more critical, for instance, of the Estonian interwar Republic, because it was only after the early 1990s that a more scholarly approach to history emerged.

4. Lagerspetz, *Constructing Post-Communism*, 74ff.

5. Tulviste and Wertsch, ('Official and Unofficial Histories, 311–29) do not limit their findings to the Estonian case: they make clear that one-dimensional or ethnocentric interpretations of history are prevalent in more established democracies as well.

6. K. Brüggemann. 2001. 'Von der Renationalisierung zur Demontage nationaler Helden. Oder: Wie schreibt man estnische Geschichte?', *Osteuropa* 7: 810–19.

7. See Ahonen's comparative study of the post-Marxist transformation of the history curricula in East Germany and Estonia, 1986–91 (Sirka Ahonen. 1992. *Clio sans Uniform: A Study of the Post-Marxist Transformation of the History Curricula in East Germany and Estonia, 1986–1991*. Soumalaisen Tiedeakatemian Toimituksia Annales Academiae Scientiarum Fennicae, Sarja-Ser. B Nide-Tom. 264. Helsinki: Suomalainen Tiedeakatemia).

8. M. Ümarik. 2001. 'Constructing the National Identity in School Textbooks: The Textbooks of Estonian History in the Soviet Estonia and in the Estonian Republic'. Paper presented at the seminar on '(Re-)nordification of Estonian Society', Tallinn, 20–22 April.

9. The books Ümarik analysed for the Soviet period were: J. Kahk, H. Palamets and S. Vahtre (1974, 1984. *Eesti NSV ajalost: lisamaterjali VII–VIII klassi NSV Liidu ajaloo kursuse juurde*. Tallinn: Kirjastus Valgus); A. Liim and K. Siilivask (1983. *Eesti NSV ajalugu IX–XI klassile: lisamaterjali NSV Liidu ajaloo kursuse juurde*. Tallinn: Kirjustas Valgus); M. Lõhmus and K. Siilivask (1975. *Esti NSV ajaloost keskoolile: lisamaterjali IX–XI klassi NSV Liidu ajaloo kursuse juurde*. Tallinn: Kirjastus Valgus); H. Palamets (1978, 1987. *Jutustusi kodumaa ajaloost:õpik IV klassile*. Tallinn: Valgus). For the transitional and re-independence period, Ümarik examined a variety of books, including S. Õispuu (1989. *Eesti ajalugu: konspektiivne õppematerjal keskkoolile*. Tallinn: Valgus); K. Arjakas, M. Laur and K. Mäesalu (1991. *Eesti ajalugu: õpik 11. Klassile*. Tallinn: Kirjastus Koolibri); A. Adamson and S. Valdmaa (1999. *Eesti ajalugu gümnaasiumlile*. Tallinn: Kirjastus Koolibri); M. Laar, M. Tilk and E. Hergauk (1997. *Ajalugu 5. klassile*. Tallinn: Kirjastus Avita); T. Toomet (1993. *Me elama ajaloos: eesti ajaloo õpik 5. Klassile*. Tallinn: Kirjastus Koolibri); and M. Laur, A. Pajur and T. Tannberg (1995. *Eesti ajalugu II*. Tallinn: Avita).

10. J. Kivimäe, 'Re-writing Estonian history', 207.

11. Tulviste and Wertsch, 'Official and Unofficial Histories', 325–29.

12. See generally, M. Bakhtin. 1981. *The Dialogic Imagination: Four Essays*, ed. Michael Holquist. Austin: University of Texas Press.

13. 'Veera'.

14. R. Hinrikus and E. Kõresaar. 2004. 'A Brief Overview of Life History Collection and Research in Estonia', in T. Kirss, T.E. Kõresaar and M. Lauristin (eds), *She Who Remembers, Survives: Interpreting Estonian Women's Post-Soviet Life Stories*. Tartu: Tartu University Press, 21.

15. Ibid., 24.

16. The theatre director Merle Karusoo and the Pirgu Development Centre have con-ducted life-history interviews since the 1980s, putting them into sociological theatre performances. Other institutions, not mentioned so far, were the Estonian Cultural

History Archive and the Estonian National Museum. For published books based on the work of the Estonian Life Histories Association, see Jaago, *Lives, Histories and Identities*; T. Anepaio and E. Kõresaar. 2001. *Kultuur ja Mälu: Konverentsi materjale.* Studia Ethnologica Tartuensia 4, Tartu: Tartu Ülikooli; Kõresaar, *Soldiers of Memory.*

17. Kirss, Kõresaar and Lauristin, *She Who Remembers Survives*, 142.
18. Hinrikus and Kõresaar, 'A Brief Overview'.
19. M. Dobson. 2009. *Khrushchev's Cold Summer: Gulag Returnees, Crime, and the Fate of Reform after Stalin.* Ithaca, NY: Cornell University Press, 54. There were also forcefully elicited biographies written during interrogations in prison cells: see ibid., 50–78.
20. J. Mark. 2010. *The Unfinished Revolution: Making Sense of the Communist Past in Central-Eastern Europe.* New Haven, CT: Yale University Press, 126–93.
21. K.G. Karlsson. 1998. 'Identity Change in the Former Soviet Union? The Roles of History', in Klas-Göran Karlsson, Bo Petersson and Barbara Törnquist-Plewa (eds), *Collective Identities in an Era of Transformations: Analysing Developments in East and Central Europe and the former Soviet Union.* Lund: Lund University Press, 16ff.
22. Kivimäe and Kivimäe, 'Geschichtsschreibung und Geschichtsforschung', 159–63.
23. Maier, 'Hot Memory … Cold Memory', 171ff.
24. Ervin.
25. This shortcoming was pointed out to me by an assistant professor of history at Tartu University ('Jaak').
26. See S.N. Eisenstadt. 1992. 'Die Mitwirkung der Intellektuellen an der Konstruktion lebensweltlicher und transzendenter Ordnung', in Aleida Assmann and Dietrich Harth (eds), *Kultur als Lebenswelt und Monument.* Frankfurt: S. Fischer, 123–32.
27. 'Kalju'.
28. Kivimäe and Kivimäe, 'Geschichtsschreibung und Geschichtsforschung'.
29. See generally U. Plath and K. Brüggemann (eds). 2000. 'Vom Tanz mit des Teufels Großmutter: Die estnische Debatte um die Zusammenarbeit von Präsident Konstantin Päts mit der SU', *Osteuropa* 50, A329–A339. Ilmjärv later published his findings in English: M. Ilmjärv. 2004. *Silent Submission: Formation of Foreign Policy in Estonia, Latvia and Lithuania, 1920–1940.* Stockholm: Almqvist & Wiksell. The biography of Päts by the Finnish author Martii Turtola, published in Estonia in 2003 with an initial run of ten thousand copies, immediately sold out, which indicates the great public interest in the former president at that time.
30. A. Kivirähk. 1995. *Ivan Orava mälestused ehk Minevik kui helesinised mäed.* Tallinn: Varrak: opening of Chapter 1, author's translation. 'Orav' means squirrel in Estonian.
31. I have quoted this respondent rather extensively to illustrate counter accounts to the dominant Estonian viewpoint; I did so primarily because of this great eloquence of his (due to his background as journalist).
32. Plath and Brüggemann, 'Vom Tanz mit des Teufels Großmutter', A 339. Kivirähk's attitude is highly cynical, as he describes the Estonians complying with the Soviet system during the day but cursing the state for all ills over a glass of schnapps in private. I identify this social strategy as 'cynical distancing'.
33. G. Gurvitch. 1964. *The Spectrum of Social Time.* Dordrecht: Reidel, 32.
34. Raun, *Estonia and the Estonians*, 45.
35. Jansen, 'Cultural or Political Nationalism?', 61.
36. See my discussion in Chapter 1 of Renan, who points to the importance of collective battles and collective sacrifices (Renan, 'Qu'est-ce qu'une nation?', 17).
37. Selective omission, prescribed amnesia and distortion have also been discussed in Chapter 1 in relation to the common social strategy of creating a positive national group image.

38. J. Laplanche and J.B. Pontalis. 1973. *The Language of Psychoanalysis*. London: Hogarth.
39. For example, D. LaCapra. 2001. *Writing History, Writing Trauma*. Baltimore, MD: John Hopkins University Press.
40. 'Siim'.
41. The interview with 'Paula' in Chapter 3 showed that lacking the experience of inter-war Estonia set her apart from the War Generation.
42. *Morgen* is a former measure of land used in Prussia, Norway and Denmark, and equals about 0.3 hectares.
43. J. Rüsen. 2001c. 'Historisch trauern – Skizze einer Zumutung', in Jörn Rüsen and Burkhard Liebsch (eds), *Trauer und Geschichte*. Cologne: Böhlau Verlag, 63–84.
44. T. Todorov. 1996. 'The Abuses of Memory', *Common Knowledge* 5(1): 14.
45. Gallerano, 'Public Use of History', 96.
46. C. Taylor (1992a. 'The Politics of Recognition', in Amy Gutman (ed.), *Multiculturalism and the Politics of Recognition*. Princeton, NJ: Princeton University Press, 25) points out that our identity is partly shaped by recognition or its absence. He argues that a person or group can suffer real damage and distortion if the people around them mirror back to them a contemptible image of themselves. This connects to the depiction of Russians in Estonian history textbooks after 1991.
47. A theme developed in G. Hosking. 2008. *Rulers and Victims: The Russians in the Soviet Union*. Cambridge, MA: Harvard University Press.
48. My discussion of collective resistance in Soviet Estonia is informed by Viktor Niitsoo's research of the resistance movement in the ESSR. He distinguishes five periods of resistance: armed resistance against Soviet occupation (1941, 1944, 1953); activities of underground youth organizations (1944–62); democratic movement activities (1968–75); open resistance (1977–85); and the independence movement (1987–91). See generally V. Niitsoo. 1997. *Vastupanu, 1955–1985*. Talinn: Tartu Ulikooli Kirjastus.
49. See generally R.J. Misiunas and R. Taagepera. 1993. *The Baltic States: Years of Dependence 1940–1990*. London: Hurst & Co; N. Hope. 1994. 'Interwar Statehood: Symbol and Reality', in Graham Smith (ed.), *The Baltic States: The National Self-Determination of Estonia, Latvia and Lithuania*. London: Macmillan, 41–60.
50. Mart Laar's book on the armed resistance of the Forest Brethren until 1955 (M. Laar. 1992. *War in the Woods: Estonia's Struggle for Survival, 1944–1956*. Washington DC: Compass Press), based solely on oral accounts, was fully in keeping with the emotional approach to national history at the time.
51. 'Zbigniew'.
52. Although I am employing the term 'collective resistance', there were actually only a few resistors and dissidents during the Soviet period; but in the context of post-Soviet Estonia more people claim to have been involved in dissident activities.
53. T. Remeikis. 1984. 'Dissent in the Baltic Republics: A Balance Sheet', *Lituanus Lithuanian Quarterly Journal of Arts and Sciences* 30(2). http://www.lituanus.org/1984_2/84_2_01.htm. See generally the studies on popular movements by A.R. Alexiev. 1983. *Dissent and Nationalism in the Soviet Baltic*. A Project AIR FORCE Report for the US Air Force. Santa Monica, CA: Rand; A. Horm. 1973. *Phases of Baltic Political Activities*. Stockholm: Mälartryckeriet AB; G. Hosking et al. 1992. *The Road to Post-Communism: Independent Political Movements in the Soviet Union, 1985–1991*. London: Pinter; H. Johnston and D.A. Snow. 1998. 'Subcultures and the Emergence of the Estonian Nationalist Opposition, 1945–1990', *Sociological Perspectives* 41(3): 473–97; H. Johnston. 2001. 'Talking the Walk: Speech Acts

and Resistance in Authoritarian Regimes'. Paper presented at the Workshop on Repression and Mobilisation, University of Maryland, 21–23 June; J.A. Trapans. 1991. 'The Popular Movement and the Soviet Union: Discussion', in J. Trapans (ed.), *Toward Independence: The Baltic Popular Movements*. Boulder, CO: Westview Press, 43–56; R. Watson (ed.). 1994. *Memory, History, and Opposition under State Socialism*. Santa Fe, NM: School of American Research Press.

54. Many dissidents from Russia proper found a niche at Tartu University, such as the Semiotician Juri Lotman. Herrmann Hesse mentions the famous Spirit of Tartu (in Estonian Tartu Vaim) in his *Glass Bead Game*.

55. The poem in question was called 'eternal arrival, or return' by the Estonian composer Tõnu Kalljuste.

56. 'Urmas'.

57. 'Vilhelm'.

58. See A. Lansky. 2005. *Outwitting History: The Amazing Adventures of a Young Man Who Rescued a Million Yiddish Books*. Chapel Hill, NC: Algonquin Books.

59. Skultans, *The Testimony of Lives*, 23ff.

60. But then again not all hidden events are of a taboo-like quality posing moral guidelines. Stanley Cohen (2001. *States of Denial: Knowing about Atrocities and Suffering*. Cambridge: Polity Press) looks at questions of denial, of blocking out the past in public histories, but also at modes of acknowledging past suffering.

61. Misiunas, 'Soviet Historiography on World War II', 181.

62. S.R. Burant and V. Zubek. 1993. 'Eastern Europe's Old Memories and New Realities: Resurrecting the Polish–Lithuanian Union', in *EEPS* 7(2): 375.

63. Christoph Dieckman, Christian Gerlach and Wolf Gruner ([eds] 2003. *Kooperation und Verbrechen. Formen der Kollaboration im östlichen Europa 1939–1945*. Göttingen: Wallstein Verlag, 11ff.) prefer the term 'cooperation under military occupation'. The Hague Convention (*Haager Landkriegsordnung*) of 1907 allowed for cooperation with the occupying power to secure the day-to-day life of civilians. However, I note that, because the main objective of the occupying power in this case was to eradicate certain segments of the civilian population, the word 'cooperation' needs to be reassessed.

64. See http://iabaeurope2011.edicypages.com/keynotes/merle-karusoo (accessed 20 Feb. 2012).

65. E.-C. Onken. 1998. *Revisionismus schon vor der Geschichte: Aktuelle lettische Kontroversen um die Judenvernichtung und Kollaboration 1941–1944*. Cologne: Wissenschaft und Politik; E.-C. Onken. 2000a. 'Zwischen kollektiver Entschuldigung und kritischer Reflexion: Die Aufarbeitung der kommunistischen Vergangenheit in Lettland', *Halbjahresschrift für südosteuropäische Geschichte, Literatur und Politik* 12(2): 5–16.

66. D.J. Smith. 2001. *Estonia: Independence and European Integration*. London: Routledge, 3.

67. Brüggemann, 'Von der Renationalisierung zur Demontage nationaler Helden', 817; M. Lagerspetz. 1999a. 'Images of the Past in Post-Socialist Politics: An Introduction', *Finnish Review of East European Studies*, Special Issue, 'Images of the Past in Post-Socialist Politics': 3–6.

68. A participant's observation during the conference on '*Reichskommissariat Ostland*. Collaboration and Resistance during the Holocaust' (18–21 April 2002, Stockholm and Uppsala, Sweden).

69. Raun, *Estonia and the Estonians*, 312.

70. K. Siemer. 2002. '"Who is Red on the Outside and White Inside?": The Topic of Soviet Rule in Estonian Life Stories', in Tiiu Jaago (ed.), *Lives, Histories and Identities: Studies on Oral Histories, Life and Family Stories*. Tartu: Estonian Literary Museum, 199.

71. Törnquist-Plewa, *The Wheel of Polish Fortune*.
72. D. Smith, Estonia, xii, 33ff. The former Estonian prime minister Mart Laar stated on BBC Radio 4, in a feature entitled 'Six Places that Changed the World: Yalta' (aired on 22 Aug. 2005), that the occupation only ended in 1994.
73. S. Drakulić. 1993. *How We Survived Communism and Even Laughed*. London: Vintage, 15.
74. This narrative trope with deep roots in both Estonian folk and Christian traditions, which is still widespread among Estonians today, initially invoked the historical memory of the British navy's intervention on behalf of Estonia during the post-1918 struggle for independence. After 1945, however, the trope encapsulates ideas of both hope and betrayal (Kivimäe, 'Estland unter der Sowjetherrschat', 593ff).
75. Rahl-Tamm, 'Deportations in Estonia', 48.
76. This moral argument has been employed by T.H. Ilves. 1999. 'Estonia and the State of Change in European Security'. Paper delivered by the foreign minister of Estonia, Chatham House, London, 4 May 1999.
77. E. Sarv (2000. 'Our Duty of Remembering'. Delivered at International Conference on Crimes of Communism, Tallinn, 14 June 2000: 36ff.). Enn Sarv (1921–2008) suffered under both totalitarian regimes, as a member of the National Committee of the Republic of Estonia (1941–44) he was deported to Stutthof and then sentenced to seven years in Vorkuta during the Soviet period. A mathematician by training, he published widely on the Soviet oppression of Estonia, and was highly decorated as a 'Freedom Fighter' in post-Soviet Estonia.
78. This argument has an ancestry: around 1900, Jaan Tõnisson denied that class struggle was of importance in Estonia, calling it 'a plant imported from abroad' that could not become domesticated in Estonia (Laur et al., *History of Estonia*, 38–52; T. Raun, *Estonia and the Estonians*, 189).
79. D. Smith, *Estonia*, xi.
80. The image of the white goose appears to be less common among Estonians today.
81. 'Paula'.
82. Andrus Kivirāk. 2000. *Rehepapp ehk November (Old Barny aka November)*. Talinn: Varrak. The book became a widely discussed bestseller and was also adopted for the stage. The images of the dandelion and juniper tree growing on sparse limestone soil also stand for the resilience of Estonians in their century-long struggle for survival (Hinrikus and Kõresaar, 'A Brief Overview').

Chapter 5

A WINNER'S TALE
The Clash of Private and Public Memories
in Post-Soviet Estonia

All history is the history of past politics.
– Frank R. Ankersmit, 'Rüsen on History and Politics'[1]

History is a back-up for the future.
– Jocelyn Létourneau, 'Digging into Historical Consciousness'[2]

Monuments must unite people.
– Andrus Ansip, *Authoritarian Backlash*[3]

It is in the public sphere that different groups compete for the inclusion of their social memories into the official narrative. I hold this struggle for public recognition to be intrinsically connected to questions of authenticity, custodianship, and ultimately collective cultural identity. This chapter continues the study of the dynamic process through which social memories are transformed into more lasting forms of political memory, and illustrates the negotiation of a new memory regime in post-Soviet Estonia. These memory regimes are formulated on the political level and can be understood as equivalent to memory laws due to their normative functions (both proscriptive and prescriptive).[4]

Earlier chapters demonstrated how, during times of socio-political transition, references to history have been used to drive the process of change. In this transitional situation, history is not reproduced for and within the academy alone; instead professional historians disseminate historical counter-accounts through political action – as already shown by the annual demonstration marking the signing of the Molotov–Ribbentrop Pact and meetings of local heritage society groups. Here, professional historians, alongside local historians, produced historical knowledge outside the academy, countering officially held Soviet interpretations of the past. These historical accounts are targeted towards a wider public; they have a public use. Gallerano holds that the public use of history consists of 'all that developed outside of the domain of scientific research in its strictest sense, outside the history of historians, which is usually written by scholars and intended for a very limited segment of the population', and is instead intended for the use of history in schools, museums, cultural associations, political parties, and so on.[5] The term 'use' implies that, alongside ethically and morally decent ways of utilizing history, there also exist misuses or abuses; but uses of history cannot be equated with manipulation or deception per se.[6] All this is intimately connected to the question of principles, rules and standards of history production and to the question of which historical facts are employed, and to what ends. In the light of Shari J. Cohen's assessment of the 'amorphous nature' of post-communist societies, these common standards of moral or historical judgement may be weak or non-existent.[7]

In this chapter I examine several contested landmarks of Estonia's contemporary historical culture linked to some of the enduring ambiguities of Estonia's recent past, such as controversial taboo topics of indigenous collaboration with the Soviet and Nazi occupiers, the fratricidal war, and other unresolved, traumatic memories of the war and post-war years. The interview material discussed in the previous chapter has illustrated that social and political memories of such controversial taboo topics possess a strong emotional and affective quality. The landmarks to be considered here are the work of the Museum of Occupations , the activities of the Estonian International Commission for the Investigation of Crimes against Humanity and the conflict over memorial monuments to different veteran groups. They serve as pre-eminent examples of historical revisionism since Estonia's transition to independence.

Five Dimensions of Public History

Before analysing these landmark examples of the politics of history in contemporary Estonia, it is helpful to distinguish in the abstract several dimensions of public history. In fact these dimensions should be understood as facets of the same story I am highlighting, rather than as clear-cut compartments. For this analysis I consider Karl-Göran Karlsson's typology as a fruitful starting point. However I have used only four of his dimensions of public history, namely the moral, ideological, political and existential, while adding the emblematic as a new category.[8] After I

	Dimension	Function
1	Moral	Rehabilitation, Legitimating
2	Ideological	Regeneration, Legitimating
3	Political	Legitimating
4	Existential	Identity reinforcing
5	Emblematic	Window dressing

Figure 5.1 The Public Uses of National History: Dimensions and Functions

point to the specific nature of public history production, I will add to my examination of these five dimensions of public history the functions these can fulfil, namely: rehabilitation, regeneration, legitimating, identity reinforcing and window dressing. This framework is set out schematically in Figure 5.1.[9]

I start with the moral dimension, which includes all the ways in which a community utilizes the past in the creation of shared values, collective norms and goals. It is found in the endeavour of the political elite to put right 'historical wrongs' in reaction to past insults. The narrative tropes of the 'Long Second World War' and the 'Return to Europe' – implying that Estonia had been wronged by history – which were utilized in the public discourse surrounding the country's accession to West European institutions, serve as examples of this moral dimension. The moral function also serves to legitimate political or legal decisions, and the use of power.

The use of history by intellectuals for purposes of national regeneration I define as the ideological dimension of history (prime examples being in national movements). Such an ideological take on history was prevalent in the programme of the Estonian Popular Front to mobilize mass support for the country's national independence. In this over-simplification, national history is reified into an intrinsically moral and metaphysical entity, based on ideas of absolute truth. Consequently history is not a gradually evolving process, but a story of mistakes that need rectifying. In practice, the ideological and the moral dimensions of history can be seen to merge into an ethno-moralistic discourse, which characterizes the public debate on Estonia's past to this day.

The political dimension denotes the rhetorically convincing use of historical arguments to critique existing socio-political shortcomings. Historical arguments are often de-contextualized and employed in a comparative, metaphorical fashion. An overbearing political dimension translates into an inflationary use of historical arguments in the public arena, for instance in political propaganda. Historical revisionism, as I define it, is connected primarily to this political dimension. In short, I understand historical revisionism as an effort to update the interpretation of historical facts in the light of new findings, such as the opening of archival collections, releasing formerly classified material. Although the term has acquired a pejorative meaning, implying manipulation and abuse, I do not view it as something negative per se. Daniel Levy notes that the proliferation of historical revisionism is associated with the 'hunger for memory' observable since the 1980s. To him 'the object of historical revisionism is to debunk those mythical substructures upon which collective identities rely'. By attacking these mythological foundations, 'revisionists thematize issues that were not previously discussed, and render them intelligible for rational debate'.[10] Historical revisionism is intimately linked to the ideological and political dimensions of history, and tends to be closely connected to the 'public use' of history. While the moral and ideological dimensions can also be employed for political legitimation, it is the primary function of the political dimension to claim and legitimize political power.

The existential dimension of public history employs past experiences, memories and historical narratives in processes of identity construction. The Hebrew saying *Zahor Lo Tishkah* ('remembering in order not to forget') hints at the role of history in reinforcing collective cultural identity. When a society is facing external or internal pressures of cultural homogenization caused by foreign domination, for instance, the existential dimension becomes accentuated. The heated conflicts over memorial monuments among different Estonian veteran groups, discussed later in this chapter, illustrate the existential use of history in the public sphere. However historical counter-accounts and their existential function rarely enter the public debate, other than in times of political crisis or transition; usually they are confined to the private sphere.

The emblematic dimension of public history can be found in the political discussion of contentious historical facts kept deliberately at a surface level of political correctness. For instance, in post-Soviet Estonia a fundamental settlement with the Soviet legacy through systematic acts of transitional justice has not been achieved. Instead the 'Estonian International Commission for the Investigation of Crimes against Humanity' was established as an official attempt to restore Estonia's moral standing in the international community. As I shall argue later in this chapter, this can be considered as a case of window dressing.

These five dimensions of public history will become clearer in the discussion of the various landmark examples of historical culture in contemporary Estonia.

The Museum of Occupations: Strategy of Victimhood

In the main entrance hall of the Museum of Occupations (hereafter 'the museum') replicas of two massive steam locomotives are displayed as a gateway to the exhibition. The models are identical, except that one displays a red star, whereas the other bears a swastika. With this motif the Estonian artist Leonhard Lapin (born 1947) places both totalitarian regimes on parallel tracks. The museum is an example of the political dimension of history, illustrating the quagmires that historical comparisons often entail. The museum was founded through the private initiative of an Estonian exile, Dr Olga Kistler, and the Kistler-Ritso Foundation, with the primary objective of collecting and exhibiting artefacts, memoirs and eyewitness accounts on the periods of occupation (1940–91), and it now showcases them to approximately 25,000 visitors per year.[11] Battered suitcases, prison doors, aluminium cutlery, a refugee boat, arrangements of mundane objects, as well as letters and newspapers, constitute the core of the exhibition.[12] In the words of one interviewee, 'Simon', who was involved in planning the museum from the very start, it 'has to be like a monument or a tombstone for the many people who have not returned. And I believe that for the people who still live, but went through this period, this [museum] would be something to make them feel a little proud; that something like this is built for them'. Equivalents to the museum can be found in Riga (the Documentation Centre of Totalitarianism, TSDC, established in 1998) and also in Vilnius (the Museum of Genocide Victims located in the cellars of the former KGB headquarters, founded in 1992).[13]

Many amateur historians and other private organizations of former victims of Soviet repressions also emerged in the 1990s, compiling lists, convening conferences, and documenting the repressions of the war and post-war years. Examples include the 'Research Centre of the Soviet Era in Estonia' (in Estonian, *S-Keskus*), the 'Memento Union', which includes the 'Estonian Association of the Former Members of the Labour Battalion', the 'Estonian Union of Political Prisoners', and the 'Estonian Repressed Persons Records Bureau'.[14]

At the time of the museum's inauguration, the president of the parliament, Toomas Savi, issued a statement on 'the crimes of the occupation regime in Estonia', with the objective of settling accounts with the past. Although both the Nazi and Soviet regimes are mentioned at the outset of the declaration, the body of the statement exclusively concerns the crimes of the Soviet occupation between 1940 and 1991, condemning the communist regime and the organizations and institutions that forcefully implemented the Soviet power. This statement assigns full accountability for all crimes committed during that period to the CP of the Soviet Union, the ECP, and their organizations – while rejecting the principle of 'collective responsibility'. It ends by labelling 'the crimes of the occupation regime in Estonia … [as] part of the inhumane activities by totalitarian regimes in the world of the twentieth century'.[15]

The experience of double occupation by the Nazis and Soviets led to an interpretation of history rather different from that which prevails, for example, in those West European countries that were 'only' occupied by Nazi Germany. When passing a 'museum of occupation' in Amsterdam, Paris or Oslo, the Western observer would assume from the name that the museum concentrates on mass deportations of Jews, Gypsies, communists and other anti-German resistance fighters; but the curators of the Museum of Occupations clearly adhere to a different logic. National suffering of ethnic Estonians during the various occupations takes centre stage here (inflicted mainly by Soviet communist atrocities), while little attention is paid to the victims of the Holocaust in Estonia.[16] The same perspective is true for the wider Estonian public, whose foremost concern is with the repression by the Soviet authorities. When asked about her personal memories of the German occupation, 'Hanneleen' of the War Generation replied:

> I know it was terrible, I accept that … all those children in the Holocaust, really we all acknowledge that. But with regard to my own memory, I know thousands, thousands of people who I saw in the mass deportations [by the Soviets]. Ten thousand on one day. Twenty thousand on another day. I have seen the railway station and many relatives and friends … Thousands! But based on my own memory, I know only two people who were victims of the Germans. And I did not know them personally. I have merely heard [of them]. And they were both members of the Communist Party.

The fact that public debate about the occupations in post-1991 Estonia is mainly concerned with the Soviet terror, while Estonian collaboration during the Nazi occupation is hardly touched upon, might be explained as an overreaction against the long-endured bias in Soviet historiography, which focused mainly on the atrocities committed during the Nazi occupation of Estonia.[17] A further cause may lie in Russia's failure to acknowledge the events of 1939–41 – specifically the annexation of Estonia in 1940 – as illegitimate acts.

In reaction to the new museum, the Russian foreign minister, Sergey Lavrov, issued a statement that in equating fascist Germany and the former Soviet Union, the museum's creation was informed by a political bias – a comment that takes us back to the political function of history. While it is crucial to avoid the possible pitfalls of historical comparison, such as appearing to relativize individual or collective suffering and injustices, it is necessary to remember that comparison deals with resemblance and difference, and that to compare does not mean a moral justification as such. The usage of the term 'totalitarianism' for both the Stalinist and Nazi systems implies they are indeed comparable, yet this does not make it permissible to equate the two systems. Nor can crimes committed in the name of Hitler's Germany be explained or justified by the atrocities committed in the name of Stalin, or vice versa.[18]

The historians' debate (*Historikerstreit*) in West Germany in the mid-1980s had the effect of making objectionable comparative approaches to understanding the totalitarian systems of Stalinism and Nazi Germany, relegating them to the fringes of public discussion – but the break-up of the Soviet bloc and German reunification engendered a moral relativism that made comparisons between the systems more in vogue. Until 1989–91, the vantage point of moral judgement in the West was fixed upon the Holocaust memory, but in parts of newly independent Eastern Europe, comparisons of the two systems were frequently employed in public debates.[19]

In response, Efraim Zuroff, head of the Jerusalem office of the Simon Wiesenthal Centre, complained that some political leaders were using the destruction of the European Jewry as a background to speak about other tragedies, such as communist crimes. Reacting to a speech by former Latvian president, Vaira Vike-Freiberga, in 2004 (at the International Forum on Preventing Genocide in Stockholm), Zuroff asserted that the mass deportations of Latvians were not a case of genocide and warned of a false symmetry that upgrades communist crimes by placing them on an equal footing with the Holocaust. It was the Baltic states who first challenged the conventional position on genocide (as codified in the 1948 UN convention) by passing national laws on genocide which, through a broader definition of the term, aimed to include specific crimes committed in the Baltic region during and after the war (1940–49). In 2003, a precedence case was created in Estonia, in which servants of the Stalinist state stood trial and were convicted. These new national laws on genocide are a legal expression of the paradigmatic shift from the anti-fascist memory regime prescribed during the Soviet period to an anti-communist one.[20]

Todorov's list of four possible responses to the comparison of the two totalitarianisms, is useful in identifying the standpoint of the individual making the comparison: (1)'Hitler's hangmen' favour the pairing with Stalinists because it serves to excuse their own actions; (2) Hitler's victims oppose a pairing, because they are aware that the 'hangmen' use it as an excuse; (3) 'Stalin's hangmen' oppose a pairing, because it is used against them as an accusation; (4) Stalin's victims favour the pairing, because they can use it as an accusation.[21] In post-Soviet Estonia there has been little hesitation about comparing the two systems, which would indicate that it is not the victims of the Nazi occupation (that is Jewish survivors or communist sympathizers) who dominated the debate but victims of Stalinism and those who believed that the Nazi occupation was the 'lesser of two evils'. In particular, respondents of the War Generation would commonly understand the Germans as 'our enemy number two' whereas the Soviets are seen as the oppressor number one.[22] 'Illar', an Estonian exile who fought with the Finnish Boys, was more reflective compared to other respondents of the War Generation: 'The Russian terror was really horrible, but the same is true for the reaction to it or the revenge for it'. Nevertheless, the predominant understanding of viewing the Germans as 'the lesser of two evils' can primarily be explained by the chronology of historical events (as outlined in Chapter 2): it was because the Soviet occupation lasted much longer, and because during the German occupation it was Jews, Roma, alleged communists and various other groups who were under constant threat of death, but not normally the ethnic Estonians. The two locomotives of the museum therefore are symbols of a profound debate in Estonian historical culture in the post-Soviet period.

A Toothless Tiger? The Estonian International Commission for the Investigation of Crimes against Humanity

Whereas the Museum of Occupations was established by a private donor, the Estonian International Commission for the Investigation of Crimes against Humanity (hereafter 'the commission') was created in 1998 through the initiative of President Lennart Meri to produce comprehensive research reports on the occupations of 1940–91.[23] In what follows I will illustrate the fraught balancing act that the commission had to strike between scholarly research, legal investigation and public history. Eva-Clarita Onken aptly remarks that 'establishing investigative commissions that are non-partisan in character and work independently from everyday politics is one way of determining guilt and responsibility for past injustices. Even if these commissions have no direct judicial or political power, their truth-seeking work and unbiased evaluation can support critical reflection, reconciliation and the feeling of justice in a post-authoritarian society'. While there was no systematic transitional justice programme in place in post-Soviet Estonia, the so-called 'historians' commission' was clearly intended to fulfil the function of restoring the 'system of moral judgement'.[24]

The Estonian case demonstrates that in societies with a strong distrust of legal and political institutions that have been discredited in the past, historians can be invested with a moral role as judges, something rarely seen in societies with more stable democracies. I argue here that besides its moral and political function, the commission played a primarily emblematic role, as it was created during the EU and NATO accession processes in reaction to increasing international pressure by the 'Nazi hunter' Efraim Zuroff, Russia and also the West. The result was a 'prescribed public remembrance' of the events surrounding the Nazi occupation and the Holocaust.

The attempt to appease international pressure by creating a nonpartisan, objective body is reflected in the international composition of the commission's board, which included well-known personalities from Germany, the UK, Finland, Sweden, Denmark and Russia, but no Estonians. On the other hand, the actual team of researchers on the ground was formed by Estonian historians. A further decision to prioritize the crimes against humanity committed during the German occupation in the research agenda (and to only subsequently study crimes committed during the Soviet occupations) can also be explained by reference to the general aim to satisfy international expectations. Consequently the first online report published in 2001 covered the events during the German occupation. Herein the myth of a 'just war' of the Estonian auxiliary police in 1941 was debunked by uncovering that the bulk of the killing of (alleged) communists during the early stages of the German occupation was done by the Estonian auxiliary police and that, in assisting the *Einsatzkommando* 1A, the police also played an active role in the extermination of the local Jewry in 1941–42. The report further mentioned that the majority of members of the destruction battalion were ethnic Estonians, thus touching on another taboo, namely the fratricidal war in Estonia. It ended on the broader note that historical events made Estonia a 'victim nation', but stated that this did 'not preclude acts of perpetration' as well. While the report attributed overall responsibility for the crimes committed during the Nazi occupation to the Germans, it identified all members of the Estonian Political Police (Department BIV) responsible for war crimes, and asserted that members of the Estonian Directorate, or Nazi client government – whose names were listed – also bore shared responsibility for war crimes committed in Estonia, and beyond its borders. It also explicitly identified the 286th, 287th and 288th police battalions as participants in crimes against humanity and acts of genocide.[25]

With regard to the difficulties of dealing with a double-totalitarian past, the commission stated: 'The main difficulty throughout the German occupation (and afterwards) was that resistance to the Germans would inevitably be construed as support for Communism and the Soviet Union; while resistance to the Soviets would be construed as support for Nazism'. Its point that there was 'very little middle ground' was also clear from my interviews with respondents of the War Generation.[26] As previously discussed, the commission was never intended as a fully fledged Truth Commission. Consequently it lacked the status of a juridical or prosecutorial body and did not initiate the tracking down of those Estonian perpetrators identified in the reports in order to hold them accountable, extradite and try them. One could however take the line of argument that since the commission is state funded, it is not just a scholarly body and so has a moral duty to pass judgement.

After discussing the commission's precarious position at the interface of scholarly research and legal investigation, let us turn to some of the immediate consequences of the publication of this first online report in 2001. Zuroff presented the contemporary Estonian Security Police with a list of sixteen members of the 36th police battalion, who had been identified in the report as having participated in the execution of Jews in Nowogrodek, Belorussia, in 1942. The Estonian Security Police concluded, however, that they had no evidence to confirm this indictment of the suspected criminals identified in the commission's report. In obvious frustration, Zuroff announced an award of $10,000 for anyone providing information leading to the arrest of these men,[27] and placed an advert in the local newspaper reading 'during the Holocaust, Estonians murdered Jews in Estonia as well as in other countries'.[28] From the commission's inaction some may conclude that its work was mainly emblematic and tailored towards a Western audience – making sure that the contentious collaboration issue was studied but without bringing to justice those identified as war criminals.

A conference paper on 'Collaboration and Resistance in Estonia 1940–1944' presented in Sweden in 2002 by Meelis Maripuu, a younger Estonian who worked as part of the commission's research team on the German occupation, seemed somewhat less balanced when compared to the commission's objectively written online report on the Nazi occupation. His presentation was marked by a selective and ethnocentric approach to the study of the Holocaust in Estonia, because he only included the genocide of Estonian Jews, while omitting the fate of those thousands of European Jews who were deported to Estonia to perish in the camps there. This imbalance allowed him to claim that fewer than a thousand Estonian Jews were killed in Estonia during the German occupation, while suggesting that the Soviet evacuation of approximately five hundred Estonian Jews to Russia can be termed the 'first act of the Holocaust'. From all this he concluded that Estonia, although the first country to declare itself *judenfrei*, was also the country in which the smallest number of Jews were exterminated under Nazi occupation.[29]

This is but one sign that the commission's carefully worded reports may not reflect the predominant opinion among professional historians, or indeed of Estonian society at large. A further indication of the existence of two different, yet interrelated, discourses – a local closed discourse and an official emblematic one, regulated and managed for the international community – is provided by the argument of an American historian of Lithuanian origin who acknowledged that while Lithuanians needed to settle accounts with their past, this could only happen in their own time, in their own way; above all, he said, they needed to discuss it among themselves and literally in their own language, because many Lithuanian words cannot be translated and are thus fundamentally unintelligible to outsiders.[30] An argument could be made that this explains the practice of a 'closed discourse', possibly as a consequence of long-term foreign rule.

The case for such a 'closed' national discourse in Estonia is substantiated by the uproar caused in 2002 by the newly appointed American ambassador to Estonia, Joseph M. De Thomas. He remarked that since re-independence no Estonian war criminal had been prosecuted for crimes committed during the Holocaust, and recommended that the Holocaust needed wider recognition as part of Estonia's national history.[31] De Thomas's comments were, however, denounced as 'interference in the internal affairs of Estonia' by the country's justice minister, who added that De Thomas's statement was like 'breaking in through an open door, since only a few states have done as much work as Estonia in investigating the crimes of the Holocaust'.[32] This furore illustrates how Estonian politicians acted as if under attack when it came to the internationally voiced demand for education in and research on the German occupation of Estonia.[33] The ambassador's comments were not entirely unfounded, because about two years earlier (in October 2000) the Estonian minister of education had declared that a Jewish Holocaust Day in schools was not required. The Estonian government came around to revising this opinion and, in 2003, 27 January was marked for the first time as International Holocaust Day in Estonian schools.[34] But because the Holocaust plays such a minor part in most family narratives and in the official narrative, this day runs the danger of serving a mostly emblematic function.

The passions generated by the coverage of the Holocaust in Estonian history textbooks are apparent in my interview with 'Nicolaij', a politician of Russian Jewish background born in Estonia in 1961. He criticized the kind of suggestive questions raised in these textbooks, such as: 'What would have been different if Hitler had not been defeated?' He stated: 'In Kiev, in Babi Yar, 33,771 Jews were killed, in Treblinka two million, in Auschwitz six million. So how can a normal person ask such a question?' After I pointed out to him that Estonians tend to see the Nazi occupation as the lesser of two evils, he replied: 'Jews who have lived here for several hundred years do not agree! Estonia was the first country that reported being "free of Jews". There were six concentration camps in Estonia where Jews from Europe were deported to and killed. Everyone has their own pain [but] these things cannot be compared'. I asked him how his mother survived the war and he explained: 'She was evacuated. In 1944 she came back. My grandmothers, three sisters and one brother were killed in concentration camps. My grandfather was in Vorkuta, in Russia, for fourteen years. Fourteen years! But survived and died in 1982. That's why SS uniforms are much more frightening to me! And there are questions on which we never argue!'

What can we say about the commission's impact on school and public debate? In answer to this question I shall consider the 1,300 pages of the final report published in 2006 under the title: 'Estonia 1940–1945: Reports of the Estonian International Commission for the Investigation of Crimes against Humanity' (hereafter 'the report').[35] Formatted like a reference book and published in English, the report is impractical for use in Estonian schools – showing once more that the work of the commission was tailored towards an international rather than a domestic audience. My reading of the report concurs largely with the judgement of historian Eva-Clarita Onken that it failed to account for the Estonian public's reception of the preliminary reports (published in 2001 and 2004). Nor did it encourage debate or reflection about these controversial themes in Estonian history. Similarly, the report did not acknowledge possible political and societal implications of the research findings (possibly due to the authors' lack of social awareness about the role of their work). While it abstained from critical analysis and contextualization, it showed a positivistic belief in 'classical historical facts' as constituting truth – this positivistic approach, adopted by historians of the Transitional Generation, was discussed in the last chapter.[36]

An example to substantiate this overall assessment of the report can be found in its rather uncritical concluding remarks on the Vaivare concentration camp:

> The actions of the members of the *Omakaitse* [the auxiliary police] and the prison [camp] guards should be considered from at least two aspects. First, they fulfilled orders coming from the German military and police authorities. At the same time, members of the *Omakaitse* and policemen were the only ones who were allowed to carry weapons besides Germans, in situations of crisis, people appear any time and any where who are prepared

to do anything and kill anyone with [a] gun in hand, not to mention cases when they will be paid for this or given free liquor. In addition, also the motive of revenge for the relatives and friends, killed, arrested or deported by Soviets must be considered.[37]

It remains problematic, therefore, to say exactly to what extent the commission helped to reconstruct a moral framework and a widely accepted political approach for dealing with the double totalitarian legacy. After publishing the last of the three online reports on the Soviet occupation in Estonia from 1944 onwards (in 2008) the commission concluded its work. This was largely due to the fact that its previously narrowly-defined mandate of focusing on crimes against humanity was not necessarily applicable to the investigation of the Soviet period up to 1991. Therefore the commission was transformed into the 'Institute of Historical Memory' (established by President Toomas H. Ilves) to extend its work and continue research into human rights violations during the Soviet period that do not fall under the narrow legal definition of 'crimes against humanity' or 'genocide'.[38]

Before turning to some monumental expressions of contemporary Estonian historical culture, I present two views from interviewees about the official ways of coming to terms with the Soviet past during the transition period. The first is by 'Oskar', of the Transitional Generation, on the intricacies of overcoming the Soviet:

> You cannot view the history of our society as one in which the Reds had been in power for half a century and now there are the Whites. No, there is a big part of our nation, which is still quite Soviet in their attitude, their worldview, and their moral principles … They still influence very much the opinion [of society] … the very basis of society has still not recovered. The very basis of a society should consist more or less of a unified understanding of the most basic moral principles … [But] sometimes it feels almost as if there are two [kinds of] Estonians … [T]hey treat the same events … differently, and this is possibly the biggest crime of Soviet rule.

Oskar goes on to describe how he sought to achieve a 'moral resolution':

> [T]hese collaborators were so afraid that they would be arrested [or] tortured … since people like me had come to power in 1992. Really those people projected their way of thinking and acting on us. They … thought we would act like them, when they were in power. But … we just wanted a moral resolution, the moral approach to things. Let's at least say what was wrong and what was right!

'Kalev' of the War Generation also emphasized that nobody was killed in retaliation: 'I thought that maybe somebody who was in prison for twenty-five years, sitting for nothing ... [might] take a landmine and vodka and ... kill some Russians. But no ... Estonians are cold. We have been slaves for so many centuries. But we resisted and are against killing'. Today, he concludes, people cannot give the Soviet occupation a word of praise, and yet

> no communist leader was in prison, and when we discussed this with peo-
> ple from Norway, who had their Quislings under the [German] occupation
> ... I said that nobody is in prison, and nobody has been killed. And this
> creates many problems. Our communist leaders can campaign and we don't
> know [which] of them are Russian agents ... Normally after an occupation
> ends, people get arrested if not killed. [But] not in our country!

Kalev's repeated statements in the interview about the atypicality of bloodshed in 1991 led me to conclude that his comparative frame for understanding the end of the Soviet occupation in 1991 were the historical events of the summer of 1941 after the Red Army's withdrawal, when Estonians lynched alleged Estonian and Russian communists in acts of revenge.

When Private Memory Goes Public:
Monumental Punch-ups

The Bronze Soldier statue, the Maarjamäe memorial complex and the Victory Cross are arguably the most compelling landmarks of contemporary Estonian historical culture. But recognition of Estonia's double-totalitarian legacy has the effect of turning memorial monuments to different veteran groups into publicly contested terrain. During the Soviet period, personal narratives of fighting side by side with the Germans against the Red Army were passed down in the private realm of many Estonian families as essentially unquestioned heroic stories of national resistance – this transmission occurred especially from the War Generation to the Transitional Generation and Freedom Children. In the 1990s not all of the privately held counter-memories resurfacing in the public domain could be integrated more permanently into the official history. As I shall show, the social memory of the veterans who fought in the German army is one example of an unofficial account that became part of the publicly debated political memories, but was pushed back again into the private sphere.

Previously I stated that a different regional logic prevails in East European societies with a double-totalitarian past, and referred to it as 'anti-communist' narrative. Enn Sarv's recollections on the situation of Estonians in early 1944 reflect this specific outlook on the past.

> In order to obtain weapons, [Estonian] men were forced to fight in German uniform ..., but they considered themselves an Estonian army. They had managed to gain the right to wear a coat of arms with the colours of the Estonian national flag on their sleeves. In February, Estonian SS fighters removed the SS symbols from their collars without authorization, and replaced them with the emblem of the Estonian Cross of Freedom ... Our main enemy, the Soviet Union, was about to invade Estonia, once again aiming to destroy our nation: so the war had become our own war.[39]

Oskar, of the Transitional Generation, related that his father and both his uncles fought in the German army. In response to my question about whether his father joined the German army voluntarily, he elaborated:

> To fight against the Russians of course! You know pretty well that the Germans had been our historical enemy and we Estonians didn't like them very much. But only one year, 1940–41, made us love the Germans so much and greet them as 'liberators'. Nazis as 'liberators', isn't it awful? But it only gives you an idea what the communist occupation had been like. Not that we are Nazis or Nazi-minded, no, never!

Oskar insisted that they did not expressly fight for the Germans or on the German side, but that they had no other choice. This is the line of argument taken by the veterans themselves. For instance, Ilmar Haalviste, a Waffen-SS veteran, exemplified this particular Estonian standpoint when he stated: 'At the end of the day there was no right or wrong side. The war was thrust upon us. We were on our side, defending our homes'. Clearly Russian veterans of the Red Army would vehemently deny this claim.[40] The specific Estonian interpretation of the Second World War and its concomitant anti-communist narrative clashed with the anti-fascist memory regime (centred on the Holocaust as single traumatic event) that predominates in the West, which is why these anti-communist narratives were subsequently pushed back to the margins of the private until after the time of successful EU accession. The Estonian government failed in its attempt to bridge these long-suppressed but now emerging anti-communist narratives, on the one hand, and the established anti-fascist Western memory regime, on the other; instead it maintained an ambiguous position. On the occasion in 1999 of the reburial of Alfons Rebane, an anti-Soviet partisan and later commander of the Estonian

Legion, the Estonian government contributed financially towards a reburial ceremony with full military honours, but only two Members of Parliament and the commander of the Estonian Defence Forces attended; most government representatives withdrew their attendance for fear of international criticism.[41]

In 2002, a privately funded memorial stone depicting an Estonian soldier in Waffen-SS uniform was put up on the initiative of Leo Tammiksaar, a local historian of the Transitional Generation who ran an organization called the 'Estonian SS Legion Museum' at the Estonian sea resort of Pärnu.[42] After it attracted a negative response from the national government the memorial was removed, and town officials ordered its redesign and the replacement of its original inscription, which had read: 'To all Estonian soldiers who fell in the Second World War to liberate their homeland and to free Europe in 1940–45'. The inference from the original inscription and from Tammiksaar's public statements is that in a heroic act of national resistance Estonian legionaries prevented the Red Army from occupying the whole of Europe. Possibly in an act of defiance the Pärnu monument was re-erected in the Estonian village cemetery of Lihula in 2004. In the words of the mayor of the Lihula parish, Tiit Madisson – a historian and former dissident leading the Hirvepark demonstration in the late 1980s – those two thousand who congregated at the monument's unveiling ceremony wished 'to honour those who chose the lesser evil'.[43] Whereas the monument still depicts a soldier wearing a German army helmet and carrying a gun, with the order of the Estonian Cross of Freedom on his collar, the amended inscription now read: 'To the Estonian men who fought in 1940–45 against Bolshevism and for the restoration of Estonian independence'.[44]

The monument provoked violent anger. Faced by an enraged stone-throwing crowd of several hundred, the police removed the monument just a fortnight after its inauguration. Afterwards a simple plaque was installed on the base stone which was the only trace remaining from the monument, reading: 'At this place the monument to the Estonian men used to stand 20.08.04–02.09.04'. The national government maintained that it was not appropriate 'to build a monument that may be interpreted as an attempt to commemorate totalitarian regimes that had occupied Estonia'. In the words of the Estonian foreign minister, Kristiina Ojuland: 'Estonia must not isolate itself from the international community and damage its reputation … Local inappropriate action often results in very serious and far-reaching international consequences … Estonia … acknowledges the need to commemorate the fallen. This must be done in a manner that does not bring forth past evils to poison the future'.[45]

In reaction to the fracas over the Lihula monument, the Estonian government established yet another commission to decide on the official representation of Estonian contemporary history. At the same time it identified as its long-term objective the gaining of more international recognition for the specific Estonian Second World War experience.[46] The removal of the Lihula monument unleashed a wave of vandalism against Soviet-built memorials all over the country.[47] There is a *longue durée* dimension to the battle over monuments in Estonia (and other East European societies) because Estonians rescued parts of monuments dating from the interwar period which had subsequently been destroyed by the new Soviet rulers, hiding them in private cellars or country houses. As discussed in the previous chapter, the social practice of laying down candles at the foundation stones of destroyed monuments to honour national heroes and the idea of national independence was a widespread form of passive cultural resistance during the Soviet period.

The Estonian Freedom Fighters' Association (hereafter 'the association') represents Estonian veterans who fought in divisions of the Waffen-SS (particularly of its 20th division, the so-called 'Estonian Legion') and also in units of anti-Soviet partisans (the 'Forest Brethren'). In 1950, a UN commission found the Baltic Legions (among them the Estonian Legion) to be neither criminal nor Nazi collaborators, but the more recent work of the Estonian International Commission allowed for a more differentiated assessment. Since the early 1990s the association has organized an annual celebration, demanding to be granted by the Estonian government the status of 'Freedom Fighters'.[48] The veterans sought state protection against Russian and Jewish organizations, labelling them as 'fascists'. In July 2004 some fifteen hundred Estonian veterans commemorated the sixtieth anniversary of the battle of the Blue Mountain against the Red Army.[49] Their identification with the 'Freedom Fighters' of a morally far less disputed war (the War of Independence) can be understood as an attempt to gain rehabilitation of their status, and legitimacy in their battle for Estonia's freedom and democracy during the Second World War.

Another impressive spatial representation of the complexity of Estonian twentieth-century history is the Maarjamäe War Memorial Complex, a vast cemetery located at Piirita on the coast north-east of Tallinn. With its overlapping layers of remembrance, Maarjamäe constitutes a truly perplexing site for any visitor, because it is the resting place of German soldiers and civilians, Estonians fighting in German army units, Estonians and Russophones fighting in the Red Army and of those who fell during the First World War and Estonian War of Independence.[50]

During the summer of 2004 the association wanted to establish a new set of memorial crosses and plaques at the Maarjamäe complex, including the names of sixteen Estonian units who had fought as parts of the Wehrmacht, and a map of the battle sites against the Red Army.[51] However, these sixteen Estonian units included the 36th Estonian Division of the Waffen-SS, which the commission had identified as having committed crimes against humanity. While the Estonian government rejected the association's initial demand, a slightly altered arrangement of three large crosses and two plaques – including references to the Estonian units that fought in the Wehrmacht – was nevertheless added to the Maarjamäe memorial site and inaugurated in the presence of President Meri in 2005.[52]

These contested monuments brought to light how individual memories of Estonians who had fought in the German army, which entered the realm of public remembrance in the 1990s, are increasingly being pushed back into the local or private sphere. This is because the Estonian government, in the course of the country's growing westward orientation and under West European pressure, holds to a publicly prescribed memory regime that does not conflict too much with the Western interpretative frame.

The Bronze Soldier and the Cross of Freedom: A Shift from Collective Suffering to Resistance

At the 60th anniversary of the end of the Second World War, tensions openly erupted around a prominent Soviet-era monument in central Tallinn, which was vandalized with paint on the morning of 9 May 2005 – the Russian Victory Day. Since 1947 the Bronze Soldier statue, known as the 'monument to the liberator of Tallinn', has commemorated Soviet soldiers who died fighting against the German army.[53] It was the venue for the annual meetings of Red Army veterans on 'Victory Day' and the 'Day of the Liberation of Tallinn' (22 September). In post-Soviet Estonia, Victory Day has become the focal point for Red Army veterans and Estonian legionaries alike, all of whom claim to have fought 'for the Estonian cause'. But whereas for Red Army veterans the date marks the 'liberation' of Estonia from Nazi occupation and fascism, to many Estonians it stands for the Soviet occupation and for the 'Long Second World War'.[54] In this struggle, the Bronze Soldier statue has increasingly turned into a field of commemorative combat over the revision of Estonia's past. Consequently, many Estonians publicly requested the removal of the monument, arguing that it serves as a reminder of five decades of Soviet rule in Estonia. For many Red Army veterans that would imply a wholesale denigration of the results of the Great Patriotic War.[55] In the furore about the Bronze Soldier statue, many Estonians understand the monument to honour only the Russian soldiers (still equating Soviet with Russian), while blanking out the memory of members of the titular nation who also fought in the Estonian Corps as Soviet soldiers.

On 9 May 2005, the controversy reached a new height when Estonian nationalists clashed with Soviet veterans and members of the Russian-speaking community waving Soviet flags.[56] In an attempt to end this divisive and ethnocentric interpretation of the past, some suggested replacing the Bronze Soldier with a monument to *all* soldiers who fell in the Second World War. But in a country with such contested memories, a single monument would be deeply problematic. Seventy years after the end of the Second World War and two decades after re-independence, the official canon on how to remember the fallen remains unresolved in Estonia; it still cannot be decided whether the fallen on *all* warring sides should be honoured, or only selected (national) groups.[57]

In the years that followed, a shift could be observed from the narrative of collective suffering (and Estonian victimhood) to an increasing use of the narrative trope of national resistance; this was also reflected in the material reinterpretation of the past leading to the disappearance or emergence of historical landmarks of post-Soviet Tallinn. Had it not been a burial site of twelve Red Army soldiers, the Bronze Soldier statue would have been removed earlier, along with many other public remnants of Estonia's Soviet past. During the run-up to the general elections of 4 March 2007 the monument turned into a hot issue. The candidate of the Reformist Party, Andrus Ansip, who had repeatedly spoken in favour of the removal of the statue because it was not unifying but dividing the Estonian people, made this his key election promise. Conversely the Centre Party under Edgar Savisaar, the mayor of Tallinn, with a strong base among the Russian-speaking community, insisted that the monument should remain in place. The excavations of the soldiers' graves (in preparation for their reburial) on 26 April 2007, soon after prime minister Ansip's election victory, resulted in two nights of extended youth riots (mainly by Russian-speakers) that were without precedent in Tallinn's recent history.[58] Other repercussions included a protest around the Estonian embassy in Moscow and an alleged 'cyber-war attack' on Estonia. The statue's relocation to the nearby cemetery for the Defence Forces (containing mainly the graves of soldiers of the War of Independence) just before the annual Victory Day celebrations can be interpreted as a deliberate practice of externalizing divisive memories and associated commemorative practices from a public space in central Tallinn to a mono-functional cemetery on the city outskirts.

The trend of eliminating those interpretations of the Second World War that are irreconcilable with the official anti-communist narrative illustrates the current government's unwillingness to allow for a pluralization of war memories – despite the fact that 40 per cent of Tallinn's inhabitants are Russian speakers.[59] In 2009 Kristina Norman, a thirty-year-old performance artist of mixed background, erected a full-size gold replica of the Bronze Soldier at the original site, encountering emotionally moving reactions from the Russian-speaking population of Tallinn.[60] The police removed the artist and her work within an hour but Norman showed this on video as part of her *After-War* show at the 53rd Venice Biennale. The title 'After-War' – instead of post-war – hints at the deep feeling of many Balts that the Second World War did not end in 1945 but lasted until 1991; and consequently that the post-Soviet decades constituted a time to finally deal with the war. When watching the video it was my impression that, in the short moment that the replica was back at its original site, it was a healing gesture: returning something to the Russian speakers that belonged to them, something they needed and that they felt had been unjustly taken from them. Watching their reactions in this video was emotionally rather touching, and it made obvious to me the open wound that the reburial and relocation had left in this community. The former site of the Bronze Soldier statue is now no more than an empty void for those busy citizens of Tallinn, few of whom bother to remember what stood there until April 2007.

Although the Soviet-era monument had disappeared from the cityscape, a new 28-metre-high Cross of Freedom glass statue was finally put up in 2009 on Tallinn's prominent Freedom Square. Initially planned as the highpoint of the ninetieth anniversary celebrations of independent Estonian statehood in 2008 – strategically omitting the Soviet period 1940–91 – it represents the formerly repressed memories of those who fought in the War of Independence of 1918–20 for the freedom of the Estonian people. The Freedom Fighters are utilized as a unifying point of reference, even though this memory can also be interpreted as a divisive once, since their fight was directed against German *and* Russian dominance. I would argue that although the statue might have been intended as a Freedom Cross it is more of a triumphant Victory Cross – akin to some of the nineteenth-century war monuments of Western Europe (such as the Berlin Victory Column and Nelson's Column). A closer look at the Freedom Cross reveals a hand brandishing a sword in its centre.[61] This is the heraldic crest of the Estonian Cross of Liberty (in Estonian, *Vabaduse Ristid*) – a medal to honour military services during the War of Independence, which is still a high state decoration in contemporary Estonia. Its inclusion in the design of the memorial column is controversial because the crest was subsequently 'highjacked' as a coat of arms by Estonians fighting in the Estonian Legion during the Second World War (to indicate that their cause was fighting for Estonian independence).

Conclusion

My preliminary analysis of recent changes to Estonia's commemorative landscape and memory regime indicates that the country's EU accession in May 2004 brought with it a new national assertiveness and confidence, leading to a shift in the core national narrative from one of struggle for freedom and collective suffering to the narrative trope of resistance. Reflecting on the various landmarks of Estonian historical culture examined in this chapter: whereas the Museum of Occupations aims at cementing the notion of Estonian suffering, the Lihula monument, the Estonian Freedom Fighters' Association and the Cross of Freedom column are all linked more to ideas of national resistance – in fact both the Bronze Soldier statue and the Cross of Freedom column are about victory. The examples of the monuments to the Estonian legionaries at Maarjamäe, and the story of the removal of the Bronze Soldier statue in particular, showed the waxing and waning of social memories in the public sphere. These various case studies made clear how battles over monuments are battles between competing interpretative frameworks, or memory regimes – that is, between the official and local Estonian points of view, the Western reading of the Second World War and, lastly, pro-Russian and dated Soviet views of the past.

In the course of the 1990s, privately held social memories of Estonian suffering and anti-Soviet resistance emerged. Both were based on the anti-communist narrative, but only those related to suffering were incorporated into the official canon, whilst those social memories of Soviet resistance deviated starkly from the Western anti-fascist memory regime, into which they could not be accommodated. As part of Estonia's integration into European institutional structures, predominantly shaped in the West, the country also yielded to the Western anti-fascist memory regime – for instance, by implementing the Estonian International Commission for the Investigation of Crimes against Humanity (1998) and introducing the Holocaust Day (2003), while more contentious memories of anti-Soviet resistance were relegated into the local or private spheres. But after EU accession and the increasing consolidation of the nation state, a shift from the theme of suffering to one of national resistance took place because, I argue, a national community cannot build its identity on suffering, victimhood or shame.

Every collective memory is anchored and unfolds in a social framework, the group, as well as in a spatial framework, such as monuments and memorial sites. I have demonstrated how the revision of history is continuously contested, and how monuments as sites of memory can turn into 'contested terrain'. Ultimately these monuments are so fiercely contested because they are sources of group identities and are therefore linked to the existential dimension of history. Because their removal or destruction causes a 'dislocation' and 'displacement' of the respective group memories (and concomitant social practices), we can speak of displaced group memories or identities in contemporary Estonia.

Notes

1. F.R. Ankersmit. 2001. 'Rüsen on History and Politics', in F.R. Ankersmit, *Historical Representation*. Stanford, CA: Stanford University Press, 279.
2. J. Létourneau. 2001. 'Digging into Historical Consciousness, Individual and Collective: Overview of a Research Trajectory'. Presented at the conference on Canadian Historical Consciousness in an International Context: Theoretical Frameworks, PWIAS, University of British Columbia, Vancouver, Canada, 26–28 August.
3. The Estonian prime minister speaking in 2007 – T. Ambrosio. 2009. *Authoritarian Backlash: Russian Resistance to Democratization in the Former Soviet Union*. Farnham: Ashgate, 99.
4. E. Langenbacher. 2003. 'Changing Memory Regimes in Contemporary Germany?', *German Politics and Society* 21(2): 46–68; J. Assmann, *Religion und kulturelles Gedächtnis*, 28. The chapter title goes back to Walter Benjamin's (1977. *Illuminationen. Gesammelte Schriften*, Vol. I. Frankfurt a. M.: Suhrkamp, 260) observation that every national history is by definition a winner's tale.
5. Gallerano, 'Public Use of History', 85.
6. Todorov, 'The Abuses of Memory', 15; K.G. Karlsson and U. Zander. 2003. *Echoes of the Holocaust: Historical Cultures in Contemporary Europe*. Lund: Nordic Academic Press, 42f.
7. Shari J. Cohen. 1999. *Politics without a Past: The Absence of History in Post-Communist Nationalism*. Durham, NC: Duke University Press, 2.
8. Karl-Göran Karlsson. 1999. *Historia som vapen: Historiebruk och samhällsupplösning i Sovjetunionen och dess efterföljarstater 1985–1995*. Stockholm: Natur och Kultur.
9. I discussed some of the conditions of history production in Soviet Estonia in Chapter 3, which is why I will only briefly refer to the work of Nancy Whittier Heer (1971. *Politics and History in the Soviet Union*. Cambridge, MA: MIT Press) who distinguished between the explicit and implicit functions of history in Soviet society. Her distinction is based on the fact that, although the legitimation of power and rationalization of policies were explicitly articulated by the highest organs of the CPSU, some other functions remained unofficial or unintended, but were nevertheless vital for sustaining socio-political order – such as using historical records against political opponents.
10. D. Levy. 1999. 'The Future of the Past: Historiographical Disputes and Competing Memories in Germany and Israel', *History and Theory* 38(1): 62–63, 65.

11. A. Velmet. 2011. 'Occupied Identities: National Narratives in Baltic Museums of Occupation', *Journal of Baltic Studies* 42(2): 191.

12. The museum also relies on the extensive use of new media, including video testimonies and a series of seven CD-ROMs covering roughly the period from 1940 to 1987, as well as the Estonian independence movement; see http://www.okupatsioon.ee.

13. Cf. J. Mark. 2008. 'Containing Fascism: History in Post-Communist Baltic Occupation and Genocide Museums', in Oksana Sarkisova and Péter Apor (eds), *Past for the Eyes: East European Representations of Communism in Cinema and Museums after 1980*. Budapest: Central European University Press, 335–69; Mark, *The Unfinished Revolution*; and Velmet, 'Occupied Identities'.

14. Kivimäe and Kivimäe, 'Geschichtsschreibung und Geschichtsforschung', 163ff. The Estonian Repressed Persons Records Bureau (ERPB) was headed by Leo Õispuu, who gathered extensive registers of names of political arrests carried out under Soviet occupation and of the deportations from Estonia to Russia. The ERPB has published several name register books as well as an electronic database on victims of repression.

15. T. Savi. 2002. Statement of the President of the Riigikogu on the Occupation Regime in Estonia, 18 June, translated in *Euro University: The Monthly Survey of the Baltic and Post-Soviet Politics* 7(109): 3–4.

16. The emphasis on national suffering is also reflected in the publications of the museum; for instance, K. Kukk and T. Raun. 2007. *Soviet Deportations in Estonia: Impact and Legacy Articles and Life Stories*. Tartu: Tartu University Press. The Museum Dungeon of the KGB in Tartu, which was termed the 'Grey House', is another site to remember the Estonians' struggle for freedom and their suffering. This museum was established in 2001; similar to the Museum of Occupations , its collection lacks any reference to the site's usage during the Nazi occupation.

17. See Misiunas, 'Soviet Historiography', 173–96.

18. Todorov, 'The Abuses of Memory', 16–19; cf. Maier, 'Hot Memory ... Cold Memory', 152–65.

19. My references to Eastern Europe pertain to the Baltic Three and also Poland, because they all share the experience of a double-totalitarian past. According to Mälksoo (*The Politics of Becoming European*), these four new member states are at the forefront of a new commemorative politics in Europe.

20. N. Naimark. 2010. *Stalin's Genocides*. Princeton, NJ: Princeton University Press, 24–25; M. Wulf. 2011b. 'Changing Memory Regimes in a New Europe', *East European Memory Studies, Memory at War Newsletter* 7 (November): 15–20. For historical revisionism in post-Soviet Latvia, see Onken, *Revisionismus schon vor der Geschichte*.

21. Todorov, 'The Abuses of Memory', 16–19.

22. Sarv, 'Our Duty of Remembering', 36.

23. Similar commissions were set up in the other Baltic states in 1998. Historians can be seen (alongside politicians and policy makers, as well as lawyers), as codifiers of these memory regimes.

24. E-C. Onken. 2007a. 'The Politics of Finding Historical Truth: Reviewing Baltic History Commissions and their Work', *Journal of Baltic Studies* 38(1): 110; Cohen, *Politics without a Past*, xx.

25. T. Hiio, M. Maripuu and I. Paalve (eds). 2006. 'Estonia 1940–1945: Reports of the Estonian International Commission for the Investigation of Crimes against Humanity'. Report Phase II. Tallinn: Estonian Foundation for the Investigation of Crimes against Humanity, xx–xxi.

26. Ibid., xxiii.

27. Already in autumn 1991, E. Zuroff (1996. *Beruf: Nazijäger. Die Suche mit dem langen Atem: Die Jagd nach den Tätern des Völkermordes*. Freiburg: Ahriman-Verlag, 318–21) failed in his attempt to arrest the Estonian Evald Mikson (who was living in Iceland at the time) for war crimes committed during the Nazi occupation of Estonia.

28. *The Baltic Times* staff, 30 Jan. 2003.

29. Meelis Maripuu ('Kollaboration und Widerstand') stated that 'the present article is only concerned with the fate of the local Jewish community during the Second World War; while the destiny of those European Jews deported to Estonia in 1942–44 is not addressed'. However in Part III of the commission's Final Report (Hiio, Maripuu and Paalve, 'Estonia 1940–1945') on the German occupation, Maripuu authored chapters on Estonian involvement in the larger Holocaust story, such as the annihilation of Czech and German Jews in Estonia in 1942–43 (pp. 705–14) and the French Jews at the Tallinn Central Prison in 1944 (pp. 717–18).

30. Participant observation at the conference on 'Reichskommissariat Ostland. Collaboration and Resistance during the Holocaust', Stockholm and Uppsala, Sweden, 18–21 April 2002.

31. De Thomas stated: 'The fact that the Soviet occupation did more direct harm in Estonia, however, does not negate the fact that the Holocaust happened here too' (28 May 2002).

32. *Leta Daily News Review*, 30 May 2002.

33. Brüggemann, 'Von der Renationalisierung zur Demontage nationaler Helden', 810–19.

34. Newsletter of the Swiss Baltic Chamber of Commerce, 27 October 2000.

35. Hiio, Maripuu and Paalve, 'Estonia 1940–1945'.

36. Onken, 'The Politics of Finding Historical Truth'; E.-C. Pettai. 2011. 'The Convergence of Two Worlds: Historians and Emerging Histories in the Baltic States', in Martyn Housden and David J. Smith (eds), *Forgotten Pages in Baltic History: Themes in Diversity and Inclusion*. New York: Rodopi, 263–80.

37. Hiio, Maripuu and Paalve, 'Estonia 1940–1945', 738.

38. The Polish Institute of National Remembrance (IPN) was established in the same years as the commission, and also set out to cover the time period from 1939 to 1989. Unlike the commission, the IPN broadened the narrow definition of genocide and crimes against humanity so as to be able to investigate crimes committed in post-totalitarian times (Naimark, *Stalin's Genocides*, 23). The IPN stated: 'Crimes against humanity are understood mainly as crimes of genocide as defined by the Convention on the Prevention and Punishment of the Crime of Genocide of December 9, 1948, as well as other forms of persecution and oppressions by official agents which were directed against people who belong to a given political, social, racial, religious or nation group' (www.ipn.gov.pl/portal/en/). These commissions and institutes of national remembrance can be found throughout central Eastern Europe; see the Platform of European Memory and Conscience, http://www.mnemosyne.ee/conscience.

39. Sarv, 'Our Duty of Remembering', 36.

40. *BBC News Week*, 9 May 2005; Itar-Tass, 27 April 2005.

41. M. Huang. 1999. 'Doing it Half Right', *Central European Review* 1(2), 5 July. http://www.ce-review.org/99/2/amber2.html

42. Alexei Gunter, 'Monumental Needs and Rethinking Estonia's Past', *The Baltic Times*, 10 June 2004.

43. BBC News World, Online Edition, 20 Aug. 2004. Only a few years later, Madisson would be fiercely campaigning for the removal of the Bronze Soldier statue in Tallinn.

44. Alexei Gunter, 'Riot Police Help Remove Controversial WWII Monument', *The Baltic Times*, 9 Sept. 2004.

45. Matthias Kolb, 'Looking for the Truth behind Lihula', *The Baltic Times*, 27 April 2005; *The Baltic Times* staff report, 2 Sept. 2004; Välisministeerium, 3 Sept. 2004.
46. Alexei Gunter, 'Estonia Sets its History Straight', *The Baltic Times*, 1 Nov. 2004.
47. D.J. Smith. 2008. '"Woe from Stones": Commemoration, Identity Politics and Estonia's "War of Monuments"', *Journal of Baltic States* 39(4): 425.
48. Michael Shafir, 'Analysis: Estonian War Veterans Provoke Russian Reaction', *Radio Free Europe, Radio Liberty*, 22 July 2004. Likewise in neighbouring Latvia, the veterans of the Latvian SS Legion (the National Soldiers' Association) organize an annual public march to the Freedom Monument in the centre of Riga on 16 March.
49. After the German troops withdrew from the Narva on 26 April 1944, soldiers of the Estonian Legion mounted a last stand against the advancing Red Army at the battle of the Blue Mountain (in Estonian, Sinimäed), 26 July – 12 August 1944. Because Estonians fought alone (and no longer side by side with the Germans) in this battle, it has been highly mythologized – for instance, in the historical documentary entitled *Sinimäed* (2006). See M. Laar. 2008. *Eesti leegion: sõnas ja pildis*. Tallinn: Grenader Publishing.
50. In 1960, on the site of a former German military cemetery, a 35-metre obelisk was erected in memory of Russian soldiers who died in 1918. In 1975 a cement park (a portal with iron figures and hands symbolizing mourning and an eternal flame) were added to honour 'those who fought for Soviet power'.
51. Jerusalem Postcom Staff, 22 May 2004.
52. Itar-Tass, 27 April 2005.
53. Until 1991 the inscription (in Russian and Estonian) read 'Eternal glory to the heroes who died for the liberation and independence of our country', and an eternal flame was lit in front because this was also the burial site of twelve Red Army soldiers.
54. Evidence of a different perception of European history became obvious during the sixtieth anniversary of the end of the Second World War, when the Estonian and Lithuanian leaders did not travel to Moscow for the celebration on 9 May. The Latvian president attended the ceremony, using the publicity to demonstrate the Baltic view on the events of the Second World War: see E.-C. Onken. 2000b. 'Geschichtsbewußtsein und nationale Identität im gesellschaftlichen Integrations- und Demokratisierungsprozeß in Lettland', in Bernard Linek and Kai Struve (eds), *Nationalismus und nationale Identität in Ostmitteleuropa im 19. und 20. Jahrhundert*. Marburg: Verlag Herder-Institut, 331–49; T. Zhurzhenko. 2007. 'The Geopolitics of Memory'. *Eurozine*, 10 May. http://www.eurozine.com/articles/2007-05-10-zhurzhenko-en.html.
55. The dispute prompted members of the Russian Duma to push for sanctions against Estonia and to denounce this 'blasphemous attitude towards the memory of those who fought against fascism' (Agence France-Presse, 22 Jan. 2007; *The Baltic Times* staff, 30 Jan. 2007).
56. In 2006, in an attempt to resolve the dispute, the Estonian parliament accepted a bill banning the display of Soviet and Nazi symbols that might incite hatred.
57. S. Kattago. 2008. 'Commemorating Liberation and Occupation: War Memorials along the Road to Narva', *Journal of Baltic Studies* 39(4): 436.
58. There is an extensive scholarly literature on the Bronze Soldier issue: see, for example, P. Petersoo and M. Tamm. 2008. *Monumental konflikt: mälu, poliitika ja identiteet tänapäeva Eestis*. Tallinn: Varrak; K. Brüggemann and A. Kasekamp. 2008. 'The Politics of History and the "War of Monuments" in Estonia', *Nationalities Papers* 36(3): 425–48; M. Lehti, M. Jutila and M. Jokisipilä. 2008. 'Never-Ending Second World War: Public Performances of National Dignity and the Drama of the

Bronze Soldier', *Journal of Baltic Studies* 39(4): 393–418; M. Ehala. 2009. 'The Bronze Soldier: Identity Threat and Maintenance in Estonia', *Jouirnal of Baltic Studies* 40(1): 139–58.

59. I would argue that a highly contentious site such as the Maarjamäe War Memorial Complex can only survive only by being on the margins of the capital.

60. K. Norman. 2009. *After-War: Estonia at the 53rd International Art Exhibition – La Biennale di Venezia 2009.* Tallinn: Estonian Centre for Contemporary Art.

61. The monument was commissioned by the Defence Ministry on the grounds that Estonia still had no landmark to symbolize liberty for its people.

Conclusion

FRAMING PAST AND FUTURE

To Europe, yes, but with our dead.
– Maria Janion, Polish literary critic[1]

The previous chapters have shown how foreign rule and catastrophic change impacted on Estonian society during the twentieth century. Using life-story interviews with professional historians and intellectuals, we have seen how memories of the Second World War and of the Soviet period continue to have a powerful effect on the country's life in the twenty-first century, framing views of both the past and the future. Following the work of Timothy Snyder, it has now become a commonplace to describe the border regions of Eastern Europe, trapped in the jaws of Nazi–Soviet antagonism, as 'bloodlands'. By tracing the dark and conflicted memories of the bloodletting in one of those countries, this book has shown how the bloodlands are also shadowlands.

In summing up the main conclusions of my work I will tease out what is specific to the Estonian case and what can be generalized, in order to increase our understanding of the challenges facing other transitional societies in the post-communist context. Similarly I will point forward to some of the wider methodological, conceptual and historical implications of my work for scholars of memory studies and East European history. In what follows I will first address the main findings on collective memory and collective cultural identity (including the concept of generations) in post-Soviet Estonia. I shall then develop a few of the key themes – namely, unresolved memories of the war and of the Soviet period, and personal strategies for regaining meaning; collective identities in the borderland (including the concepts of cultural hybridity and liminality); the importance of transcending national historiography in post-conflict societies; and finally the prospects of a shared European memory after 1989.

Let us turn first to the main theoretical and empirical findings on collective memory and collective cultural identity in post-Soviet Estonia: collective memories are not simply split along ethno-cultural fault lines but instead consist of many overlapping and competing group memories. I analysed the complexity of group identities in post-Soviet Estonia, reflecting the country's borderland character between Teuton and Slav, and suggested that generational solidarities (based on shared social and formative historical experiences, as well as on social milieu and political affiliation) might at times supersede ethno-cultural affinities. I also argued that the study of generational identity proves particularly fruitful in the case of post-conflict societies. It is therefore no coincidence that the pioneers in the field of generational research, such as José Ortega y Gasset and Karl Mannheim, drawing on lessons from the Great War, hoped to transcend nationalistic thinking by launching 'generation' as an alternative category of identification. I have proposed the importance of going beyond the artificial distinction of myth and history – or history and memory – by adapting Jörn Rüsen's inclusive concept of 'historical culture'. With regard to the interrelation of collective cultural identity and memory, I then showed how collective memory can enforce identity as much as restricting it, and suggested that it is the collective memories of formative historical events that link national identity to collective memory. Based on Estonian historiography and the historians' personal accounts, I singled out three categories of foundational histories – events of collective suffering, events of collective resistance and collective taboo issues – that, I argue, together constitute the building blocks of Estonian national identity.

Let us turn back to the important category of generation: what has the life-story material revealed about generational identities in Estonia? I suggested that we could discern four generations among intellectuals and historians in Estonia today: the War Generation, Post-War Children, the Transitional Generation and Freedom Children. Some of this is already familiar to scholars, but identification of the third generational group identity – the Transitional Generation, brought forward by the specific historical and political conditions of Estonian history – is another key finding of this book. In terms of intergenerational differences we saw that the War Generation acted as guardians of the authentic social memories during the Soviet period, but rarely transmitted their accounts to the Post-War Children to avoid jeopardizing the latter's schooling and careers; on the contrary, they encouraged the Post-War Children to integrate into the new society. The Transitional Generation in turn deplored the Post-War Children as having been morally corrupted by the Soviet system, and looked instead to the War Generation for moral integrity and historical meaning. One respondent of the Post-War Children, 'Ülle-Mai', described her own generation as operating with a 'double consciousness' or 'double mental standard', and clearly this generational group displayed great inconsistencies and dissonances when telling their life stories. Consequently the political reorientation after 1991, involving a fundamental reassessment of moral values and cultural norms, was in many ways most painful for this specific generation. With regard to the intergenerational dynamic at work during Estonia's transition process of the late 1980s, I underlined the importance of the founding alliance between the War Generation and the Transitional Generation, which subsequently formed the motor of the Estonian independence movement.

To what extent, then, can the generational model that I have developed for the Estonian context be generalized for Eastern Europe as a whole? From the intergenerational dynamic discussed in this book, it became obvious that a sharp break in the generational chain, as found for instance in the 1968 movement in post-war West Germany, was absent in Estonia. Instead we can observe a marginalization of the Post-War Children, in that they were not considered by either the previous or the subsequent generations to be guardians of authentic social memories or bearers of the national values and traditions. While my analysis of the intergenerational dynamic might also be applicable to the other Baltic states, it differs from the case of communist Poland because of the more systematic eradication of the old national elite during the Second World War and also the political events of 1956, 1970 and 1980 – Soviet-era crises that were absent in the Baltic republics.[2]

What can we say about the unresolved memories of victims and perpetrators lingering on in the shadowlands? The interview material made clear that outsiders can hardly imagine the often momentous choices facing people in Estonia during the war and post-war years – evoked by the image of the 'piano player' who is obliged to play a set repertoire. At times the choices were starkly black or white, with not much space for a grey zone. Either one fought in a German uniform or in that of the Red Army; the only alternative was to leave family and even homeland to fight in the forests or in Finland. Whereas for the War Generation these unresolved memories are linked to issues of collaboration during the war, the Post-War Children are more troubled by their accommodation to and complicity with the post-totalitarian regime. This brings us back to the metaphor of colours. Red and white figured prominently in the interviews that I conducted: in an attempt to distance themselves from the Soviet mindset, respondents often referred to themselves as white. For males in the War Generation the colour of the uniform worn at the end of the war became decisive for the rest of their lives, for instance because it prompted deportation or the need to flee the homeland.

Other unresolved memories are connected to trauma, loss and mourning. We saw that both the War Generation and Post-War Children share the experience of loss, but the former – which I labelled the Lost Generation – relate it more to the devastating human and material impact of the war years, whereas the latter – which I labelled the Fatherless Generation – connect it more to a loss of ideological belief. In this concluding chapter I shall delineate six personal strategies, or ways of talking about one's past, which the War Generation and the Post-War Children employed to make sense of loss and to regain meaning, which I entitle *resignation, distancing, denial, apologetics, glorification* and *destiny*.[3]

Each of these strategies requires a little additional comment. Some respondents would state that the situation during the war simply could not be communicated, being impossible to convey or comprehend: this brought with it a sense of resignation. Resignation was experienced after the war in relation to the losses that had been experienced (opportunities, freedom, beliefs and so on); but, more generally, it is a mode of talking about the past because respondents felt they had reached their limits when relating these painful experiences to me. Distancing was accomplished through jokes or other forms of intellectual abstraction (also through subtle changes in tone of voice during the interview). Respondents described their encounters with the KGB as 'games' of successfully outsmarting the system's oppressive institution, and testing its boundaries. Distancing oneself from oppression in this way allows the respondent to maintain an illusion of the power of the powerless. Another common phrase among my respondents (particularly Post-War Children) was, 'I knew it all the time, but I did not actualize it' – signifying a form of denial or 'double think', and making it appear as if they were not permitted at the time to draw their own conclusions.[4] Denial is often a defensive reaction caused by irritation and shame. Juhan Kahk, author of the official history of the ESSR, for instance, retrospectively claimed that it was due to his lack of knowledge that he interpreted the events of 1940 as a 'revolution' rather than an 'occupation'.[5] It is clear that at times compliance and active cooperation with the regime were a matter of sheer survival. Many respondents used the slightly apologetic expression 'people have to live' as a personal strategy of self-justification.[6] I referred to the image of the 'radish' – which connects back to the revolutionary-era colours of red and white – and the remarkable distinction between those real Bolsheviks who were red on the outside and the inside as opposed to the average Estonian communist party members who were red only on the outside.[7] The fifth strategy, glorification, is exemplified in the idea that all

'Estonians were resistance fighters', surviving against overwhelming odds, and is also found in many of the oral accounts of Estonian historians. The personal strategies of glorification and of apologetics were also evident on the level of official history writing, as discussed in Chapter 5. Finally, respondents employed metaphysical explanations to make sense of their life experiences: 'It was my destiny to go to prison camp' aptly captures the essence of this strategy and provides my shorthand for it.[8] Another respondent understood it as her 'fate' to live in Estonia, a fate she cannot and does not wish to change.[9] Because it is through 'talking about the past' that the respondents construct identity, these personal, verbal strategies of *resignation, distancing, denial, apologetics, glorification* and *destiny* provide some insight into different post-Soviet identities in Estonia today.

What does all this suggest for issues of collective cultural identity in the Baltic borderland, most notably in Estonia? What are the 'newly emerging identities', to borrow Mannheim's phrase from 1928? We saw that in contemporary Estonia the reconfiguration of identities and the codification of an official history are far from being consolidated: 'memory work', coping with loss, the regaining of meaning and the potential for reconciliation are all ongoing processes. Moreover, the inter-ethnic make-up of Estonian society and the effects of Soviet communism produced forms of cultural hybridity that are striking – though not unique to a post-Soviet setting, when we think for instance of the various effects of globalization; I pointed, for example, to Estonian Russians of the War Generation, and also to the diaspora identity of the Post-War Children of Russian settlers. The concept of cultural hybridity can also be applied to the notions of 'double consciousness' during the Soviet period, in that a sense of 'hybridization of identity' was determined also by the degree to which the individual was willing to accommodate to the Soviet system. These 'adaptive mechanisms' make the national 'myth of authenticity' redundant, because long-term occupation inevitably creates cultural hybridity, or what in the Estonian case the exile historian 'Siim' referred to as a 'Soviet Estonian mindset'.

A concept closely connected to cultural hybridity is 'liminality', which I consider instrumental for grasping the transitional nature of Estonian society today. Similar to a 'cultural hybrid', the (Estonian) 'liminary' is situated 'betwixt and between' the margin and the centre. This is an ambiguous state of limbo, no longer belonging to the 'Soviet' society, but *not yet* incorporated into the new society still in gestation.[10] I demonstrated that cultural hybridity has ethno-cultural, socio-political and ideological roots. As examples of newly emerging post-Soviet hybrid identities, we could point, first, to younger respondents of mixed ethno-cultural background who were forced by the changing political environment to reflect on and define their identity more carefully during the transition period, in the process making an innovative and critical contribution to Estonian society. A second example of post-Soviet hybrid identity is constituted by younger Russian speakers in Estonia, who label themselves not 'Estonian Russians' but 'Euro Russians' or 'Baltic Russians', thereby connecting back to the Baltic German legacy of the region.

Shadowlands demonstrates the importance of moving beyond nationalistic history writing, especially in post-conflict societies with divided and divisive memories. Going outside Estonia we can also think of Turkey, Cyprus, former Yugoslavia, Northern Ireland, Spain and Israel. Such a move is all the more important because this study suggests that the ethnic category is only one among a spectrum of group identifications, and that at times generational group identity can supersede ethnic belonging. We saw that in post-1991 Estonia the climate of the nationalizing state produced a shift from 'class' as a central category of identification to 'nation'. Consequently the new national historiography of the 1990s was soon fashioned around the ethnic binary of Estonian victims (the resisters and survivors) on one side and Soviet Russian perpetrators (the occupiers) on the other. This book highlights the importance of transcending such a reductive, exclusive national historiography and of publicly recognizing the multi-vocality of the different accounts of Estonia's troubled history, rather than reaching back into the shadowlands of a glorified past. Such a new form of historiography may do justice to the complexity of recent events by recognizing the criminal nature of the Soviet regime while also including a more balanced approach to the role of the Red Army as liberators from Nazism and to the complicity of Estonians with both of the totalitarian regimes.

And so, in line with Jörn Rüsen, I argue for a multi-faceted narrative, allowing a variety of perspectives and voices, in which the national culture should not be portrayed as a single and singular success story.[11] The integration of the Russian-speaking community within contemporary Estonia could be facilitated by transcending this reductive distinction between 'us' (good Estonians, victims) and 'them' ('bad' Russians, perpetrators).[12] But today the 'category of victimhood' (and to a growing extent that of resistance) is constitutive for Estonian identity, impeding real change in such stereotyping. In many ways it would be uncomfortable to admit that not all Russians have been 'villains', because in so doing Estonians would have to amend their textbooks and acknowledge the historical reality of (ethnic) Estonians who sympathized with and supported the Stalinist regime or Nazi Germany, and also that Estonians killed or deported other Estonians. Omar Bartov's discussion of the complexity of victimhood is revealing. He calls 'the victim trope a central feature of our time', and points out that 'it is a dangerous prism through which to view the world, for victims are produced by enemies, and enemies eventually make for more victims'.[13] In other words, pronounced collective suffering is a cyclical process, breeding the urge to look for one culprit after another. Bartov therefore suggests dropping the trope of victimhood altogether.

Although historical 'truth' can have healing properties, in reality these are often limited. The pursuit of truth and justice among professional historians (as exemplified through the Estonian Historians Commission's work) may be in conflict rather than in harmony with the purpose of inter-ethnic reconciliation, for often there is no chance that both warring sides will recognize the same truth. Moreover, history in Estonia has long been an 'existential' matter of national survival, with certain *lieux de mémoire* made into sacred taboo topics (proscriptive function of cultural memory), precluding any mediation of differences in historical interpretation.[14] Here, 'Zahkar' holds:

> When you take a small nation such as the Estonians of one million, then a national myth is a question of survival. Without it the Estonian nation would not exist and this makes the debate about the deconstruction of myth a somewhat delicate undertaking … If you tell an Estonian that he is also a relic of the homo sovieticus, he takes it as a personal offence, since a homo sovieticus is par excellence only a Russian. And a Russian is automatically a communist … To find your way [through this] as an individual – I always place myself … in no man's land.

This 'no man's land' lies between the various binaries and stereotypes that I have analysed. Ultimately I would argue for inter-ethnic and intergenerational reconciliation, and maintain with Rüsen that only through an open treatment of the past in the history textbooks, for example, and through public forgiving, can these dichotomies to gradually be transcended.[15] There is a lot to be said about the importance of coming to terms with a traumatic past. Certainly the moral duty to give a voice to those who suffered during Soviet communism is a worthy cause, but the story of Germany's *Vergangenheitsbewältigung* since 1945 suggests that the process will be painful and protracted.[16] It also raises challenging questions of intention and motive: we have to ask whether such memory politics is oriented towards the past or the future and, equally important, *cui bono?* – that is, who is benefiting from it? History came alive in the 1980s, when people's interest in 'their' history was rekindled, and revelations about the past mobilized them. Politicians, such as former prime minister Mart Laar, would connect to the people's existential need to become masters of their own past and to gain public recognition for what they perceive to be their historical truth. History was not 'dead'; this was certainly not the 'end of history' but rather its 'rebirth'. However, in post-1991 Estonia this process of restoration and rehabilitation of historical knowledge was always guided by a future orientation: to mobilize for and legitimize the new state.

Finally, then, let us move from the national level of history rewriting to the European plane. Undoubtedly the past that post-1945 Western Europe had to come to terms with is very different from the past that burdens post-1989 Eastern Europe. In an ostensibly united Europe of twenty-seven nation states, that asymmetrical double burden of memory has to be acknowledged and reconciled, otherwise the shadowlands of the past will haunt the politics of the future. Here this book may perhaps serve as a kind of a manual, helping West European and American readers to grasp the pain and complexity of the East European experience of the Second World War, and the resulting different interpretations that are little understood or even known in the West. I have sought to convey the conflicted sense of double occupation and the difficulties faced by Estonians in traversing their dangerous borderland between Teuton and Slav. That Janus-like historical experience raised the challenge of having to define one's national self into two directions.

What, in practical terms, are the prospects for developing a shared European memory and, by extension, a shared European identity? Recent initiatives in Eastern Europe reveal the strong – almost existential – desire of some of the new East European member states to enfold their account of Soviet communist crimes in a shared European memory of the war, and thus to gain recognition for their definition of historical truth.[17] The Estonian Historians' Commission and memorial culture, discussed in the previous chapter, is one example. Yet this bid for inclusivity is resisted by the West because it fundamentally shakes up the long-established anti-fascist narrative, centred on the Holocaust as the single most traumatic event of the twentieth century. By 2008 the signatories of the 'Prague Declaration' were already demanding a common European approach regarding the crimes of all totalitarian regimes, together with an acknowledgement of the common legacy of Soviet communism and Nazism. In line with the 'Prague process', an open letter to the European Union's justice commissioner was authored two years later by six post-communist states (the Czech Republic, Hungary, Romania, Bulgaria, Latvia and Lithuania) requiring that the denial of any totalitarian crime should be treated as equivalent to Holocaust denial.[18] And on 14 October 2011 in Prague, organizations from thirteen EU states – mostly from the former communist bloc but including Germany, Sweden and the Netherlands – established the Platform of

European Memory and Conscience, to 'encourage a broad, European-wide discussion about the causes and consequences of totalitarian rule, as well as about common European values, with the aim of promoting human dignity and human rights'.[19]

To be sure, on the official level political memories of the specific East European experience of the war and post-war years have been increasingly integrated into a wider shared European understanding of the Second World War. This is reflected in official commemorative speeches in the European Parliament and the European Commission.[20] On the level of political ritual, for example, the president of the European Parliament, Jerzy Buzek, delivered a speech marking the anniversary of the outbreak of the war at the Polish Westerplatte in September 2009. That same year the European Parliament passed a resolution to designate 23 August as the European Day of Remembrance of the victims of *all* totalitarian and authoritarian regimes, this being the date of the signing of the Molotov–Ribbentrop Pact in 1939. But these very cautious attempts to reconcile the diverse European experiences of the war and post-war years are considerably removed from the demands of the 'Prague process' and other post-communist countries to place the two totalitarian regimes on an explicitly equal footing.[21]

Yet again, in East European countries such as Estonia that share a double-totalitarian past, attempts at post-1991 national myth making are highly contentious because they involve redefining the categories of victim and hero.[22] These countries turn out to be particularly challenged when pushed to accept the anti-fascist narrative with the Holocaust as its central traumatic event. The notion of 'double genocide' was therefore increasingly appropriated as a strategy of historical revisionism to counter the imposition of the dominant Western narrative on their political memory.[23] But this is not acceptable to many groups in the West, particularly those who insist on the uniqueness of the Nazis' 'Final Solution'.[24]

Ultimately then, in post-Soviet Eastern Europe as in post-war Western Europe, coming to terms with the troubled past is a matter of time. In Estonia since 1991, discussing Estonian victimhood in an open way is still a sacrilege. Private family memories of the war have acquired truth-like qualities during the fifty years of Soviet rule, and the national history has an existential force for the collective cultural identity. So these notions can only change ever so gradually, as subsequent generations of historians move away from the valley of the shadow of war. But such social change requires that a more inclusive treatment of the complexities of the past is allowed to develop in the future – on both the national and the European levels. *Shadowlands* is offered as a small step in this long journey.

Notes

1. Referring to Poland's EU accession (in Snyder, *Bloodlands*, 406).
2. Here I am referring particularly to the Katyn massacre, in which 21,857 Poles – mostly reserve officers and professionals, such as doctors, lawyers and academics – were executed as a result of Stalin's order of 4 March 1940 in a deliberate targeting of the Polish elite (L. Rees. 2008. *World War Two behind Closed Doors: Stalin, the Nazis and the West*. London: BBC Books, 53, 55). Snyder (*Bloodlands*, 406) estimates that Poland lost 1.1 million non-Jewish civilians due to Soviet actions during the war, and another million in atrocities committed by the Germans.
3. Cf. H. Welzer, S. Moller and K. Tschuggnall. 2002. *'Opa war kein Nazi': Nationalsozialismus und Holocaust im Familiengedächtnis*. Frankfurt a. M.: S. Fischer.
4. 'Ülle-Mai'.
5. Kahrk, in M. Kerner and S. Stopinski. 1990. *Die Unabhängigkeit der baltischen Staaten in historischer Bilanz und als aktuelle Perspektive: Betrachtungen und Gespräche zu kontroversen Fragen der Innen- und Außenpolitik Litauens, Lettlands und Estlands sowie zum Stand der wissenschaftlichen Forschung*. Berlin: Berghof Stiftung für Konfliktforschung, 29.
6. 'Hanneleen'.
7. 'Ülle-Mai'.
8. 'Ervin'.
9. 'Ülle-Mai'.
10. But liminality must not be confused with marginality. My respondents were not alienated underdogs but very much part of society.
11. Rüsen in Imry Schweiger. 2002. 'Konflikte der Kulturen. Braunschweig: Historiker Jörn Rüsen im Georg Eckert Institut', *Braunschweiger Zeitung*, 30 Nov. 2002. See also Ricoeur ('Memory and Forgetting', 10–11) on writing a parallel history of the victims and the victors.
12. Cf. M. Zimmermann. 2002. 'Täter-Opfer-Dichitomien als Identitätsformen', in Konrad Jarausch (ed.), *Verletztes Gedächtnis: Erinnerungskultur und Zeitgeschichte im Konflikt*. Frankfurt. a. M: Campus Verlag, 199–216.
13. O. Bartov. 1998. 'Defining Enemies, Making Victims: Germans, Jews, and the Holocaust', *American Historical Review* 103(3): 811.
14. J. Jedlicki. 1999. 'Historical Memory as a Source of Conflict in Eastern Europe', *Communist and Post-Communist Studies* 32: 230–31.
15. Adam Michnik's famous slogan: 'amnesty yes … amnesia no'.
16. See Mary Fulbrook (*German National Identity*; and 2011. *Dissonant Lives: Generations and Violence through the German Dictatorship*. Oxford: Oxford University Press); and Norbert Frei (2005. *1945 und wir: Das Dritte Reich im Bewusstsein der Deutschen*. Munich: C.H. Beck).
17. http://www.memoryandconscience.eu/ (accessed 8 February 2012).
18. http://www.radio.cz/en/section/curraffrs/czech-mep-throws-damper-on-appeal-for-eu-ban-on-denial-of-communist-crimes (accessed 30 September 2011).
19. See http://www.memoryandconscience.eu/ (the declaration can be found under 'declarations') (accessed 8 February 2012).
20. This is based on a qualitative analysis of remembrance speeches related to the Second World War in the EP and EC between 1995 and 2010 conducted by L. van Suijlekom (2011. 'A Shared European History? Dealing with Divided Memory within the European Union', Universiteit Maastricht, MA thesis, June).

21. East European countries chose a different wording, namely the 'European Day of Remembrance of the Victims of Stalinism and Nazism'.
22. See Bartov, 'Defining Enemies'.
23. James Mark speaks acutely of 'double-genocide revisionism'. Diaspora historians started using the term 'Soviet genocide' to describe the repressions of Baltic people during the Stalinist era; another interrelated strategy is referring to the Nazi occupation as the 'lesser evil' when compared to Stalinist crimes; and lastly, the strategy of 'containing fascism', which places the Jewish suffering outside the national history unless it supports the national anti-communist narrative (Mark, 'Containing Fascism', 335, 362, 364; Mark, *Unfinished Revolution*, 93–125).
24. See, for instance, Peter Novick (1999. *The Holocaust in American Life*. New York: Mariner Books, 280), on the strategic decision of the American Jewish leadership in support of an embattled Israel to depict the Holocaust as a unique event and the emblematic Jewish experience.

APPENDICES

Appendix A:
Principal narrators quoted in chapters 5 and 6

1) **Birgit** (f.), b. 1965, Estonian, researcher in ethnography, living in Tartu (G 3).
2) **Class of Estonian students**, EHI, Tallinn Pedagogical University, 7 Oct. 2003.
3) **Eduard** (m.), b. 1950, Russian Armenian, linguist, intellectual, living in Tallinn (G 2).
4) **Elena** (f.), b. 1941, Russian, manual worker, municipal politician, living in Narva (G 2).
5) **Ervin** (m.), b. 1952, Estonian, architect, heater, former dissident, historian, works in the Estonian Immigration Office, living in Tallinn (G 2).
6) **Evgeny** (m.), b. 1957, Russian, historian, works at Narva Museum, living in Narva (G 2).
7) **Franka** (f.), b. 1965, Estonian, history teacher at the Estonian gymnasium, living in Narva (G 3).
8) **Hanneleen** (f.), b. 1936, Estonian, history teacher, teacher training, Professor at Tallinn Pedagogical University, living in Tallinn (G 1).
9) **Hariton** (m.), b. 1933, Russian, Professor emeritus of Linguistics, living in Tartu (G 1).
10) **Henrik** (m.), b. 1960, American Estonian, journalist (G 2)
11) **Iivo** (m.), b. 1925, Estonian exile, Professor emeritus of History, living in Uppsala (G 1).
12) **Illar** (m.), b. 1921, Estonian exile, PhD in Political Science, archivar, librarian, living in Uppsala (G 1).
13) **Indrek** (m.), b. 1965, Estonian, historian, journalist, living in Tallinn (G 3).
14) **Jaak** (m.), b. 1965, Estonian Canadian, Assistant Professor of History, living in Tartu (G 3).

15) **Juhan** (m.), b. 1953, Estonian Swede, Professor of Linguistics, living in Uppsala (G 2).
16) **Kalev** (m.), b. 1930, Estonian, Professor emeritus of History, living in Tartu (G 1).
17) **Kalju** (m.), b. 1955, Estonian, PhD in History, living in Tartu (G 3).
18) **Kalle** (m.), b. 1973, Swede of Estonian parents, PhD in Geography, living in Uppsala (G 3).
19) **Nelli** (f.), b. 1944, Estonian, sociologist, theatre director, living in Tallinn (G 2).
20) **Nicolaij** (m.), b. 1961, Russian, philologist, Estonian language teacher, MP, living in Tallinn (G 3).
21) **Niils** (m.), b. 1969, Estonian, historian, MP, member of EMS, living in Tallinn (G 4).
22) **Nikitor** (m.), b. 1952, Estonian Russian, senior researcher in Philosophy, living in Tallinn (G 2).
23) **Nora** (f.), b. 1945, Estonian, literature critic, writer, living in Tallinn (G 2).
24) **Olavi** (m.), b. 1973, Estonian, PhD in History, publisher, living in Tallinn (G 4).
25) **Oskar** (m.), b. 1960, Estonain, PhD in History, member of EMS, living in Tallinn (G 3).
26) **Paula** (f.), b. 1933, Estonian Russian, former minister in ESSR, Professor of Political Science at the Tallinn Pedagogical University, living in Tallinn (G 1).
27) **Pauls** (m.), b. 1948, Latvian, PhD in History, researcher, living in Stockholm (G 2).
28) **Pille** (f.), b. 1971, Estonian, sociologist, PhD in Psychology, living in Tartu (G 4).
29) **Polina** (f.), b. 1976, Estonian Russian, historian, living in Tallinn (G 4).
30) **Rein** (m.), b. 1929, Estonian, technical engineer, amateur historian, member of EMS, living in Narva (G 1).
31) **Siim** (m.), b. 1943, Estonian exile, Professor of History, former Minister of Defence in post-Soviet Estonia, living in Gothenburg and Kiel (G 2).
32) **Simon** (m.), b. 1956, Estonian, chimney sweeper, former dissident, worked for Radio Free Europe (Munich), now Occupation Museum, living in Tallinn (G 2).
33) **Tiina** (f.), b. 1970, Estonian, PhD in Psychology, living in Tartu (G 4).
34) **Ülle-Mai** (f.), b. 1948, Estonian, Professor of Social Science, living in Tallinn (G 2).

35) **Urmas** (m.), b. 1926, Estonian, Professor emeritus of History, politician after 1991, living in Tartu (G 1).
36) **Veera** (f.), b. 1971, Estonian, PhD in Ethnography, living in Tartu (G 4).
37) **Vilhelm** (m.) b. 1932, Estonian, Professor emeritus of History, living in Tallinn (G 1).
38) **Vilma** (f.), b. 1921, Estonian, Professor emeritus of History, living in Tallinn (G 1).
39) **Zahkar** (m.) b. 1963, Estonian Russian, historian, journalist, living in Tallinn (G 3).
40) **Zbigniev** (m.), b. 1950, Russian, tailor, amateur historian, living in Tallinn (G 2).
41) **Zinovij** (m.), b. 1973, Estonian Russian, PhD in history, former member EMS, living in England (G 4).

Appendix B:
Questionnaires

(A) Questionnaire for historians in Estonia (Estonians, Russians, Estonian Russians)

Personal background

1. Your family background? Siblings? Profession of parents? Where and when were you born? Where did you grow up? Where did you go to school? Where, when, what did you study and why (professional research interest)?

The past

2. The role of memories, history, culture in Estonia during foreign rule, occupation, Soviet Estonia, the transition, and today?
3. Personal memories of the inter-war period, of the Second World War (or the stories told by grandparents, parents, relatives and friends).
4. How did you learn about history? In school, at university, at home, through relatives, neighbours, friends? Can you give me examples?

National identity, national pride

5. How were Estonians able to preserve and transmit their cultural identity? Were they?

6. How did you learn about what it means to be Estonian?
7. What is at the base of Estonian national identity, what is it made of? What does it mean to be Estonian for you? How do you define your identity?
8. Could you single out events, places, figures connected to national pride?

Events of collective resistance

9. Can you think of events of collective resistance?
10. Who were the carriers of the true Estonian culture/identity during foreign rule, occupation, the Soviet period?
11. Did historians or intellectuals (teachers, professors, writers) in general play a special role in preserving or transmitting what it means to be Estonian (i.e. a counter-history and counter-memory)? The role of the Estonian Heritage Society in the transition?
12. Was dissent possible? What is dissent or resistance for you (e.g. partisans, dissidents)?
13. How did the political changes come about?
14. How do you view the role of Estonian exile historians for the social and political developments in Estonia?

Collective Suffering

15. Can you name events of collective suffering?
16. Were there cases of lustration in post-Soviet Estonia? How do you define collaboration? Who are the collaborators? What should be done with them? How to do justice, how to reconcile?
17. What is occupation? Do you call it occupation all the way from 1939 to 1991/94?

Taboo, shame, conflict

18. What changed in the interpretation of history since the late 1980s, after 1991?
19. Who is writing the official history in Estonia today?
20. Which events, which facts needed to be uncovered/discussed after 1991?
21. Whose history was destroyed after 1991?
22. What was deliberately forgotten during the Soviet period, taboo issues?
23. What is deliberately forgotten today? Any taboo issues or controversies?

24. What are the sources of conflict in Estonian society today? Social, political, historical, ethnic?
25. The Russian-speaking minority? How is reconciliation and integration possible?

Prospects for the future

26. What would you stress in children's history textbooks today?

(B) Questionnaire for Estonian intellectuals abroad (in Sweden and Germany)

Personal background

1. Your family background? Siblings? Profession of parents? Where and when were you born? Where did you grow up? Where did you go to school? Where, when, what did you study and why (professional research interest)?

Exile

2. How, when, why did you come to Sweden/Germany? Early memories?
3. Could your parents keep any ties with family members and friends or colleagues in Estonia during the Soviet period?
4. How did your parents explain their choice to live in exile?
5. How did you learn about history? School, university, home, through family, relatives, friends?
6. How did you learn about what it means to be Estonian?
7. Describe your integration into Swedish/German society. How was your education and professional life in Sweden/Germany?
8. How did the Estonians in Sweden/Germany preserve and maintain their memory of Estonia, their national identity since the mid-1940s (role of organization, schools, Church, other institutional networks)?
9. Were there conflicts (of a political nature) within the Estonian exile community in Sweden/Germany?
10. When did you first visit, or come back to Estonia? How are your memories about that? First impressions, experience?
11. Did Estonian intellectuals in exile play a role for Estonians in the ESSR? And if so, how? Did they play a part to bring about the change?
12. Is the Estonian community in Sweden/Germany different from other Estonian exile communities (Canada, USA, etc.)?

13. Can you point out differences in identity between homeland Estonians and those who lived abroad? Were there any conflicts? About what?

Changes

14. How did you experience the changes in 1990?
15. Did you think of returning (moving back) to Estonia after 1991? How often do you go back? How is your impression of the political changes?

Exile identity

16. How do you describe your own identity (e.g. hyphenated, émigré, exile, political refugee, expatriate)?
17. How did you learn about what it means to be Estonian?

On homeland Estonians

18. How were Estonians able to preserve or transmit their cultural identity during foreign rule?
19. Who is/was the carrier of the true Estonian culture/history during the Soviet period?
20. Did intellectuals, historians, dissidents play a special role in preserving this counter-history?

Present and future

21. Which events, which facts needed to be uncovered and officially discussed in post-Soviet Estonia? Examples of controversial topics? How do you view those political changes/developments in Estonia?
22. Future prospects for Estonia? Your vision?

BIBLIOGRAPHY

PRIMARY SOURCES

Schedule of Interviews

1. Class, group discussion, Tallinn, 7 Oct. 2003 (in English).
2. Eduard, interview, Tallinn, 11 Sept. 1996 (in English).
3. Elena, interview, Narva, 6 June 2002 (interpreter, in Russian).
4. Ervin, interview, Tallinn, 2 Oct. 2003 (in English).
5. Evgeny, interview, Narva, 6 June 2002 (interpreter, in Russian).
6. Franka, interview, Narva, 5 June 2002 (interpreter, in Estonian).
7. Hanneleen, interview, Tallinn, 13 June 2002 (in English).
8. Hariton, interview, Tartu, 2 June 2002 (interpreter, in Russian).
9. Henrik, interviews, London, 30 March, 20–21 April 2003 (in English and German).
10. Iivo, interview, Uppsala, 17 July 2002 (in German).
11. Illar, interview, Uppsala, 9 July 2002 (in English).
12. Indrek, interiew, Tallinn, 7 June 2002 (in English).
13. Jaak, interview, Tartu, 2 June 2002 (in English).
14. Juhan, interview, Tallinn, 26 Sept. 2003 (in English).
15. Kalev, interview, Tallinn, 3 June 2002 (in English).
16. Kalju, interview, Tartu, 6 Oct. 2003 (in German).
17. Kalle, interview, Uppsala, 11 July 2002 (in English).
18. Nelli, interview, Tallinn, 5 Oct. 2003 (in English).
19. Nicolaij, interview, Tallinn, 8 Oct. 2003 (interpreter, in Estonian).
20. Niils, interview, Tallinn, 11 June 2002 (in English).
21. Nikitor, interview, Tallinn, 2 Oct. 2003 (in English).
22. Nora, interview, Tallinn, 8 Oct. 2003 (in German).
23. Olavi, interview, Tallinn, 2 Oct. 2003 (in English).

24. Oskar, interview, Tallinn, 1 Oct. 2003 (in English).
25. Paula, interview, Tallinn, 9 Oct. 2003 (in English).
26. Pauls, interview, Stockholm, 19 July 2002 (in German).
27. Pille, interview, Tartu, 6 Oct. 2003 (in English).
28. Polina, interview, Tallinn, 5 Oct. 2003 (in English).
29. Rein, interview, Narva, 4 June 2002 (interpreter, in German and Estonian).
30. Siim, interview, Berlin, 17 April 2004 (in English).
31. Simon, interview, Tallinn, 7 June 2002 (in English).
32. Tiina, interview, Tartu, 6 Oct. 2003 (in English).
33. Ülle-Mai, interview, Tallinn, 8 June 2002 (in English).
34. Urmas, interview, Tartu, 7 Oct. 2003 (in German).
35. Veera and Biirgit, interview, Tartu, 10 June 2002 (in English).
36. Vilhelm, interview, Tallinn, 12 June 2002 (in German).
37. Vilma (and husband), interview, Tallinn, 11 June 2002 (in English and German).
38. Zahkar, interview, Tallinn, 12 June 2002 (in German).
39. Zbigniew, interview, Tallinn, 3 Oct. 2003 (interpreter, in Estonian and Russian).
40. Zinovij, interview, Tallinn, 18 Sept. 2003 (in English).

SECONDARY SOURCES

Aarelaid-Tart, Aili. 2001 'Estonian's Adaptation to New Cultural Realities after WWII', in 'Visions and Divisions: Challenges to European Sociology'. The 5th Conference of the European Sociological Association. Abstracts, University of Helsinki.

Aarelaid-Tart, Aili. 2003. 'Estonian-inclined Communists as Marginals', in R. Humphrey, R. Miller and E. Zdravomyslova (eds), *Biographical Research in Eastern Europe: Altered Lives and Broken Biographies*. Aldershot: Ashgate, 71–100.

Aarelaid-Tart, Aili. 2006. *Cultural Trauma and Life Stories*. Helsinki: Kikimora Publications, University of Helsinki.

Aarelaid-Tart, Aili, and Indrek Tart. 1995. 'Culture and the Development of Civil Society', *Nationalities Papers* 23(1): 153–66.

Aaskivi, Signe. 2001. 'Idea of Nation-State and Integration of Minorities as Two Competing Logics'. Paper presented at the seminar on '(Re-)nordification of Estonian Society', Tallinn, 20–22 April.

Abrahams, Ray. 1999. 'Nation and Identity: A View from Social Anthropology', in Michael Branch (ed.) *National History and Identity: Approaches to the Writing of National History in the North-East Baltic Region, Nineteenth and Twentieth Centuries*, Studia Fennica Ethnologica 6. Helsinki: Finnish Literature Society, 34–47.

Abrams, Dominic, and Michael Hoog (eds). 1991. *Social Identity Theory*. New York: Springer.

Adamson, A., and S. Valdmaa. 1999. *Eesti ajalugu gümnaasiumlile*. Tallinn: Kirjastus Koolibri.

Adorno, Theodor W. 1973. *Studien zum autoritären Charakter*. Frankfurt a. M.: Suhrkamp [first publ. in English 1950].

Agar, Michael H. 1996. *The Professional Stranger: An Informal Introduction to Ethnography*, 2nd edn. San Diego: Academic Press.

Ahonen, Sirka. 1992. *Clio sans Uniform: A Study of the Post-Marxist Transformation of the History Curricula in East Germany and Estonia, 1986–1991*. Soumalaisen Tiedeakatemian Toimituksia Annales Academiae Scientiarum Fennicae, Sarja-Ser. B Nide-Tom. 264. Helsinki: Suomalainen Tiedeakatemia.

Alapuro, Risto (ed.). 1985. *Small States in Comparative Perspective: Essays for Erik Allardt*. Oslo: Norwegian University Press.

Alexiev, Alexander R. 1983. *Dissent and Nationalism in the Soviet Baltic*. A Project AIR FORCE Report for the US Air Force. Santa Monica, CA: Rand.

Alexopoulos, Golfo, Julie Hessler and Kiril Tomoff (eds). 2011. *Writing the Stalin Era: Sheila Fitzpatrick and Soviet Historiography*. Basingstoke: Palgrave Macmillian.

Alheit, Peter. 1989. 'Zählform und "soziales Gedächtnis": Beispiel beginnender Traditionsbildung im autobiographischen Erinnerungsprozess', in Peter Alheit and Erika M. Hoerning (eds), *Biographisches Wissen. Beiträge zu einer Theorie lebensgeschichtlicher Erfahrung*. Frankfurt: Campus Verlag, 123–47.

Alheit, Peter. 1996. 'Changing Basic Rules of Biographical Construction: Modern Biographies at the End of the 20th Century', in Ansgar Weymann and Walter R. Heinz (eds), *Society and Biography: Interrelationships between Social Structure, Institutions and the Life Course*. Weinheim: Deutscher Studien Verlag, 111–28.

Ambrosio, Thomas. 2009. *Authoritarian Backlash: Russian Resistance to Democratization in the Former Soviet Union*. Farnham: Ashgate.

Anderson, Benedict. 1991. *Imagined Communities: Reflections on the Origin and Spread of Nationalism*. London: Verso.

Anderson, Edgar. 1969. 'The Role of Baltic Historians Abroad: Present Situation and Perspectives', in Ivar Ivask (ed.), 'Association for the Advancement of Baltic Studies: First Conference on Baltic Studies, Summary of Proceedings'. Tacoma, WA: Pacific Lutheran University, 48–51.

Andriansen, Inge, and Birgit Jenvold. 1998. 'Dänemark: Für Fahne, Sprache und Heimat', in Monika Flacke (ed.), *Mythen der Nationen. Ein Europäisches Panorama*. Berlin: Deutsches Historisches Museum, 83–86.

Anepaio, Terje. 2001. 'Trauma and Memory: Repressed Estonians Coping with the Past', in Anepaio and Kõresaar (eds), *Kultur ja Mälu*, 198–215.

Anepaio, Terje. 2002. 'Past Shared and Erased: The Obliteration of Tragic Experience in the Social Memory of Estonians'. Paper presented at conference on 'The Presence of the Past: Transformation and Dealing with the Past in Eastern and Central Europe', 23–25 March, Humboldt University Berlin.

Anepaio, Terje, and Ene Kõresaar (eds). 2001. *Kultuur ja Mälu: Konverentsi materjale*. Studia Ethnologica Tartuensia 4, Tartu: Tartu Ülikooli.

Ankersmit, F.R. 1998. 'Hayden White's Appeal to the Historians', *History and Theory* 37(2): 194–219.

Ankersmit, F.R. 2001. 'Rüsen on History and Politics', in F.R. Ankersmit, *Historical Representation*. Stanford, CA: Stanford University Press, 262–80.

Appleby, Joyce, Lynn Hunt and Margaret Jacob. 1994. *Telling the Truth about History*. New York: Norton.

Arendt, Hannah. 1986. *Elemente und Ursprünge totaler Herrschaft*. Munich: Pieper.

Arjakas, K., M. Laur and K. Mäesalu. 1991. *Eesti ajalugu: õpik 11. Klassile*. Tallinn: Kirjastus Koolibri.

Armstrong, John. 1968. 'Collaboration in World War II: The Integral Nationalist Variant in Eastern Europe', in *Journal of Modern History* 40(3): 396–410.

Armstrong, John. 1982. *Nations before Nationalism*. Chapel Hill: University of North Carolina Press.

Assmann, Aleida. 1986. 'Opting In and Opting Out', in H.U. Gumbrecht and K.L. Pfeiffer (eds), *Stil: Geschichten und Funktionen eines Kulturwissenschaftlichen Diskurselements*. Frankfurt a. M.: Suhrkamp, 127–43.

Assmann, Aleida. 1993. *Arbeit am nationalen Gedächtnis. Eine kurze Geschichte der deutschen Bildungsidee*. Frankfurt a. Main: Campus Verlag.

Assmann, Aleida. 1995. 'Funktionsgedächtnis und Speichergedächtnis – Zwei Modi der Erinnerung', in Kristin Platt and Mihran Dabag (eds), *Generation und Gedächtnis. Erinnerungen und kollektive Identitäten*. Opladen: Leske & Budrich, 169–85.

Assmann, Aleida. 1998. 'Wozu 'nationales Gedenken?', in Ewa Kobylinska and Andreas Lawaty (eds), *Erinnern, vergessen, verdrängen. Polnische Erfahrungen*. Wiesbaden: Harrassowitz Verlag, 111–32.

Assmann, Aleida. 1999. *Erinnerungsäume: Formen und Wandlungen des kulturellen Gedächtnisses*. Munich: C.H. Beck.

Assmann, Aleida. 2001. 'Wie wahr sind Erinnerungen?', in Harald Welzer (ed.), *Das soziale Gedächtnis. Geschichte Erinnerung Tradierung*. Hamburg: Hamburger Edition diskord, 103–22.

Assmann, Aleida. 2006. *Der Lange Schatten der Vergangenheit*. Munich: C.H. Beck.

Assmann, Aleida, and Jan Assmann. 1990. 'Aspekte einer Theorie des unkommunikativen Handelns', in Jan Assmann and Dietrich Harth (eds), *Kultur und Konflikt*. Frankfurt: S. Fischer, 11–48.

Assmann, Aleida, and Ute Frevert (eds). 1999. *Geschichtsvergessenheit, Geschichtsversessenheit. Vom Umgang mit deutschen Vergangenheiten nach 1945*. Stuttgart: DVA.

Assmann, Aleida, and Heidrun Friese (eds). 1998. *Identitäten*. Frankfurt a. M.: Suhrkamp.

Assmann, Aleida, and Dietrich Harth (eds). 1991. *Kultur als Lebenswelt und Monument*. Frankfurt: S. Fischer.

Assmann, Jan. 1988. 'Kollektives Gedächtnis und kulturelle Identität', in Jan Assmann and Toni Hölscher (eds), *Kultur und Gedächtnis*. Frankfurt a. M.: Suhrkamp, 9–19.

Assmann, Jan. 1995. 'Erinnern, um dazu zugehören. Kulturelles Gedächtnis, Zugehörigkeitsstruktur und normative Vergangenheit', in Kristin Platt and Mihran Dabag (eds), *Generation und Gedächtnis. Erinnerung und Kollektive Identitäten*. Opladen: Leske & Budrich, 51–75.

Assmann, Jan. 1997. *Das kulturelle Gedächtnis. Schrift, Erinnerung und politische Identität in frühen Hochkulturen*. Munich: C.H. Beck.

Assmann, Jan. 2007. *Religion und kulturelles Gedächtnis*. Munich: C.H. Beck.

Assmann, Jan. 2011. *Cultural Memory and Early Civilization: Writing, Remembrance, and Political Imagination*. Cambridge: Cambridge University Press.

Assmann, Jan, and Dietrich Harth. 1992. 'Frühe Formen politischer Mythomotorik. Fundierende, kontrapräsentische und revolutionäre Mythen', in Jan Assmann and Ditriech Harth (eds), *Revolution und Mythos*. Frankfurt a. M.: Suhrkamp, 39–62.

Augstein, Rudolf, et al. 1987. *Historikerstreit, Dokumentation der Kontroverse um die Einzigartigkeit der nationalsozialistischen Judenvernichtung*. Munich: Piper.

Bakhtin, Mikhail. 1981. *The Dialogic Imagination: Four Essays*, ed. Michael Holquist. Austin: University of Texas Press.

Balibar, Etienne. 1991. 'Is there a Neo-racism?', in Etienne Balibar and Immanuel Wallerstein, *Race, Nation, Class*. London: Verso.

Barrera, José Carlos Bermejo. 2001. 'Making History, Talking about History', *History and Theory* 40(2): 190–205.

Barth, Frederik. 1970. *Ethnic Groups and Boundaries: The Social Organisation of Culture Difference*. London: George Allen & Unwin.

Barthes, R. 1983. 'Inaugural Lecture, College de France', in Susan Sonntag (ed.), *Barthes: Selected Writings*. London: Fontana.

Bartlett, Charles. 1967. *Remembering: A Study in Experimental and Social Psychology*. Cambridge: Cambridge University Press.

Bartov, Omar. 1998. 'Defining Enemies, Making Victims: Germans, Jews, and the Holocaust', *American Historical Review* 103(3): 771–816.

Bartov, Omar. 2000. *Mirrors of Destruction: War, Genocide, and Modern Identity*. New York: Oxford University Press.

Baumann, Zygmut. 1987. 'Intellectuals in Eastern Europe: Continuity and Change', in *East European Politics and Society* 1(2): 162–86.

Baumeister, Roy F., and Stephen Hastings. 1997. 'Distortions of Collective Memory: How Groups Flatter and Deceive Themselves', in J. Pennebaker, Dario Paez and Bernard Rimé (eds), *Collective Memory of Political Events: Social Psychological Perspectives*. Mahwah, NJ: Lawrence Erlbaum Associates, 277–94.

Bédarida, Francois. 2000. 'The Historian's Craft, Historicity, and Ethics', in Joep Leerssen and Ann Rigney (eds), *Historians and Social Values*. Amsterdam: Amsterdam University Press, 69–76.

Beissinger, Mark. 1995. *Nationalist Mobilization and the Collapse of the Soviet State*. Cambridge: Cambridge University Press.

Bellelli, Guglielmo, and Mirella A.C. Amatulli. 1997. 'Nostalgia, Immigration and Collective Memory', in J. Pennebaker, Dario Paez and Bernard Rimé (eds), *Collective Memory of Political Events: Social Psychological Perspectives*. Mahwah, NJ: Lawrence Erlbaum Associates, 209–20.

Benjamin, Walter. 1991. *Das Passagen-Werk. Gesammelte Schriften*, Vol. V. Frankfurt a. M.: Suhrkamp.

Benjamin, Walter. 1977. *Illuminationen. Gesammelte Schriften*, Vol. I. Frankfurt a. M.: Suhrkamp.

Bennich-Björkman, Li. 2001. '"Our generation is the same everywhere...": Investigating the Tenacity of Political Culture among the Estonian Inter-war Generation in Exile and at Home'. Conference paper at the seminar on '(Re-)nordification of Estonian Society', Tallinn, 20–22 April.

Bennich-Björkmann, Li. 2007. 'Civic Commitment, Political Culture and the Estonian Inter-War Generation', in *Nationalities Papers* 35(1): 1–21.

Benz, Wolfgang, and Juliane Wetzel (eds). 1998. *Solidarität und Hilfe für Juden während der NS-Zeit: Regionalstudies 2, Ukraine, Frankreich, Böhmen und Mähren, Österreich, Lettland, Litauen, Estland*. Berlin: Metropol.

Berghe, Pierre van den. 1978. 'Race and Ethnicity: A Socio-biological Perspective', *Ethnic and Racial Studies* 1(4): 401–11.

Berquist, William H., and Berne Weiss. 1994. *Freedom! Narratives of Change in Hungary and Estonia*. San Francisco: Jossey-Bass Inc.

Beyrau, Dietrich. 2000. 'Nationalsozialistisches Regime und Stalin-System. Ein riskanter Vergleich', in *Osteuropa* 50(6): 709–29.

Bhabha, Homi K. (ed.). 1990a. *Nation and Narration*. London: Routledge.

Bhabha, Homi K. 1990b. 'DissemiNation: Time, Narrative, and the Margins of the Modern Nation', in Homi K. Bhabha (ed.), *Nation and Narration*. London: Routledge, 289–322.

Bhabha, Homi K. 1994. *The Location of Culture*. London: Routledge.

Bhabha, Homi K. 1996. 'Culture's In-Between', in Stuart Hall and Paul du Gay (eds), *Questions of Identity*. London: Sage, 53–60.

Billig, Michael. 1997. *Banal Nationalism*. London: Sage.

Birn, Ruth Bettina. 2001. 'Collaboration with Nazi Germany in Eastern Europe: The Case of the Estonian Security Police', in *Contemporary European History* 10(2): 181–98.

Bollerup, Soren Rinder, and Christian Dons Christensen. 1997. *Nationalism in Eastern Europe: Causes and Consequences of the National Revivals and Conflicts in Late 20th Century Eastern Europe*. London: Macmillan.

Bonnell, Victoria (ed.). 1996. *Identities in Transition: Eastern Europe and Russia after the Collapse of Communism*. Berkeley: University of California, Center for Slavic and East European Studies, Research Series, Number 93.

Borst, Arno. 1979. 'Barbarossas Erwachen – zur Geschichte der Deutschen Identität', in Odo Marquard and Karlheinz Stierle (eds), Identität: Kolloquium der Forschungsstelle 'Poetik und Hermeneutik', Munich: Fink, 17–60.

Bourdieu, Pierre. 1977. *Outline of a Theory of Practice*. Cambridge: Cambridge University Press.

Bourdieu, Pierre. 1990a. *In Other Words, Essays Towards a Reflexive Sociology*. Cambridge: Polity Press.

Bourdieu, Pierre. 1990b. *The Logic of Practice*. Cambridge: Polity Press.

Bourdieu, Pierre. 1993. *The Field of Cultural Production: Essays on Art and Literature* (ed. Randal Johnson). Cambridge: Polity Press.

Brady, Henry E., and Cynthia S. Kaplan. 2001. 'Subjects to Citizens: From Nonvoting, to Protesting, to Voting in Estonia during the Transition to Democracy', in *Journal of Baltic Studies* 32: 347–78.

Branch, Michael. 1994. 'The Invention of a National Epic', in Michael Branch and Celia Hawkesworth (eds), *The Uses of Tradition: A Comparative Enquiry into the Nature, Uses and Functions of Oral Poetry in the Balkans, the Baltic, and Africa*. London: SSEES, 195–212.

Brass, Paul R. 1991. *Ethnicity and Nationalism: Theory and Comparison*. New Delhi: Sage.

Brockmeier, Jens, and Qi Wang. 2002. 'Autobiographical Remembering as Cultural Practice: Understanding the Interplay between Memory, Self and Culture', in *Culture and Psychology* 8(1): 45–65.

Broszat, Martin, Hans-Adolf Jacobsen and Helmut Krausnick (eds). 1965. *Anatomie des SS-Staates. Konzentrationslager, Kommisarbefehl, Judenverfolgung*, Vol. II. Olten & Freiburg i. Br.: Walter Verlag.

Brown, R., and J. Kulik. 1977. 'Flashbulb Memories', *Cognition* 5(1): 73–99.

Brubaker, Rogers. 1996. *Nationalism Reframed: Nationhood and the National Question in the New Europe*. Cambridge: Cambridge University Press.

Brubaker, Rogers. 2004. *Ethnicity without Groups*. Cambridge, MA: Harvard University Press.

Brüggemann, Karsten. 1995. 'Von der führenden Schicht zur nationalen Minderheit. Zur Klärung der Rolle der estländischen deutschen Minderheit bei der Begründung der Republik Estlands 1918–1919', in 'Estland und seine Minderheiten: Esten, Deutsche, Russen im 19. und 20. Jahrhundert', *Nord Ost Archiv* 4(2): 453–79.

Brüggemann, Karsten. 1997. 'Die deutsche Minderheit in Estland und Konstituierung des Estnischen Staates', in Boris Meissner et al. (eds), *Die Deutsche Volksgruppe in Estland. Während der Zwischenkriegszeit und Aktuelle Fragen des deutsch-estnischen Verhältnisses*. Hamburg: Bibliotheca Baltica.

Brüggemann, Karsten. 1998. 'Von der Sezession zur Okkupation: Die Entwicklung der Estnischen Republik und ihre Beziehungen zur SU 1920–1940', in Jörg Hakmann (ed.), *Estland – Partner im Ostseeraum*. Lübeck: Ostseeakademie, 57–74.

Brüggemann, Karsten. 2001. 'Von der Renationalisierung zur Demontage nationaler Helden. Oder: Wie schreibt man estnische Geschichte?', *Osteuropa* 7: 810–19.

Brüggemann, Karsten, and Andres Kasekamp. 2008, 'The Politics of History and the "War of Monuments" in Estonia', *Nationalities Papers* 36(3): 425–48.

Brundage, James A. 1961. *The Chronicle of Henry of Livonia*. Madison: University of Wisconsin Press.

Brunn, Gerhard. 1992. 'Historical Consciousness and Historical Myths', in Andreas Kappeler (ed.), *The Formation of National Elites, Comparative Studies on Government and Non-dominant Ethnic Groups in Europe, 1850–1940*. New York: New York University Press, 327–38.

Bubnys, Arunas. 2003. 'Die litauische Hilfspolizeibataillone und der Holocaust', in Vincas Bartusevicius, Joachim Tauber and Wolfram Wette (eds), *Holocaust in Litauen. Krieg, Judenmorde und Kollaboration im Jahre 1941*. Cologne: Böhlau, 117–31.

Bude, Heinz. 1995. *Das Altern einer Generation. Die Jahrgänge 1938–1948*. Frankfurt a. M.: Surhkamp.

Bude, Heinz. 2000. 'Die biographische Relevanz der Generationen', in M. Kohli and M. Szydkij (eds), *Generationen in Familie und Gesellschaft*. Opladen: Leske & Budrich, 19–35.

Burant, Stephen R., and Voytek Zubek. 1993. 'Eastern Europe's Old Memories and New Realities: Resurrecting the Polish–Lithuanian Union', in *EEPS* 7(2): 370–93.

Burg, Steven L. 1994. 'Nationalism Redux: Through the Glass of the Post Communist States Darkly', in Minton F. Goldman (ed.), *Russia, the Eurasian Republics, and Central Eastern Europe*. Guilford, CT: Dushkin, 162–66.

Burke, Peter. 1989. 'History as Social Memory', in Thomas Butler (ed.), *Memory: History, Culture and the Mind*. Oxford: Blackwell, 97–113.

Burke, Peter. 1991. 'Geschichte als soziales Gedächtnis', in Aleida Assmann and Dietrich Harth (eds), *Mnemosyne, Formen und Funktionen kultureller Erinnerung*. Frankfurt: S. Fischer, 289–305.

Burke, Peter. 1998. *Offene Geschichte. Die Schule der 'Annales'*. Frankfurt a. M: S. Fischer, 37–57.

Burke, Peter. 2004. *What is Cultural History?* Cambridge: Polity.

Burleigh, Michael. 1988. *Germany Turns Eastwards: A Study of Ostforschung in the Third Reich*. Cambridge: Cambridge University Press.

Butenschön, Marianna. 1992. *Estland, Lettland, Litauen. Das Baltikum auf dem langen Weg in die Freiheit*. Munich: Piper.

Calhoun, Craig. 1997. *Concepts in Social Science: Nationalism.* Buckingham: Open University Press.

Carr, David. 1997. 'Die Realität der Geschichte', in Klaus E. Müller and Jörn Rüsen (eds), *Historische Sinnbildung. Problemstellungen, Zeitkonzepte, Wahrnehmungshorizonte, Darstellungsstrategien.* Reinbek bei Hamburg: Rowohlt-Taschenbuch-Verlag, 309–27.

Carr, E.H. 1990. *What is History?* London: Penguin Books.

Cassese, Antonio. 2006. 'Balancing the Prosecution of Crimes against Humanity and Non-Retroactivity of Criminal Law: The Kolk and Kislyiy v. Estonia Case before the ECHR', in *Journal of International Criminal Justice* 4(2): 410–18.

Chartier, Robert. 1988. 'Geistesgeschichte oder histoire des mentalités?', in Dominik LaCapra and Steven L. Kaplan (eds), *Geschichte denken. Neubestimmung und Perspektiven moderner europäischer Geistesgeschichte.* Frankfurt a. M: S. Fischer, 11–44.

Chartier, Roger. 1988. *Cultural History: Between Practices and Representations.* Cambridge: Polity Press.

Chartier, Roger. 1989. 'Text, Printings, Readings', in Lynn Hunt (ed.), *New Cultural History.* Berkeley: University of California Press, 154–75.

Chernevych, Andriy. 2000. *Victory Day in the USSR: Shaping the Memory of the Great Patriotic War.* MA thesis, Central European University, Budapest.

Christiansen, Eric. 1980. *The Northern Crusades: The Baltic and the Catholic Frontier 1100–1525.* London: Macmillan.

Chubarov, Alexander. 2001. *Russia's Bitter Path to Modernity: A History of the Soviet and Post-Soviet Eras.* London: Bloomsbury.

Cipolla, Carlo. 1969. *Literacy and Development in the West.* Harmondsworth: Penguin.

Clemens, Walter C. Jr. 1990. *Baltic Independence and Russian Empire.* London: Macmillan.

Cohen, Shari J. 1999. *Politics without a Past: The Absence of History in Post-Communist Nationalism.* Durham, NC: Duke University Press.

Cohen, Stanley. 2001. *States of Denial: Knowing about Atrocities and Suffering.* Cambridge: Polity Press.

Colley, Linda. 1992. *Britons: Forging the Nation, 1707–1837.* New Haven, CT: Yale University Press.

Connelly, John. 2000. *Captive University: The Sovietization of East German, Czech, and Polish Higher Education, 1945–56.* Chapel Hill: University of North Carolina Press.

Connerton, Paul. 1989. *How Societies Remember.* Cambridge: Cambridge University Press.

Connor, Walker. 1990. 'When is the Nation?', *Ethnic and Racial Studies* 13(1): 92–103.

Conway, Martin. 1997a. *Recovered Memories and False Memories*. Oxford: Oxford University Press.

Conway, Martin. 1997b. 'Inventory of Experience: Memory and Identity', in James Pennebaker, Dario Paez and Bernard Rimé (eds), *Collective Memory of Political Events: Social Psychological Perspective*. Mahwah, NJ: Lawrence Erlbaum Associates, 21–45.

Conze, Werner. 1985. 'Ethnogenese und Nationsbildung – Ostmitteleuropa als Beispiel', in *Studien zur Ethnogenese*. Opladen: Westdeutscher Verlag, 189–206.

Cooperm, J.C. (ed.). 1986. *Illustriertes Lexikon der traditionellen Symbole*. Leipzig: Dre Lillien Verlag.

Coser, Lewis A. (ed.). 1992. *Maurice Halbwachs: On Collective Memory*. Chicago: University of Chicago Press.

Creuzberger, Stefan, Ingo Mannteufel and Jutta Unser. 2000. 'Kommunismus und Terror. Das Schwarzbuch des Kommunismus – Hauptthesen und Argumente', *Osteuropa* 50(6): 585–92.

Croce, Benedetto. 1949. *My Philosophy, and Other Essays on the Moral and Political Problems of our Time*. London: Allen & Unwin.

Crowley, David, and Susan E. Reid (eds). 2002. *Socialist Spaces: Sites of Everyday Life in the Eastern Bloc*. New York: Berg.

Cushman, Thomas. 1997. 'Collective Punishment and Forgiveness: Judgements of Post-communist National Identities by the "Civilised West"', in S.G. Mestrovic (ed.), *Genocide after Emotion: The Postemotional Balkan War*. London: Routledge, 184–94.

Cutler, William. 1996. 'Accuracy in Oral History Interviewing', in David K. Dunaway and Willa K. Baum (eds), *Oral History: An Interdisciplinary Anthology*, 2nd Edition. Walnut Creek, CA: AltaMira Press, 99–106.

Dabag, Mihran. 1995. 'Tradionelles Erinnern und historische Verantwortung', in Kristin Platt and Mihran Dabag (eds), *Generation und Gedächtnis: Erinnerung und Kollektive Identitäten*. Opladen: Leske & Budrich, 76–106.

Dallin, Alexander. 1978. 'The Baltic States between Nazi Germany and Soviet Russia', in V. Stanley Vardys and Romuald J. Misiunas (eds), *The Baltic States in Peace and War, 1917–1945*. University Park: Pennsylvania State University Press, 97–109.

Davis, Fred. 1979. *Yearning for Yesterday: A Sociology of Nostalgia*. New York: The Free Press.

Davies, Norman. 1997. *Europe: A History*. London: Pimlico.

Davies, Norman. 2011. *Vanished Kingdoms: The History of Half-Forgotten Europe*. London: Penguin.

Dehio, Georg. 1927. 'Vom baltischen Deutschtum', *Mitteilungen der Akademie zur wissenschaftlichen Erforschung und zur Pflege des Deutschtums* 10: 341–45.

Denzin, Norman K. 1989. *Interpretive Biography: Qualitative Research Methods*. London: Sage.

Denzin, Norman K. 2000. 'The Practices and Politics of Interpretation', in Norman K. Denzin and Yvonna S. Lincoln (eds), *Handbook of Qualitative Research*, 2nd edn. London: Sage, 897–922.

Dieckmann, Christoph, Christian Gerlach and Wolf Gruner (eds). 2003. *Kooperation und Verbrechen. Formen der Kollaboration im östlichen Europa 1939–1945*. Göttingen: Wallstein Verlag.

Dietsch, Johan. 2006. *Making Sense of Suffering: Holocaust and Holodomor in Ukrainian Culture*. Lund: Lund University Press.

Diner, Dan (ed.). 1988. *Ist der Nationalsozialismus Geschichte? Zu Historisierung und Historikerstreit*. Frankfurt: S. Fischer.

Diner, Dan. 2000. 'Gedächtnis und Erkenntnis: Nationalismus und Stalinismus im Vergleichsdiskurs', *Osteuropa* 50(6): 698–708.

Dirks, Nicholas B., Geoff Eley and Sherry B. Ortner (eds). 1994. *Culture/Power/History: A Reader in Contemporary Social Theory*. Princeton, NJ: Princeton University Press.

Dobson, Miriam. 2009. *Khrushchev's Cold Summer: Gulag Returnees, Crime, and the Fate of Reform after Stalin*. Ithaca, NY: Cornell University Press.

Dohrn, Verena. 1994. *Baltische Reise. Vielvölkerlandschaft. Das Alte Europa*. Frankfurt am Main: S. Fischer.

Donskis, Leonidas. 1999. 'Concepts of Nationalism in 20th Century Lithuania', in Christopher Williams and Thanasis D. Sfikas (eds), *Ethnicity and Nationalism in Russia, the CIS and the Baltic States*. Aldershot: Ashgate, 324–50.

Douglas, Mary. 1966. *Purity and Danger: Analysis of Concepts of Pollution and Taboo*. New York: Praeger.

Douglas, Mary. 1975. *Implicit Meanings: Essays in Anthropology*. London: Routledge & Kegan Paul.

Douglas, Mary. 1986. *How Institutions Think*. London: Routledge & Kegan Paul.

Drakulić, Slavenka. 1993. *How We Survived Communism and Even Laughed*. London: Vintage.

Dreifelds, Juri. 1996. *Latvia in Transition*. Cambridge: Cambridge University Press.

Drobizheva, L.M. 1991. 'The Role of the Intelligentsia in Developing National Consciousness among the Peoples of the USSR under Perestroika', *Ethnic and Racial Studies* 14(1): 87–99.

Dudwick, Nora. 2000. 'Postsocialism and the Fieldwork of War', in Nora Dudwick and Hermine G. De Soto (eds), *Fieldwork Dilemmas: Anthropologists in Postsocialist States*. Madison: University of Wisconsin Press, 13–32.

Duijzings, Ger. 1992. 'De Egyptenaren in Kosovo en Macedonië', *Amsterdams Sociologisch Tijdschrift* 18(4): 24–38.

Dunaway, David K. 1996. 'Introduction: The Interdisciplinary of Oral History', in David K. Dunaway and Willa K. Baum (eds), *Oral History: An Interdisciplinary Anthology*, 2nd edn. Walnut Creek, CA: AltaMira Press, 7–22.

Duncan, W. Raymond, and Paul Holman, Jr. (eds). 1994. *Ethnic Nationalism and Regional Conflict*. Boulder, CO: Westview Press.

Durkheim, Emile. 1964. *The Elementary Forms of the Religious Life*. London: Allen & Unwin.

Eco, Umberto. 2000a. 'Between Author and Text', in Norman K. Denzin and Yvonna S. Lincoln (eds), *Handbook of Qualitative Research*. 2nd edition. London: Sage Publications, 67–88.

Eco, Umberto. 2000b. 'Overinterpreting Texts', in Norman K. Denzin and Yvonna S. Lincoln (eds), *Handbook of Qualitative Research*. 2nd edn. London: Sage Publications, 45–66.

Eder, K., and W. Spohn (eds). 2005. *Collective Memory and European Identity: Effects of Integration and Enlargement*. Aldershot: Ashgate.

Ehala, M. 2009. 'The Bronze Soldier: Identity Threat and Maintenance in Estonia', *Journal of Baltic Studies* 40(1): 139–58.

Eisenstadt, Shmuel N. 1991. 'Die Mitwirkung der Intellektuellen an der Konstruktion lebensweltlicher und transzendenter Ordnung', in Aleida Assmann and Dietrich Harth (eds), *Kultur als Lebenswelt und Monument*. Frankfurt: S. Fischer, 123–32.

Eisenstadt, Shmuel N. 2000. 'Multiple Modernities', in *Daedalus* 129(1): 1–29.

Elias, Norbert. 1989. *Studien über die Deutschen: Machtkämpfe und Habitusentwicklung im 19. und 20. Jahrhundert*. Frankfurt: Suhrkamp.

Ellis, Carolyn, and Arthur P. Bochner. 2000. 'Autoethnography, Personal Narrative, Reflexivity: Researcher as Subject', in Norman K. Denzin and Yvonna S. Lincoln (eds), *Handbook of Qualitative Research*. 2nd edn. London: Sage Publications, 733–68.

Ellrich, Lutz. 1999. *Verschriebene Fremdheit. Die Ethnographie kultureller Brüche bei Clifford Geertz und Stephen Greenblatt*. Frankfurt and New York: Campus.

Estonian State Commission on the Examination of the Policies of Repression. 2005. The White Book. Losses Inflicted on the Estonian Nation by Occupation Regimes 1940–91. Tallinn: Estonian Encyclopedia Publishers.

Evans, Richard J. 1989. *In Hitler's Shadow: West German Historians and the Attempt to Escape the Nazi Past*. London: I.B. Taurus.

Fara, Patricia, and Karalyn Patterson (eds). 1998. *Memory*. Cambridge: Cambridge University Press.

Feest, David. 1998. 'Die Entstehung der estnischen Nation', in Jörg Hackmann (ed.), *Estland – Partner im Ostseeraum*. Lübeck: Ostseeakademie, 19–40.

Feest, David. 2000. 'Terror und Gewalt auf dem estnischen Dorf', *Osteuropa* 50(6): 656–71.

Fein, Elke. 2000a. 'Zwei Schritte vor, einen zurück. Widersprüchliche Haltungen zur Vergangenheitsbewältigung in Rußland', in *Osteuropa* A271–A280.

Fein, Elke. 2000b. *Geschichtspolitik in Russland Chancen und Schwierigkeiten einer demokratisierenden Aufarbeitung der sowjetischen Vergangenheit am Beispiel der Tätigkeit der Gesellschaft Memorial*. Münster: LIT Verlag.

Feldman, Gregory. 2000. 'Shifting the Perspective on Identity Discourse in Estonia', in *Journal of Baltic Studies* 31(4): 406–28.

Fentress, James, and Chris Wickham. 1992. *Social Memory*. Oxford: Blackwell.

Finkenauer, Catrin, Lydia Gisle and Oliver Luminet. 1997. 'When Individual Memories are Socially Shaped: Flashbulb Memories of Sociopolitical Events', in J. Pennebaker, Dario Paez and Bernard Rimé (eds), *Collective Memory of Political Events: Social Psychological Perspective*. Hillsdale, NJ: Lawrence Erlbaum Associates, 191–208.

Finnegan, Ruth. 1996. 'A Note on Oral Tradition and Historical Evidence', in David K. Dunaway and Willa K. Baum (eds), *Oral History: An Interdisciplinary Anthology*. 2nd Edition. Walnut Creek, CA: AltaMira Press, 126–34.

Fischer, Fritz. 1994. *Griff nach der Weltmacht. Die Kriegszielpolitik des kaiserlichen Deutschlands 1914/1918*. Düsseldorf: Droste.

Fischer, Fritz. 1998. *Hitler war kein Betriebsunfall. Aufsätze*. 4th edn. Munich: C.H. Beck.

Fishman, Joshua. 1996. 'Language and Nationalism', in Stuart Woolf (ed.), *Nationalism in Europe, 1815 to the Present: A Reader*. London: Routledge, 155–70.

Flacke, Monika. 1998. 'Die Begründung der Nation aus der Krise', in Monika Flacke and Rainer Rother (eds), *Mythen der Nationen: Ein Europäisches Panorama*. Munich: Koehler & Amelang, 101–28.

Flood, C. 2001. *Political Myth*. London: Routledge.

Forty, Adrian, and Susanne Kuchler (eds). 1999. *The Art of Forgetting*. Oxford: Berg.

Franck, Julia. 2011. *Rücken an Rücken*. Frankfurt a. M: S. Fischer.

Francois, Etienne, and Hagen Schulze. 1998. 'Das emotionale Fundament der Nationen', in Monika Flacke (ed.), *Mythen der Nationen: Ein Europäisches Panorama*. Munich: Berlin DHM, 17–32.

Freeman, Mark. 1993. *Rewriting the Self: History, Memory, Narrative*. London: Routledge.

Frei, Norbert. 2005. *1945 und wir: Das Dritte Reich im Bewusstsein der Deutschen*. Munich: C.H. Beck.

Friedlander, Peter. 1996. 'Theory, Method, and Oral History', in David K. Dunaway and Willa K. Baum (eds), *Oral History: An Interdisciplinary Anthology*. 2nd edn. Walnut Creek, CA: AltaMira Press, 150–60.

Fritz, Peter. 2002. 'Militärinternierte der deutschen Wehrmacht in Schweden 1945: Ihre Aufnahme und Unterbringung, Seperatum', in Harald Knoll, Peter Ruggenthalter and Barbara Stelz-Marx (eds), *Konflikte und Kriege im 20. Jahrhundert. Aspekte und Folgen*. Graz: Veröffentlichungen des Ludwig Boltzmann-Instituts für Kriegsfolgen-Forschung, Sonderband 3, 47–57.

Fukuyama, Francis. 1992. *The End of History and the Last Man*. Harmondsworth: Penguin.

Fulbrook, Mary. 1995. *Anatomy of a Dictatorship: Inside the GDR 1949–1989*. Oxford: Oxford University Press.

Fulbrook, Mary. 1999. *German National Identity after the Holocaust*. Cambridge: Polity Press.

Fulbrook, Mary. 2011. *Dissonant Lives: Generations and Violence through the German Dictatorship*. Oxford: Oxford University Press.

Gaier, U. (ed.). 1990. *Herder, Volkslieder, Übertragungen, Dichtungen*, Vol. 3. Frankfurt a. M.: Deutscher Klassiker Verlag.

Gallerano, Nicola. 1994. 'History and the Public Use of History', in François Bédarida (ed.), 'The Social Responsibility of the Historian', *Diogenes* 42(4): 85–102.

Garleff, Michael. 1976. *Deutschbaltische Politk zwischen den Weltkriegen: Die parlamentarische Tätigkeit der deutschbaltischen Parteien in Lettland und Estland*. Bonn: Wissenschaftliches Archiv.

Garleff, Michael. 2001. *Die baltischen Staaten, Estland, Lettland, Litauen, vom Mittelalter bis zur Gegenwart*. Regensburg: Verlag Friedrich Pustet.

Gaunt, David, Paul A. Levine and Laura Palosuo (eds). 2004. *Collaboration and Resistance during the Holocaust: Belarus, Estonia, Latvia, Lithuania*. Bern: Peter Lang.

Gay, Peter. 1978. *Freud, Jews and other Germans: Master and Victims in Modernist Culture*. Oxford: Oxford University Press.

Geertz, Clifford. 1973. *Local Knowledge: Further Essays in Interpretive Anthropology*. New York: Basic Books.

Geistlinger, Michael, and Aksel Kirch. 1995. *Estonia – A New Framework for the Estonian Majority and the Russian Minority*. Vienna: Braunmüller.

Gellner, Ernest. 1964. *Thought and Change*. London: Weidenfeldt & Nicolson.

Gellner, Ernest. 1983. *Nations and Nationalism*. Oxford: Basil Blackwell.

Gellner, Ernest. 1988. *State and Society in Soviet Thought*. Oxford: Basil Blackwell.

Gellner, Ernest. 1994. *Conditions of Liberty: Civil Society and its Rivals*. London: Hamish Hamilton.

Gellner, Ernest. 1996. 'Ernest Gellner's Reply: Do Nations have Navels?', *Nations and Nationalism* 2(3): 366–70.

Gennep, Arnold von. 1960. *The Rites of Passage*. Chicago, IL: University of Chicago Press.

Gerner, Kristian, and Stefan Hedlund. 1993. *The Baltic States and the End of the Soviet Empire*. London: Routledge.

Giddens, Anthony. 1978. *Durkheim*. London: Fontana.

Giesen, Bernhard (ed.). 1992. *Nationale und kulturelle Identität*. Frankfurt a. M.: Suhrkamp.

Giesen, Bernhard. 1999. *Kollektive Identität. Die Intellektuellen und die Nation*. Frankfurt a. M.: Suhrkamp.

Gilbert, Martin. 1995. *Endlösung: Die Vertreibung und Vernichtung der Juden. Ein Atlas*. Hamburg: Rowohlt.

Gillis, John R. 1994. *Commemorations: The Politics of National Identity*. Princeton, NJ: Princeton University Press.

Giordano, Christian. 1997. 'Lex Talionis: Citizens and Stateless in the Baltic Countries', in *Anthropological Journal on European Cultures* 6(1): 101–24.

Giordano, Christian. 2005. *Die post-sozialistische Transition ist beendet, weil sie nie angefangen hat. Zur Archäologie eines gescheiterten Entwicklungsmodells*. Brauncschweig: Georg-Eckert Institut für internationale Schulbuchforschung.

Glenny, Misha. 1993. *The Rebirth of History: Eastern Europe in the Age of Democracy*. Harmondsworth: Penguin.

Goody, Jack. 1991. 'Time: Social Organization', in D.L. Sills (ed.), *International Encyclopaedia of Social Sciences* 16, 30–42. New York: Macmillan.

Götz, Norbert, and Jörg Hackmann (eds). 2003. *Civil Society in the Baltic Sea Region*. Aldershot: Ashgate.

Graubner, Hans. 1994. 'Spättaufklärer im aufgeklärten Riga: Hamann und Herder', *Zeitschrift für Ostforschung* 43: 517–33.

Greenblatt, Stephen, and Catherine Gallagher. 2000. *Practicing New Historicism*. Chicago: University of Chicago Press.

Greenblatt, Stephen, Istvan Rev and Randolph Starn. 1995. 'Introduction', *Representations* 49, Special Issue, 1–14.

Greenfeld, Liah. 1992. *Nationalism: Five Roads to Modernity*. Cambridge MA: Harvard University Press.

Griffin, Roger. 1995. *Fascism*. Oxford: Oxford University Press.

Gross, Jan Tomasz. 2001. *Neighbours: The Destruction of the Jewish Community in Jedwabne, Poland*. Princeton, NJ: Princeton University Press.

Große-Kracht, Klaus. 1996. 'Gedächtnis und Geschichte: Halbwachs – Pierre Nora', *Geschichte und Wissenschaft im Unterricht* 47(1): 21–31.

Gumbrecht, Hans Ulrich. 2001. 'On the Decent Uses of History', *History and Theory* 40(1): 117–27.

Gurin-Loov, Eugenia. 1994. *Holocaust of Estonian Jews 1941*. Tallinn: Eesti Juudi Kogukond.

Gurin-Loov, Eugenia. 1996. 'Verfolgung der Juden in Estland (1941–44) Rettungsversuche und Hilfe', in Wolgang Benz and Juliane Wetzel (eds), *Solidarität und Hilfe für Juden während der NS-Zeit, Regionalstudien 2, Ukraine, Frankreich, Böhmen und Mähren, Lettland, Litauen, Estland*. Berlin: Metropol, 295–308.

Gurvitch, Georges. 1964. *The Spectrum of Social Time*. Dordrecht: Reidel.

Gutman, Israel (ed.). 1990. *The Encyclopaedia of the Holocaust*. New York: Macmillan.

Gutschow, Niels. 1993. 'Stadtplanung im Warthegau 1939–1944', in Mechthild Rössler and Sabine Schleiermacher (eds), *Der Generalplan Ost, Hauptlinen der nationlasoziaistischen Planungs- und Vernichtungspolitik*. Berlin: Akademie Verlag, 232–70.

Habermas, Jürgen. 1996. *Between Facts and Norms, Contributions to a Discourse Theory of Law and Democracy*, transl. William Rehg. Cambridge: Polity Press.

Haffner, Sebastian. 1994. *Der Teufelspakt. Die deutsch-russischen Beziehungen vom Ersten zum Zweiten Weltkrieg.* Zürich: Manesse.

Halbwachs, Maurice. 1966. *Gedächtnis und seine sozialen Bedingungen.* Berlin: Luchterhand.

Halbwachs, Maurice. 1980. *The Collective Memory.* New York: Harper & Row.

Halbwachs, Maurice. 1985. *Gedächtnis und seine sozialen Bedingungen.* Revised edn. Frankfurt a. M.: Suhrkamp.

Halbwachs, Maurice. 2003. *Stätten der Verkündung im Heiligen Land. Eine Studie zum kollektiven Gedächtnis.* Konstanz: UVK.

Hall, John A. (ed.). 1998. *The State of the Nation, Ernest Gellner and the Theory of Nationalism.* Cambridge: Cambridge University Press.

Hall, Stuart. 1994. *Die Frage der kulturellen Identität. Rassismus und Identität.* Hamburg: Argument.

Hall, Stuart. 1996a. 'Ethnicity: Identity and Difference', in Geoff Eley and Ronald G. Suny (eds), *Becoming National: A Reader.* New York: Oxford University Press, 339–49.

Hall, Stuart. 1996b. 'The New Ethnicities', in John Hutchinson and Anthony D. Smith (eds), *Ethnicity.* Oxford: Oxford University Press, 161–68.

Hall, Stuart, and Paul du Gay (eds). 1996c. *Questions of Identity.* London: Sage.

Hallik, Klara. 2002. 'Nationalising Policies and Integration Challenges', in Marju Laurestin and Mati Heidmets (eds), *The Challenge of the Russian Minority: Emerging Multicultural Democracy in Estonia.* Tartu: Tartu University Press, 65–88.

Hamm, Michael F. 1998. 'Introduction', *Nationalities Papers* 26(1): 9–14.

Hanko, Lauri. 1999. 'Traditions in the Construction of Cultural Identity', in Michael Branch (ed.), *National History and Identity: Approaches to the Writing of National History in the North-East Baltic Region, Nineteenth and Twentieth Centuries.* Helsinki: Finnish Literature Society, 19–33.

Hareven, Tamara. 1996. 'The Search for Generational Memory', in David K. Dunaway and Willa K. Baum (eds), *Oral History: An Interdisciplinary Anthology,* 2nd edn. Walnut Creek, CA: AltaMira Press, 241–56.

Hartmann, Geoffrey (ed.). 1994. *Holocaust Remembrance: The Shapes of Memory.* Oxford: Basil Blackwell.

Hasselblatt, Cornelius. 1995. 'Nationalbewegung und Staatbildung', in Robert Maier (ed.), *Nationalbewegung und Staatsbildung. Die baltische Region im Schulbuch.* Frankfurt a. M.: GEI, 59–68.

Hasseblatt, Cornelius. 1998. 'Die Bedeutung des Nationalepos "Kalevipoeg" für das nationale Erwachen der Esten', in Jörg Hackmann (ed.), *Estland – Partner im Ostseeraum.* Lübeck: Ostseeakademie, 41–56.

Hastings, Adrian. 1997. *The Construction of Nationhood: Ethnicity, Religion and Nationalism.* Cambridge: Cambridge University Press.

Havel, Václav, et al. 1985. *The Power of the Powerless: Citizens against the State in Central-Eastern Europe*, John Keane (ed.). London: Hutchinson.

Hechter, Michael. 1987. *Principles of Group Solidarity*. Berkeley: University of California Press.

Heer, Nancy Whittier. 1971. *Politics and History in the Soviet Union*. Cambridge, MA: MIT Press.

Heidmets, Mati, and Marju Lauristin. 2002. 'Learning from the Estonian Case', in Heidmets and Lauristin (eds), *The Challenge of the Russian Minority: Emerging Multicultural Democracy in Estonia*. Tartu: Tartu University Press, 319–22.

Helemäe, Yelena, and Ellu Saar. 1995. 'National Reconstruction and Social Restratification', *Nationalities Papers* 23(1): 127–40.

Helme, Rein. 1995. 'Die estnische Historiographie', in Michael Garleff (ed.), *Zwischen Konfrontation und Kompromiß, Oldenburger Symposium: Interethnische Beziehungen in Ostmitteleuropa als historiographisches Problem der 1930er/40er Jahre*. Munich: Oldenbourg, 139–54.

Helme, Sirje. 2000. 'Mitteametlik kunst: Vastupanuvormid eesti kunstis', *Kunstiteaduslikke Uurimusi* [Talinn] 10: 253–73.

Herf, Jeffery. 1997. *Divided Memory: The Nazi Past in the Two Germanys*. Cambridge, MA: Harvard University Press.

Hess, Remi, and Christoph Wulf (eds). 1999. *Grenzgänge: Über den Umgang mit dem Eigenen und dem Fremden*. Frankfurt: Campus.

Hiden, John. 1970. *German Policy towards the Baltic States of Estonia and Latvia, 1920–1926*. PhD dissertation, London University.

Hiio, T., M. Maripuu and I. Paalve (eds). 2006. 'Estonia 1940–1945: Reports of the Estonian International Commission for the Investigation of Crimes against Humanity'. Tallinn: Estonian Foundation for the Investigation of Crimes against Humanity.

Hilberg, Raul (ed.). 1992. *Täter, Opfer, Zuschauer. Die Vernichtung der Juden 1933–1945*. Frankfurt a. M.: S. Fischer.

Hilberg, Raul. 1994. *Die Vernichtung der europäischen Juden*, Vols. 1–3. Frankfurt a. M.: S. Fischer.

Hinrikus, Rutt, and Ene Kõresaar. 2004. 'A Brief Overview of Life History Collection and Research in Estonia', in T. Kirss, T.E. Kõresaar and M. Lauristin (eds), *She Who Remembers, Survives: Interpreting Estonian Women's Post-Soviet Life Stories*. Tartu: Tartu University Press, 19–34.

Hint, Mati. 1991. 'The Changing Language Situation: Russian Influences on Contemporary Estonian', in *Journal of Multilingual and Multicultural Development* 12(1/2): 111–17.

Hint, Mati. 1995. 'Das Problem von Mehrheit und Minderheit im estnischen Kontext', in 'Estland und seine Minderheiten: Esten, Deutsche und Russen im 19. und 20. Jahrhundert', in *Nordost-Archiv* 4(2): 627–33.

Hobsbawm, Eric J. 1972. 'The Social Function of the Past: Some Questions', in *Past & Present* 55(1): 3–17.

Hobsbawm, Eric J. 1990. *Nations and Nationalism after 1780*. Cambridge: Cambridge University Press.

Hobsbawm, Eric J. 2003. *Gefährliche Zeiten*. Munich: Carl Hanser Verlag.

Hobsbawm, Eric J., and Terence Ranger (eds). 1983. *The Invention of Tradition*. Cambridge: Cambridge University Press.

Hockerts, Hans-Günther. 2002. 'Zugänge zur Zeitgeschichte: Primärerfahrung, Erinnerungskultur, Geschichtswissenschaft', in Konrad H. Jarausch (ed.), *Verletztes Gedächtnis: Erinnerungskultur und Zeitgeschichte im Konflikt*. Frankfurt a. M.: Campus Verlag, 39–74.

Hoffmann, Alice. 1996. 'Reliability and Validity in Oral History', in David K. Dunaway and Willa K. Baum (eds), *Oral History: An Interdisciplinary Anthology*. 2nd edn. Walnut Creek, CA: AltaMira Press, 87–93.

Höhnle, Heinz. 1978. *Der Orden unter dem Totenkopf. Die Geschichte der SS*. Munich: Bertelsmann.

Hölscher, Lucian. 1995. 'Geschichte als "Erinnerungskultur"', in Kristin Platt and Mihran Dabag (eds), *Generation und Gedächtnis. Erinnerung und Kollektive Identitäten*. Opladen: Leske & Budrich, 146–68.

Hope, Nicholas. 1994. 'Interwar Statehood: Symbol and Reality', in Graham Smith (ed.), *The Baltic States: The National Self-Determination of Estonia, Latvia and Lithuania*. London: Macmillan, 41–60.

Horm, Arvo. 1973. *Phases of Baltic Political Activities*. Stockholm: Mälartryckeriet AB.

Horowitz, Donald L. 2000. *Ethnic Groups in Conflict*. Berkeley: University of California Press.

Hösch, Edgar. 1991. 'Die kleinen Völker und ihre Geschichte: Zur Diskussion über Nationswerdung und Staat in Finnland', in Manfred Alexander et al. (eds), *Kleine Völker in der Geschichte Osteuropas*. Stuttgart: Franz Steiner Verlag, 22–32.

Hosking, Geoffrey. 1992. 'Popular movements in Estonia', in Geoffrey A. Hosking et al. (eds), *The Road to Post-Communism: Independent Political Movements in the Soviet Union, 1985–1991*. London: Pinter, 180–201.

Hosking, Geoffrey. 2008. *Rulers and Victims: The Russians in the Soviet Union*. Cambridge, MA: Harvard University Press.

Hroch, Miroslav. 1985. *Social Preconditions of National Revival in Europe: A Comparative Analysis of the Social Composition of Patriotic Groups among the Smaller European Nations*. Cambridge: Cambridge University Press, 76–85.

Hroch, Miroslav. 1990. 'How Much does Nation Formation Depend on Nationalism?', *East European Politics and Society* 4(1): 101–15.

Hroch, Miroslav. 1996. 'From National Movement to the Fully Formed Nation: The Nation-Building Process in Europe', in Geoff Eley and Ronald Grigor Suny (eds), *Becoming National: A Reader*. New York: Oxford University Press, 60–78.

Hroch, Miroslav. 1999. 'Historical Belles-lettres as a Vehicle of the Image of National History', in Michael Branch (ed.), *National History and Identity, Approaches to the Writing of National History in the North-East Baltic Region, Nineteenth and Twentieth Centuries*. Helsinki: Finnish Literature Society, 97–108.

Huang, Mel. 1999. 'Doing it Half Right', *Central European Review* 1(2), 5 July. http://www.ce-review.org/99/2/amber2.html

Hutchinson, John. 1987. *Dynamics of Cultural Nationalism: The Gaelic Revival and the Creation of the Irish Nation State*. London: Allen & Unwin.

Hutchinson, John, and Anthony D. Smith (eds). 1995. *Nationalism*. Oxford: Oxford University Press.

Hutnik, Nimni. 1991. *Ethnic Minority Identity: A Social Psychological Perspective*. Oxford: Oxford University Press.

Huttenbach, Henry R. (ed.). 1990. *Soviet Nationality Policies: Ruling Ethnic Groups in the USSR*. London: Mansell.

Igartua, Juanjo, and Dario Paez. 1997. 'Art and Remembering Traumatic Collective Events: The Case of the Spanish Civil War', in James Pennebaker, Dario Paez and Bernard Rimé (eds), *Collective Memory of Political Events: Social Psychological Perspectives*. Hillsdale, NJ: Lawrence Erlbaum Associates, 79–101.

Iggers, Georg G. 1983. *The German Conception of History: The National Tradition of Historical Thought from Herder to the Present*. Middletown, CT: Wesleyan University Press.

Ignatieff, Michael. 1993. *Blood and Belonging: Journeys into the New Nationalism*. London: Chatto & Windus.

Ignatieff, Michael. 1999. 'Nationalism and the Narcissism of Minor Differences', in Ronald Reiner (ed.), *Theorizing Nationalism*. New York: State University of New York Press, 91–102.

Ilja, Merit. 1994. 'Estonian Literature in a Time of Change', *Slovo* 7(1): 30–38.

Ilmjärv, Magnus. 1993. *Nõukogude Liidu ja Saksamaavahel. Balti rigid ja Soome 1934–1940*. Tallinn: Eesti Teaduste Akadeemia.

Ilmjärv, Magnus. 1999. 'Konstantin Päts ja Nõukogude Liidu Tallinna saatkond: aastad 1925–1934', *Acta Historica Tallinnensia* 3: 156–223.

Ilmjärv, Magnus. 2004. *Silent Submission: Formation of Foreign Policy in Estonia, Latvia and Lithuania, 1920–1940*. Stockholm: Almqvist & Wiksell.

Ilves, Toomas Hendrik. 1991. 'Reaction: The Inter-Movements in Estonia', in Jan Arveds Trapans (ed.), *Toward Independence: The Baltic Popular Movements*. Boulder, CO: Westview Press, 71–84.

Ilves, Toomas Hendrik. 1999. 'Estonia and the State of Change in European Security'. Paper delivered by the foreign minister of Estonia, Chatham House, London, 4 May 1999.

Irwin-Zarecka, Iwona. 1989. *Neutralising Memory: The Jew in Contemporary Poland*. New Brunswick, NJ: Transaction Books.

Irwin-Zarecka, Iwona. 1994. *Frames of Remembrance: Dynamics of Collective Memory*. New Brunswick, NJ: Transaction Books.

Isakov, Sergej G. 1998. 'Die russische nationale Minderheit in Estland: Vergangenheit, Gegenwart, Zukunft', in Jörg Hakmann (ed.), *Estland – Partner im Ostseeraum*. Lübeck: Ostsee-Akademie.

Jaago, Tiiu (ed.). 2002. *Lives, Histories and Identities: Studies on Oral Histories, Life and Family Stories*. Tartu: University of Tartu Estonian Literary Museum.

Jackson, J. Hampden. 1941. *Estonia*. London: George Allen & Unwin.

Jankowski, Stansilaw. 1990. 'Warsaw: Destruction, Secret Town Planning, 1939–44, and Post-war Reconstruction', in Jeffery M. Diefendorf (ed.), *Rebuilding Europe's Bombed Cities*. Basingstoke: Macmillan, 77–93.

Jansen, Ea. 1985. 'On the Economic and Social Determination of the Estonian National Movement', in Aleksander Loit (ed.), *National Movements in the Baltic Countries during the 19th Century*. Stockholm: Centre for Baltic Studies, 41–57.

Jansen, Ea. 1990. 'Estonian Culture – European Culture in the Beginning of the 20th Century', in Aleksander Loit (ed.), *The Baltic Countries 1900–1914*. Stockholm: Centre for Baltic Studies, 311–26.

Jansen, Ea. 1997. 'Die nicht-deutsche Komponente', in Wilfried Schlau (ed.), *Sozialgeschichte der Baltischen Deutschen*. Cologne: Mare Baltikum, 233–43.

Jansen, Ea. 2000a. 'Cultural or Political Nationalism? (On The Development of Estonian Nationalism in the 19th Century)', in Anu-Mai Köll (ed.), *Time and Change in the Baltic Countries: Essays in Honour of Aleksander Loit*. Stockholm: Stockholm University Press, 57–79.

Jansen, Ea. 2000b. 'Autobiographical data' [first published as Eesti rahva elulood I]. Tallinn: Tänapäev, 224–39.

Jarausch, Konrad H. 2002. 'Zeitgeschichte und Erinnerung. Deutungskonkurrenz oder Interdependenz?', in Konrad Jarausch (ed.), *Verletztes Gedächtnis: Erinnerungskultur und Zeitgeschichte im Konflikt*. Frankfurt a. M: Campus Verlag, 9–38.

Järve, Priit. 2002. 'Two Waves of Language Laws in the Baltic States: Changes of Rationale', *Journal of Baltic Studies* 33(1): 78–110.

Jedlicki, Jerzy. 1998. 'Kollektives Gedächtnis und historische Gerechtigkeit', in Ewa Kobylinska and Andreas Lawaty (eds), *Erinnern, vergessen, verdrängen. Polnische Erfahrungen*. Wiesbaden: Harrassowitz Verlag, 133–44.

Jedlicki, Jerzy. 1999. 'Historical Memory as a Source of Conflict in Eastern Europe', *Communist and Post-Communist Studies* 32: 225–32.

Jenkins, Richard. 1994. 'Rethinking Ethnicity: Identity, Categorisation and Power', *Ethnic and Racial Studies* 17(2): 197–223.

Jesse, E. 1999. *Totalitarismus im 20. Jahrhundert: eine Bilanz der internationalen Forschung*. Bonn: Bundeszentrale für Politische Bildung.

Jessen, Ralph. 2002. 'Zeithistoriker im Konfliktfeld der Vergangenheitspolitik', in Konrad H. Jarausch (ed.), *Verletztes Gedächtnis: Erinnerungskultur und Zeitgeschichte im Konflikt*. Frankfurt a. M.: Campus Verlag, 153–76.

Johnston, Hank. 1992a. 'Religion and Nationalist Subcultures in the Baltics', *Journal of Baltic Studies* 23(2): 133–48.

Johnston, Hank. 1992b. 'The Comparative Study of Nationalism: Six Themes from the Baltic States', *Journal of Baltic Studies* 23(2): 95–104.

Johnston, Hank. 2001. 'Talking the Walk: Speech Acts and Resistance in Authoritarian Regimes'. Paper presented at the Workshop on Repression and Mobilisation, University of Maryland, 21–23 June.

Johnston, Hank, and Aili Aarelaid-Tart. 2000. 'Generations, Microcohorts, and Long-term Mobilization in the Estonian National Opposition 1939-1991', *Sociological Perspectives* 43(4): 671–95.

Johnston, Hank, and David A. Snow. 1998. 'Subcultures and the Emergence of the Estonian Nationalist Opposition, 1945–1990', *Sociological Perspectives* 41(3): 473–97.

Jonsson, Anna. 1999. 'Nationalising State-Building and Language: The Case of Estonia'. Department of East European Studies, Uppsala, Working Paper, 50.

Jordanova, Ludmilla. 2000. *History in Practice*. London: Arrowsmiths.

Joyner, Charles. 1996. 'Oral History as Communicative Event', in David K. Dunaway and Willa K. Baum (eds), *Oral History: An Interdisciplinary Anthology*, 2nd edn. Walnut Creek, CA: AltaMira Press, 292–97.

Judt, Tony. 1990. 'The Rediscovery of Central Europe', *Daedalus* 119(1): 23–54.

Judt, Tony. 1992. 'The Past is Another Country: Myth and Memory in Post-war Europe', *Daedalus* 121(4): 83–118.

Judt, Tony. 2005. *Postwar: A History of Europe since 1945*. London: Penguin.

Jung, Carl G. 1991. *The Archetypes and the Collective Unconscious*. 2nd edn. London: Routledge.

Jünger, Friederich Georg (ed.). 1957. *Gedächtnis und Erinnerung*. Frankfurt a. M.: Klostermann Vittorio.

Jurgaitienè, Kornelija, and Priit Järve. 1997. 'The Baltic States: Re-nationalisation of Political Space', in P. Jonniemi (ed.), *Neo-nationalism or Regionality: The Restructuring of Political Space around the Baltic Rim*. Stockholm: NordREFO, 119–38.

Kahk, Juhan. 1990. 'Peasant Movements and National Movements in the History of Europe', in Aleksander Loit (ed.), *The Baltic Countries 1900–1914*. Stockholm: Centre for Baltic Studies, 15–23.

Kahk, J., H. Palamets and S. Vahtre. (1974, 1984). *Eesti NSV ajalost: lisamaterjali VII–VIII klassi NSV Liidu ajaloo kursuse juurde*. Tallinn: Kirjastus Valgus.

Kallas, Kristina. 2002. 'The Formation of Interethnic Relations in Soviet Estonia: Host–Immigrant Relationship'. MA thesis. Budapest: Central European University.

Kalmus, Veronika. 2002. 'Ethno-Political Discourse in Estonian School Textbooks', in Marju Laurestin and Mati Heidmets (eds), *The Challenge of the Russian Minority: Emerging Multicultural Democracy in Estonia*. Tartu: Tartu University Press, 225–64.

Kangeris, Karlis. 1994. 'Kollaboration vor der Kollaboration? Die baltischen Emigranten und ihre "Befreiungskomitees" in Deutschland 1940/1941', in *Europa unterm Hakenkreuz: Okkupation und Kollaboration (1938–1945), Beiträge zu Konzepten und Praxis der Kollaboration in der deutschen Okkupationspolitik.* Bundesarchiv, Berlin & Heidelberg: Hüthig Verlagsgesellschaft, 165–90.

Kaplinski, Jaan. 1987. *The Wandering Border.* Port Townsend, NY: Copper Canyon Press.

Kaplinski, Jaan. 1993. 'The Future of National Cultures in Europe', in K. Livonen (ed.), *The Future of the Nation State in Europe.* Aldershot: Edward Elgar.

Kappeler, Andreas (ed.). 1992. *The Formation of National Elites.* New York: European Science Foundation.

Karjahärm, Toomas. 1998. 'Konfessionen und Nationalismus in Estland zu Beginn des 20. Jahrhunderts', in *Nordost-Archiv: Zeitschrift für Regionalgeschichte* 7(2): 533–53.

Karklins, Rasma. 1994. *Ethnopolitics and Transition to Democracy: The Collapse of the USSR and Latvia.* Baltimore, MD: Johns Hopkins University Press.

Karlsson, Klas-Göran. 1998. 'Identity Change in the Former Soviet Union? The Roles of History', in Klas-Göran Karlsson, Bo Petersson and Barbara Törnquist-Plewa (eds), *Collective Identities in an Era of Transformations: Analysing Developments in East and Central Europe and the former Soviet Union.* Lund: Lund University Press, 10–28.

Karlsson, Klas-Göran. 1999. *Historia som vapen: Historiebruk och samhällsupplösning i Sovjetunionen och dess efterföljarstater 1985–1995.* Stockholm: Natur och Kultur.

Karlsson, Klas-Göran. 2002. 'History in Swedish Politics – The "Living History" Project', in Attila Pok et al. (eds), *European History: Challenges for a Common Future.* Hamburg: Körber Stiftung, 145–62.

Karlsson, Klas-Göran, and Kristian Gerner. 2001. Draft paper, 'International Comparative Study on the Holocaust and the European Historical Culture'.

Karlsson, Klas-Göran, and Ulf Zander. 2003. *Echoes of the Holocaust: Historical Cultures in Contemporary Europe.* Lund: Nordic Academic Press.

Karusoo, Merle. 2002. 'Kein Mainstream', Forum Festwochen, Vienna, 48–50.

Kasekamp, Andres. 1993. 'The Estonian Veterans' League: A Fascist Movement?', *Journal of Baltic Studies* 24(3): 263–314.

Kasekamp, Andres. 1999. 'Radical Right-Wing Movements in the North-East Baltic', *Journal of Contemporary History* 34(4): 587–600.

Kasekamp, Andres. 2000. *The Radical Right in Interwar Estonia.* London: Macmillan.

Kasekamp, Andres. 2010. *A History of the Baltic States.* New York: Palgrave Macmillan.

Kattago, Siobhan. 2008. 'Commemorating Liberation and Occupation: War Memorials along the Road to Narva', *Journal of Baltic Studies* 39(4): 431–49.

Kattago, Siobhan. 2009. 'Agreeing to Disagree on the Legacies of Recent History: Memory, Pluralism and Europe after 1989', *European Journal of Social Theory* 12(3): 375–95.

Kearney, Richard (ed.). 1995. *Paul Ricoeur: The Hermeneutics of Action*. London: Sage Publications.

Kearney, Richard, and Mark Dooley (eds). 1999. *Questioning Ethics: Contemporary Debates in Philosophy*. London: Routledge.

Keegan, John. 1981. *Die Waffen SS*. Munich: Moewig.

Kellas, James G. 1991. *The Politics of Nationalism and Ethnicity*. London: Macmillan.

Kenéz, Csaba János (ed.). 1990. *Zur Unabhängigkeitsbewegung in Estland*. Marburg: Johann-Gottfried-Herder Institut.

Kennedy, Michael (ed.). 1999. *Intellectuals and the Articulation of the Nation*. Ann Arbor: University of Michigan Press.

Kerner, Manfred, and Sigmar Stopinski (eds). 1990. *Die Unabhängigkeit der baltischen Staaten in historischer Bilanz und als aktuelle Perspektive: Betrachtungen und Gespräche zu kontroversen Fragen der Innen- und Außenpolitik Litauens, Lettlands und Estlands sowie zum Stand der wissenschaftlichen Forschung*. Berlin: Berghof Stiftung für Konfliktforschung.

Kerner, Manfred, and Sigmar Stopinski. 1991. 'Vom Umgang mit der eigenen Geschichte', *Osteuropa* 6(41): 602–10.

Kettler, David, Voler Meja and Nico Stehr (eds). 1989. *Politisches Denken in Studien zu Karl Mannheim*. Frankfurt a. M.: Suhrkamp.

Kiaupa, Zigmatas, et al. (eds). 1999. *The History of the Baltic Countries*. Tallinn: Avita.

Kionka, Riina, and Raivo Vetik. 1996. 'Estonians', in Graham Smith (ed.), *Nationalities Questions in the Post-Soviet States*. London: Longman, 129–46.

Kirby, David. 1995. *The Baltic World, 1772–1993: Europe's Northern Periphery in an Age of Change*. London: Longman.

Kirby, William Forsell (transl.). 1985. *Kalevala: The Land of the Heroes*. London: Athlone Press.

Kirch, Aksel, Iris Brökling and Mart Kivimäe. 2001. 'Estonia: Images of Europe – The Country Study Estonia', *Newsletter, Social Science in Eastern Europe*, Special Edition, 70–82.

Kirch, Aksel, Marika Kirch and Tarmo Tuisk. 1993. 'Russians in the Baltic States: To Be or Not To Be?', *Journal of Baltic Studies* 24(2), 173–88.

Kirch, Aksel, and Marika Kirch. 1995. 'Estonians and Non-Estonians', *Nationalities Papers* 23(1): 43–60.

Kirch, Marika, David D. Laitin and Vello A. Pettai (eds). 1994. *Changing Identities in Estonia: Sociological Facts and Commentaries*. Tallinn: Estonian Science Foundation.

Kirschbaum, Engelbert. 1994. *Lexikon der christlichen Ikonographie*. 8 vols. Freiburg: Verlag Herder.

Kirss, Tiina. 2000. 'Playing the Fool in the Territory of Memory: Jaan Kross' Autobiographical Fictions of the Twentieth Century', *Journal of Baltic Studies* 31(3): 273–94.

Kirss, Tiina, Ene Kõresaar and Marju Lauristin (eds). 2004. *She Who Remembers Survives: Interpreting Estonian Women's Post-Soviet Life Stories.* Tartu: Tartus University Press.

Kittsteiner, Heinz Dieter. 2000. 'Die Krise der Historiker-Zunft', in Rainer Maria Kiesow and Dieter Simon (eds), *Auf der Suche nach der verlorenen Wahrheit. Zum Grundlagenstreit in der Geschichtswissenschaft.* Frankfurt a. M.: Campus Verlag, 71–87.

Kivimäe, Jüri. 1995. 'Aus der Heimat ins Vaterland: Die Umsiedlung der Deutschbalten aus dem Blickwinkel estnischer nationaler Gruppierungen', *Nordost Archiv* 4(2): 501–20.

Kivimäe, Jüri. 1999. 'Re-writing Estonian History', in Michael Branch (ed.), *National History and Identity: Approaches to the Writing of National History in the North-East Baltic Region, Nineteenth and Twentieth Centuries.* Helsinki: Finnish Literature Society, 205–11.

Kivimäe, Jüri, and Sirje Kivimäe. 1987. 'Estnische Geschichtsforschung an der Universität Tartu 1920–1940: Ziele und Ergebnisse', in Gert v. Pistolkors et al. (eds), *Die Universitäten Dorpat/Tartu, Riga und Wilna/Vilnius 1529–1979. Beiträge zu ihrer Geschichte und ihrer Wirkung im Grenzbereich zwischen Ost und West,* 277–92.

Kivimäe, Jüri, and Sirge Kivimäe. 2002. 'Geschichtsschreibung und Geschichtsforschung in Estland 1988–2001', *Österreichische Osthefte* 44(1/2): 159–70.

Kivimäe, Sirje. 1995. 'Estland unter der Sowjetherrschat 1941/44–1954', *Nordostarchiv* 4(2): 577–600.

Kivimäe, Sirje. 1999. 'Were These the Same Women? Life in the Socialist Structures in Estonia', in S. Bridger (ed.), *Women and Political Change: Perspectives from East-Central Europe.* London: Routledge, 60–74.

Kivirähk, Andrus. 1995. *Ivan Orava mälestused ehk Minevik kui helesinised mäed.* Tallinn: Varrak.

Kivirähk, Andrus. 2000. *Rehepapp ehk November.* Tallinn: Varrak.

Kleiner, Jack. 1977. 'On Nostalgia', in Charles W. Socarides (ed.), *The World of Emotions: Clinical Studies of Affects and their Expression.* New York: International Universities Press.

Kleßmann, Christoph. 1988. *Zwei Staaten, Eine Nation: Deutsche Geschichte 1955–1970.* Göttingen: Vandenhoeck & Ruprecht.

Koebner, Richard. 1990. 'Die Idee der Zeitwende (1941–43)', in Koebner, *Geschichte, Geschichtsbewußtsein und Zeitwende: Vorträge und Schriften aus dem Nachlass.* Gerlingen: Bleichner, 147–93.

Kohl, J.G. 1841. *Die deutsch-russischen Ostseeprovinzen.* 2 vols. Dresden: Arnold.

Kohn, Hans. 1944. *The Idea of Nationalism.* New York: Macmillan.

Kõll, Anu-Mai. 2000. 'The Narva Region in Soviet Industrialisation, 1945–1952'. Paper presented at 'Narva in the Mirror of History' conference, Narva, 17–20 November.

Kõll, Anu-Mai. 2002. 'State Sponsored Research on Crimes of Communism'. Paper presented at the Round Table Conference 'Contemporary Historians, Professional Standards and the Public Use of History', at Södertörns University College, Sweden, 29–31 August.

Kolstø, Pål. 1995. *Russians in the Former Soviet Republics.* London: Hurst & Company.

Kolstø, Pål. 1996. 'The New Russian Diaspora – An Identity of its Own? Possible Identity Trajectories for Russians in the Former Soviet Republic', *Ethnic and Racial Studies* 19(3): 609–39.

Konrád, György. 1979. *Intellectuals on the Road to Class Power.* Brighton: Harvester Press.

Konrád, György. 1982. *The Loser.* Orlando, FL: HBJ.

Konrád, György. 1994. *Antipolitics: An Essay.* London: Quartet Books.

Kõresaar, Ene. 2002a. 'Interpretation of the Biographical Past as a Project for a National Future: The Relationship between State and Individual in the Biographies of Elderly Estonians in the 1990s'. Paper presented at conference on 'The Presence of the Past: Transformation and Dealing with the Past in Eastern and Central Europe', Humboldt University, Berlin, 23–25 May.

Kõresaar, Ene. 2002b. 'The Farm as the Symbol of the State: Metaphorical Depiction of the Nation and the State in the Childhood Memories of Older Estonians', in Tiiu Jaago (ed.), *Lives, Histories and Identities: Studies on Oral Histories, Life and Family Stories.* Tartu: University of Tartu Estonian Literary Museum, 169–87.

Kõresaar, Ene. 2003. 'Lapsepõlv kuiajaloopilt. Rahvuse ja riigi metafooriline kujutamnie vanemate eestlaste lapsepõlve mälestustes', in E. Kõresaar and T. Anepaio (eds), *Mälu kui kultuuritegur. Etnoloogilisi perspektiive.* Tartu: Tartu Ülikooli Kirjastus, 60–91.

Kõresaar, Ene (ed.). 2011. *Soldiers of Memory: World War II and its Aftermath in Estonian Post-Soviet Life Stories.* Amsterdam: Radolphi.

Kõresaar, Ene, and Rutt Hinrikus. 2004. 'A Brief Overview of Life History Collection and Research in Estonia', in Tiina Kirss, Ene Kõresaar and Marju Lauristin (eds), *She Who Remembers Survives: Interpreting Estonian Women's Post-Soviet Life Stories.* Tartu: Tartu University Press, 19–34.

Korn, Salomon. 1999. *Geteilte Erinnerung. Beiträge zur deutsch-jüdischen Gegenwart.* Berlin: Philo.

Koselleck, Reinhart. 2000a. 'Stetigkeit u. Wandel aller Zeitschichten', in Reinhart Koselleck and Hans Georg Gadamer, *Zeitschichten: Studien zur Historik.* Frankfurt a. M.: Suhrkamp, 246–64.

Koselleck, Reinhart. 2000b. 'Erinnerungsschleusen u. Erfahrungsschichten', in Reinhart Koselleck and Hans Georg Gadamer, *Zeitschichten: Studien zur Historik*. Frankfurt a. M.: Suhrkamp, 265–84.

Krausnick, Helmut, and Hans-Heinrich Wilhelm. 1981. *Die Truppe des Weltanschauungskrieges, Die Einsatzgruppen der Sicherheitspolizei und des SD 1938–1942*. Stuttgart: DVA.

Kreindler, Isabelle. 1985. *The Soviet Deported Nationalities: A Summary and an Update*. Jerusalem: Hebrew University.

Krepp, Endel. 1981. *Mass Deportations of Population from the Soviet-occupied Baltic States*. Stockholm: Estonian Information Centre.

Kreutzwald, Friedrich (ed.). 1982. *Kalevipoeg: An Ancient Estonian Tale*. Moorestown, NJ: Symposia Press.

Krezeminkski, Adam. 1998. 'Wie sich Völker erinnern', in Ewa Kobylinska and Andreas Lawaty (eds), *Erinnern, Vergessen, Verdrängen: Polnische Erfahrungen*. Wiesbaden: Harrassowitz Verlag, 87–99.

Kross, Jaan. 1994. *Der Verrückte des Zaren: Historischer Roman*. Munich: dtv.

Kross, Jaan.1995a. *Zwischen drei Pestseuchen. Roman des Balthasar Rüssow*. Munich: Hanser.

Kross, Jaan. 1995b. *Ausgrabungen*. Frankfurt a. M.: dipa-Verlag.

Kross, Jaan. 1999. *Das Leben des Balthasar Rüssow*. Munich: dtv.

Kruus, Raul (ed.). 1962. *People be Watchful!* Tallinn: Estonian State Publishing House.

Kuczynski, Jürgen. 1989. 'Lügen, Verfälschungen, Auslassungen, Ehrlichkeit und Wahrheit: Fünf verschiedene und für den Historiker gleich wertvolle Elemente in Autobiographien', in Peter Alheit and Erika Hoerning (eds), *Biographisches Wissen. Beiträge zu einer Theorie lebensgeschichtlicher Erfahrung*. Frankfurt: Campus Verlag, 24–37.

Kühne, Olaf. 2001. 'Geographie der nationalen Stereotypen: Fallbeispiel Mittel- und Osteuropa', *Osteuropa* 51(11/12): 1416–34.

Kukk, K., and T. Raun. 2007. *Soviet Deportations in Estonia: Impact and Legacy Articles and Life Stories*. Tartu: Tartu University Press.

Kulakauskas, Antanas. 1999. 'Rediscovery of the History of Lithuania in the Nineteenth and Early Twentieth Centuries', in Michael Branch (ed.), *National History and Identity: Approaches to the Writing of National History in the North-East Baltic Region, Nineteenth and Twentieth Centuries*. Helsinki: Finnish Literature Society, 259–64.

Küng, Andres. 1980. *A Dream of Freedom: Four Decades of National Survival versus Russian Imperialism in Estonia, Latvia and Lithuania 1940–80*. Cardiff: Boreas Publishing House.

Kurman, George. 1968. *The Development of Written Estonian*. Bloomington: Indiana University Press.

Küttler, Wolfgang, Jörn Rüsen and Ernst Schulin (eds). 1997. *Geschichtsdiskurs: Krisenbewußtsein, Katastrophenerfahrungen und Innovation 1880–1945, Band 4*. Frankfurt a.M.: S. Fischer.

Laar, Mart. 1992. *War in the Woods: Estonia's Struggle for Survival, 1944–1956*. Washington DC: Compass Press.

Laar, Mart. 2008. *Eesti leegion: sõnas ja pildis*. Tallinn: Grenader Publishing.

Laar, Mart, Maria Tilk and Eha Hergauk. 1997. *Ajalugu 5. klassile*. Tallinn: Kirjastus Avita.

Labov, William (ed.). 1980. *Locating Language in Time and Space*. New York: Academic Press.

LaCapra, Dominick. 1988. 'Geistesgeschichte und Interpretation', in Dominick LaCapra and Steven L. Kaplan (eds), *Geschichte denken: Neubestimmung und Perspektiven moderner europäischer Geistesgeschichte*. Frankfurt: S. Fischer, 45–86.

LaCapra, Dominick. 2001. *Writing History, Writing Trauma*. Baltimore, MD: John Hopkins University Press.

Lagerspetz, Mikko. 1996. *Constructing Post-Communism: A Study in the Estonian Social Problems Discourse*. Turku: Turun Yliopisto.

Lagerspetz, Mikko. 1999a. 'Images of the Past in Post-Socialist Politics: An Introduction', *Finnish Review of East European Studies*, Special Issue, 'Images of the Past in Post-Socialist Politics': 3–6.

Lagerspetz, Mikko. 1999b. 'The Cross of the Virgin Mary's Land: A Study in the Construction of Estonia's "Return to Europe"', *Finnish Review of East European Studies*, Special Issue, 'Images of the Past in Post-Socialist Politics', 17–28.

Lagerspetz, Mikko. 1999c. 'Post-Socialism as a Return: Notes on a Discursive Strategy', *East European Politics and Societies* 13(2): 377–90.

Lagrou, Pieter. 2000. *The Legacy of Nazi Occupation: Patriotic Memory and National Recovery in Western Europe, 1945–1965*. Cambridge: Cambridge University Press.

Laitin, David D. 1992. 'Language Normalisation in Estonia and Catalonia', *Journal of Baltic Studies* 23(2): 149–64.

Laitin, David D. 1995. 'Identity Formation: The Russian-Speaking Nationality in Estonia and Bashkortostan', *Studies in Public Policy* 249, Centre for the Study of Public Policy, University of Strathclyde.

Laitin, David D. 1998. *Identity in Formation: The Russian-Speaking Populations in the Near Abroad*. Ithaca, NY: Cornell University Press.

Lambek, Michael. 1996. 'The Past Imperfect: Remembering as Moral Practice', in P. Antze and M. Lambek (eds), *Tense Past: Cultural Essays in Trauma and Memory*. London: Routledge, 235–56.

Lane, Nicholas. 1995. 'Estonia and its Jews: Ethical Dilemma', *East European Jewish Affairs* 25(1), 3–16.

Langenbacher, Eric. 2003. 'Changing Memory Regimes in Contemporary Germany?', *German Politics and Society* 21(2): 46–68.

Lansky, Aaron. 2005. *Outwitting History: The Amazing Adventures of a Young Man Who Rescued a Million Yiddish Books*. Chapel Hill, NC: Algonquin Books.

Laplanche, Jean, and Jean-Bertrand Pontalis. (1973) 1983. *The Language of Psychoanalysis*. London: Hogarth.

Laul, Endel. 1985. 'Die Schule und die Geburt der Nation', in Aleksander Loit (ed.), *National Movements in the Baltic Countries during the 19th Century*. Stockholm: Centre for Baltic Studies, 293–309.

Laur, Mati, et al. (eds). 2002. *History of Estonia*. Tallinn: Avita.

Laur, Mati, A. Pajur and T. Tannberg. 1995. *Eesti ajalugu II*. Tallinn: Avita.

Lauristin, Marju. 1991. 'Estonia: A Popular Front Looks to the West', in Jan Arveds Trapans (ed.), *Toward Independence: The Baltic Popular Movements*. Oxford: Westview Press, 145–52.

Lauristin, Marju, et al. (eds). 1997. *Return to the Western World: Cultural and Political Perspectives on the Estonian Post-Communist Transition*. Tartu: Tartu University Press.

Lauristin, Marju, and Mati Heidmets. 2002. 'The Russian Minority in Estonia as a Theoretical and Political Issue', in Marju Lauristin and Mati Heidmets (eds), *The Challenge of the Russian Minority: Emerging Multicultural Democracy in Estonia*. Tartu: Tartu University Press, 19–30.

Leede, V., A. Matsulevits and B. Tamm (eds). 1963. *Die Deutschfaschistische Okkupation in Estland (1941–1944), Sammlung von Dokumenten und Materialien*. Tallinn: Institut für Parteigeschichte beim Zentralkomitee der Kommunistischen Partei Estlands.

Le Goff, Jacques. 1992. *History and Memory*. New York: Columbia University Press.

Lehti, Marko, Matti Jutila and Markku Jokisipilä. 2008. 'Never-Ending Second World War: Public Performances of National Dignity and the Drama of the Bronze Soldier', *Journal of Baltic Studies* 39(4): 393–418.

Lehtmets, Ann, and Douglas Hoile. 1994. *Sentence Siberia: A Story of Survival*. Kent Town, South Australia: Wakefield Press.

Leibbrandt, Georg (ed.). 1942. *Die Völker des Ostraumes*. Berlin: Verlagsanstalt Otto Stollberg.

Leitsch, Walter. 1991. 'Die Esten und die Probleme der Kleinen', Manfred Alexander et al. (eds), *Kleine Völker in der Geschichte Osteuropas: Festschrift für Günther Stökl zum 75. Geburtstag*. Stuttgart: Franz Steiner Verlag, 149–58.

Lemberg, H.L. 1971. 'Kollaboration in Europa mit dem 3. Reich um das Jahr 1941', in Karl Bosl (ed.), *Das Jahr 1941 in der europäischen Politik*. Munich: R. Oldenbourg.

Leonard, Wolfgang. 1955. *Die Revolution entlässt Ihre Kinder*. Cologne: Kiepenheuer and Witsch.

Létourneau, Jocelyn. 2001. 'Digging into Historical Consciousness, Individual and Collective: Overview of a Research Trajectory'. Presented at the conference on Canadian Historical Consciousness in an International Context: Theoretical Frameworks, PWIAS, University of British Columbia, Vancouver, Canada, 26–28 August.

Levin, Dov. 1994. *Baltic Jews under the Soviets, 1940–1946*. Jerusalem: Centre for Research and Documentation of East European Jewry, Avraham Harman Institute of Contemporary Jewry, Hebrew University of Jerusalem.

Lévi-Strauss, Claude. 1974. *The Savage Mind*. London: Weidenfeld & Nicolson.

Levy, Daniel. 1999. 'The Future of the Past: Historiographical Disputes and Competing Memories in Germany and Israel', *History and Theory* 38(1): 51–66.

Lieven, Anatol. 1994. *The Baltic Revolution: Estonia, Latvia, Lithuania and the Path to Independence*. New Haven, CT: Yale University Press.

Lieven, Anatol. 1998. *Chechnya – Tombstone of Russian Power*. New Haven, CT: Yale University Press.

Liim, Allan, and Karl Siilivask. 1983. *Eesti NSV ajalugu IX–XI klassile: lisamaterjali NSV Liidu ajaloo kursuse juurde*. Tallinn: Kirjustas Valgus.

Lilla, Mark. 2001. *The Reckless Mind: Intellectuals in Politics*. New York: New York Review Books.

Lipinsky, Jan. 2000. 'Sechs Jahrzehnte Geheimes Zusatzprotokoll zum Hitler-Stalin-Pakt: Sowjetrussische Historiographie zwischen Leugnung und Wahrheit', *Osteuropa* 50(10): 1123–48.

Lira, Elizabeth. 1997. 'Remembering: Passing through the Heart', in James Pennebaker, Dario Paez and Bernard Rimé (eds), *Collective Memory of Political Events: Social Psychological Perspectives*. Mahwah, NJ: Lawrence Erlbaum Associates, 223–36.

Litvin, Alter L. 2001. *Writing History in 20th Century Russia: A View from Within*. Basingstoke: Palgrave.

Loeber, Dietrich Andre. 1972. *Diktierte Option: Die Umsiedlung der Deutsch-Balten aus Estland und Lettland 1939–41*. Neumünster: Karl Wachholtz Verlag.

Lõhmus, Marta, and Karl Siilivask. 1975. *Esti NSV ajaloost keskoolile: lisamaterjali IX–XI klassi NSV Liidu ajaloo kursuse juurde*. Tallinn: Kirjastus Valgus.

Loit, Aleksander (ed.). 1985. *National Movements in the Baltic Countries during the 19th Century*. Stockholm: Centre for Baltic Studies.

Loit, Aleksander. 1990. 'Die nationalen Bewegungen im Baltikum während des 19. Jahrhunderts in vergleichender Perspektive', in Aleksander Loit (ed.), *The Baltic Countries, 1900–1914*. Stockholm: Centre for Baltic Studies, 59–81.

Loit, Aleksander. 1998a. 'Nationale Bewegungen und regionale Identität im Baltikum', in *Nordost-Archiv: Zeitschrift für Regionalgeschichte*, Neue Folge, 7(1): 219–33.

Loit, Aleksander (ed.). 1998b. *Entwicklung der Nationalbewegungen in Europa 1850–1914*. Berlin: Duncker & Humboldt.

Lovell, David W. 2001. 'Trust and the Politics of Postcommunism', *Communist and Post-Communist Studies* 34(1): 27–38.

Lowenthal, David. 1985. *The Past is a Foreign Country*. Cambridge: Cambridge University Press.

Lowenthal, David. 1998. *The Heritage Crusade and the Spoils of History*. Cambridge: Cambridge University Press.

Lübbe, Herrmann. 1979. 'Zur Identitätspräsentation von Historie', in Odo Marquard and Karlheinz Stierle (eds), *Identität: Kolloquium der Forschungsstelle 'Poetik und Hermeneutik'*. Munich: Fink, 277–92.

Lucius-Hoene, Gabriele, and Arnulf Deppermann. 2002. *Rekonstruktion narrativer Identität. Ein Arbeitsbuch zur Analyse narrativer Interviews*. Opladen: Leske & Budrich.

Lundin, Ingvar. 2000. *Baltiska judar. Fördrivna, Förföljda, Förintade*. Stockholm: Warne Förlag.

Lux, Markus. 2000. 'Der 16 März und die lettischen Legionäre. Vom problematischen Umgang mir der Geschichte in Estland', Osteuropa-archiv, *Osteuropa*, January, A1–A2.

MacQueen, Michael. 2003. 'Einheimische Gehilfin der Gestapo: Die litauische Sicherheitspolizei', in Vincas Bartusevicus, Joachim Tauber and Wolfram Wette (eds), *Holocaust in Litauen: Krieg, Judenmorde und Kollaboration im Jahre 1941*. Cologne: Böhlau, 103–16.

Maier, Charles S. 2002. 'Hot Memory … Cold Memory: On the Political Half-Life of Fascist and Communist Memories', *Transit* 22: 153–65.

Maier, Konrad. 1995. 'Nationalbewegung und Staatsbildungsprozesse in Estland im Spiegel aktueller Schulbücher', in Robert Maier (ed.), *Nationalbewegung und Staatsbildung: Die baltische Region im Schulbuch*. Frankfurt a. M.: GEI, 79–94.

Maier, Konrad. 2002. 'Geschichtsschreibung und Geschichtsforschung in Estland – Zwischenbilanz von 1988–2001: Ein Kommentar', *Österreichische Osthefte* 44(1/ 2): 171–78.

Mälksoo, Maria. 2010. *The Politics of Becoming European: A Study of Polish and Baltic Post-Cold War Security Imaginaries*. London: Routledge.

Mann, Michael. 1995. 'A Political Theory of Nationalism and its Excesses', in Sukumar Periwal (ed.), *Notions of Nationalism*. Budapest: Central European University, 44–64.

Mannheim, Karl. 1928. 'Das Problem der Generationen', in *Kölner Vierteljahreszeitschrift für Soziologie* 28(7): 309–30.

Mannheim, Karl. 1952. *Essays on the Sociology of Knowledge*. London: Routledge & Kegan.

Marandi, Rein. 1991. 'Must-valge lipu all, Vabadussõjalaste liikumine Eestis 1929–1937, I. Legaalne periood (1929–1934)', *Studia Baltica Stockholmiensia* 6: 519–51.

Marandi, Rein. 1997. 'Must-valge lipu all, Vabadussõjalaste liikumine Eestis 1929–1937, II. Illegaalne vabadussõjalus (1934–1937)', in *Studia Baltica Stockholmiensia* 18: 225–37.

Maripuu, Meelis. 2002. 'Kollaboration und Widerstand in Estland 1940–1944'. Paper presented at the conference on 'Reichskommissariat Ostland: Collaboration and Resistance during the Holocaust', Stockholm and Uppsala, Sweden, 18–21 April 2002.

Mark, James. 2008. 'Containing Fascism: History in Post-Communist Baltic Occupation and Genocide Museums', in Oksana Sarkisova and Péter Apor (eds), *Past for the Eyes: East European Representations of Communism in Cinema and Museums after 1980*. Budapest: Central European University Press, 335–69.

Mark, James. 2010. *The Unfinished Revolution: Making Sense of the Communist Past in Central-Eastern Europe*. New Haven, CT: Yale University Press.

Marquard, Odo. 1979. 'Identität – Autobiographie – Verantwortung (ein Annährungsversuch)', in Odo Marquard and Karlheinz Stierle (eds), *Identität: Kolloquium der Forschungsstelle 'Poetik und Hermeneutik'*. Munich: Fink, 690–99.

Marquard, Odo, and Karlheinz Stierle. 1979. 'Stetigkeit und Wandel aller Zeitschichten', in Odo Marquard and Karlheinz Stierle (eds), *Identität: Kolloquium der Forschungsstelle 'Poetik und Hermeneutik'*. Munich: Fink, 246–64.

Masso, Iivi. 2001. 'What is Nordic about Estonia? Politics, Discourse, Culture'. Paper presented at the seminar on '(Re-)nordification of Estonian Society', Tallinn 20–22 April.

Mattusch, Katrin. 1998. 'Estlands Bevölkerung auf dem Weg zur demokratischen Gesellschaft?', in Jörg Hakmann (ed.), *Estland – Partner im Ostseeraum*. Lübeck: Ostseeakademie, 75–98.

McCracken, Grant (ed.). 1988. *The Long Interview (Qualitative Research Methods)*. London: Sage Publications.

McCrone, David. 1998. 'The Unforeseen Revolution: Post-communist Nationalism', in David McCrone (ed.), *The Sociology of Nationalism: Tomorrow's Ancestors*. London: Routledge, 149–68.

McKinlay, Andy, Jonathan Potter and Margaret Whetherell. 1993. 'Discourse Analysis and Social Representations', in Glynis. M. Breakwell and David. V. Canter (eds), *Empirical Approaches to Social Representation*. Oxford: Claredon Press, 39–62.

Meinecke, Friedrich. 1946. *The German Catastrophe: Reflection and Recollections*. Cambridge, MA: Harvard University Press.

Meinecke, Friedrich. 1969. *Weltbürgertum und Nationalstaat*, in *Werke*, Vol. 5. Munich: R. Oldenbourg.

Meissner, Boris. 1956. *Die Sowjetunion, die baltischen Staaten und das Völkerrecht*. Cologne: Verlag für Politik und Wirtschaft.

Meissner, Boris. 1991. 'Die staatliche Kontinuität, völkerrechtliche Stellung und außenpolitische Lage der baltischen Länder', in Boris Meissner (ed.), *Die baltischen Nationen: Estland, Lettland, Litauen*, 2nd edn. Cologne: Markus-VG, 270–335.

Mendeloff, David. 2002. 'The Causes and Consequences of Historical Amnesia: The Annexation of the Baltic States in Russian Popular History and Political Memory', in Kenneth Christie and Robert Cribb (eds), *Historical Injustice and Democratic Transition in Eastern Asia and Northern Europe: Ghosts at the Table of Democracy*. London: Routledge Curzon.

Mendelsohn, Ezra. 1983. *The Jews of East Central Europe between the World Wars*. Bloomington: Indiana University Press.

Meri, Lennart. 1999. *Botschaften und Zukunftsvisionen. Reden des estnischen Präsidenten*. Bonn: Bouvier Verlag.

Merkel, Garlieb Helwig. (1796) 1998. *Die Letten, vorzüglich in Liefland, am Ende des philosophischen Jahrhunderts, ein Beitrag zur Völker und Menschenkunde*. Wedemark: H. von Hirschheydt.

Merridale, Catherine. 2001. *Night of Stone: Death and Memory in 20th Century Russia*. New York: Viking.

Merton, Robert K., and Patricia L. Kendall. 1979. 'Das fokussierte Interview', in Christel Hopf and Elmar Weingarten (eds), *Qualitative Sozialforschung*. Stuttgart: Klett-Cotta, 171–204.

Mettan, Colin W., and Stephen Wyn Williams. 1998. 'Internal Colonialism and Cultural Divisions of Labour in the Soviet Republic of Estonia', *Nations and Nationalism* 4(3): 363–88.

Michel, Gabriele. 1985. *Biographisches Erzählen – zwischen individuellem Erlebnis und kollektiver Geschichtentradition*. Tübingen: Max Niemeyer Verlag.

Michlic, Joanna Beata. 2006. *Poland's Threatening Other: The Image of the Jew from 1880 to the Present*. Lincoln: University of Nebraska Press.

Michnic-Coren, Joanna. 1999. 'The Troubling Past: The Polish Collective Memory of the Holocaust', *East European Jewish Affairs* 29(1/2): 75–84.

Middleton, David, and Derek Edwards (eds). 1990. *Collective Remembering*. London: Sage.

Miljan, Toivo. 2004. *Historical Dictionary of Estonia*. Lanham, MD: Scarecrow.

Milosz, Czeslaw. 2001. *The Captive Mind*. London: Penguin.

Mintz, Sidney. 1996. 'The Anthropological Interview and the Life History', in David K. Dunaway and Willa K. Baum (eds), *Oral History: An Interdisciplinary Anthology*. 2nd edn. Walnut Creek, CA: AltaMira Press, 298–305.

Misiunas, Romuald J. 1978. 'Soviet Historiography on World War II and the Baltic States, 1944–1974', in V. Stanley Vardys and Romuald J. Misiunas (eds), *The Baltic States in Peace and War 1917–1945*. Univerersity Park: Pennsylvania State University Press, 173–96.

Misiunas, Romuald J., and Rein Taagepera. 1993. *The Baltic States: Years of Dependence 1940–1990*. London: Hurst & Co.

Mitscherlich, Alexander, and Margarete Mitscherlich. 2004. *Die Unfähigkeit zu Trauern. Grundlagen kollektiven Verhaltens*. Munich: Piper.

Molik, Witold. 1998. 'Noch ist Polen nicht veloren', in Monika Flacke (ed.), *Mythen der Nationen: Ein Europäisches Panorama*. Munich: Koehler & Amelang, 301–5.

Mommsen, Wolfgang J. 1995. 'Die moralische Verantwortlichkeit des Historikers', in Kristin Platt and Mihran Dabag (eds), *Generation und Gedächtnis: Erinnerung und Kollektive Identitäten*. Opladen: Leske & Budrich, 131–45.

Moscovici, Serge. 1983. 'The Phenomenon of Social Representations', in Robert M. Farr and Serge Moscovici (eds), *Social Representations*. Cambridge: Cambridge University Press, 3–70.

Mosse, George L. 1975. *The Nationalization of the Masses*. New York: Howard Fertig.

Mosse, George L. 1993. *Confronting the Nation: Jewish and Western Nationalism*. Hanover, NH: University Press of New England.

Motyl, Alexander J. 1993. *Dilemmas of Independence: Ukraine after Totalitarianism*. New York: Council of Foreign Relations Press.

Mühlmann, Wilhelm E. 1985. 'Ethnogenie und Ethnogenese: Theoretisch-ethnologische und ideologische Studie', in *Studien zur Ethnogenese*. Opladen: Westdeutscher Verlag, 9–28.

Müssener, Helmut. 1971. *Die kulturelle deutschsprachige Emigration nach Schweden 1933–1945*. Stockholm: Tyska Institutionen.

Myllyniemi, Seppo. 1973. *Die Neuordnung der baltischen Länder 1941–1944: Zum nationalsozialistischen Inhalt der deutschen Besatzungspolitik*. Helsinki: Suomen Historiallinen Seura.

Myllyniemi, Seppo. 1979. *Die baltische Krise 1938–1941*. Stuttgart: Deutsche Verlagsanstalt.

Myllyniemi, Seppo. 1996. 'Enttäuschter Nationalismus im Baltikum', in Wolfgang Benz, Johannes Houwink ten Cate and Gerhard Otto (eds), *Anpassung, Kollaboration, Widerstand. Kollektive Reaktionen auf die Okkupation*. Berlin: Metropol, 171–302.

Myllyniemi, Seppo. 1997. 'Die Deutsche Besatzung Estlands nach der sowjetischen Annexion und ihre Auswirkung auf die deutsch-estnischen Beziehungen', in Boris Meissner et al. (eds), *Die Deutsche Volksgruppe in Estland. Während der Zwischenkriegszeit und aktuelle Fragen des deutsch-estnischen Verhältnisses*. Hamburg: Bibliotheca Baltica, 213–27.

Naimark, Norman. 2010. *Stalin's Genocides*. Princeton, NJ: Princeton University Press.

Narusk, Anu (ed.). 1995a. *Everyday Life and Radical Social Changes in Estonia: A Sociological-Empirical Overview of Changes in Estonians' Life Values, Attitudes, Living Conditions and Behaviour during the Transition from Soviet to Post-Soviet*. Tallinn: Eesti Teaduste Akadeemia Kirjastus.

Narusk, Anu. 1995b. 'The Estonian Family in Transition', *Nationalities Papers* 23(1): 141–52.

Narusk, Anu, and Leeni Hansson. 1999. *Estonian Families in the 1990s: Winners and Losers*. Tallinn: Estonian Academy Publishers.

Nationalities Papers. 1989. Special edition on 'The International Status of the Baltic States: The Baltic Republics Fifty Years after the Molotov–Ribbentrop Pact', *Nationalities Papers* 17(2): 156–203.

Neitzel, Sönke, and Harald Welzer. 2011. *Soldaten: Protokolle vom Kämpfen, Töten und Sterben*. Frankfurt a M.: S. Fischer Verlag.

Nekrich, Alexander. 1991. *Forsake Fear: Memory of an Historian*. Boston: Unwin Hyman.

Neumann, Iver B. 1996. *Russia and the Idea of Europe: A Study in Identity and International Relations*. London: Routledge.

Neumann, Iver B., and Jennifer M. Welsh. 1991. 'The Other in European Self-Definition: An Addendum to the Literature on International Society', *Review of International Studies* 17(4): 327–48.

Ney, Gottlieb. 1959. *Zur Ethnogenese des estnischen Volkes, hauptsächlich im Lichte der neueren estnischen Forschung*. Bonn: Baltisches Forschungsinstitut.

Niedermüller, Peter. 1994. 'Politics, Culture, and Social Symbolism: Some Remarks on the Anthropology of Eastern European Nationalism', *Ethnologia Europaea* 24: 21–33.

Niedermüller, Peter. 1997. 'Zeit, Geschichte, Vergangenheit: Zur kulturellen Logik des Nationalismus im Postsozialismus', *Historische Anthropologie* 5(2): 245–67.

Nielsen, Kai. 1999. 'Cultural Nationalism: Neither Ethnic nor Civic', in Ronald Reiner (ed.), *Theorizing Nationalism*. New York: State University of New York Press, 119–30.

Niethammer, Lutz. 1999. *Deutschland danach: Postfaschistische Gesellschaft und Nationales Gedächtnis*, eds Ulrich Herbert and Dirk van Laak. Bonn: Dietz-Verlag.

Niethammer, Lutz (ed.). 2000. *Kollektive Identität. Heimliche Quellen einer unheimlichen Konjunktur*. Reinbeck: Rohwolt.

Nietzsche, Friedrich. 1995. 'On the Uses and Disadvantages of History for Life' (1874), in Nietzsche, *Untimely Meditations*. Cambridge: Cambridge University Press, 57–123.

Niitsoo, Viktor. 1997. *Vastupanu, 1955–1985*. Talinn: Tartu Ulikooli Kirjastus.

Nisbet, H. Barry. 1999. 'Herder's Conception of Nationhood and its Influence on Eastern Europe', in Roger Bartlett and Karen Schönwälder (eds), *The German Lands and Eastern Europe: Essays on the History of their Social, Cultural and Political Relations*. London: Macmillan, 115–35.

Nodel, Emanuel. 1971. 'Life and Death of the Estonian Jewry', in Rimvydas Silbajoris, Arvids Ziedonis and Edgar Anderson (eds), 'Association for the Advancement of Baltic Studies, Second Conference on Baltic Studies, Summary of Proceedings'. Norman: University of Oklahoma Press, 227–36.

Nolte, Ernst. 1965. *The Three Faces of Fascism*. London: Weidenfeld & Nicolson.

Nora, Pierre (ed.). 1996. *Realms of Memory: Rethinking the French Past, vol. 1, Conflicts and Divisions* (translated by Arthur Goldhammer). New York: Columbia University Press.

Norman, Kristina. 2009. *After-War: Estonia at the 53rd International Art Exhibition – La Biennale di Venezia 2009*. Tallinn: Estonian Centre for Contemporary Art.

Novick, Peter. 1999. *The Holocaust in American Life*. New York: Mariner Books.

Oberländer, Erwin. 2001. 'Die Präsidialdiktaturen in Ostmitteleuropa – Gelenkte Demokratie?' in Oberländer (ed.), *Autoritäre Regime in Ostmittel – und Südosteuropa 1919–1944*. Paderborn: F. Schönigh, 3–18.

Oinas, Felix. 1990. 'Legends of Kalevipoeg', in Aleksander Loit (ed.), *The Baltic Countries, 1900–1914*. Stockholm: Centre for Baltic Studies, 495–99.

Õispuu, Leo (ed.). 1996, 1998. *Political Arrests in Estonia 1940–1988*. 2 vols. Tallinn: Leo Õispuu.

Õispuu, Leo (ed.). 1999. *Deportation from Estonia to Russia. Deportation in March 1949, Vol. 5, Part 2*. Tallinn: Leo Õispuu.

Õispuu, Leo (ed.). 2001. *Deportation from Estonia to Russia: June Deportation in 1941 and Deportations in 1940–1953*. Tallinn: Leo Õispuu.

Õispuu, Silvia. 1989. *Eesti ajalugu: konspektiivne õppematerjal keskkoolile*. Tallinn: Valgus.

Okihiro, Gary Y. 1996. 'Oral History and the Writing of Ethnic History', in David K. Dunaway and Willa K. Baum (eds), *Oral History: An Interdisciplinary Anthology*, 2nd edn. Walnut Creek, CA: AltaMira Press, 187–98.

Olavi, Arens. 1969. 'Soviet Estonian Historiography with Special Reference to the Treatment of the 1917–18 Revolutionary Period', in Ivar Ivask (ed.), 'AABS, First Conference on Baltic Studies, Summary of Proceedings'. Tacoma, WA: Pacific Lutheran University, 51–52.

Olick, Jeffrey K., and Daniel Levy. 1997. 'Collective Memory and Cultural Constraint: Holocaust Myth and Rationality in German Politics', *American Sociological Review* 62(6): 921–36.

Olick, Jeffrey K., and Joyce Robbins. 1998. 'Social Memory Studies: From "Collective Memory" to Historical Sociology of Mnemonic Practices', *Annual Review of Sociology* 24: 105–40.

Onken, Eva-Clarita. 1998. *Revisionismus schon vor der Geschichte: Aktuelle lettische Kontroversen um die Judenvernichtung und Kollaboration 1941–1944*. Cologne: Wissenschaft und Politik.

Onken, Eva-Clarita. 2000a. 'Zwischen kollektiver Entschuldigung und kritischer Reflexion: Die Aufarbeitung der kommunistischen Vergangenheit in Lettland', *Halbjahresschrift für südosteuropäische Geschichte, Literatur und Politik* 12(2): 5–16.

Onken, Eva-Clarita. 2000b. 'Geschichtsbewußtsein und nationale Identität im gesellschaftlichen Integrations- und Demokratisierungsprozeß in Lettland', in Bernard Linek and Kai Struve (eds), *Nationalismus und nationale Identität in Ostmitteleuropa im 19. und 20. Jahrhundert*. Marburg: Verlag Herder-Institut, 331–49.

Onken, Eva-Clarita. 2003. *Demokratisierung der Geschichte in Lettland. Staatsbürgerliches Bewußtsein und Geschichtspolitik im ersten Jahrzehnt der Unabhängigkeit*. Hamburg: Reinhold Krämer Verlag.

Onken, Eva-Clarita. 2007a. 'The Politics of Finding Historical Truth: Reviewing Baltic History Commissions and their Work', *Journal of Baltic Studies* 38(1): 109–16.

Onken, Eva-Clarita. 2007b. 'The Baltic States and Moscow's 9 May Commemoration: Analysing Memory Politics in Europe', *Europe–Asia Studies* 59(1): 23–46.

Onken, Eva-Clarita, Norbert Götz and Gottfried Hanne. 1998. 'Ethnopolitik', in Heike Graf and Manfred Kerner (eds), *Handbuch Baltikum heute*, Nordeuropäische Studien 14. Berlin: Verlag Arno Spitz, 299–334.

Oplatka, Andreas. 1999. *Lennart Meri. Ein Leben für Estland. Dialog mit dem Präsidenten*. Zürich: NZZ Buchverlag.

Oras, Ants. 1948. *Baltic Eclipse*. London: Gollancz.

Overing, Joanna. 1997. 'The Role of Myth: An Anthropological Perspective, or the Reality of the Really Made-up', in Geoffrey Hosking and George Schöpflin (eds), *Myths and Nationhood*. London: Hurst, 1–18.

Overy, Richard. 2003. *Russlands Krieg 1941–1945*. Hamburg: Rowohlt.

Owen, Alwyn, and Jack Perkings. 1986. *Speaking for Ourselves: Echoes from New Zealand's Past, from the Award-winning 'Spectrum' Radio Series*. Auckland: Penguin.

Ozouf, Mona. 1988. *Festivals and the French Revolution*. Cambridge, MA: Harvard University Press.

Paez, Dario, Nekane Basabe and Jose Luis Gonzalez. 1997. 'Social Processes and Collective Memory: A Cross-Cultural Approach to Remembering Political Events', in James Pennebaker, Dario Paez and Bernard Rimé, *Collective Memory of Political Events: Social Psychological Perspective*. Hillsdale, NJ: Lawrence Erlbaum Associates, 147–74.

Pajupuu, Hille. 1994. 'A Nation's Autostereotype', in Oral Memory & National Identity. Papers of the conference organized by the Institute of Language and Literature of the Estonian Academy of Sciences and the National Language Board of the Republic of Estonia, 18–19 September 1993, Tallinn, 31–38.

Pajur, Ago. 2001. 'Die "Legitimierung" der Diktatur des Präsidenten Päts und die öffentliche Meinung in Estland', in Erwin Oberländer (ed.), *Autoritäre Regime in Ostmittel – und Südosteuropa 1919–1944*. Paderborn: F. Schönigh, 163–214.

Palamets, Hillar. 1978, 1987. *Jutustusi kodumaa ajaloost:õpik IV klassile*. Tallinn: Valgus.

Parekh, Bhikhu. 1994. 'Discourses on National Identity', *Political Studies* 42(3): 492–504.

Parekh, Bhikhu. 1995. 'The Concept of National Identity', *New Community* 21(2): 255–68.

Parekh, Bhikhu. 1999a. 'Defining National Identity in a Multicultural Society', in Edward Mortimer (ed.), *People, Nation and State: The Meaning of Ethnicity and Nationalism*. London: I.B. Tauris, 66–74.

Parekh, Bhikhu. 1999b. 'The Incoherence of Nationalism', in Ronald Reiner (ed.), *Theorizing Nationalism*. New York: State University of New York Press, 295–326.

Parekh, Bhikhu. 2000. *Rethinking Multiculturalism: Cultural Diversity and Political Theory*. London: Palgrave.

Park, Andrus. 1994. 'Ethnicity and Independence: The Case of Estonia in Comparative Perspective', *Europe–Asia Studies* 46(1): 69–87.

Park, Andrus. 1995. 'Fighting For the Mini-State: Four Scenarios', *Nationalities Papers* 23(1): 67–78.

Parming, Tõnu. 1977. 'Roots of Nationality Differences', in Edward Allworth (ed.), *Nationality Group Survival in Multi-ethnic States: Shifting Support Patterns in the Soviet Baltic Region*. New York: Praeger, 24–57.

Pearson, Raymond. 1993. 'Fact, Fantasy, Fraud: Perceptions and Projections of National Revival', *Ethnic Studies* 10(1–3): 43–64.

Pearson, Raymond. 1999. 'History and Historians in the Service of Nation-Building', in Michael Branch (ed.), *National History and Identity: Approaches to the Writing of National History in the North East Baltic Region, Nineteenth and Twentieth Centuries*. Helsinki: Finnish Literature Society, Helsinki, 63–77.

Peck, M. Scott. 1990. *The Road Less Travelled*. London: Arrow.

Penikis, Jani J. 1991. 'Soviet Views of the Baltic Emigration: From Reactionaries to Fellow Countrymen', in Jan Arveds Trapans (ed.), *Toward Independence: The Baltic Popular Movements*. Oxford: Westview Press, 153–64.

Penikis, Janis J. 1990. 'Mass Receptivity to Nationalist Appeals: Theoretical Considerations in the Cases of Baltic Nationalist Movements', in Aleksander Loit (ed.), *The Baltic Countries 1900–1914*. Stockholm: Centre for Baltic Studies, 25–32.

Pennebaker, James, and Becky L. Banasik. 1997. 'On the Creation and Maintenance of Collective Memory: History and Social Psychology', in James Pennebaker, Dario Paez and Bernard Rimé (eds), *Collective Memory of Political Events: Social Psychological Perspective*, Hillsdale, NJ: Lawrence Erlbaum Associates, 14–20.

Perels, Joachim. 1998. 'Die Zerstörung von Erinnerung als Herrschaftstechnik. Adornos Analysen zur Blockierung der Aufarbeitung des NS-Vergangenheit', in Helmut König et al. (eds), *Vergangenheitsbewältigung am Ende des 20. Jahrhunderts*. Opladen: Westdeutscher Verlag, 53–68.

Petersoo, Pille. 2007. 'Reconsidering Otherness: Constructing Estonian Identity', *Nations and Nationalism* 13(1): 117–33.

Petersoo, Pille, and Marek Tamm (eds). 2008. *Monumental konflikt: mälu, poliitika ja identiteet tänapäeva Eestis*. Tallinn: Varrak.

Petersson, Bo. 2002. *National Self-Images and Regional Identities in Russia*. Aldershot: Ashgate.

Pettai, E.-C. 2011. 'The Convergence of Two Worlds: Historians and Emerging Histories in the Baltic States', in Martyn Housden and David J. Smith (eds), *Forgotten Pages in Baltic History: Themes in Diversity and Inclusion*. New York: Rodopi, 263–80.

Pettai, Vello A. 1993. 'Estonia: Old Maps and New Roads', *Journal for Democracy* 4(1): 117–25.

Pettai, Vello A. 1995. 'Shifting Relations, Shifting Identities: The Russian Minority in Estonia after Independence', *Nationalities Papers* 23(1): 405–11.

Piirimäe, Helmut. 1991. 'Some Basic Conceptions of History Teaching in Estonian Schools: Its Past and Present', in *Geschichtsbild in den Ostseeländern 1990*. Stockholm: UHÄ.

Piirimäe, Helmut. 1995. 'Die Behandlung der estnischen nationalen Bewegung und der Gründung der Estnischen Republik in den Lehrbüchern während der sowjetischen Okkupation', in Robert Maier (ed.), *Nationalbewegung und Staatsbildung: Die baltische Region im Schulbuch*. Frankfurt a. M.: GEI, 69–78.

Pistohlkors, Gert von. 1993. 'Inversion of Ethnic Group Status in the Baltic Region: Governments and Rural Ethnic Conflict in Russia's Baltic Provinces and the Independent States of Estonia and Latvia, 1850–1940', in David Howell (ed.), *Roots of Rural Ethnic Mobilisation*. Dartmouth: European Science Foundation, New York University Press, 169–220.

Plath, Ulrike, and Karsten Brüggemann (eds). 2000. 'Vom Tanz mit des Teufels Großmutter: Die estnische Debatte um die Zusammenarbeit von Präsident Konstantin Päts mit der SU', *Osteuropa* 50, A329–A339.

Plato, Alexander von. 1990. 'Einleitung zum Schwerpunkt: Oral History in der SU', *BIOS* 3(1): 1–7.

Plato, Alexander von. 1991. 'Oral History als Erfahrungswissenschaft: Zum Stand der "mündlichen Geschichte" in Deutschland', *BIOS* 4(1): 97–119.

Plato, Alexander von. 1999. 'Opferkonkurrenten?', in Elisabeth Domansky and Harald Welzer, *Eine offene Geschichte: Zur kommunikativen Tradierung der nationalsozialistischen Vergangenheit*. Tübingen: Kimmerle, 74–92.

Plato, Alexander von. 2000. 'Zeitzeugen und die historische Zunft: Erinnerung, kommunikative Tradierung und kollektives Gedächtnis – ein Problemaufriß', *BIOS* 13(1): 5–29.

Platt, Kirstin, and Mihran Dabag (eds). 1995. *Generation und Gedächtnis. Erinnerung und Kollektive Identitäten*. Opladen: Leske & Budrich.

Pohl, Otto J. 2000. 'Stalin's Genocide against the "Repressed Peoples"', *Journal of Genocide Research* 2(2): 267–93.

Priedite, Aija. 1999. 'National Identity and Cultural Identity: The History of Ideas in Latvia in the Nineteenth and Twentieth Century', in Michael Branch (ed.), *National History and Identity: Approaches to the Writing of National History in the North-East Baltic Region, Nineteenth and Twentieth Centuries*. Helsinki: Finnish Literature Society, 229–44.

Prusin, Alexander. 2010. *The Lands Between: Conflict in the East European Borderlands, 1870–1992*. Oxford: Oxford University Press.

Puhvel, Madi. 1999. *Symbol of Dawn: The Life and Times of the 19th Century Estonian Poet Lydia Koidula*. Tartu: Tartu University Press.

Pullerits, Albert (ed.). 1937. *Estonia, Population, Cultural and Economic Life*. Tallinn: Tallinna Eesti Kirjastis-Ühisuse trükikoda.

Raag, Raimo. 1990. 'The Linguistic Development of Estonian between 1900 and 1914', in Aleksander Loit (ed.), *The Baltic Countries 1900–1914*. Uppsala: Centre for Baltic Studies, 425–42.

Raag, Raimo. 1999. 'One Plus One Equals One: The Forging of Standard Estonian', *International Journal of the Sociology of Language* 139: 17–38.

Raag, Raimo. 2010. 'Eestlased ja eesti keel rootsis', in Kristina Praakli and Jüri Viikberg (eds), *Eestlased ja eesti keel välismaal*. Talinn: Eesti Keele Sihtasutus, 385–432.

Radstone, Susannah (ed.). 2000. *Memory and Methodology*. Oxford: Berg.

Rahl-Tamm, A. 2007. 'Deportations in Estonia, 1941–1951', in K. Kukk and T. Raun (eds), *Soviet Deportations in Estonia: Impact and Legacy. Articles and Life History*. Tartu: Tartu University Press, 9–54.

Rajangu, Väino. 1994. 'Sprachsituation in Estland: Zu Veränderungen im Gebrauch der estnischen und russischen Sprache im Bildungssytem', *Osteuropa* 44: 938–44.

Ranke, Leopold von. 1973 edn. *The Theory and Practice of History*. Indianapolis: Bobbs-Meriill.

Rappaport, Joanne. 1998. *The Politics of Memory*. Durham, NC: Duke University Press.

Ratner, Carl. 2002. 'Subjectivity and Objectivity in Qualitative Methodology', *Forum Qualitative Sozialforschung* 3(3): art. 16.

Rauch, Georg von. 1986. *Geschichte der baltischen Staaten*. Hannover-Döhren: Harro v. Hirschheydt.

Raud, Irina. 1998. 'Materialisiertes Gedächtnis in Estland. Wunsch nach Symbolen?', in *Denkmale und kulturelles Gedächtnis nach dem Ende der Ost-West-Konfronation*. Berlin: Akademie der Künste, 61–64.

Raun, Toivo. (1987) 2001. *Estonia and the Estonians*. Stanford, CA: Hoover Institution Press.

Raun, Toivo. 1990. 'The Estonian and Latvian National Movements: An Assessment of Miroslav Hroch's Model', *Journal of Baltic Studies* 21(2): 131–44.

Raun, Toivo. 1991. 'Perestroika and Baltic Historiography', *Journal of Soviet Nationalities* 2: 52–62.

Raun, Toivo. 1997. 'Democratization and Political Development in Estonia 1987–1996', in Bruce Parrot and Karen Dawisha (eds), *Democratic Changes and Authoritarian Reactions in Russia, Ukraine, Belarus and Moldova*. Cambridge: Cambridge University Press, 334–74.

Raun, Toivo. 1999. 'The Image of the Baltic German Elites in 20th Century Estonian Historiography: The 1930s vs. the 1970s', *Journal of Baltic Studies* 30(4): 338–51.

Raun, Toivo. 2001. 'Estonia in the 1990s', *Journal of Baltic Studies* 32(1): 19–42.

Raun, Toivo. 2003. 'Nineteenth- and Early Twentieth-Century Estonian Nationalism Revisited', *Nations and Nationalism* 9(1): 129–48.

Realo, Anu. 1998. 'Collectivism in an Individualist Culture: The Case of Estonia', *Trames* No. 1, Vol. 2(52/47): 19–39.

Realo, Anu. 2003. 'Comparison of Public and Academic Discourses: Estonian Individualism and Collectivism Revisited', *Culture and Psychology* 9(1): 47–77.

Rees, Laurence. 2008. *World War Two behind Closed Doors: Stalin, the Nazis and the West*. London: BBC Books.

Reiber, Alfred J. 2000. 'Repressive Population Transfers in Central, Eastern and South-Eastern Europe: A Historical Overview', *Journal of Communist Studies and Transition Politics* 16(1/2): 1–27.

Remeikis, Thomas. 1984. 'Dissent in the Baltic Republics: A Balance Sheet', *Lituanus Lithuanian Quarterly Journal of Arts and Sciences* 30(2).

Renan, Ernest. 1994. 'Que'est-ce qu'une nation?' in John Hutchinson and Antony Smith (eds), *Nationalism*. Oxford: Oxford University Press, 17–18.

Richardson, Stephen A., Barbara Snell Dohrenwend and David Klein. 1979. 'Die "Suggestivfrage": Erwartungen und Unterstellungen im Interview', in Christel Hopf and Elmar Weingarten (eds), *Qualitative Sozialforschung*. Stuttgart: Klett-Cotta, 205–32.

Ricoeur, Paul. 1997. 'Gedächtnis – Vergessen – Geschichte', in Klaus E.Muller and Jörn Rüsen (eds), *Historische Sinnbildung. Problemstellungen, Zeitkonzepte, Wahrnehmungshorizonte, Darstellungsstrategien*. Hamburg: Rowohlt, 433–54.

Ricoeur, Paul. 1998. *Das Rätsel der Vergangenheit. Erinnern – Vergessen – Verzeihen*. Göttingen: Wallstein.

Ricoeur, Paul. 1999a. 'Memory and Forgetting', in Richard Kearny and Mark Dooley (eds), *Questioning Ethics*. London: Routledge, 5–11.

Ricoeur, Paul. 1999b. 'Imagination, Testimony and Trust: A Dialogue with Paul Ricoeur', in Richard Kearny and Mark Dooley (eds), *Questioning Ethics*. London: Routledge, 11–17.

Ricoeur, Paul. 2002. 'Zwischen Gedächtnis und Geschichte', *Transit-Europäische Revue* 22: 3–17.

Ries, Nancy. 2000. 'Foreword: Ethnography and Postsocialism', in Hermine G. De Soto and Nora Dudwick (eds), *Fieldwork Dilemmas: Anthropologists in Postsocialist States*. Madison: University of Wisconsin Press, ix–xi.

Rikmann, Erle. 1999. 'Retroactive History and Personal Memory', Idäntutkimes: *Finnish Review of East European Studies* 6(3/4): 60–73.

Ritter, Gerhard. 1948. *Europa und die deutsche Frage*. Munich: Münchner Verlag.

Rodin, David. 2002. *War and Self-Defense*. Oxford: Oxford University Press.

Röhr, Werner. 2000. 'Okkupation und Kollaboration', in Rohr (ed.), *Europa unterm Hakenkreuz. Okkupation und Kollaboration (1938–1945): Beiträge zu Konzepten und Praxis der Kollaboration in der deutschen Okkupationspolitik*. Berlin: Hüthig Verlagsgesellschaft, 59–87.

Roos, Aarand. 1985. *Estonia: A Nation Unconquered*. Baltimore, MD: Estonian World Council, Inc.

Roos, Aarand. 1993. *Words for Understanding Ethnic Estonians*. Tallinn: Kommunaalprojekt.

Rosch, Leah, and Eberhad Jäckel. 1990. *Der Tod ist ein Meister aus Deutschland: Deportation und Ermordung der Juden. Kollaboration und Verweiterung in Europa*. Hamburg: Hoffmann and Campe.

Rose, Richard. 1995. 'New Baltics Barometer II: A Survey Study', *Studies in Public Policy* 251. University of Strathclyde, Centre for the Study of Public Policy.

Rose, Richard, and William Maley. 1994a. 'Nationalities in the Baltic States: A Survey Study', *Studies in Public Policy* 222. University of Strathclyde, Centre for the Study of Public Policy.

Rose, Richard, and William Maley. 1994b. 'Conflict or Compromise in the Baltic States: What do the Peoples there Think?', *Studies in Public Policy* 231. University of Strathclyde, Centre for the Study of Public Policy.

Rosenfeld, Alla, and Norton T. Dodge (eds). 2002. *Art of the Baltics: The Struggle for Freedom of Artistic Expression under the Soviets, 1945–1991*. London and New Brunswick, NJ: Rutgers University Press.

Rosenthal, Gabriele. 1992. 'Kollektives Schweigen zu den Nazi-Verbrechen: Bedingungen der Institutionaisierung einer Abwehrhaltung', *Psychosozial* 15(3): 22–33.

Rosenthal, Gabriele. 1995. *Erlebte und erzählte Lebensgeschichte: Gestalt und Struktur biographischer Selbstbeschreibungen*. Frankfurt a. Main: Campus.

Rosenthal, Gabriele. 1997. 'Zur interaktionellen Konstitution von Generationen: Generationenabfolgen in Familien von 1890–1970 in Deutschland', in Jürgen Mansel, Gabriele Rosenthal and Angelika Tölke (eds), *Generationen-Beziehungen, Austausch und Tradierung*. Opladen: Westdeutscher Verlag, 57–73.

Rosenthal, Gabriele. 2000. 'Historische und familiale Generationenabfolge', in Martin Kohli and Marc Szydlik (eds), *Generationen in Familie und Gesellschaft*. Opladen: Leske & Budrich, 162–78.

Rosimannus, Rain. 1995. 'Political Parties: Identity and Identification', *Nationalities Papers* 23(1): 29–42.

Roth, Philip. 1980. 'The Most Original Book of the Season', *New York Times*, 30 November 1980.

Rüsen, Jörn. 1983. *Historische Vernunft: Grundzüge einer Historik, Band I*. Göttingen: Vandenhoeck & Ruprecht.

Rüsen, Jörn. 1984. 'Geschichtsbewusstsein und menschliche Identität', *Aus Politik und Zeitgeschichte* 41 (B14/84): 3–10.

Rüsen, Jörn. 1994a. *Historische Orientierung: über die Arbeit des Geschichtsbewußtseins, sich zurechtzufinden*. Cologne: Böhlau Verlag.

Rüsen, Jörn. 1994b. 'Was ist Geschichtskultur? Überlegungen zu einer neuen Art, über Geschichte nachzudenken', in Jörn Rüsen, Klaus Füßmann and H.T. Grütter (eds), *Historische Faszination. Geschichtskultur Heute*. Cologne: Böhlau Verlag, 3–25.

Rüsen, Jörn. 2001a. *Zerbrechende Zeit. Über den Sinn der Geschichte*. Cologne: Böhlau Verlag, 279–300.

Rüsen, Jörn. 2001b. 'Holocaust, Erinnerung, Identität: Drei Formen generationeller Praktiken des Erinnerns', in Harald Welzer (ed.), *Das soziale Gedächtnis: Geschichte Erinnerung Tradierung*. Hamburg: Hamburger Edition, 243–59.

Rüsen, Jörn. 2001c. 'Historisch trauern – Skizze einer Zumutung', in Jörn Rüsen and Burkhard Liebsch (eds), *Trauer und Geschichte*. Cologne: Böhlau Verlag, 63–84.

Rüsen, Jörn, and Friedrich Jäger. 2001. 'Erinnerungskultur', in Karl-Rudolf Korte and Werner Weidenfeld (eds), *Deutschland TrendBuch: Fakten und Orientierungen*. Opladen: Leske and Budrich, 397–428.

Ruutsoo, Rein. 1995. 'Introduction: Estonia on the Border of Two Civilizations', *Nationalities Papers* 23(1): 13–16.

Ruutsoo, Rein. 1997. 'The Estonians: Identity and Small Nation in Past and Present', *Anthropological Journal on European Cultures* 6(1): 73–100.

Ruutsoo, Rein. 2002. 'Discursive Conflict and Estonian Post-Communist Nation-Building', in Marju Lauristin and Mati Heidmets (eds), *The Challenge of the Russian Minority: Emerging Multicultural Democracy in Estonia*. Tartu: Tartu University Press, 31–54.

Sabrow, Martin. 2002. 'Der Historiker als Zeitzeuge: Autobiographische Umbruchsreflexionen deutscher Fachgelehrter nach 1945 und 1989', in Konrad H. Jarausch (ed.), *Verletztes Gedächtnis: Erinnerungskultur und Zeitgeschichte im Konfliktt*. Frankfurt a. M.: Campus Verlag, 125–52.

Salo, Vello. 2002. *Population Losses 1940–41: Citizens of Jewish Nationality*. Tallinn: Estonian State Commission on Examination of the Policies of Repression.

Salumets, Thomas. 2000. 'Introduction', *Journal of Baltic Studies* 31(3): 225–36.

Sarv, Enn. 2000. 'Our Duty of Remembering'. Delivered at International Conference on Crimes of Communism, Tallinn, 14 June 2000. http://www.isamaaliit.ee/isamaa2/eng_4_2.html

Savi, Toomas. 2002. Statement of the President of the Riigikogu on the Occupation Regime in Estonia, 18 June, translated in *Euro University: The Monthly Survey of the Baltic and Post-Soviet Politics* 7(109): 3–4.

Schacter, Daniel L. 1996. *Searching for Memory: The Mind, the Brain, and the Past*. New York: Basic Books.

Schacter, Daniel L. 1999a. *Wir sind Erinnerung: Gedächtnis und Persönlichkeit*. Hamburg: Rowolt.

Schacter, Daniel L. 1999b. *The Cognitive Neuropsychology of False Memory*. Hove: Psychology Press

Schäfer, Kristin Anne. 2003. 'Völkerschlacht', in Etienne François and Hagen Schulze (eds), *Deutsche Gedächtnisorte, Band II*. Munich: C.H. Beck, 185–201.

Schlau, Wilfried (ed.). 1997. *Sozialgeschichte der Baltischen Deutschen*. Cologne: Mare Baltikum.

Schlesinger, Philip. 1987. 'On National Identity: Some Conceptions and Misconceptions Criticised', *Social Science Information* 26(2): 219–64.

Schlink, Bernhard. 1998. 'Die Bewältigung von Vergangenheit durch Recht', in Helmut König et al. (eds). *Vergangenheitsbewältigung am Ende des 20. Jahrhunderts*. Opladen: Westdeutscher Verlag, 433–51.

Schmidt, Alexander. 1992. *Geschichte des Baltikums: Von den alten Göttern bis zur Gegenwart*. Munich: Piper.

Schmitt, Jean-Carl. 1994. 'Die Geschichte der Außenseiter', in Jacques LeGoff et al. (eds), *Die Rückeroberung des historischen Denkens. Grundlagen der Neuen Geschichtswissenschaft*. Frankfurt a. M.: S. Fischer, 201–43.

Schöpflin, George. 1991. 'Nationalism and National Minorities in East and Central Europe', *Journal of International Affairs* 45(1): 51–65.

Schöpflin, George. 1993. *Politics in Eastern Europe, 1945–92*. Oxford: Blackwell.

Schöpflin, George. 1997. 'The Functions of Myth and a Taxonomy of Myths', in George Schöpflin and Geoffrey Hosking (eds), *Myths and Nationhood*. London: Hurst, 19–35.

Schöpflin, George. 1999. 'Uses of the Past in Inter-Ethnic Relations', in *Finnish Review of East European Studies* 6(3/4): 7–16.

Schöpflin, George. 2000. *Nations, Identity, Power: The New Politics of Europe*. London: Hurst.

Schotter, John, and Kenneth J. Gergen (eds). 1989. *Texts of Identity*. London: Sage.

Schudson, Michael. 1995. 'Dynamics of Distortion in Collective Post-Communist Europe', in Daniel L. Schacter (ed.), *Memory Distortion: How Minds, Brains, and Societies Reconstruct the Past*. Harvard: Harvard University Press.

Schulin, Ernst. 1997. *Arbeit an der Geschichte: Etappen der Historisierung auf dem Weg zur Moderne*. Frankfurt a. M.: Campus.

Schweiger, Imry. 2002. 'Konflikte der Kulturen. Braunschweig: Historiker Jörn Rüsen im Georg Eckert Institut', *Braunschweiger Zeitung*, 30 Nov. 2002

Sharp, Joanne P. 2000. 'Women, Nationalism and Citizenship in Post-communist Europe', in Angela Dimitrakaki, Pam Skelton and Mare Tralla (eds), *Private Views: Spaces and Gender in Contemporary Art from Britain and Estonia*. London: WAL, 100–9.

Shils, Edward. 1957. 'Primordial, Personal, Sacred and Civil Ties', *British Journal of Sociology* 8(2): 130–45.

Shils, Edward. 1981. *Tradition*. Chicago: University of Chicago Press.

Shteppa, Konstantin F. 1962. *Russian Historians and the Soviet State*. New Brunswick, NJ: Rutgers University Press.

Siemens, Christof. 2001. 'Jäger der Erinnerung: Die Esten suchen nach ihrer Identität, erfinden neue Sportarten, singen viel und bauen ein Okkupationsmuseum', *Die Zeit*, 5 July, 35.

Siemer, Kaari. 2002. '"Who is Red on the Outside and White Inside?": The Topic of Soviet Rule in Estonian Life Stories', in Tiiu Jaago (ed.), *Lives, Histories and Identities: Studies on Oral Histories, Life and Family Stories*. Tartu: Estonian Literary Museum, 188–203.

Silverman, David. 2000. 'Analyzing Talk and Text', in Norman K. Denzin and Yvonna S. Lincoln (eds), *Handbook of Qualitative Research*, 2nd edn. London: Sage, 821–34.

Silverman, David. 2001. *Interpreting Qualitative Data: Methods for Analysing Talk, Text and Interaction*. London: Sage.

Simmonds-Duke, E.M. 1987. 'Was the Peasant Uprising a Revolution? The Meanings of a Struggle over the Past', *East European Politics and Society* 1(2): 187–223.

Skultans, Vieda. 1998. *The Testimony of Lives: Narrative and Memory in Post-Soviet Latvia*. London: Routledge.

Smith, Anthony D. 1986. *The Ethnic Origins of Nations*. Oxford: Blackwell.

Smith, Anthony D. 1991. *National Identity*. Harmondsworth: Penguin.

Smith, Anthony D. 1992. 'Chosen Peoples: Why Ethnic Groups Survive', *Ethnic and Racial Studies* 15(3): 436–56.

Smith, Anthony D. 1995a. 'The Formation of National Identity', in Henry Harris, *Identity*. Oxford: Clarendon, 129–51.

Smith, Anthony D. 1995b. *Nations and Nationalism in a Global Era*. Cambridge: Polity.

Smith, Anthony D. 1996a. 'Opening Statement: Nations and Their Pasts', *Nations and Nationalism* 2(3): 358–64.

Smith, Anthony D. 1996b. 'Memory and Modernity: Reflections on Ernest Gellner's Theory of Nationalism', *Nations and Nationalism* 2(3): 371–88.

Smith, Anthony D. 1997. 'Nation and Ethnoscapes', *Oxford International Review* 8(2): 11–18.

Smith, Anthony, D. 1998. *Nationalism and Modernism: A Critical Survey of Recent Theories of Nations and Nationalism*. London: Routledge.

Smith, Anthony D. 1999. *Myths and Memories of the Nation*. New York: Oxford University Press.

Smith, David J. 1998. 'Russia, Estonia and the Search for a Stable Ethno-Politics', *Journal of Baltic Studies* 29(1): 3–18.

Smith, David J. 1999. 'The Restorationist Principle in Post Communist Estonia', in Christopher Williams and Thanasis D. Sfikas (eds), *Ethnicity and Nationalism in Russia, the CIS and the Baltic States*. Aldershot: Ashgate, 287–323.

Smith, David J. 2001. *Estonia: Independence and European Integration*. London: Routledge.

Smith, David J. 2002. 'Framing the National Question in Central and Eastern Europe: A Quadratic Nexus?', *Global Review of Ethnopolitics* 2(1): 3–16.

Smith, David J. 2008. '"Woe from Stones": Commemoration, Identity Politics and Estonia's "War of Monuments"', *Journal of Baltic States* 39(4): 419–30.

Smith, Gordon B. 1992. *Soviet Politics: Struggling with Change*. New York: St Martin's Press.

Smith, Graham (ed.). 1994. *The Baltic States: The National Self-Determination of Estonia, Latvia and Lithuania.* London: Macmillan.

Smith, Graham. 1996a. 'The Ethnic Democracy Thesis and the Citizenship Question in Estonia and Latvia', *Nationalities Papers* 24(2): 199–216.

Smith, Graham. 1996b. 'When Nations Challenge and Nations Rule: Estonia and Latvia as Ethnic Democracies', *Coexistence* 33(1): 25–41.

Smith, Graham (ed.). 1996c. *Nationalities Questions in the post-Soviet States.* London: Longman.

Smith, Graham et al. 1998. *Nation-Building in the Post-Soviet Borderlands: The Politics of National Identities.* Cambridge: Cambridge University Press.

Smolar, Alexander. 1999/2000. 'Vergangenheitspolitik nach 1989: Eine vergleichende Zwischenbilanz der Entkommunisierung', *Transit-Europäische Revue* 18: 81–101.

Snyder, Jack, and Karen Ballentine. 1996. 'Nationalism and the Marketplace of Ideas', *International Security* 21(2): 5–40.

Snyder, Timothy. 2010. *Bloodlands: Europe between Hitler and Stalin.* London: Bodley Head.

Socor, V. 2007. 'Bronze Soldier Set to Leave Tallinn as Last Soviet Soldier', *Eurasia Monitor Daily*, 12 January.

Sontag, Susan. 2003. 'The Power of Principle', *Guardian* (London), Review, 26 April, 4–6.

Squire, Larry R., and Eric R. Kandel. 2000. *Memory: From Mind to Molecules.* Basingstoke: Palgrave.

Staab, Andreas. 1998. *National Identity in Eastern Germany: Inner Unification or Continued Separation?* Westport, CT: Praeger.

Stalin, Joseph. (1994). 'The Nation', in Anthony D. Smith and J. Hutchinson (eds), *Nationalism Reader, Oxford Readers.* Oxford and New York: Oxford University Press, 18–21.

Starr, Louis. 1996. 'Oral History', in David K. Dunaway and Willa K. Baum (eds), *Oral History: An Interdisciplinary Anthology.* 2nd edn. Walnut Creek, CA: AltaMira Press, 39–61.

Strods, Heinrihs, and Matthew Kott. 2000. 'The Files on Operation "Priboi": A Re-Assessment of the Mass Deportations of 1949', *Journal of Baltic Studies* 33(2): 1–36.

Stukuls, Daina. 1997. 'Imagining the Nation: Campaign Posters of the First Communist Elections in Latvia', *East European Politics and Society* 11(1): 131–54.

Sugar, Peter F. 1994. 'External and Domestic Roots of Eastern European Nationalism', in Peter F. Sugar and Ivo J. Lederer (eds), *Nationalism in Eastern Europe.* Seattle: University of Washington Press, 3–54.

Suijlekom, L. van. 2011. 'A Shared European History? Dealing with Divided Memory within the European Union'. Universiteit Maastricht, MA thesis.

Szacki, Jerzy. 1994. *Liberalism after Communism*. Budapest: Central European University Press.

Sztompka, Piotr. 1991. 'The Intangibles and the Imponderables of the Transition to Democracy', *Studies in Comparative Communism* 24(3): 295–311.

Taagepera, Rein. 1984. *Softening without Liberalization in the Soviet Union: The Case of Jüri Kukk*. Lanham, MD: University Press of America.

Taagepera, Rein. 1993. *Estonia: Return to Independence*. Boulder, CO: Westview Press.

Tägil, Sven. 1995. *Ethnicity and Nation Building in the Nordic World*. London: Hurst & Co.

Tägil, Sven (ed.). 1999. *Regions in Central Europe: The Legacy of History*. London: Hurst & Co.

Tajfel, Henri. 1981. *Human Groups and Social Categories*. Cambridge: Cambridge University Press.

Tajfel, Henri (ed.). 1982. *Social Identity and Intergroup Relations*. Cambridge: Cambridge University Press.

Talve, Ilmar. 1952. *Maja lumes*. Lund: Eesti Kirjanike Kooperative.

Taube, Arved Baron. 1937. *Landespolitik und Volkswerdung: Betrachtungen zur Entwicklung der nationalen Frage in der Geschichte Estlands*. Tallinn: F. Wassermann.

Tauber, Joachim. 2003. '14 Tage im Juni: Zur kollektiven Erinnerung von Litauern und Juden', in Vincas Bartusevicius, Joachim Tauber and Wolfram Wette (eds), *Holocaust in Litauen: Krieg, Judenmorde und Kollaboration im Jahre 1941*. Cologne: Böhlau Verlag, 40–50.

Taylor, Charles. 1989. *Sources of the Self: The Making of the Modern Identity*. Cambridge: Cambridge University Press.

Taylor, Charles. 1992a. 'The Politics of Recognition', in Amy Gutman (ed.), *Multiculturalism and the Politics of Recognition*. Princeton, NJ: Princeton University Press.

Taylor, Charles. 1992b. *The Ethics of Authenticity*. Cambridge, MA: Harvard University Press.

Taylor, Charles. 1999. 'Nationalism and Modernity', in Ronald Reiner (ed.), *Theorizing Nationalism*. New York: State University of New York Press, 219–46.

Thaden, Edward. 1981. *Russification in the Baltic Provinces and Finland, 1855–1914*. Princeton, NJ: Princeton University Press.

Theroux, Alexander. 2011. *Estonia: A Ramble through the Periphery of Europe*. Seattle: Fantagraphics.

Tillett, Lowell. 1969. *The Great Friendship: Soviet Historians on the non-Russian Nationalities*. Chapel Hill: University of North Carolina Press.

Tishkov, Valery. 1997. *Ethnicity, Nationalism and Conflict in and after the Soviet Union*. London: Sage.

Todorov, Tzvetan. 1996. 'The Abuses of Memory', *Common Knowledge* 5(1): 6–26.

Tonkin, Elizabeth. 1992. *Narrating our Pasts: The Social Construction of Oral History*. Cambridge: Cambridge University Press.

Toomet. T. 1993. *Me elama ajaloos: eesti ajaloo õpik 5. Klassile*. Tallinn: Kirjastus Koolibri.

Törnquist-Plewa, Barbara. 1992. *The Wheel of Polish Fortune: Myth in Polish Collective Consciousness during the First Years of Solidarity*. Lund: Lund University.

Törnquist-Plewa, Barbara. 1998. 'Cultural and National Identification in Borderlands: Reflections on Central Europe', in Klas-Göran Karlsson, Bo Petersson and Barbara Törnquist-Plewa (eds), *Collective Identities in an Era of Transformations: Analysing Developments in East and Central Europe and the Former Soviet Union*. Lund: Lund University Press, 79–107.

Torpey, John C. 1995. *Intellectuals, Socialism, and Dissent: The East German Opposition and Its Legacy*. Minneapolis: University of Minnesota Press.

Trapans, Jan Arveds. 1991. 'The Popular Movement and the Soviet Union: Discussion', in J. Trapans (ed.), *Toward Independence: The Baltic Popular Movements*. Boulder, CO: Westview Press, 43–56.

Trouillot, Michel-Rolph. 1995. *Silencing the Past: Power and the Production of History*. Boston: Beacon Press.

Truska, Liudas. 2003. 'Litauische Historiographie über den Holocaust in Litauen', in Vincas Bartusevicius, Joachim Tauber and Wolfram Wette (eds), *Holocaust in Litauen. Krieg, Judenmorde und Kollaboration im Jahre 1941*. Cologne: Böhlau Verlag, 262–76.

Tulviste, P., and J.V. Wertsch. 1994. 'Official and Unofficial Histories: The Case of Estonia', *Journal of Narrative and Life History* 4(4): 311–29.

Tumarkin, Nina. 1994. *The Living and the Dead: The Rise and Fall of the Cult of World War Two in Russia*. New York: Basic Books.

Turner, Victor W. 1986. 'Betwixt and Between: The Liminal Period in Rites de Passage', in Turner, *The Forest of Symbols: Aspects of Ndembu Ritual*. Ithaca, NY: Cornell University Press, 93–111.

Uibopuu, Henn-Jüri. 1990. 'Die Entwicklungen des Freistaates Estland', in Boris Meissner (ed.), *Die Baltischen Nationen, Estland – Lettland – Litauen, Nationalitäten- und Regionalprobleme in Osteuropa, vol 4*. Cologne: Markus-Verlag, 52–62.

Ümarik, Meril. 2001. 'Constructing the National Identity in School Textbooks: The Textbooks of Estonian History in the Soviet Estonia and in the Estonian Republic'. Paper presented at the seminar on '(Re-)nordification of Estonian Society', Tallinn, 20–22 April.

Unwin, Tim. 1999. 'Place, Territory, and National Identity in Estonia', in Guntram H. Herb and David H. Kaplan (eds), *Nested Identities: Nationalism, Territory, and Scale*. Boston: Rowman & Littlefield, 151–74.

Uustalu, Evald. 1952. *The History of Estonian People*. London: Boreas.

Uustalu, Evald. 1976. 'The National Committee of the Estonian Republic', *Journal of Baltic Studies* 7(3): 209–19.

Vahtre, Sulev. 1996. 'Die Geschichtskunde und die Historiker in Estland in den kritischen Jahren 1918/1919 und 1987/1989', in Eberhard Demm, Roger Noel and William Urban (eds), *The Independence of the Baltic States: Origins, Causes, and Consequences. A Comparison of the Crucial Years: 1918–1919 and 1990–1991*. Chicago: Lithuanian Research and Studies Center, 131–37.

Valk, Aune. 2001. *Two Facets of Ethnic Identity: Pride and Differentiation*. Tartu: Tartu University Press.

Vansina, Jan. 1965. *Oral Tradition*. Harmondsworth: Penguin.

Vardys, Stanley V. 1978. 'The Rise of Authoritarian Rule in the Baltic States', in Stanley V. Vardys and Romuald J. Misiunas (eds), *The Baltic States in Peace and War 1917–1945*, University Park: Pennsylvania State University Press, 65–80.

Vasara, Vesa. 1995. 'Das estnische Parlament und die Deutschbalten. Zu den Debatten bis zur Verabschiedung der Kulturautonomie 1925', *Nordost-Archiv* 4(2): 479–500.

Velliste, Trivimi. 1995. 'Ethnic Issues in Estonia: A Personal View', *World Affairs* 157(3): 137–41.

Velmet, Aro. 2011. 'Occupied Identities: National Narratives in Baltic Museums of Occupation', *Journal of Baltic Studies* 42(2): 189–211.

Venner, Dominique. 1974. *Söldner ohne Sold: Die Deutschen Freikorps 1918–23*. Berlin: Paul Neff Verlag.

Verdery, Katherine. 1999. *The Political Lives of Dead Bodies: Reburial and Postsocialist Change*. New York: Columbia University Press.

Verschik, Anna. 1999a. 'The Yiddish Language in Estonia: Past and Present', *Journal of Baltic Studies* 30(2): 117–28.

Verschik, Anna. 1999b. 'Some Aspect of the Multilingualism of Estonian Jews', *International Journal of the Sociology of Language* 139: 49–67.

Vetik, Raivo, Gerli Nimmerfelt and Marti Taru. 2006. 'Reactive Identity versus the EU Integration', *Journal of Common Market Studies* 44(5): 1079–1102.

Vidal-Naquet, Pierre. 1996. 'Memory and History', *Common Knowledge* 5(2): 14–20.

Vihalemm, Peeter. 1999. 'Changing Baltic Space: Estonia and its Neighbours', *Journal of Baltic Studies* 30(3): 250–69.

Vihalemm, Triin. 1999. 'Group Identity Formation Process among Russian-Speaking Settlers of Estonia: A Linguistic Perspective', *Journal of Baltic Studies* 30(1): 18–39.

Vihalemm, Triin. 2002a. 'On the Perspectives of Identity Formation among the Estonian Russians', in Marju Lauristin and Mati Heidmets (eds), *The Challenge of the Russian Minority: Emerging Multicultural Democracy in Estonia*. Tartu: Tartu University Press, 219–26.

Vihalemm, Triin. 2002b. 'Usage of Language as a Source of Societal Trust', in Marju Lauristin and Mati Heidmets (eds), *The Challenge of the Russian*

Minority: Emerging Multicultural Democracy in Estonia. Tartu: Tartu University Press, 199–218.

Vihalemm, Triin, and Anu Masso. 2002. 'Patterns of Self-identification among the Younger Generation of Estonian Russians', in Marju Laurestin and Mati Heidmets (eds), *The Challenge of the Russian Minority: Emerging Multicultural Democracy in Estonia.* Tartu: Tartu University Press, 185–98.

Viirlaid, Arved. 1972. *Graves without Crosses.* Toronto: Clarke, Irwin & Co.

Vorvelle, Michel. 1994. 'Die Geschichtswissenschaft und die "longue durée"', in Jacques LeGoff et al. (eds), *Die Rückeroberung des historischen Denkens. Grundlagen der Neuen Geschichtswissenschaft.* Frankfurt a. M.: S. Fischer, 103–36.

Wallerstein, Immanuel. 1977. 'Geschichte und Sozialwissenschaften: Die longue duree', in Claudia Honegger (ed.), *Schrift und Materie der Geschichte.* Frankfurt a. M.: Suhrkamp, 47–85.

Walzer, Michael. 1982. *Exodus and Revolution.* New York: Basic Books.

Walzer, Michael. 2000. *Just and Unjust Wars: A Moral Argument with Historical Illustrations.* New York: Basic Books.

Watson, Rubie S. (ed.). 1994. *Memory, History, and Opposition under State Socialism.* Santa Fe, NM: School of American Research Press.

Weber, Eugen J. 1976. *Peasants into Frenchmen: The Modernization of Rural France, 1870–1914.* Stanford, CA: Stanford University Press.

Weber, Max. 1947. *Essays in Sociology.* London: Routledge & Kegan.

Weiss-Wendt, Anton. 1997. *Must Valge Linn. Schwarz Weiße Stadt, Vana Narva Fotoajalugu.* Tallinn: Fotogeschichte Alt Narvas.

Weiss-Wendt, Anton. 2003. 'Extermination of Gypsies in Estonia during World War II: Popular Images and Official Policies', *Holocaust and Genocide Studies* 17(1): 31–61.

Weiss-Wendt, Anton. 2009. *Murder without Hatred: Estonians and the Holocaust.* Syracuse, NY: Syracuse University Press.

Welzer, Harald. 1998. 'Erinnern und weitergeben: Überlegungen zur kommunikativen Tradierung von Geschichte', *BIOS*, 11(2): 155-170.

Welzer, Harald. 2000. 'Das Interview als Artefakt. Zur Kritik der Zeitzeugenforschung', *BIOS* 13(1): 51–63.

Welzer, Harald. 2001a. 'Das gemeinsame Verfertigen von Vergangenheit im Gespräch', in Welzer (ed.), *Das soziale Gedächtnis: Geschichte Erinnerung Tradierung.* Hamburg: Hamburger Edition, 160–78.

Welzer, Harald. 2001b. 'Kumulative Heroisierung. Nationalismus und Krieg im Gespräch zwischen den Generationen', *Mittelweg 36*: 57–73.

Welzer, Harald. 2002. *Das kommunikative Gedächtnis: Eine Theorie der Erinnerung.* Munich: C.H. Beck.

Welzer, Harald, Sabine Moller and Karoline Tschuggnall (eds). 2002. *'Opa war kein Nazi': Nationalsozialismus und Holocaust im Familiengedächtnis.* Frankfurt a. M.: S. Fischer.

Welzer, Harald, Robert Montau and Christine Plass. 1997. 'Was wir für böse Menschen sind': Der Nationalsozialismus im Gespräch zwischen den Generationen. Tübingen: Edition diskord.

Welzer, Harald et al. (eds). 1999. Auf den Trümmern der Geschichte. Tübingen: Edition diskord.

Wengraf, Tony. 2001. Qualitative Research Interviewing: Biographic Narrative and Semi-Structured Methods. London: Sage.

Wertsch, James V. 1994. 'Introduction: Historical Representation', Journal of Narrative and Life History 4(4): 247–55.

Wertsch, James V. 2002. Voices of Collective Remembering. New York: Cambridge University Press.

Wertsch, James V., and Peeter Tulviste. 1994. 'Official and Unofficial Histories: The Case of Estonia', Journal of Narrative and Life History 4(4): 311–29.

White, Hayden. 1987. Content of the Form: Narrative Discourse and Historical Representation. Baltimore, MD: John Hopkins University Press.

White, Hayden. 2000. 'Historische Modellierung (emplotment) und das Problem der Wahrheit', in Rainer Kiesow et al. (eds), Auf der Suche nach der verlorenen Wahrheit: Zum Grundlagenstreit in der Geschichtswissenschaft. Frankfurt a. M.: Campus Verlag, 142–68.

Wiegandt, Manfred H. 1995. 'The Russian Minority in Estonia', International Journal on Group Rights 3: 109–43.

Wilson, Andrew. 1996. 'The Post-Soviet States and the Nationalities Question', in Graham Smith (ed.), Nationalities Questions in the post-Soviet States. London: Longman, 23–43.

Wilson, Andrew. 1997a. Ukrainian Nationalism in the 1990s: A Minority Faith. Cambridge: Cambridge University Press.

Wilson, Andrew. 1997b. 'Myths of National History in Belarus and Ukraine', in Geoffrey Hosking and George Schöpflin (eds), Myth & Nationhood. London: Hurst, 182–97.

Wilson, Andrew. 2000. The Ukrainians: Unexpected Nation. London: Yale University Press.

Wineburg, Sam. 2001. 'Sinn machen: Wie Erinnerung zwischen den Generationen gebildet wird', in Harald Welzer (ed.), Das soziale Gedächtnis: Geschichte, Erinnerung, Tradierung. Hamburg: Hamburger Edition, 179–218.

Winter, Jay. 2006. Remembering War: The Great War between Memory and History in the Twentieth Century. New Haven, CT: Yale University Press.

Winter, Jay, and Antoine Prost. 2005. The Great War in History: Debates and Controversies, 1914–Present. Cambridge: Cambridge University Press.

Winter, Jay, and Emmanuel Sivan (eds). 2000. War and Remembrance in the Twentieth Century. Cambridge: Cambridge University Press.

Wischermann, Clemens (ed.). 1996. Die Legitimität der Erinnerung und die Geschichtswissenschaft. Stuttgart: F. Steiner Verlag.

Wolf, Christa. 1999. *Kindheitsmuster*. Munich: dtv.

Wolff, Larry. 1996. *Inventing Eastern Europe: The Map of Civilisation on the Mind of Enlightenment*. Stanford, CA: Stanford University Press.

Wolfrum, Edgar, and Petra Bock. 1999. *'Umkämpfte Vergangenheit': Geschichtsbilder, Erinnerungen und Vergangenheitspolitik im internationalen Vergleich*. Göttingen: Vandenhoeck & Ruprecht.

Wöll, Alexander, and Harald Wydra (eds). 2008. *Democracy and Myth in Russia and Eastern Europe*. London: Routledge.

Wood, Nancy. 1994. 'Memory's Remains: Les Lieux de Mémoire', *History and Memory* 6: 123–49.

Wood, Nancy. 1999. *Vectors of Memory: Legacies of Trauma in Postwar Europe*. Oxford: Berg.

Woods, Shirley A. 1999. 'Ethnicity and Nationalism in Contemporary Estonia', in Christopher Williams and Thanasis D. Sfikas (eds), *Ethnicity and Nationalism in Russia, the CIS and the Baltic States*. Aldershot: Ashgate, 265–86.

Wrobel, Piotr. 1997. 'Double Memory: Poles and Jews after the Holocaust', *East European Politics and Society* 11(3): 560–74.

Wulf, Meike. 2005. 'Book Review of Tiina Kirss et al. (eds), She Who Survives Remembers: Interpreting Estonian Women's Post-Soviet Life Stories', *Journal of Baltic Studies* 36(2): 237–42.

Wulf, Meike. 2008. 'The Struggle for Official Recognition of Displaced Group Memories in post-Soviet Estonia', in Michal Kopecek (ed.), *Past in the Making: Recent History Revisions and Historical Revisionism in Central Europe after 1989*. Budapest: CEU Press, 217–41.

Wulf, Meike. 2009. 'Locating Estonia: Homeland and Exile Perspectives', in Peter Gatrell and Nick Baron (eds), *Warlands: Population Resettlement and State Reconstruction in Soviet Eastern Europe, 1945–50*. Basingstoke: Palgrave Macmillan, 231–54.

Wulf, Meike. 2010. 'Politics of History in Estonia: Changing Memory Regimes 1987–2009', in Mihail Neamtu (ed.), *History of Communism in Europe, Vol. I: Politics of Memory in post-Communist Europe*. Bucharest: Zeta Books, 243–65.

Wulf, Meike. 2011a. 'Review of Maria Mälksoo's The Politics of Becoming European', *Journal of Baltic Studies* 42(2): 307–9.

Wulf, Meike. 2011b. 'Changing Memory Regimes in a New Europe', *East European Memory Studies, Memory at War Newsletter* 7 (November): 15–20.

Wulf, Meike, and Pertti Grönholm. 2010. 'Generating Meaning across Generations: The Role of Historians in the Codification of History in Soviet and Post-Soviet Estonia', *Journal of Baltic Studies* 41(3): 351–82.

Yates, Frances A. 1966. *The Art of Memory*. London: Routledge & Kegan Paul.

Young, James E. 1993. *The Texture of Memory: Holocaust Memorials and Meaning*. New Haven, CT: Yale University Press.

Young, James E. 1997. 'Between History and Memory: Voices of Historian and Survivor', *History and Memory* 9(1/ 2): 47–58.

Young, James E. 2001. 'Zwischen Geschichte und Erinnerung: Über die Wiedereinführung der Stimme der Erinnerung in die historische Erzählung', in Harald Welzer (ed.), *Das soziale Gedächtnis: Geschichte Erinnerung Tradierung*. Hamburg: Hamburger Edition, 41–62.

Yurchak, Alexei. 2006. *Everything Was Forever, Until It Was No More: The Last Soviet Generation*. Princeton, NJ: Princeton University Press,

Zerubavel, Eviatar. 1977. 'The French Republican Calendar: A Case Study in the Sociology of Time', *American Sociological Review* 42(6): 868–77.

Zerubavel, Eviatar. 1995. 'Reading the Past against the Grain: The Shape of Memory Studies', *Critical Studies in Mass Communication* 12: 214–39.

Zerubavel, Yael. 1995a. 'The Multivocality of a National Myth: Memory and Counter-Memories of Masada', *Israel Affairs* 1(3): 110–28.

Zerubavel, Yael. 1995b. *Recovered Roots: Collective Memory and the Making of Israeli National Tradition*. Chicago: University of Chicago Press.

Zetterberg, Seppo. 1971. 'Finland und der estnische Freiheitskrieg', in Rimvydas Silbajoris, Arvids Ziedonis and Edgar Anderson (eds), 'Association for the Advancement of Baltic Studies: Second Conference on Baltic Studies, Summary of Proceedings'. Norman, OK: University of Oklahoma Press, 157–66.

Zhurzhenko, Tatiana. 2007 'The Geopolitics of Memory'. *Eurozine*, 10 May. http://www.eurozine.com/articles/2007-05-10-zhurzhenko-en.html

Zimmermann, Moshe. 2002. 'Täter-Opfer-Dichitomien als Identitätsformen', in Konrad Jarausch (ed.), *Verletztes Gedächtnis: Erinnerungskultur und Zeitgeschichte im Konflikt*. Frankfurt. a. M: Campus Verlag, 199–216.

Zizek, Slavoj. 1994. 'Genieße Deine Nation wie Dich selbst! Der Andere und das Böse. Vom Begehren des ethnischen "Dings"', in Joseph Vogl (eds), *Gemeinschaften: Positionen zu einer Philosophie des Politischen*. Frankfurt: Suhrkamp, 133–66.

Zizek, Slavoj. 2001. *Did Somebody Say Totalitarianism? Five Interventions in the (Mis)use of a Notion*. London: Verso.

Zubok, Vladislav. 2009. *Zhivago's Children: The Last Russian Intelligentsia*. Cambridge MA: The Belknap Press.

Zuroff, Efraim. 1996. *Beruf: Nazijäger. Die Suche mit dem langen Atem: Die Jagd nach den Tätern des Völkermordes*. Freiburg: Ahriman-Verlag.

INDEX

A

Aarelaid-Tart, Aili, 79
Afghanistan War, 71, 84, 91
After-War show, 162
Agar, Michael, 68
agricultural economy, 48
Alexander I (Tsar), 41
Alexander III (Tsar), 42
Alien Law of 1993, 55
allusions, 67
alphabets, 50. *See also* language
amnesia, collective, 127-30
anecdotal evidence, 67
Ankersmit, Frank, 65
Ansip, Andrus, 160
apologetics, 173
Armistice of 11 November 1918, 43
assimilation, 107
Assmann, Aleida, 10, 13, 16
    formats of memory, 27
Assmann, Jan, 10, 12, 19
    canons of groups, 23
    concept of memory, 27
Atlantic Charter in 1941, 133
Auschwitz, 154
autobiographical memory, 12
autobiographical texts, 111
automatic citizenship, 54
auxiliary police, 46
The Avenger, 120

B

Bakhtin, Mikhail, 110
Baltic Chain, 135
Baltic Charter (1979), 121
Baltic Germans, 39, 50, 131
Baltic Legions, 159
Baltic Soviet regimes (1918-19), 106
Baltic States, occupation of, 52
Barbarossa, Frederick, 16
Batov, Omar, 174
Battle of Võnnu (1919), 120

Bédarida, François, 65
Bhabha, Homi K, 90
biographical interviews, 67
Björkmann, Li Bennich, 79
bloodlands, 6, 169
Bolshevik leadership, 44
books, destruction of, 126
borderland, concept of, 36
bourgeois Estonia, 76
Brezhnev, Leonid, 36, 49
    Russification policies, 114
    Sovietization policies (1970s), 71, 91
Bronze Soldier statue, 156, 160-63
brotherhood in arms, 117
Burke, Peter, 15

C

Canada, as destination of refugees, 47
canon, 22-24
catastrophes, 1
Catholic Church, criticism of, 64
Centre Party, 160
change in collective memory, 12-13
Christianity, 24
    Protestant Reformation, 38
Christmas, celebration of, 126, 127
Citizen's Committee, 52, 54
citizenship
    application of, 83
    automatic, 54
cognitive framing, 107
Cohen, Shari J., 144
Cold War, 3, 4, 88
    historians during, 63
collaboration
    with Nazis, 159
    of occupying powers, 85
'Collaboration and Resistance in Estonia
    1940-1944', 152
collective amnesia, 127-30
collective ego, 132
collective identities, 146

collective memory, 9–34, 69, 170
    community and change in, 12–13
    in Eastern Europe, 25–28
    functions of cultural memory, 22–24
    generational group memories, 16–18
    group conflicts, 15–16
    levels of, 12
    mechanisms of, 10–12
    national identity and, 18–22
    sites of memory, 13–15
collective resistance, 120–27
collectivization policies (1940s), 72
colonialism, 38
communicative memory, 22, 65
Communist Party, 83
    choice of joining, 76
    Post-War Children and support of, 92
community
    in collective memory, 12–13
    of common destiny, 117
    and national identity, 20
concentration camps
    Auschwitz, 154
    Klooga, 78, 129
Congress of People's Representatives, 42
constitutions, 54
continuity of groups, 12
Cooper, James Fennimore, 81
corporal punishment, 114
counter-memories, 15–16
Cross of Freedom, 160–63
cultural hybridity, 173
cultural memory, 12, 13, 19, 65, 69, 114, 115, 128
    functions of, 22–24
cultural resistance, 124
culture, 15, 19, 35, 37–43, 82
Cyrillic alphabet, 50
Czechoslovakia, 84

D
Davies, Norman, 1, 2, 44
declaration of independence (1918), 53
decolonization (1919), 44
democracy, 159
demographics, 2, 82
denial, 173
Denmark, 151
Department of Scientific Communism, 73
deportations
    of Gypsies, 148
    of Jews, 47
    mass (1941), 114, 132
    to Siberia, 114
desertion of country, 81
destabilization tactics, 52

destiny, 173
destruction of books, 126
De Thomas, Joseph M., 153
distancing, 173
Dobson, Miriam, 111
Documentation Centre of Totalitarianism (TSDC), 147
documentation of repression, 147
Double Other (identity formation), 37–43
double totalitarian rule, 45–47
Dylan, Bob, 86

E
Eastern Europe, 1, 5
    collective memory in, 25–28
    historical experience of, 6
education, 82
    destruction of books, 126
    history textbooks, 108
    resistance, 125
Eighth Estonian Rifle Corps, 46
Eisler, Hans, 64
emergence of Estonian Republic (1920), 114
emerging post-Soviet identities, 96–98
empirical case studies, 69–70
equality, new society based on, 86
era of silence (1934-40), 45
Estonia,
    history, 1–4, 35–56
    independence, 43–44, 114
Estonia, cultural history, 35–56, 131–32, 144-46, 150, 155–56
Estonian auxiliary police, 151, 154
Estonian awakening, 40
Estonian Communist Party (ECP), 48, 49
Estonian Cross of Liberty, 162
Estonian Cultural History Archive, 111
Estonian Defense Forces, 158
Estonian Encyclopedia, 126
Estonian farmers (kulaks), 48
Estonian Freedom Fighters' Association, 159
Estonian Heritage Society, 52, 53, 93, 110, 111
Estonian Historians Commission, 175
Estonian International Commission for the Investigation of Crimes against Humanity, 144, 146, 150-56, 159
Estonian Life History Organization, 111
Estonian Literary Museum, 110
Estonian National Committee, 77
Estonian National Museum, 45
Estonian National Progressive Party, 42
Museum of Occupations , 126, 144, 147-50
Estonian Political Police (Department BIV), 151
Estonian Popular Front, 52, 145
Estonian Security Police, 152
Estonian Soviet Socialist Republic (ESSR), 46

Estonian Soviet Socialist Republic (ESSR), 46
ethnicity, 16
ethnic nationalism, 21
ethno-cultural identities, 108
European Day of Remembrance, 177
European Union (EU), 133, 151
events
        of collective suffering, 116–20
        typology of formative, 114–16
exile, 3, 117. *See also* deportations
ex negativo identity, 51

F
Faehlmann, Friedrich Robert, 16
fathers, absence of, 85
Final Act of the Helsinki Conference on
        Security and Cooperation in Europe
        (1975), 49
Finland, 46, 47, 151
Finnish Boys, 47
First Republic, 43–45
First World War, 36
        national identity before, 41
        writing of history about, 77
five dimensions of public history, 144–46
foreign rule, 2, 35, 135
        oral history of, 66
Forest Brethren, 107, 120, 121, 129, 159
formative events
        collective resistance, 120–27
        of collective suffering, 116–20
        typology of, 114–16
framing the past and future, 169–77
Freedom Children, 71, 93–96
Freedom Fighters, 44, 123
Freedom Square, 162
French Revolution, 13
Freud, Sigmund, 114
frozen family memories, 110
Furtwängler, Wilhelm, 5
future, framing the past and, 169–77

G
Gallerano, Nicola, 66, 144
Gasset, José Ortegay, 170
generational group identities, 70–71
generational group memories, 16–18
generational style, 18
Genghis Kahn tradition, 90
genocide, 114, 149. *See also* Holocaust
Germany, 13. 22
        collapse of Kaisserreich (1918), 43
        historical memory in, 25, 149,
        171, 175
        occupation of (WWII), 3, 151
        power struggle with Russia, 2, 35–47

glasnost, 51. *See also* Gorbachev, Mikhail
globalization, 173
glorification, 173
Goebbels, Heiner, 1
golden age of independence period, 107
Gorbachev, Mikhail, 4, 28, 51, 54
Gorbachev Generation, 93
graves, excavations of, 161
gray Barons, 40
Great Northern War of 1700-21, 41, 132
Great Patriotic War, 160
Great Terror of the 1930s, 128
groups
        conflicts, 15–16
        generational group identities, 70–71
        post-Soviet Estonia identities, 170
Gründgens, Gustav, 5
Gypsies, deportations of, 148

H
Haalviste, Ilmar, 157
Halbwachs, Maurice, 10, 11
        collective memory, 12
        topographical memories, 14
Havel, Vaclav, 27
Heine, Heinrich, 24
Heller, Agnes, 118
Herder, Johann Gottfried, 37, 39
Herguak, Eha, 106
hidden events, collective amnesia of,
        127–30
Hirvepark, demonstrations in, 122
historians (as carriers of meaning), 63–104
        emerging post-Soviet identities,
        96–98
        empirical case studies, 69–70
        Freedom Children, 93–96
        generational group identities, 70–71
        history production in Soviet era,
        71–79
        life-story interviews, 64–67
        methods of life-story interviews,
        67–69
        Post-War Children, 85–91
        Transitional Generation, 91–93
        War Generation, 78–85
historical culture, concept of, 15, 19, 137,
        144, 146, 150, 155–56, 170
historical memory, 12
historical revisionism, 144, 145
historical truth, 175
history
        excursions based on, 93
        fact-based idea of, 14
        five dimensions of public, 144–46
        post-Soviet histories, 105–42

production in Soviet era (1945-91),
71–79
reframing, 130–37
textbooks, 108
History Circle, 92, 93
History Task Force, 110
Hitler, Adolf, 45, 46. *See also* Germany
Hitler Youth, 46
holidays, celebration of, 126, 127
Holocaust, 17, 23, 36
as taboo, 128
Homeland History (1989), 106, 108
human rights, 49
humiliation, 114–116
Hupel, August Wilhelm, 40
Hurt, Jakob, 40

I
identities, 106
collective. *See also* collective
identities
Double Other, 37–43
emerging post-Soviet, 96–98
ethno-cultural, 108
First Republic, 43–45
generational group, 70–71
national, 9–34. *See also* national
identity
post-Soviet Estonia, 170
reconfiguration of, 173
Ilves, Toomas H., 155
independence
declaration of (1918), 53
golden age of, 107
path to, 51–55
restoration of, 63
industrialization, 48
Institute for Jewish Research (YIVO), 126
Institute of Historical Memory, 155
International Forum on Preventing Genocide
(2004), 149
interviews
life-story, 64–67
oral traditions. *See* oral traditions
interwar period, 76, 80
Iron Curtain, 114
Italy, 13

J
Jakobson, Carl Robert, 40, 106
Jannsen, Jahann Voldemar, 40
Jansen, Ea, 72
jestlased, 129, 135
Jews. *See also* Holocaust
converting to Christianity, 24
killing of as taboo, 128

rescue of, 47
Wannsee conference of 1942, 47
jokes, 67

K
Kahk, Jüri, 108
Kaiser Wilhelm I, 16
Kalevipoeg, 40
Kaplinski, Jaan, 54
Karlsson, Karl-Göran, 144
Karusoo, Merle, 86, 129, 130
Kelam, Tune, 64
Kerensky, Aleksander, 43
Khrushchev, Nikita, 36, 85
end of occupation, 107
Soviet consumerism, 86
kidnapped Europe, 132
Kiev Rus', 23
Kirss, Tiina, 111
Kistler, Olga, 147
Kistler-Ritso Foundation, 147
Kivirähk, Andrus, 113
Klooga concentration camp, 78, 129
Kõidula, Lydia, 124
Komsomol youth organization, 26, 84
Konrád, György, 64
Kukk, Jüri, 121

L
Laar, Mart, 64, 93, 106, 109, 175
labour camps, 77
Lagerspetz, Mikko, 107
Laidoner, Juhan, 44, 45
landmarks
memories through, 13
public disputes, 156
language, 82
post-Stalin era, 49
Russian speaking populations, 53, 95
standardization of, 38
as symbol of nationalism, 41
Language Law, 55
Lapin, Leonhard, 147
Latvia, 53, 96
resistance, 130
Soviet, 66
Laur, Mati, 109
Lavrov, Sergey, 148
Leaden Time (1978), 86
*The Legendary Topography of the Gospels in the
Holy Land*
Le Goff, Jacques, 10, 26, 65
Letter of the Forty, 123
levels of collective memory, 12
Levy, Daniel, 146
liberalization, 94

liberation, 133
libraries as transmission of memories, 11
life-story interviews, 64–67
    empirical case studies, 69–70
    methods of, 67–69
liquidation units (German), 129
literary traditions, 126
Livonian Wars (1558-1629), 38
loss, 114–116
Luiga, Georg Eduard, 44
Lukas, Tõnu, 109
Lutheran German civilization, 37

M
Maarjamäe memorial complex, 156, 159
Maier, Charles, 22
Mannheim, Karl, 17, 18, 63, 170, 173
Mark, James, 111
mass deportations (1941), 132
May, Karl, 81
mechanisms of collective memory, 10–12
The Memoirs of Ivan Orav, 113
memory, 65, 69
    collective, 9–34, 170
    community and change in, 12–13
    counter-memories, 15–16
    cultural, 12–13, 19, 22–24, 65, 69, 114, 115, 128
    difference between types of, 109
    in Eastern Europe, 25–28
    generational group memories, 16–18
    group conflicts, 15–16
    levels of collective, 12
    limitations of, 14
    mechanisms of collective, 10–12
    national identity and, 18–22
    private/public memories, 143–68
    sites of, 13–15
    as source of truth, 66
    War Generation, 79
Meri, Arnold, 3
Meri, Lennart, 3, 93, 132, 150, 160
Merkel, Garlieb, 40
Messianism, 107
methods of life-story interviews, 67–69
military occupations, 2
Molotov-Ribbentrop Pact (1939), 45, 49, 52, 121, 122, 128, 143
Mommsen, Wolfgang, 65
monuments, 158. See also landmarks
mourning, 118
Müller, Heiner, 86
mythomoteurs, 115
myths, 16, 22–24

N
narratives. See also history
    new national, 106–14
    tropes, 130–37
national history writing, 106. See also post-Soviet histories
national identity, 35–55, 134
    collective memory and, 9–34
    Double Other, 37–43
    double totalitarian rule, 45–47
    First Republic, 43–45
    path to independence, 51–55
    Soviet-style domination, 48–51
National Independence Party, 54
national pride, sources of, 120–27
national unification, 13
Nazi Hunters, 151
Nazi occupation, 36
    accusations of collaboration, 72
    collaboration, 159
new national narratives, 106–14
Nietzsche, Friedrich, 12
Niklus, Mart-Olav, 121
Nora, Pierre, 10, 14
Norman, Kristina, 162
North Atlantic Treaty Organization (NATO), 133, 155

O
occupation, 36. See also Germany; Russia
    of Baltic States, 52
    Soviet, 46
Occupied Eastern Territories, 46
Õispuu, Silvia, 109
Old Barny aka November, 135
Olick, Jeff, 10
Onken, Eva-Clarita, 150, 154
oral traditions, 12, 66, 67
    shift from, 13
Other, concept of, 36

P
Palamets, Hillar, 108
Parek, Lagle, 121
Parekh, Bhikhu, 18, 20, 21
Pärnu Courier, 40
Pärnu monument, 158
passive cultural resistance, 124
past and future, framing the, 169–77
past experiences, 12
Pastior, Oskar, 5
path to independence, 51–55
Päts, Konstantin, 43, 45
peasant boys, 80
peasant uprisings, 39, 40
perestroika, 51. See also Gorbachev, Mikhail

Petrograd Duma, 42
Piast, 23
Pietism, spread of, 38
Piirimäe, Helmut, 76, 92
Poe, Edgar Allan, 1
police
    Estonian auxiliary, 151, 154
    Estonian Political Police, 151
    Estonian Security Police, 152
policies
    collectivization (1940s), 72
    Russification, 114
    Sovietization (1970s), 71
political freedom, 118
politicization of memories, 27, 28
politics, historians involved in, 64
populations, 82
post-authoritarian societies, 150
Postimees (The Postman), 112
post-Soviet Estonia, 4
    group identities, 170
private/public memories, 143–68
post-Soviet histories, 105–42
    collective amnesia, 127–30
    collective resistance, 120–27
    events of collective suffering, 116–20
    new national narratives, 106–14
    reframing history, 130–37
    typology of formative events, 114–16
Post-War Children, 71, 75, 85–91, 170–73
Power of the Powerless, 27
Prague Spring, 84
private/public memories, 143–68
    crimes against humanity, 150–56
    Museum of Occupations , 147–50
    five dimensions of public history, 144–46
    public disputes, 156–60
    shift to resistance, 160–63
propaganda, 145
    Soviet Union, 72
Protestant Reformation, 38
Prusin, Alexander V., 42
public history, five dimensions of, 144–46
public libraries, transmission of memories, 11

R
Raag, Raimo, 77
radio broadcasts, 87
radish, trope of, 135
Rahi-Tamm, Aigi, 133
Raun, Toivo, 77
reconstruction, 90
    of national identity, 107
Red Army, 3, 44, 46, 160
    liberation by, 72
    recaptured by, 48

War Generation, 78
reframing history, 130–37
refugees, destinations of, 47
rehepaplus (old-barnyism), 135
Renan, Ernest, 21
repression, documentation of, 147
resignation, 173
resilience, 116, 135
resistance, 116, 135
    collective, 120–27
    Latvia, 130
    shift to, 160–63
restorationist path (1989-93), 54
Return to Europe, 131, 145
revisionism, historical, 144, 145
Riefentstahl, Leni, 5
Roman alphabet, 50
Romulus and Remus, 23
Rosenthal, Gabriele, 17
Rüsen, Jörn, 15, 118, 143, 170, 174, 175
Russia, 151. *See also* Soviet era
    collective memory of, 25
    as influence to, 2
    post-Soviet Estonia, 4
    power struggle with Germany, 35–43
Russian dissidents, 123
Russian speaking populations, 53
Russification policies, 114
Russified Estonians, 129
Russified' Estonians, 48
Rüssow, Balthasar, 64
Ruutsoo, Rein, 37

S
Sandberger, Martin, 47
Sarv, Enn, 157
Savisaar, Edgar, 160
schools as transmission of memories, 11
Schöpflin, George, 25
script cultures, 13
Second World War, 3, 23, 28
    biographical interview questions, 60
    concept of long Second World War,
      132, 145, 160
    eliminating interpretations of, 161
    landmarks, 158
    social experiences of, 36
shame (national), 127–37
shock battalions, 114
Siberia, 110
    deportations to, 114
Siemer, Kaari, 132
Siilivask, Karl, 108
Simon Wiesenthal Centre, 149
Singing Revolution (1987), 36, 52, 95, 124, 135
sites of memory, 13–15

sites of memory, 13-15
Skultans, Vieda, 67, 126
slavery, 106, 115
Smith, Anthony D., 13, 19, 21, 42
Smith, David, 134
Snyder, Timothy, 6, 169
social change, 2
socialism, 80, 83
social memory, 11, 69. *See also* memory
    of resistance, 120
    of veterans, 156
social strategies, reframing history, 130-37
socio-political transitions, 143
soldiers' graves, excavations of, 161
Solidarity movement, 91
Soviet consumerism, 86
Soviet era, 3
    history production in (1945-91), 71-79
Soviet Estonian Encyclopedia (ENE), 126
Sovietization policies (1970s), 71, 91
Soviet Latvia, 66
Soviet occupation, 46
Soviet-style domination, 48-51
Soviet Union, 1. *See also* Russia
    emerging post-Soviet identities, 96-98
    interpretation of history, 109, 110
    post-Soviet histories, 105-42
    propaganda, 72
    spatial frameworks (memory), 13-15
Stagna, 86, 87
Stalin, Joseph, 36, 45
    death of, 48
    destruction of books, 126
    War Generation, 78
Stalinism. *See also* Stalin, Joseph
    horrors of, 88
    victims of, 119
Stalinist terror, 117
statehood, restoration of, 105, 106
strategies
    reframing history, 130-37
    of victimhood, 147-50
subjectivity of historians, 66
suffering, 116
events of collective suffering, 116-20
Sweden, 151
    refugees, destinations of, 47
Sword Brethren (or Teutonic Knights), 38
Szabó, István, 5
Sztompka, Piotr, 26

T
Taagepera, Rein, 91
taboos, 113, 127-30
Tallinn, demonstrations in, 49
Tarto, Enn, 121

Tartu Peace Treaty (1920), 44, 120
Teutonic Knights, 38, 132
textbooks, history, 108
Theroux, Alexander, 1, 2
Tilk, Maria, 106
Tõnisson, Jan, 42
Tonkin, Elizabeth, 10-12
topographical memories, 14
totalitarian regimes, 147
totalitarian rule, 45-47
transgression, narrative of, 89
Transitional Generation, 71, 75, 91-93, 105,
    170-73
resistance, 123
trauma, 114-16
Treaty of Nystad (1721), 41
trope of the radish, 135
tropes, narrative, 130-37
truth
    historical, 75, 175
    memory as source of, 66
Truth Commission, 152
Tsar Alexander I, 41
Tsar Alexander III, 42
Tsarist Russia, 41. *See also* Russia
typology of formative events, 114-16

U
Ümarik, Meril, 108
United Council of Workers' Collectives, 53
United Kingdom (UK), 151
United Nations (UN), 49
Uustalu, Evald, 77

V
Vahrtre, Sulev, 76, 108
Vahtre, Lauri, 64
Vahtre, Sulev, 92
Väljas, Vaino, 52
Vanished Kingdoms, 1
Velliste, Trivimi, 53
Vergangenheitsbewältigung, 175
victimhood
    category of, 174
    strategies of, 147-50
victimization, 132
Victory Cross, 156
Victory Day, 45, 120, 160-61
Vike-Freiberga, Vaira, 149
von Buxhöveden, Albert, 38
von Humboldt, Alexander, 66
Voyage in the Year, 39. *See also* Herder, Johann
    Gottfried

W
Waffen-SS, 130, 160

Waggoners, 129
Wannsee conference of 1942, 47
War Generation, 71, 75, 78–85, 96, 105, 109,
    117, 152, 170–73
War of Independence (1918-20), 44, 124
War of Independence Veterans' League, 45
Western Europe, 22
White, Hayden, 69
White Book, 3
Winter, Jay, 11
wisdom, 22–24

Y
Yates, Francis A., 10
Years of Dependence, 120
Yeltsin, Boris, 54
Young Communist League, 84
Young Tartu movement, 91

Z
Zeitgeist, 18
Zuroff, Efraim, 149, 152